Contents

Acknowledgements

Introduction

Administrative reorganisation and place-names

Map of counties before local government reorganisation in 1972

Map of counties after United Kingdom local government reorganisation

Abbreviations

Dictionary of place-names

Glossary of common place-name elements

Appendix: Regions, counties and districts in Great Britain and Northern Ireland

Bibliography

Acknowledgements

I wish to thank many friends for their kind advice and unstinting aid. Dr Margaret Gelling, John Dodgson, and the late Professor Melville Richards provided much useful information in the early stages of the compilation of this book. Individual problems have been discussed with them and with Professor Kenneth Cameron, Dr Gillian Fellows Jensen, and David Mills. The late Eamonn de hÓir, of the Irish Ordnance Survey, Mrs Deirdre Flanagan and Professor Tomas Ó Máille have been most generous in their assistance with Irish names. Ian Fraser kindly supplied information and guidance on Scottish names, and Professor Charles Thomas (through Oliver Padell, whose help is also gratefully acknowledged) elucidated a number of Cornish names.

Warm thanks are due also to John Parfitt, Head of Library Services at Dacorum College, and his colleagues Miss M. Fraser, Miss S. Rickard, and Mrs D. Grogan for their efficient and friendly service. Without their help, access to some of the works listed in the Bibliography and to many other sources of information would have been far more difficult. My wife has, as always, given me constant encouragement, and I here place on record my thanks to her for her tolerance in sharing her home with a book, and for help with many matters of detail in its preparation.

Place-Names
of
Great Britain and Ireland

John Field

DAVID & CHARLES
Newton Abbot London

British Library Cataloguing in Publication Data

Field, John, b.1921
Place-Names of Great Britain and Ireland.
1. Names, Geographical – Great Britain – Dictionaries
I. Title
914.1'003   DA645
ISBN 0–7153–7439–7

First published 1980
Second impression 1990

Typeset by Tata Press Limited India
and printed in Great Britain
by Redwood Press Limited, Melksham
for David & Charles plc
Brunel House Newton Abbot Devon

Introduction

Places and their Names

This book sets out to interpret and discuss a selection of place-names from all parts of Great Britain and Ireland. It is not intended for the specialist, for whom larger and more detailed works already exist, but for the general reader or ordinary traveller — who may be one and the same person. Much can be learnt from names in their present form, but it is never possible to arrive at a reliable interpretation unless the earliest spellings can be studied. Both name and place must be seen in their historical and geographical context, otherwise the name remains a mere verbal label and its connexion with the place an inexplicable accident.

An interest in place-names may originate in a variety of ways. A name fortuitously observed on a signpost in the depths of the country may strike the traveller as peculiarly inappropriate, and so set him off on a quest for its history. Sometimes a name previously thought to be unique may be found to be duplicated in another county. Groups of names occur within restricted areas (eg The Rodings in Essex or The Langtons in Leicestershire), drawing attention to themselves by their similarity or their variety. Names commemorating dead kings or queens (eg Harold Wood, Edith Weston) may lead the historically-minded wayfarer to try to find how and why the place came to bear the person's name.

The discussion of a place-name starts with an investigation of the origin of the word. The earliest spellings of the name are inspected and analysed, and the language or languages of its root-words identified; this part of the process may well be limited to those who have been appropriately trained. But the meaning of the name is not the limit of the discussion. Behind and beyond the meaning will be the place itself and the people who first established the settlement or recognised the natural feature and its need for a particular name. History (both national and local) and geography will have their own contributions to make. The geologist may find that certain groups of names have a particular significance in the study of soil types; the historical geographer will note the relation between particular names and patterns of settlement, evidence of practices such as summer-pasturing, and the light that the history of the landscape and the names of the area shed on each other.

The area with which this book is concerned may be only a very small fraction of the surface of the earth, but the names to be found there are very numerous indeed. In view of the great numbers, an attempt to make a truly representative selection would be impossibly ambitious, and several quite different reasons have influenced the choice.

The largest towns have of course been considered, together with the names of counties and other large territorial units, including Districts brought into being by local-government reorganisation in the United Kingdom. Other names have been chosen because the places are historically important or otherwise interesting. The names of some very small places have been included because of their similarity to those of more famous localities or because of some special features of the names themselves. Space has been found for a number of river-names and the names of mountains and other natural features. Here again, size has not been the dominant criterion, but it would seem culpable to have omitted Shannon, Snowdon, Thames, or Ben Nevis.

Scope of the Work

This book examines a selection of names from the two large islands of Ireland and Great Britain, with their outlying isles and islets, and the Isle of Man. Politically, Ireland is at present two-fold: the Republic of Ireland comprises the ancient provinces of Leinster, Munster, and Connaught, with part of the fourth, Ulster; in the north-east, the Six Counties of Northern Ireland (most of the province of Ulster) are part of the United Kingdom. Great Britain contains the two kingdoms of Scotland and England (the original United Kingdom) and the Principality of Wales. The Isle of Man is not part of the United Kingdom, though it is subject to the British crown. The Channel Islands, however, lie outside the scope of this book.

Immigrants and Invaders

The traditional divisions — England, Wales, Scotland, Ireland, Isle of Man — correspond, in a very limited way, to linguistic areas due to successive immigrations.

Two varieties of Celtic language occur. The first, Brittonic, is particularly associated with Wales; but there are large outcrops in Cumbria, southern Scotland, and Cornwall, as well as sporadic remnants in all parts of England. The characteristic 'Welshness' of such names as Caerwent or Abergavenny is easily recognised; but Wendover, Lympne, and Carlisle represent the considerable number of places in England whose names have an origin

6

in the ancient British language. Ochiltree, Lanark, and Methuen are a small sample of Scottish names derived from this variety of Celtic, as are many river-names throughout Britain.

The other variety of Celtic—Goidelic or Gaelic—is found in Ireland and Scotland as a living language, and also occurs in the place-names of Man. Inverness, Eigg, Crieff, and Kilchattan are characteristic Gaelic names from Scotland; Inishmore, Kildare, and Clonmel are examples from Ireland.

Before the Irish immigrants (known as Scots) brought Gaelic to Caledonia, however, the Pictish language was spoken over a large area of the north. This seems to have been a hybrid tongue in which a Brittonic element was combined with some earlier language of unknown origin. In the absence of Pictish literary evidence, the recognition of this derivation is necessarily difficult, and the arguments complicated. The numerous names with the prefix Pit- are almost certainly connected with this mysterious people, though it is worth noticing that the second components in most of these names are Gaelic words. Only three or four other elements have been suggested as probably of Pictish origin; these include *pevr*, 'radiant, beautiful' (as in Strathpeffer) and *lanerc*, 'glade', on which a comment is made in the entry for Lanark.

Germanic invaders, settling in various parts of Britain and Ireland during the first millennium AD, in turn left their mark on place-names. From the evidence of these names, we can conclude that they settled in greater numbers in eastern Britain than elsewhere. Anglo-Saxon names (eg Hastings, Birmingham, Kingston, Dryburgh, Hawick) are found in all parts of England and Scotland, but their number diminishes north of the Forth and west of the Severn. Scandinavian names, representing settlement between 860 and about 1060, have a different distribution. Names of Danish origin occur in north and eastern England; Grimsby, Lowestoft, Derby, and Copmanthorpe — with their rather limited range of terminal elements — are a fair sample. Norwegian names are found in Scotland (eg, Helmsdale, Sutherland, Staffa), in Shetland and Orkney, in the Isle of Man, in Cumbria, along the Welsh coast (eg, Swansea, Skokholm) and on the east and south-east coasts of Ireland.

The next invaders to arrive were Normans. They were descendants of Scandinavians who had settled in northern France a century or so before 1066, but were French-speaking when they came to Britain. Conquerors rather than settlers, they were not obliged to name newly established villages. Their contribution was to supplement existing nomenclature by

7

bringing into existence 'manorial' or 'feudal' additions (eg, Stansted Mountfitchet, Stogursey), by modifications of spellings (eg, Nottingham, Jarrow, Trafford), by the occasional replacement of existing Anglo-Saxon names in England (eg, Richmond), and by a characteristic description of the sites of castles and manor houses (eg, Belvoir, Belper, Montacute). Examples of the last category are found throughout the British Isles; the Normans' fondness for complimentary descriptions encouraged much later imitation, however, and not every Belmont or Beaulieu can be ascribed to them. Still less do we owe to them all names in England and Scotland terminating in -*ville*, many of which are creations of the past two hundred years. Earlier names with this ending originally had -*feld* or another Old English element as their second component. Recent coinages include Coalville and Bournville; among early names are Enville and Turville.

Nothing has so far been said of the Latin element in the names of the area. It might be thought that four centuries of Roman occupation would have left their mark on the place-names of Britain. In fact, very few names indeed can be traced directly to the Romans, who were present as military occupiers, not as settlers. Such Latin names as they tried to impose were soon forgotten after their departure; their attempt to rename Londinium, for instance, was unsuccessful. Augusta did not seem to be in any way superior to the name already in use.

Traces of Latin in names brought into existence during later centuries are attributable to the use of that language in legal documents, (eg, Pontefract), or occasionally to its employment for monastic sites and properties (eg, Cerne Abbas).

The language to which a place-name belongs must obviously be considered in interpreting the name. But there are implications beyond this, into the fields of politics and national aspirations. On the lips of speakers of alien tongues—whether they be visitors, colonisers, traders or conquerors—names take on new forms, often unrecognisable by the natives of the place and sometimes a cause of understandable resentment. Changes in the political regime in some countries have led to widespread alterations in the names themselves, and not merely their forms. In the Celtic parts of these islands, including Cornwall, place-names have become an issue in a growing national consciousness in recent decades. Anglicised forms and spellings of Irish and Welsh names have now largely been discarded in favour of authentic local forms (Aberafan for Aberavon, for instance) and historic names have been restored in place of

8

later names imposed by English-speaking government agencies (eg, Cobh for Queenstown). Similarly, Gaelic names in the Highlands of Scotland now appear on maps in authentic spellings rather than a lame Anglicised orthography, as used to be customary. This book attempts to take due note of such changes.

The Process of Naming

A solitary inhabitant has little need of place-names, but communication with others requires that the place of settlement should be set off from other places, by means of some label alluding to the settlers or their home, or by referring the site to some natural feature.

Early settlers often used their tribal name as that of their territory. Many 'folk names' survive; Suffolk and Norfolk are obvious examples, but Sussex, Essex, Hitchin, the revived Dyfed, Jarrow, Ripon, and Northumbria were all originally the names of the inhabitants rather than of their territory. Natural objects — rivers, hills, ravines — would be among the earliest things to be named by settlers, though the names are likely to be repetitive if movement was restricted. Thus, *The Hill* will serve satisfactorily to designate a slight eminence or a veritable mountain, if no other exists in the vicinity. With greater mobility, however, the settlers would need a more complex system of naming, giving rise to such forms as *Red Hill, Round-Topped Hill,* or *Fairy Hill,* when it was necessary to distinguish between a number of features in the neighbourhood.

Rivers seem to preserve some of the most ancient names. Many, it is true, bear names interpreted disappointingly as 'river', 'stream', 'flowing one', or even 'water'. Others are described in some way; many names allude to qualities, eg, 'foaming', 'roaring', 'sluggish', or 'dark'. Other names are metaphorical, eg, Gele, 'blade' — referring probably to the brightness of the water. Yet others are those of animals — either because of some aspect of the river or for some deeper reason associated with totemism. Colwyn Bay and Banff were named from streams called respectively 'whelp' and 'little pig'. Occasionally, a religious or divine connexion is less obscure. Don, Dee, and Aeron, among many others identify particular rivers with Celtic goddesses and gods. Rivers often further contribute to the naming-process by giving rise to settlement names associated with them. Fords, for instance, are important enough features to be named in the designation of four English county-towns and an Irish national capital. Estuaries also provide important sites, and names prefixed by *Aber-*, restricted to Wales and Scotland, constitute an interesting collection. Gaelic *Inver-* names, perhaps in some instances supplanting *Aber-* names in Scotland, also incorporate much older river-names, such as Ness, or keep such a name in being while themselves suffering extinction; Ayr embodies an ancient river name, and is all that is left of the former *Inberair*.

Personal names, apart from the tribal names already referred to, also make an important contribution. The named person is usually no longer identifiable, important though he may have been when the place was established. Sometimes, of course, the personal name is that of the saint to whom the church is dedicated.

After 'What does that name mean?' and, perhaps, 'Why does it mean that?' may occur the question 'How did the early form of the name become what we have today?' A full answer may require a detailed exploration of the history of language in terms of sound changes, semantic development, and numerous other features. It may be necessary to turn aside occasionally to note the difficulties occurring when a place receives a transferred name, or the vagaries of folk etymology. It is symptomatic of human curiosity about place-names that popular explanations of their origin are frequently circulated, and sometimes the names are altered either to fit the spurious explanation or to adjust them to recognisable forms or words. A rather similar process occurs in 'back-formation'. River-names are often older than settlement names and frequently have a part in the formation of the latter. Back-formation is said to occur when a river-name is contrived by a shortening or wrong analysis of a settlement-name, eg, by deriving the river-name Wandle from Wandsworth.

Sound changes are a fact of linguistic history; for instance Modern English *road, rope, load,* and *oak* may be compared with Old English *rād rāp, lād,* and *āc.* But other modifications also occur in the regular use of the language at any one time, and English-speakers often find the consonant changes occurring in the Celtic languages particularly hard to follow. Both kinds of change may be seen in the formation of place-names. The sounds of the earlier language will have been modified during the period of development, and particular consonants are likely to be altered when combined with others in adjacent elements in a name.

Many examples of these features of name development will be found throughout this book. Within the little space available in a single entry, the information provided is intended to show how the elements concerned came to combine and interact and so produce the modern form of the name.

Arrangement of the Dictionary

Names discussed are in alphabetical order, each followed immediately by an abbreviation of the name of the county in which the place is located. This information is important for anyone seeking further information in the county volumes of the English Place-Name Survey, or reference works for the other countries. Recent boundary changes are occasionally noted by a double entry. eg, Sr/GL, signifying that the place (eg, Peckham) was formerly in Surrey but is now in Greater London. Generally such changes are ignored, but some new names created or revived in the most recent reorganisation have themselves been included as separate entries. The names of Districts are fully listed, under the names of reorganised Counties or Regions, in the Appendix.

Occasionally the head-word is followed by a date; this is a convenient way of indicating that the present spelling of the name was first recorded in that year. The meaning of the name(s) then follows, with brief observations.

Lastly, within square brackets, dated early forms of the name are quoted, followed by the elements (apart from personal names). When names are grouped, early forms are numbered to correspond with the order of the names in the group. For very common names, marked *freq*, 'of frequent occurrence', early forms are not usually given.

In the interests of brevity, meanings follow particular patterns: '....'s farm or village', 'settlement of the followers of ....', 'grove or wood by ....', and so on. This practice obviates the need to give a detailed explanation each time particular elements occur. The citation of the element is a suggestion that further details may be obtained under that heading in a larger work of reference. Comparisons and further information are sometimes indicated by cross-references.

A select list of common elements will be found at the end of the book (pp 195-201). This Glossary may serve as a guide in interpreting names not included in this work, though it is necessary to repeat the warning that the present form of a place-name is often an unreliable indication of its basic structure.

A fuller discussion of many of the names contained in this work will be found in books listed in the Bibliography.

Administrative Reorganisation and Place-Names

During the 1970s, changes took place in the structure of local government in all parts of the United Kingdom. New Counties were created in England and Wales; in Scotland the country was divided into large areas known as Regions. Sub-divisions of these Counties and Regions, known as Districts, were also newly organised. In Northern Ireland, the division was immediately into Districts.

For many of the new areas names were required. Freshly created Counties received various designations: the Metropolitan Counties frequently took over existing names previously informally applied to economic regions, such as Merseyside, South Yorkshire, and West Midlands. Other new Counties and Regions assumed historic names that differed only slightly from their previous titles, such as Lothian and Cumbria. Wales adopted names of former provinces, such as Dyfed, Gwent, and Gwynedd.

Most names of new Districts were chosen from existing names either of large towns and cities, or of former administrative areas, such as rural districts. In addition, some ancient Hundred names were revived, for instance Broxtowe and Bassetlawe in Nottinghamshire, Dacorum in Hertfordshire, and Uttlesford in Essex.

In the Dictionary, District-names are marked with an obelisk (†), but no indication is there given of the County in which the District lies; in many cases, of course, it will be unchanged from what is stated. For the sake of comprehensiveness and accuracy a complete list of Counties, Regions, and Districts is given in the Appendix. Names defined in the Dictionary are printed in capital letters, but a name partly in capitals means that reference may be made to the main body of the work for the meaning of that part, the remainder being either self-explanatory or defined in the Appendix.

Counties before Local Government Reorganisation in 1972

ORKNEY

SHETLAND

on same scale

0 10 20 30 40 50   100 miles

N

WESTERN
ISLES

HIGHLAND   GRAMPIAN

TAYSIDE

CENTRAL   FIFE

LOTHIAN

STRATHCLYDE   BORDERS

DONEGAL

DUMFRIES
& GALLOWAY   NORTHUMBERLAND

TYNE & WEAR

CUMBRIA   DURHAM   CLEVELAND

ISLE
OF MAN

NORTH YORKSHIRE

SLIGO

MAYO

LEITRIM

ROSCOMMON

LONGFORD

CAVAN

MONAGHAN

LOUTH

MEATH

WESTMEATH

GALWAY

OFFALY

DUBLIN

KILDARE

WICKLOW

CLARE

LAOIS

LIMERICK   TIPPERARY   KILKENNY   CARLOW

WEXFORD

KERRY   CORK   WATERFORD

LANCASHIRE   WEST
YORKSHIRE   HUMBERSIDE

MERSEYSIDE   GREATER
MANCHESTER   SOUTH
YORKSHIRE

CHESHIRE   DERBY   LINCOLN

GWYNEDD   CLWYD   NOTTINGHAM

STAFFORD   LEICESTER   NORFOLK

SHROPSHIRE   WARWICK   NORTHAMPTON   CAMBRIDGE   SUFFOLK

POWYS   HEREFORD
& WORCESTER   BEDFORD   HERTFORD   ESSEX

BUCKINGHAM

GLOUCESTER   OXFORD   GREATER
LONDON

DYFED   GWENT

1 WEST GLAMORGAN
2 MID GLAMORGAN
3 EAST GLAMORGAN

1   2   AVON   BERKSHIRE   SURREY   KENT

3   WILTSHIRE   HAMPSHIRE   WEST
SUSSEX   EAST
SUSSEX

SOMERSET

DEVON   DORSET   ISLE OF
WIGHT

CORNWALL

ISLES OF
SCILLY

Counties after United Kingdom Local Government Reorganisation

Abbreviations

1 County names

In most main entries no account is taken of local government reorganisation in the United Kingdom, and places are accordingly assigned to pre-1972 counties. Transfers to Greater London from adjacent counties are usually noted. Names of new counties, when referred to, are not abbreviated.

Abd	Aberdeenshire, Scotland	ELo	East Lothian, Scotland
Agl	Anglesey, Wales	ERY	East Riding of Yorkshire, England
Ang	Angus (Forfarshire), Scotland		
Ant	Antrim, Northern Ireland	Ess	Essex, England
Arg	Argyllshire, Scotland		
Arm	Armagh, Northern Ireland	Fif	Fife, Scotland
Ayr	Ayrshire, Scotland	Flt	Flintshire, Wales
		Fmn	Fermanagh, Northern Ireland
Bd	Bedfordshire, England		
Ber	Berwickshire, Scotland	Gal	Galway, Republic of Ireland
Bk	Buckinghamshire, England	Gl	Gloucestershire, England
Bnf	Banffshire, Scotland	GL	Greater London, England
Bre	Brecknockshire, Wales	Glm	Glamorgan, Wales
Brk	Berkshire, England		
Bte	Buteshire, Scotland	Ha	Hampshire, England
		He	Herefordshire, England
C	Cambridgeshire, England	Hrt	Hertfordshire, England
Cai	Caithness, Scotland	Hu	Huntingdonshire, England
Car	Carlow, Republic of Ireland		
Cav	Cavan, Republic of Ireland	Inv	Inverness-shire, Scotland
Ch	Cheshire, England	IOM	Isle of Man
Cla	Clare, Republic of Ireland		
Clk	Clackmannanshire, Scotland	K	Kent, England
Co	Cornwall, England	Kcb	Kirkcudbrightshire, Scotland
Crd	Cardiganshire, Wales	Ker	Kerry, Republic of Ireland
Crk	Cork, Republic of Ireland	Kld	Kildare, Republic of Ireland
Crm	Carmarthenshire, Wales	Klk	Kilkenny, Republic of Ireland
Crn	Caernarvonshire, Wales	Knc	Kincardineshire, Scotland
Cu	Cumberland, England	Knr	Kinross-shire, Scotland
D	Devon, England	La	Lancashire, England
Db	Derbyshire, England	Lei	Leicestershire, England
Den	Denbighshire, Wales	Lfd	Longford, Republic of Ireland
Dmf	Dumfriesshire, Scotland	LHo	Parts of Holland, Lincolnshire, England
Dnb	Dunbartonshire, Scotland		
Do	Dorset, England	Lim	Limerick, Republic of Ireland
Don	Donegal, Republic of Ireland	LKe	Parts of Kesteven, Lincolnshire, England
Du	Durham, England		
Dub	Dublin, Republic of Ireland	LLi	Parts of Lindsey, Lincolnshire, England
Dwn	Down, Northern Ireland		

16

Lnk	Lanarkshire, Scotland	Tip	Tipperary, Republic of Ireland
Lon	Londonderry, Northern Ireland	Tyr	Tyrone, Northern Ireland
Lth	Louth, Republic of Ireland		
Ltm	Leitrim, Republic of Ireland	W	Wiltshire, England
Lx	Laoighis (Leix), Republic of Ireland	Wa	Warwickshire, England
		Wat	Waterford, Republic of Ireland
		We	Westmorland, England
Mer	Merionethshire, Wales	Wex	Wexford, Republic of Ireland
Mgm	Montgomeryshire, Wales	Wic	Wicklow, Republic of Ireland
Mhn	Monaghan, Republic of Ireland	Wig	Wigtownshire, Scotland
MLo	Midlothian, Scotland	WLo	West Lothian, Scotland
Mon	Monmouthshire, Wales	Wme	Westmeath, Republic of Ireland
Mor	Morayshire, Scotland	Wo	Worcestershire, England
Mth	Meath, Republic of Ireland	WRY	West Riding of Yorkshire, England
Mx	Middlesex, England		
Myo	Mayo, Republic of Ireland	Wt	Isle of Wight, England
Nb	Northumberland, England	Zet	Shetland, Scotland
Nf	Norfolk, England		

2 General

AN	Anglo-Norman
B	British (language)
C	Celtic
c	century (12c, 'twelfth century')
c	*circa*, 'about' (c 1250, 'about 1250')
cf	compare
Co	Cornish
comp	comparative degree
Cu	Cumbric (language)
dat	dative case
DB	Domesday Book
dial	dialect(al)
dim	diminutive
E	English
e g	for example
F	French
FN	field-name(s)
freq	frequent(ly)
G	Gaelic
gen	genitive case
I	Irish
i e	that is
isld	island
L(at)	Latin
lke	lake
M	Middle (ME: Middle English, etc)
Midl	Midland(s)
Mn	Modern (MnI: Modern Irish, etc)

Nrn	Nairnshire, Scotland
NRY	North Riding of Yorkshire, England
Nt	Nottinghamshire, England
Nth	Northamptonshire, England
O	Oxfordshire, England
Off	Offaly, Republic of Ireland
Ork	Orkney, Scotland
Pbl	Peeblesshire, Scotland
Pmb	Pembrokeshire, Wales
Pth	Perthshire, Scotland
R	Rutland, England
Rad	Radnorshire, Wales
Rcm	Roscommon, Republic of Ireland
Rnf	Renfrewshire, Scotland
Ros	Ross and Cromarty, Scotland
Rox	Roxburghshire, Scotland
Sa	Shropshire, England
Sf	Suffolk, England
Sli	Sligo, Republic of Ireland
Slk	Selkirkshire, Scotland
So	Somerset, England
Sr	Surrey, England
St	Staffordshire, England
Stl	Stirlingshire, Scotland
Sut	Sutherland, Scotland
Sx	Sussex, England

mtn	mountain	sg	singular
N	Norse	Std E	Standard English
NCy	North Country (England)	superl	superlative degree
n d	no date	s v	*sub verbo*, 'under the word'
NED	*A New English Dictionary* ('The Oxford English Dictionary')		('refer to the matter discussed under the stated head-word')
NG	Norse-Gaelic	v	*vide*, 'see'
O	Old (OC: Old Celtic, etc)	viz	*videlicet*, 'namely'
P	Pictish (language)	W	Welsh
pl	plural	WCy	West Country (England)
PN	place-name(s)	WS	West Saxon
q v	*quod vide*, 'which see' ('refer to the name in the appropriate place') (plural: qq v)	*	a postulated form, i e a word found as a place-name element but not occurring in literature
riv	river	<	derived from
S	South(ern)	>	becomes
Sc	Scottish	†	District name (UK)
SCy	South Country (England)	††	Name of a new county (UK)

Dictionary of Place-Names

Abbas Combe So, '(land in a) narrow valley held by an abbess', in the tenure of the Abbess of Shaftesbury in the eleventh century [*Cumbe* 1086, *Coumbe Abbatisse* 1327: OE *cumb*, L *abbatissa*].

Abbess Roding Ess, 'township in The Rodings (q v) held by an abbess'. The Abbess of Barking owned this place [*Roinges Abbatisse* 1237, *Abbeys Rothyng* 1518: L *abbatissa*].

Abbots Bromley St. See Kings Langley.

Abbotsford Rox, '(land by) ford held by an abbot', referring to the Abbot of Melrose [OE *abbod, ford*].

Abbots Langley Hrt. See Kings Langley.

Abbots Salford Wa. See Salford O.

Aberaeron Crd, '(place at the) mouth of river Aeron', named after the goddess of war [OW *aber*].

Aberafan Glm 1606, '(place at the) mouth of river Afan (q v)'. Confusion with the fairly common river name Avon led to the adoption of the spelling Aberavon [OW *aber*].

†Aberconwy Crn (District, Gwynedd). See Conway.

Aberdare Glm, 'mouth of the river Dâr, i e oak river'. Both in Wales and in Scotland, some names with the prefix *aber-* occur at the confluence of a river and its tributary. **Abertillery** Mon, for instance, stands at the junction of the Teleri and the Ebwy Fach [1. *Aberdar* 1203, 2. *Teleri* 1332: OW *aber, dâr, ty*].

Aberdaugleddyf Pmb. See Milford Haven.

†Aberdeen Abd, '(place at the) mouth of the Don'. The river bears the name of Devona, a Celtic goddess [*Aberdon* c 1187: P *aber*].

Aberdour Fif, 'mouth of the river Dour, i e waters', the river-name being related to Micheldever, Andover, and Dover (qq v) [*Abirdaur* 1226: P *aber, *dubro-*].

Aberfeldy Pth, 'confluence of Peallaidh', naming an *uruisg* or water-sprite said to haunt the place where the Moness Burn enters the Tay [P *aber*].

Aberfoyle Pth, 'confluence of the streams' [*Abirfull* 1481: P *aber*, G *poll*, gen. *phuill*].

Abergavenny Mon, 'confluence of river Gefenni (i e river called The Smith)'— situated where that river joins the Usk [*Gobannio* 4c, *Abergavenni* 1175: OW *aber, gobannion*].

Abergele Den 1257, 'mouth of the river Gele, i e the blade', alluding to the brightness and straightness of the river [OW *aber, gelau*].

Abergwaun Pmb, 'mouth of the river Gwaun, i e marsh (river)', the Welsh name for Fishguard (q v) [*Fisse-gard id est Aber gweun* 1210: OW *aber, gwaun*].

Abernethy Pth, 'mouth of the Nethy, i e the pure one', referring to a tributary which joins the Tay at this point [*Aburnethige* c 970: P *aber, *nectona*].

Aberpennarth Glm c 1780, 'mouth of the Pennarth, i e stream from the height'. This was the original name of the place now called Mountain Ash. The modern name was first used by J. B. Pryce in the early nineteenth century [*Aber Pennarthe* 1570: W *aber, pennardd*].

Aberporth Crd 1284, 'mouth of the port' [OW *aber, porth*].

Abertillery Mon. See Aberdare.

Aberystwyth Crd, 'mouth of the Ystwyth, i e winding river', naming the situation of the castle about two miles from the modern town, which is actually at the mouth of the Rheidol [*Aberestuuth* 1232: OW *aber, ystwyth*].

Abingdon Brk, '(place by) Æbba's hill', doubtless alluding to the higher ground to the north of the town, which is itself at river-level [*Abbandune* 968: OE *dūn*].

Aboyne Abd, '(place by) white cow river' [*Obyne* 1260: G *abh, bo, fionn*].

Accrington La, 'acorn farm', probably not where acorns were harvested, but, being on the edge of Rossendale Forest, where they were stored [*Akarinton* 12c: OE *æcern, tūn*].

Achnashellach Forest Ros, 'field of willows' [*Auchnashellicht* 1543: G *achadh, seilach*].

Achray Forest Pth, 'forest by shaking ford', in the neighbourhood of a quaking bog [G *àth, chrathaidh*].

Acklam ERY, —NRY. See Acle.

Ackton WRY, **Acton** *freq*: 'village or farm with or by oak trees'. **Acton** Do, however, is 'farm for young sheep', the first element being OE *tacca, initial *t-* being lost as in Elstree Hrt (q v) [1. *Acitone* 1086, 3. *Tacatone* 1086: OE *āc*, **tacca, tūn*].

Acle Nf, 'oak wood or clearing', the second element being OE *lēah*, found in the dative plural in **Acklam** ERY and **Acklam** NRY, 'at the oak woods' [1. *Acle* 1086, 2. *Aclun* 1086, 3. *Achelum* 1086: OE *āc, lēah*].

Acton *freq*. See Ackton.

Adlestrop Gl, 'Tætel's hamlet', with loss of initial *T* as in Elstree (q v) [*Tatelstrop* 12c: OE *þrop*].

†**Adur** *riv* Sx, back-formation adapted from *Portus Adurni*, 'Adurnos's harbour',

identified by Drayton with the mouth of this river. The name is now also applied to a District in West Sussex.

Aerfen, Llyn *lke* Mer, 'Aerfen's lake', alternative name for Bala Lake. Aerfen was the Celtic goddess of war [*i lynn Aerfen* 15c: W *llyn*].

†**Afan** *riv* Glm, probably derived from a personal name. Afan was also the name of the commote (medieval administrative area) and now designates the District in West Glamorgan through which the river flows [*Auan* c 1150]. See also Aberafan.

Affric *riv* Inv, 'dappled (river)' [*Afraic* n d: G *ath* (intensive), *breac*].

Airdrie Lnk, —Nrn: 'high slope' [2. *Ardruigh* n d: G *ard, ruighe*].

Aire *riv* WRY, 'strong river' [*Yr* 959: B *isarā].

Akeman Street Gl-Hrt, 'paved road leading to Bath'. Bath was known in Anglo-Saxon times as *Acemannes cæstre*, 'Akeman's Roman station' [*Akemanestrete* c 1260: OE *strǣt*].

Alba, Albion, 'the world', the old name for Britain. The term also occurs with the meaning 'Scotland' (as distinct from 'Land of the Picts') and is found in Breadalbane (q v). Though Professor Jackson pointed out as long ago as 1948 that the term could not be 'white land' many writers repeat this fallacious interpretation [*Albion* c AD 50 *Alba* c 900: B *albio-*].

Albury Hrt, —O, —Sr, **Aldborough** Nf, —WRY, **Aldbrough** ERY, —NRY, **Aldbury** Hrt, **Aldeburgh** Sf: 'old fortification' [1. *Eldeberie* 1086, 2. *Eldeberie* 1086, 3. *Aldburi* 675, 4. *Aldeburg* 1086, 5. *Aldeburgh* 1316, 6. *Aldenburg* 1086: OE *ald, burh*].

Alcester Wa, 'Roman station by the river Alne, i e the very white river'. A Roman road passes through the town, near which was one of the series of forts aligned parallel to the Fosse Way [*Alencestre* 1138: OE *ceaster*].

Aldborough Nf. See Albury.

Alde *riv* Sf, back-formation from Aldeburgh Sf (See Albury).

Aldershot Ha, 'projecting alder copse,' an instance of the numerous names in -*shot* (OE *scēat*) occurring in eastern Hampshire and the adjoining part of Surrey [*Alreshete* 1248: OE *alor, scēat*].

Aldridge St, 'outlying farm among alder-trees' [*Alrewic* 1086: OE *alor, wīc*].

Alfoxton So, 'Ælfeah's farm' [*Alfagestone* 1086: OE *tūn*].

Alice Holt Forest Ha, 'Aelfsige's wood' [*Alfsiholt* 1169: OE *holt*].

Allan *riv* Stl, **Allen** *riv* Co, **Allen** *riv* Flt, **Aln** *riv* Nb, **Alness** *riv* Ros, **Alun** *riv* Glm, **Alun** *riv* Mon: 'holy one' or 'mighty one', [2. *Alan* 1199, 3. *Alom* 1312, 4. *Alaunon* c 150, *Alne* c 730, 5. *Alune* 1227: B **Alaun*-].

Allerton WRY. See Northallerton NRY.

Alloa Clk, **Alloway** Ayr, **Alva** Clk, **Alvah** Bnf: 'plain of the rocks' [1. *Alveth* 1357, 2. *Auleway* 1324, 3. *Alweth* 1489, 4. *Alveth* 1308: G *allmhagh*].

Alne *riv* Wa. See Alcester.

Alnmouth Nb, 'mouth of river Aln'. For the river-name, see s v Allan. The river rises near **Alnham**, 'homestead on Aln', and passes through †**Alnwick**, 'outlying farm on Aln' 1. *Alnemuth* 1201, 2. *Alneham* 1228, 3. *Alaunos* c 150, *Alnewyk* 1157: OE *mūþa, hām, wīc*].

Alsop en le Dale Db, 'Ælli's little valley', with the explanatory phrase 'in the valley' added, perhaps when -*hop* was no longer understood in this sense. The full French form *en le* (found also in Chapel en le Frith Db and Stretton en le Field Lei) is rare, *le* alone being normally all that remains, as in Newton le Willows, Chester le Street, or Poulton le Fylde (qq v) [*Elleshope* 1086, *Alsope in le dale* 1535: OE *hop, dæl*, OF *en, le*].

Alton Ha, **Alton Barnes** W, **Alton Pancras** Do, **Alton Priors** W: 'farm by the source of a river', Alton Ha being by the source of the river Wey, and Alton Pancras near that of the Piddle. Pancras alludes to the patron saint of the church, Alton Barnes to the feudal tenure of the Berners family, and Alton Priors to St Swithun's Priory in Winchester [1. *Aultone* 1086, 2. *Aweltun* 825, 4. *Aulton prioris* 1199: OE *æwiell, tūn*].

Altrincham Ch, 'homestead of Aldhere's people' [*Aldringeham* 1290: OE -*ingas, hām*].

Alva Clk. See Alloa.

†**Alyn and Deeside** (District: Clwyd). See Allen *riv* Flt (s v Allan), Dee.

Amber *riv* Db, a pre-Celtic name of uncertain meaning. The Sanskrit word *ambhas* means 'water', and this may be the significance of the name. The District of †**Amber Valley** is drained by this river [*Ambre* c 1195].

Ambleside We, 'shieling by Amel, i e river-sandbank', a name referring to the practice of transhumance—the transfer of flocks to upland pastures in the summer and the setting up of temporary shelters, shielings, on the mountain sides. The ON element appears as -*side* in a number of names in Sutherland, as -*setter* in Orkney and Shetland, and as -*shader* in the Hebrides. Spellings ending in -*side* for Ambleside are relatively late

[*Ameleseta* c 1095, *Amylside* c 1400: ON *á*, *melr*, *sǽtr*].

Amersham Bk 1675, 'Ealhmund's village'. In names of this type, it cannot be assumed that the named person was the founder of the settlement, but he or she may have held a position of authority in the early years of its history [*Agmodesham* 1066, *Elmodesham* 1086: OE *hām*].

Amlwch Agl, '(place) near the swamp' [*Anulc* 1254: W *am*, *llwch*].

Ammanford Crm, '(place by) ford over river Aman, i e pig', a recent name for a town which grew up in the nineteenth century [*Amman* 1541: W *banw*, OE *ford*].

Ampleforth NRY, '(place by) ford where sorrel grew' [*Ampreforde* 1086: OE *ampre*, *ford*].

Andover Ha, '(place by) river called Ann, i e ash-tree stream'. The river is now called the Anton, through an eighteenth-century antiquarian's error; a reference in Tacitus to the Trent as *Trisanton* was misread as *Anton* and taken to refer to Andover [*Andeferas* 955: B **onno-*, **dubro-*].

Andreas IOM. See Llanandras.

Anglesey 1248, 'Ongull's island'. The personal name and the second element are both Scandinavian; the Welsh name for the island is Môn [*ynys uon* 815, *Anglesege* 1098, *Ongulsey* 13c: ON *ey*].

†**Angus**, '(territory of) Angus', alluding to Angus, son of Fergus, the eighth-century king of the Picts. As a county name, Angus replaced Forfarshire; it is now a District of Tayside Region [*Enegus* 12c].

Annan Dmf, **Annan** *riv* Dmf, †**Annandale** Dmf: '(place by/valley of) the river'. The non-committal interpretation reflects the obscurity of the name's linguistic history; the valley has been successively *ystrad* (Cumbric), *srath* (Gaelic), and *dale* (< ON *dalr* or OE *dæl*). Annandale is now combined with Eskdale as a District in the Galloway and Dumfries Region [*Annava* 7c, *Estrahanent* 1124, *Stratanant* 1152, *Annandesdale* 1179].

Anstey Do, —Ha, —Hrt, —Lei, —W: 'narrow footpath', the first element indicating a track wide enough for only one person [1. *Anstigan* 942, 2. *Hanstige* 1086, 4. *Anstige* 1086, 5. *Anestige* 1086: OE *ān*, *stig*]. See also West Anstey.

Anstruther Fif, 'the little stream'. A small river enters the sea here [*Anestrothir* c 1205: G *an* (= 'the'), *sruthair*].

Anton *riv* Ha. See Andover.

†**Antrim**, 'solitary farm' [I *cen*, *treabh*].

Appin Arg, 'abbey land' owned by Ligmore Abbey in the Middle Ages [*Apuinn* n d: MI *apdaine*].

Applecross Ros, 'mouth of the Crosan, i e little cross river' [*Aporcrosan* c 1080: P *aber-*, G *cros*].

Aran Island Don, **Aran Islands** Gal: 'ridged place', the Irish word meaning literally 'kidney', with the secondary sense '(arched) back'. The group in Galway Bay consists of three larger islands and a number of much smaller ones. The largest is **Inishmore**, 'great island'; next to it lies **Inishman**, 'middle island', to the landward of which is **Inisheer**, 'eastern island, [1. *Ara Mhor* 20c, 2. *Arainn* 20c: I *ara*, dat. *arainn*, *inis*, *mór*, *meadhon*, *ear*].

Arbroath Ang, 'mouth of river Brothock, i e seething one'. Readers of Southey's poem, *The Inchcape Rock*, will be glad to find that the form he uses is an authentic medieval version of the name [*Aberbrothok* 1178, P *aber*, G *brothach*].

Ardee Lth, 'ford of Ferdia', referring to a hero said to have been killed by Cuchullin at this place [*Ath-Fhirdia* n d: I *àth*].

Arden Wa, 'steep place', almost certainly a British name for a notable natural region, related to the continental forest-name, Ardennes [*Eardene* 1088: B **ardu-*].

Ardersier Inv, 'height of Rosser, i e eastern promontory' [*Ardrosser* 1227, *Arderosseir* 1257: G *ard, ros, ear*].

Ardglass Dwn, 'green height' [I *ard, glas*].

Ardmore Wat, **Ardmore Point** (Islay) Arg: 'great height' [G *ard, mór*].

Ardnamurchan Arg 1500, meaning uncertain. The earliest spellings suggest an association with piracy ('sea sins'), which has some support from actual events, but later forms are taken to mean 'height or point of sea otters' [*Art Muirchol* c 700, *Ardnamurchin* 1309: G *ard, muir, chol, muirchon*].

Ardnaneane Lim, 'height of the birds' [I *ard, en*].

Ardross Ros, 'height of the moorland' or 'height of the promontory' [G *ard, ros*].

Ardrossan Ayr, 'height of the little promontory', the latter being the lower land on which Saltcoats now stands [*Ardrossane* c 1320: G *ard, ros, an*].

†**Ards** (District, Northern Ireland), 'heights'. The District takes its name from Ards Peninsula, east of Strangford Lough, at the head of which is Newtownards. The District includes some territory to the west of the lough [I *ard*].

†**Arfon** (District, Gwynedd), 'opposite Anglesey'. The District name, like many in Wales, is an ancient one, being that of the cantref in which Caernarvon (q v) was situated. *Arfon* also illustrates the way in which consonants in Welsh words change with the addition of prefixes etc, the *M* of *Môn* ('Anglesey') here becoming *f* following the preposition *ar* [*Aruon* 1269: W *ar*].

†**Argyll**, 'country of the Gaels'—the kingdom of the Scots (Dalriada) in Pictish territory. The invaders gained entry through Kintyre. Argyll (with its offshore islands) is now combined with Bute (apart from Arran) as a District in Strathclyde Region [*Arregaithel* c 970, *Argail* 1292: OI *airer*].

Arklow Wic, 'Arnkel's meadow', the Scandinavian owner of the personal name not being identified [*Herketelou* 1177: ON *ló*].

Arley *freq*, 'eagle wood or clearing' [OE *earn, lēah*].

Armadale (Skye) Inv, **Armadale** Sut: 'elongated valley', the first element denoting an arm-shaped piece of land. **Armadale** WLo is a transferred name, from its former owner, Lord Armadale, who derived his title from the Sutherland place [*Armidill* 1723: ON *armr, dalr*].

†**Armagh**, 'height of Macha' [*Altitudo Machae* 807, *Ard Macha* n d: I *ard*].

Armitage St, 'hermitage' [*Armytage* 1520: OF *ermitage*].

Arnold ERY,—Nt 1474: 'eagles' nook of land' [1. *Ærnhale* 1190, 2. *Ernehale* 1086: OE *earn, halh*].

Arran Bte, meaning unknown.

Asby Cu, **Great & Little Asby** We, **Ashby** *freq:* 'farm by or with ash trees'. Forms with additions include **Canons Ashby** Nth, which alludes to the priory founded there in the twelfth century; **Ashby Folville** Lei, **Ashby Mears** Nth, **Ashby de la Launde** LLi, and **Ashby de la**

Zouch Lei bear the names of feudal tenants. **Ashby Puerorum** LLi provided support for the young choristers of Lincoln Cathedral. Possibly only the rare **Asby** names represent the true Scandinavian compound, the numerous examples of **Ashby** being perhaps Scandinavianised forms of the even more common **Ashton** (q v) [1. *Askeby* 1234, 2. *Aschaby* c 1160, 3. *Esseby Canonicorum* 1254, 6. *Ascebi* 1086, *Esseby la Zusche* 1241, 7. *Aschebi* 1086, *Askeby ... parvorum chori Lincoln'* 1291: OE *æsc*, ON *askr, bý*].

Ascot Brk,—O, **Ascot d'Oilly** O, **Ascot under Wychwood** O, **Ascott** Bk: 'eastern cottage'. The affix d'Oilly is manorial; Wido de Oileo held the place in the late eleventh century [1. *Estcota* 1177, 2. *Ascote Doilly* 1327, 4. *Estcota* 1220: OE *ēast, cot*]. See Wychwood.

Ash *freq*, '(place with or by) ash tree(s)' [OE *æsc*].

Ashby. See Asby.

†**Ashfield** Nt, 'open land with ash trees', until recently a 'lost', i e disused, name apart from its occurrence in **Sutton-in-Ashfield** and **Kirkby-in-Ashfield** Nt. It has now been revived to designate a District formed by local government reorganisation [*Esfeld* 1216: OE *æsc, feld*].

Ashford D,—Db, —Sa. See Ashford Mx.

†**Ashford** K, 'ford by an ash copse', the modern form concealing either the suffix meaning 'clump of . . .'(OE -*et*) or the element that appears in Aldershot Ha and Exceat Sx (qq v), [*Essetesford* 1046: OE *æscet/æsc, scēat, ford*].

Ashford Mx, possibly 'ford by *Ecles, i e pasture with or by oak trees'. Whatever this name means, it is certainly not 'ford by ash trees', although **Ashford** D,

Ashford Db, and **Ashford Bowdler** and **Carbonel** Sa, can be so interpreted. The Middlesex place is at a ford over a stream called *Eclesbroc* in the tenth century, and it has been suggested that the stream name is the foundation on which the habitation name is built; the interpretation now proposed implies that both the stream-name and the ford-name derive from **Ecles*, ultimately *æcen-lǣs*, the phonetic development from which to the modern form seems quite normal [*Ecelesford* 969: OE *æcen, lǣs, ford*].

Ashridge Hrt, 'long hill covered with ash trees', indicating that the area was even more thickly wooded in earlier centuries than it is now. **Asheridge** Bk lies across the valley of the river Bulbourne, less than six miles away [1. *Assherugge* c 1200, 2. *Esregge* 1200, *Asherugge* 1535: OE *æsc, hrycg*].

Ashtead Sr, 'ash-tree place' [*Estede* c 1150: OE *æsc, stede*].

Ashton *freq*, 'farm with or by ash trees', occasionally with various affixes. These are topographical in **Ashton on Mersey** Ch, **Ashton under Hill** Gl. **Ashton in Makerfield** La, and **Ashton under Lyne** La. The Hill referred to is Bredon Hill Wo; **Makerfield** is 'open land by the ruin'; the region known as The Lyme, perhaps 'elm-grown place', is alluded to in numerous place-names in Lancs, Cheshire, Staffordshire, and Shropshire [OE *æsc, tūn*]. See also Asby.

Askeaton Lim, 'Gephtine's cataract' [*Eas-Gephtine* n d: I *eas*].

Aspatria Cu, '(place by) Patrick's ash tree'. The order of the elements here—the personal name following the generic word—is Celtic, and due to the Irish-Norse settlers in Cumbria, who brought with them a Norse dialect greatly influenced by Irish. Other examples of this word order are Brigsteer We, 'Styr's bridge' and Stone Arthur, in Grasmere We 'Arthur's stone' (*Askpatrik* 1291: ON *askr*).

Aston *freq*, usually 'eastern farm', but a few instances are variants of Ashton (q v); these are **Aston He** (but not **Aston Ingham** He), **Aston on Clun** Sa, and **Cold Aston** Gl [1. *Esscetuna* 1123, 4. *Assheston* 1291, *Æsctun* 931: OE *ēast*, *æsc*, *tūn*].

Aston Juxta Mondrum Ch. See Mondrum.

Athlone Wme, 'ford of Luan' [*Áth Luain* n d: I *àth*].

Atholl Pth. See Blair Atholl.

Athy Kld, 'ford of Ae', named after a Munster chieftain who took part in a battle here [*Ath-I* n d: I *àth*].

Auchinleck Ayr, 'field of the flat stones' [*Auechinlec* 1239: G *achadh*, *leac*].

Auchterarder Pth, 'upland of high water' [*Vchterardouere* c 1200: G *uachdar*, *ard*, *dobhar*].

Auchtermuchty Fif, 'upland of the pig place' [*Vchtermuckethin* c 1210: G *uachdar*, *muccatu*].

Auckland. See Bishop Auckland.

Aughrim   Gal,—Wic: 'horse   ridge' [2. *Aghrym* c 1500: I *each*, *dhruim*].

Aughton ERY,—La (x 2),—WRY: 'oak farm', a northern variant of Acton (q v) [1. *Actun* 1086, 2. *Achetun* 1086, 3. *Aghton* c 1330, 4. *Actone* 1086: OE *āc*, *tūn*].

Aultbea Ros, 'birch glen' [G *allt*, *beith*].

Avebury W, 'Afa's fortified place' [*Avreberie* 1086: OE *burh*].

Avoca *riv* Wic, a modern name, adapting without warrant Ptolemy's *Oboka* to a length of the river Avonmore (q v), viz the parts immediately above and below the meeting of the waters, where the Avonmore is joined by the Avonbeg ('little water').

Avon *riv* Bnf,—*riv* Ha,—*riv* Nth-Wo,—*riv* W-Gl,—*riv* W-Ha—*riv* WLo: 'river' [1. *Ovania* 756, 2. *Auene* 813, 3. *Afen* c 705, 4. *Abon* 688, 5. *Afene* 672, 6. *Hæfe* 710, *Avin* c 1128: B *abonā*].

††**Avon,** new English county named after the Bristol, or Lower, Avon.

Avonmore *riv* Wic, 'great water', said by W. J. Watson to have been formerly *Dea*, 'goddess' (cf Dee) [*The Great Water* 1599, *River of Owenmore* 1660: OI *abhainn, mhór*].

Awe, Loch *lke* Arg, **Loch Awe** *lke* Sut: 'lake of a river called Awe', the river name being a Gaelic variant of Avon (q v) [1. *Aba* 700, *Lochaue* 1292; G *abh*].

Axe *riv* Do-D,—*riv* So-D: 'water, river', related to Esk, Exe, and Usk (qq v) [1. *Axan* 1005, 2. *Aesce* 712: B *iscā*].

Axminster D, 'monastery or large church by river Axe (q v), [*Ascanamynster* c 900: OE *mynster*].

Aylesbury Bk, 'Ægel's fortified place', with a personal name which occurs also in **Aylesford** K, **Aylestone** Lei, and **Aylesworth** Nth, respectively '.. ford', 'farm', and 'enclosure'. The **Three Hundreds of Aylesbury**, marked on Ordnance Survey maps, are the Aylesbury, Stone, and Risborough Hundreds—a grouping similar to that found in the Chiltern Hundreds (q v) [*Aegelesburh* c 900: OE *burh*].

Aylesford K, **Aylestone** Lei, **Aylesworth** Nth. See Aylesbury.

Ayot St Lawrence Hrt, **Ayot St Peter**
Hrt: 'Æga's gap', no reference to an
island being possible here, though a
derivation from OE *iggoð* has been often
suggested. Etymological considerations,
as well as topography, support the interpretation here proposed; OE *geat*
develops to *yott* in field-names in this
county (cf EFN 265), and this derivation
is consistent with the earliest spellings
of both the Ayots. The 'gap' is probably
the one between the two places, which
are on hills rising to more than 100m.
The affixes refer to the dedications of the
churches [1. *Aiegete* c 1060, *Ægete* 1065,
Aette de Sco Laur' 1255, 2. *Eyotte Sci
Petri* 1535: OE *geat*].

Ayr Ayr, '(place at mouth of) river'—
strictly speaking 'of river called Ayr.
i e river', necessary for the interpretation
of the former name *Inverayr*. The river-
name is an ancient one, with continental
counterparts, e g Aar and Ahr,
tributaries of the Rhine [*Ar* 1177:
B *Arā*].

Ayston R, 'Æþelstan's village or farm'
[*Æðelstanestun* 1046: OE *tūn*].

Azerley WRY, 'Azur's wood or clearing',
a hybrid, the personal name being
Scandinavian and the second element
Old English [*Assterle*, *Haserlai* 1068:
OE *lēah*].

Babbacombe D, 'Babba's valley' [*Babbe-
cumbe* c 1200: OE *cumb*].

Backway D. See Bakewell.

Bacup La, 'small valley by a ridge',
evidently noted for its muddiness in the
thirteenth century (OE *fūl* 'foul, dirty')
[*Fulebachope* c 1200, *Bacop* 1324: OE
fūl, *bæc*, *hop*].

†**Badenoch** Inv, 'submerged land', i e land
subject to inundation [*Badenach* 1229: G
baideanach < *baithte*, 'drowned'].

Badminton Gl. See Great Badminton.

Baginton Wa. See Bakewell.

Bagley *freq*, **Baguley** Ch: 'woodland fre-
quented by badgers' [1. *Bacgan leah* 955,
Bagaleia 1086 etc; 2. *Baglelei* 1086,
Baguley 1398: OE *bagga*, *lēah*].

Bagshot Sr, 'patch of woodland
frequented by badgers' [*Bagshete* 1165:
OE *bagga*, *scēat*].

Baile Atha Cliath Dub, 'town at the hurdle
ford'. The name *Dublin* itself is of respect-
able antiquity and Celtic origin, but the
ancient *Ath-Cliath* is preferred by speakers
of current Irish, remembering not the
'black pool' of the Liffey (cf Dublin)
but the means by which the obstacle of
the river was overcome—the artificial
ford of woven withies. The causeway
allowed unbroken passage of the road
from Wicklow to Tara [I *baile*, *àth*,
cliath].

Bakewell Db 1330, 'Beadeca's spring'.
This personal name is found also in
Baginton Wa ('farm associated with
Beadeca' *Badechitone* 1086), **Barkfold** Sx
('Beadeca's enclosure'), and **Backway** D
(in Shebbear parish: 'Beadeca's way or
path', *Badekeweye* 1330) [*to Bedecan
wiellon* 924, *Badequella* 1086: OE *wella*].

Bala Mer 1878, 'outlet'. The town stands
at the place where the river Dee leaves
the lake, known in English as Bala Lake
and in Welsh as **Llyn Tegid**, 'lake of
Tegid'. Tegid is a personal name. To the
bards, the lake was Llyn Aerfen (q v)
[W *bala*, 'outlet'].

Balbriggan Dub, 'Brecan's farm' [I
baile].

Balcomie Fif, 'Colman's village' [*Bal-
colmie* 1253: G *baile*].

Baldock Hrt, 'Baghdad', founded and
named by the Knights Templars in the

12th century, to whom the Arabian city was known as *Baldac* [*Baldoce* c 1140, *Baldac* 1168].

Baldrine IOM, 'blackthorn farm' [G *baile, draighionn*].

Balemartine (Tiree) Arg, 'Martin's village' [*Balmartin* 1654: G *baile*].

Balerno MLo, 'sloe-tree homestead' [*Balhernoch* 1280: G *baile, airneach*].

Balfour Knc,—(Shapinsay) Ork: 'pasture farm' [G *baile, pór*].

Balgowan Inv, **Balgown** (Skye) Inv, **Balgown Point** Wig: 'smith's farm' [G *baile, gobhan*].

Balham Sr/GL, 'smooth meadow' [*Bælgenham* 957: OE *bealg, hamm*].

Balintore Ang,—Ros: 'bleaching village' [G *bailean, todhair*].

Ballantrae Ayr, 'village on the shore' [G *baile, traigh*].

Ballina Myo, 'ford-mouth of the wood' [I *Bel-atha-an-fheadha*].

Ballycastle Ant, 'farm by a castle' [I *baile*, E *castle*].

Ballycastle May, 'farm by a stone fort' [I *Baile-an-chaisil*]. See Cashel.

†Ballymena Ant, 'middle town' [I *baile, meadhonach*].

†Ballymoney Ant, 'homestead by a thicket' [I *baile, muine*].

Ballynahinch Dwn,—Tip, 'homestead by an island' [I *baile, inis*].

Balmoral Abd, 'farm of the big clearing' [*Bouchmorale* 1451: G *baile, mór; B ial*, 'open space'].

Balnakiel Slk. See Buccleuch.

Bamburgh Nb, 'Bebba's fortified place'. Bebba, or Bebbe, was the wife of king Æþelfrið of Northumbria, who ruled between 593 and 617 [*Bebbanburh* c 875, *Banburg* 1212: OE *burh*].

Banbury O, 'Bana's fortified place' [*Banesberie* 1086; OE *burh*].

†Banff Bnf, 'little pig'. Affectionate animal names are occasionally applied to rivers, and it is possible that this name was an alternative appellation of the river Deveron. Banff is now combined with Buchan (q v) as a District in Grampian Region [*Banb* c 1150: G *banbh*].

Bangor Crn 1191—Dwn,—Flt 1277: 'rod in a wattled fence'. The cryptic interpretation normally given makes it necessary to explain that these were all sites of monastic establishments, enclosed within plaited fences. The Welsh name in Ulster is due to Bangor Dwn being a daughter foundation of Bangor Crn [1. *Benchoer* 634, 3. *Bancor* 8c: W *bangor*].

Bannockburn Stl 1314, 'stream from Bannock, i e peaked hill' [*Bannokburne* 1654: OW *bannauc*, OE *burna*].

Bantry Crk, '(place of) Beann's people'. Beann was one of the sons of Conor mac Nessa, the first-century king of Ulster [I *Beanntraighe*, 'the race of Beann'].

Bard Head (Bressay) Zet. See Burwick.

Barkfold Sx. See Bakewell.

Barking Ess. '(place of) Berica's people' [*Berecingas* 695: OE *-ingas*].

Barle *riv* So, 'hill stream' [*Bergel* 1219: OE *beorg, wella*].

Barmouth Mer, '(place at) mouth of river Mawddach'. This name bristles with anomalies. The current English form looks like a word of Anglo-Saxon origin, whereas both elements are Celtic. The modern Welsh forms include one (Y Bermo) in which the first syllable has been replaced by the definite article. The confusion stems primarily from the fact that Barmouth is at the mouth of a river whose name, Mawdd, resembles the English word *mouth*. The spelling *Abermowth* 1410 places these difficulties in perspective. Regular (but in this instance, erroneous) accentuation of the penultimate syllable would produce the English-sounding 'Bermouth', developing to the present form Barmouth. Welsh sound changes account for the development to Abermo, misunderstood as Y Bermo [*Abermau* 1284: W *aber*]. See also Mawddach.

Barnes Sr/GL, 1387, '(place by) a barn or barns'. Early spellings vary between singular and plural forms, as do those of **Berne** Do, which has settled down to the singular at the present day [1. *of Bærnun* c 1000, *Berne* 1086, *Bernes* 1222, 2. *La Berne* 1281, *Le Bernes* 1431: OE *bere-ærn*].

Barnet Hrt/GL 1196: 'burnt place'. Several places in the area bear the name, distinguished by prefixes: **Chipping Barnet** ('Barnet with a market') or **High Barnet, East Barnet, New Barnet,** and **Friern Barnet** ('Barnet of the brethren'). Friern Barnet was held by the Knights of St John of Jerusalem and so was placed in Middlesex when the medieval county boundaries were determined [1. *Barneto* c 1070, 2. *Chepyng Barnet* 1329, 4. *Chipping Barnet al. High Barnet* 1628, 6. *Freron Barnet* 1460: OE *bærnet, cieping* ME *frere*].

Barnsley Do, —Gl, †—WRY, —Wt: 'Beorn's woodland clearing'. The exact form of the personal name is different in each instance, as can be inferred from the early spellings: 1. *Bernardeslega* 1178 (Beornheard), 2. *Barmodeslea* c 802

(Beornmōd), 3. *Berneslai* 1086 (Beorn), 4. *Benverdeslei* 1086 (Beornfriŏ) [OE *lēah*].

Barnstaple D 1675, 'bearded pile', alluding to a post marked with a bunch of twigs or something similar, used to indicate a mooring place or navigation channel. In some Latin documents, and on old maps and milestones, the form *Barum* is found. This is the same kind of abbreviation as *Sarum* for Salisbury (q v) [*Beardastapol, Bardanstapol* c 1000, *Barnestaple* 1086, *Ecclesia Barum* 1291: OE *beard, stapol*].

Baron's Court GL, possibly an arbitrary name applied without historical warrant in the late nineteenth century.

Barra *isld* Inv. 'hill island' [*Barru* c 1090, *Barey* c 1200: OC **barro-*. ON *ey*].

Barrhead Rnf, 'head headland', a tautologous form combining Gaelic and English synonyms [G *barr*, 'top', MnE *head*].

Barrow *freq*, '(place in or by) a wood'. Exceptions are Barrow in Furness (q v) and **Barrow** R. The latter, like one of several Barrows in Somerset, means 'hill' [Gl: *Berwe* 12c, Sa: *Barwe* 1267, Sf: *Baro* 1086, R: *Berghes* 1206, So: *La Bergh* 1232: OE *bearu, beorg*].

†**Barrow in Furness** La, 'headland island in Furness, i e buttock promontory'. The elements in Barrow are identical with those in Barra but OC *barro-* in this name has the sense 'tip of a promontory', rather than 'peak'. The town is now in Cumbria and provides the name for a District (*Barrai* 1190, *Futhþernessa* c 1150: OC **barro-*, ON *ey, fuŏ, nes*).

Barrowby LKe, —WRY (x 2): 'farm on the hills' [1. *Bergebi* 1086, 2. *Berghebi* 1086: ON *berg, bý*].

Barry Glm 1176, 'hill place' [*Barri* c 1190: OW *barr*].

Barton *freq*, 'barley farm' or possibly 'corn farm', used of an outlying settlement, subsidiary to a main village, manor, or monastery. Names with distinctive additions include **Barton Bendish** Nf ('within the ditch', i e the Devil's Ditch), **Barton in the Clay** Bd, **Barton on the Heath** Wa, and **Barton le Willows** NRY [OE *beretūn*].

Basing Ha, '(place of) Basa's folk'. **Basingstoke** Ha is 'secondary settlement of the Basings' [1. *æt Basengum* 871 2. *Onem* ('just by') *Basinga stoc* 990: OE *ing, stoc*].

Bassenthwaite Lake Cu, 'lake by Bastun's clearing', earlier called Bastunwater, this is the only stretch of water in the English Lake District which has the word *Lake* in its name [*Bastunwater* c 1220: OE *wæter*, ON *þveit*, ME *lake*].

†**Bassetlaw** Nt, possibly 'mound or hill of the dwellers in the burnt place'. Formerly the name of a large wapentake in the north of Nottinghamshire, it is now applied to the District covering almost the same area [*Bernesedelaue* 1086: OE *bærnet, sæte, hlāw*].

†**Bath** So, 'baths'. The general sense of the OE word is 'pool, bathing place', but the strong associations of this particular place suggest elegant buildings constructed for purposes of bathing. In other place-names, e g **Bathley** Nt or **Simonsbath** So, the sense is less specialised; the first syllable in **Batheaston** So, **Bathford** So, and **Bathwick** So merely refers to proximity to the town of Bath [1. *æt Baþum* 796, 2. *Badeleie* 1086, 3. *Simonsbath* 1550, 4. *Estun* 1086, *Batheneston* 1258, 5. *æt Forda* 957, 6. *Wiche* 1086: OE *bæð, lēah, ēast, tūn ford, wīc*].

Batheaston So, **Bathford** So. See Bath.

Bathgate WLo, 'boar wood', a Celtic, but not a Gaelic, name, belonging instead to the Brittonic 'Cumbric' language. The second element is related to that found in Lichfield (q v) [*Batket* c 1160: Cu **badd, *ceto-*].

Bathley Nt, **Bathwick** So. See Bath.

Batley WRY 'Bata's wood' [*Bateleia* 1086: OE *lēah*].

Battersea Sr/GL, 'Beaduric's island'. Confusion of the personal name with Patric occurs in DB and other early documents, and this may account for the *-t-* in the modern form of the name [*Batriceseg ante* 1066, *Patricesy* 1086: OE *ēg*].

Battle Sx, 'place of battle'. An abbey was founded in memory of the battle of Hastings, near the site of the conflict. Less well known is **Battlefield** Sa, where a college of secular canons was established by Henry IV to commemorate the Battle of Shrewsbury (1403) [1. *La batailge* 1086, 2. *St Mary Magdalene of Batelfeld* 1415: OF *bataille*].

Beachy Head Sx, 'fine headland headland,' a tautologous hybrid name. Being that of a coastal feature, the name was associated with *beach*. **Beauchief** Db has the same origin, retains more evidence of its French ancestry, and has not been provided with a redundant *Head* [1. *Beuchef* 1279, 2. *Be(a)uchef* c 1179: OF *beau, chef*].

†**Beaconsfield** Bk, 'open land near a beacon' [*Bekenesfeld* 1185: OE *bēacon, feld*].

Beadlow Bd. See Beaulieu.

Beamish Du, 'fine mansion' [*Bewmis* 1288: OF *beau, mes*].

Beamond Bk. See Beaumont.

Beane riv Hrt, 'little goddess' [*Bene ficcan* 913: OW *ben, *bicc].

Bear Park Du, **Beaurepaire** Ha, **Belper** Db 1577: 'fine retreat' [1. *Beaurepayre* 1267, 2. *Beaurepeir* 1346, 3. *Be(a)urepeir* 1231, *Belpare* 1520: OF *beau*, *repaire*].

Beauchamp Roding Ess, 'Roding (q v) in the tenure of the de Beauchamp family'. An earlier name alluded to the dedication of the church to St Botolph [*Rothyng Bothulf* 1254, *Roynges Beuchamp* 1238: OE *-ingas*].

Beauchief Db. See Beachy Head.

Beaudesert St, 1293, —Wa 1227: 'fine wilderness' [2. *Beldesert* 1181: OF *beau*, *desert*].

Beaufront Nb, 'beautiful (hill-) brow' [*Beaufroun* 1356: OF *beau*, *front*].

Beaulieu Ha, **Beauly** Inv 1300, **Bewdley** Wo, **Bewley** Du: 'fine place'. Bewley Du and Bewdley Wo show varying degrees of Anglicisation, taken a step further in **Beadlow** Bd (in the parish of Clophill). **Bewley Castle** We 1609 is a transferred name from Beaulieu Ha, one of whose abbots, Hugh, became Bishop of Carlisle and resided here in the early thirteenth century [1. *Bellus Locus Regis* 1205, 2. *Prioratus de bello loco* 1230, 3. *Beuleu* 1275, *Bellum Locum* 1308, 4. *Bellus Locus* c 1335, 5. *Beaulieu* 1254, *Bedlowe* 1578, 6. *Bellum Locum in Westmeria* 1250, *Bellewe* 1274: OF *beau*, *lieu*].

Beaumanor Lei, 'fine estate' [*Beumaner* 1265: OF *beau*, *maner*].

Beaumaris Agl 1296, 'fine marsh' [*Bello Marisco* 1284: OF *beau*, *marais*].

Beaumont Cu, —Ess, —La: 'fine hill'. The pronunciation of these names varies between 'bo-' in the Essex and Lancs examples and 'bee-' in the Cumberland name, a pronunciation actually represented in the spelling of **Beamond** Bk, which also belongs here. It is uncertain how far these complimentary names in *Beau-* and *Bel-* designate genuinely beautiful landscapes; in at least one instance a less flattering name has been replaced by a *Beau-* form, the Essex example having been changed from a name meaning 'foul pit' [1. *Beaumund* 1292, 2. *Fulepet* 1086, *Bealmont* c 1177, 3. *Bellus Mons* 1190, *Belmunt* 1218: OF *beau*, *mont*].

Beaurepaire Ha. See Bear Park.

Beccles Sf, 'pasture by a stream', the town being beside the river Waveney [*Becles* 1086: OE *bæce*, *læs*].

Beckenham K/GL, 'Beohha's homestead' [*Biohhahema* 862, *Bacheham* 1086; OE *hām*].

Beckery Island So, 'little Ireland', a name bestowed by Irish monks [*Bekeria* 971: OI *bec-Eriu*].

Bedale NRY 1086, 'Beda's nook of land' [OE *halh*].

Beddgelert Crn 1791, 'Celert's grave', referring to an unidentified hero of Irish origin. The association of the place with Gelert, Llewelyn's hound, is based on the fortuitous similarity of the names [*Bekelert* 1258, *Bedkelerd* 1269: W *bedd*].

Beddington Sr, 'farm associated with a man called Beadda' [*Beaddinctun* c 905: OE *-ingtūn*].

†**Bedford** Bd 1198, 'Beda's ford'. The county name, like most in central England, combines OE *scir* with the name of the county town [1. *Bedanford* 918, 2. *Bedanfordscir* 1011: OE *ford*, *scir*].

Bedford Levels C: areas of Fenland drained under the direction of Francis, Earl of Bedford [*Great Level of the Fens* 1632].

Beeston Bd, —Nf, —Nt 1181, —WRY 1180: 'village where bent-grass grew'. There are three other examples in Norfolk: **Beeston Regis** 1207, **Beeston St Andrew**, and **Beeston St Lawrence** [1. *Bistone* 1086, 2. *Bestone* 1254, 3. *Bestune* 1086, 4. *Bestone* 1086, 5. *Besentuna* 1086, 6. *Bes(e)tuna* 1086, 7. *Bestone* c 1045: OE **bēos, tūn*].

Beith Ayr, 'birch (place)' [G *beither*].

Belasis Du 1305, **Bellasis** Du, —Nb, **Bellasize** ERY, **Belsars** C, **Belses** Rox, **Belsize** Hrt 1840, —Nf, —Nth: 'fine residence or seat' [2. *Belasis* 14c, 3. *Beleassis* 1279, 4. *Belasize* 1312, 8. *Belas(s)ise* c 1220: OF *bel, assis*].

†**Belfast** Ant, 'sandbank ford', alluding to the stretch of sand, uncovered at low tide, by which the river could be crossed (*Belfeirsde* n d: OI *bel, fearsad*).

Belmont *freq*, 'fine hill', found throughout the British Isles, from Shetland (Unst) to Offaly, Lancs, and Surrey. The places are usually very small, and most records of the name, a variant of Beaumont (q v), quite late. Belmont Hrt, in East Barnet, is on record from 1811, replacing Mount Pleasant, found from 1636 onwards [OF *beau, bel, mont*].

Belper Db. See Bear Park.

Belsars C, **Belses** Rox, **Belsize** Hrt. See Belasis.

Belvoir Lei, 'fine view' [*Belveder* 1130, *Beluueir* c 1175: OF *beau, bel, vedeir*].

Bembridge Wt, '(place) within the bridge' [*Bynnebrygg* 1316: OE *binnan, brycg*].

Benbecula *isld* Inv, perhaps 'hill of the fords' [*Beanbeacla* 1449: G *beinn-na-fhaodla*].

Benbeg *mtn* Gal, 'little hill' [I *beinn, beag*].

Benbrack *mtn* Ayr, —*mtn* Cav, —*mtn* Dmf-Kcb, —*mtn* Kcb: 'speckled hill' [G *beinn, breac*].

Benburb Tyr, 'bold peak'. The settlement developed near a cliff overhanging the river Blackwater [I *bheann-bhorb*].

Ben Cruachan *mtn* Arg, 'mountain of the stacks' [*Crechanben* c 1375: G *beinn, cruach*].

Benderloch Arg, 'hill between two lochs' [*Bintaloch* 1654: G *beinn eader da loch*].

Benenden K, 'swine pasture of Bionna's folk'. The numerous place-names ending in -*den* in this county recall the agricultural practice of the early English settlers of Kent, who utilised the upland forest of the Weald as detached pasture territory appended to settlements elsewhere. Sometimes the pasture was at a considerable distance from the home area; Tenterden, for instance 'swine pasture of the men of Thanet', is about forty miles from that area. Bionna's people, therefore, may well have settled a long way from Benenden [*Bynidene* 993, *Benindene* 1086: OE *denn*].

Bengeo Hrt 1517, 'spur of land of the dwellers by the river Beane (q v)'. The same river-name is embodied in **Bennington** Hrt, 1638 'village of dwellers by river Beane' [1. *Belingehou* 1086, *Beningeho* c 1220, *Bengeho* 1378, 2. *Beljntone* 1086, *Beninton(e)* 1086: *hōh, -ing, tūn*].

Ben Glas *mtn* Pth, 'grey mountain' [G *beinn, glas*].

Ben Lomond *mtn* Stl. See Lomond.

Ben More *mtn freq*, 'great mountain' [G *beinn, mór*].

Ben Nevis *mtn* Inv, 'mountain by the river Nevis, i e the spiteful one'. References in Gaelic literature to the river and its glen are in uncomplimentary terms [*Gleann Nibheis* 16c: G *nemess*].

Bennington Hrt. See Bengeo.

Bentley *freq*, 'clearing in which bent-grass grew'. These names are parallel to the Beeston names; the latter contain OE **beos*, whereas Bentley is from the more usual *beonet*. **Fenny Bentley** Db 1271 and **Hungry Bentley** Db 1464 have additions descriptive of the soil—marshy and infertile respectively. **Bentley Pauncefote** Wo, which for a short time was also known as Stretch Bentley, alludes to the families of Richard Panzeuot, who held land here in 1185, and of Streche, the owners of an estate in 1275 [1. *Benedlege* 1086, *Fennibent(e)ley(e)* 1271, 2. *Beneleie* 1086, *Hungrybentele* 1269, 3. *Beneslei* 1086, *Benetlege Pancevot* 1212, 4. *Stretch Bentley* 1578: OE *beonet, lēah*].

Ben Vorlich *mtn* Dnb, —*mtn* Pth: 'mountain of the sea-bag'. 'Sea-bag' is the picturesque name given to bays in the lochs adjacent to mountains [G *beinn, murbhlag*, gen. *mhur' laig*].

Berkeley Gl: 'birch wood or clearing' [*Beorclea* 824, *Berchelai* 1086: OE *beorc, lēah*].

Berkhamsted Hrt, 'homestead by a hill'. The interpretation 'birch-tree homestead' has been suggested in the past, supported by the abundance of birches in the vicinity, but not confirmed by the early spellings [*æt Beorhðanstædæ* c 875, *Beorhhamstede* c 1100: OE *beorg, hāmstede*].

Berkshire, 'county about the wood of *Barroc*, i e hilly place', an exception among county names in not having a town-name as its first element. The wood was probably near Hungerford [*Berrocscire, Bearrocscire* 893, *Barrocscire* 11c, *Barkssire* c 1300: B **barrŏg*, OE *scīr*].

Bermondsey Sr/GL, 'Beornmund's island', a path of dry ground amid the marshes of the lower Thames valley [*Vermundesei* c 712, *Bermundesye* 1086: OE *ēg*].

Berne Do. See Barnes.

Bernwood Forest Bk. See Wotton.

Berrynarbor D, 'Nerebert's holding at the fortified place'. For some time during the Middle Ages the place was simply Bury, though in Domesday Book it is recorded as *Hurtesberia*, 'Heort's fortified place'. The name of the Nerebert or Narbert family was later appended as a feudal addition [*Hertesberie* 1121, *Biri* 1167, *Bury juxta Ilfredcumbe* 1281, *Berri Neyberd* 1281, *Byry in Arberd* 1394: OE *burh*].

Berwick *freq*, 'barley farm', usually implying 'outlying lands of a manor retained for the lord's use'. Various additions are found, such as **Berwick Maviston** Sa and **Berwick Bassett** W, alluding to the families of Malveisin and Basset respectively. Other Wiltshire Berwicks include **Berwick St James, Berwick St John**, and **Berwick St Leonard**; all these indicate the dedication of the church. †**Berwick upon Tweed** Nb has the distinction of providing a name for the shire, now a District, in the Borders Region of Scotland [OE *berewīc*].

Bethel Crn, **Bethesda** Crn, **Bethlehem** Crm: names of Biblical places applied to Methodist chapels around which settlements developed.

Bettyhill Cai, 'hill named in honour of Betty', a hamlet commemorating Margaret, Marchioness of Stafford.

Betws-y-Coed Crn, 'chapel in the wood'. W *betws* is a loanword from Middle English and represents *bed-hūs*, 'bead house, oratory' [*Betus* 1254, *Bettws y Coed* 1727: W *coed*].

†**Beverley** ERY, 'beaver stream' [*Beferlic* c 1000: OE *beofor*, *lecc].

Bewcastle Cu, 'shelter at a Roman station'. Destroyed and rebuilt several times during the Roman occupation, this outpost north of Hadrian's Wall offered a supply of useful materials for the construction of temporary shelters for sheep or shepherds. The variant form -*castle* occurs also in **Horncastle** L and **Pabcastle** Cu,'Roman station on a tongue of land (between rivers)' and 'Roman station occupied by a hermit' [1. *Buchecastre* c 1178, *Bothecaster* 1272, *Bothecastell* 1327, 2. *Hornecastre* 1086, 3. *Papecastre* 1267: OE *ceaster*, ON *búð*, OE *horn*, ON *papi*].

Bewdley Wo, **Bewley** Du. See Beaulieu.

Bexhill Sx, **Bexley** K: 'box wood'. The confusion with -*hill* in the first name doubtless first arose from the misreading of a form like '*Bixele*', taking the final -*e* as a mere grammatical termination instead of an essential component of the element *lēah* [1. *Bexlea* 772, *Bexelei* 1086, *Bixel* 1278, *Byxhell* 1496, 2. *Bixle* c 780 *Byxlea* 814: OE *byxe, *lēah*].

Biddulph St, '(place) beside a quarry' [*Bidolf* 1086, *Bydulf* 1291: OE *bi*, 'by', *dylf].

Bideford D, probably 'Byda's ford'. The meaning of the second element is confirmed by the geography. A personal name, Byda or Bieda, seems most likely as the first element [*Bedeford* 1086, *Budiford* 1232, *Bydiford* 1238: OE *ford*].

Biggar Lnk, possibly 'barley plot' [*Bigir* 1170: ON *bygg*, *geiri*, 'triangular patch of ground'].

Biggleswade Bd c 1585, 'Biccel's ford'. Spellings with -*g*- date only from 1486, but gradually prevailed over forms with -*c*- [*Pichelesuuade* 1086, *Bic(h)leswade* 1175, *Bygelswade* 1486: OE (*ge*)*wæd*].

Birdoswald Cu, 'Oswald's fold'. The word-order in this name is Celtic [*Borddosewald* c 1200: W *buarth*].

Birkenhead Ch, 'birch-grown promontory'. It has been suggested that Woodside Ferry adjoins the site of the birch wood from which this place was named. The name is English in origin, but the form has been influenced by Old Norse. The earliest spellings developed to a form *Birket* current in the sixteenth and seventeenth centuries. The spelling *Birchened* 1325 must be seen alongside *Birkened*, *Birkenhed* 1278 to appreciate the way in which the ON forms gradually prevailed [*Bircheveth* c 1200, *Byrkeheveht* 1259, *Berkhened* 1639: OE *birce*, *bircen*, *hēafod*, ON *birki*, *hǫfuð*].

†**Birmingham** Wa, 'village of Beorma's family'. The popular pronunciation *Brummagem* is in line with the history of the name as attested by early spellings, though the spelling *Bromwicham*, current in the seventeenth century, makes a connexion with the name Bromwich (q v) which is fallacious. Beorma is a hypocoristic or pet-name form of Beornmund [*Bermingeham* 1086, *Bremingeham* 1166, *Brimingeham* 1169: OE -*ing*,-*ingas*, *hām*].

Birnie Mor, 'marshy place' [*Brennach* c 1190: G *braonach*].

Birstall Lei, — WRY: 'site of a fort' [1. *Burstelle* 1086, 2. *Birstale* 12c: OE *burh*, *steall*].

Birtsmorton Wo. See Moreton.

Bishop Auckland Du, 'Bishop's holding at the rock on the Clyde'. To the Scandinavian settlers the British name *Alclit* was sufficiently near to a significant Norse expression *auki-land* 'additional land' to be acceptable with a slight modification, but the river name *Clit* was replaced by an ON descriptive name, *Gagnlaus* (now Gaunless) 'useless'. The identity of the British name with the old name for Dumbarton (q v) is noteworthy but indicates no special connexion between the two places; duplication of river names is by no means uncommon, and beside the modern Clyde (q v) may be placed the several rivers in Wales called Clydach, derived from the same word. Bishop Auckland was a possession of the Bishop of Durham; sharing the main name are also West Auckland and Auckland St Andrew and St Helen [*Alclit* c 1050, *Auclent* 1202, *Aucland* 1254: B *Alclut*, 'rock-on-Clyde'].

Bishop's Stortford Hrt, **Bishop's Tachbrook** Wa, **Bishop's Tawton** D, **Bishopsteignton** D, **Bishopstoke** Ha, **Bishops Waltham** Ha: 'bishop's holding at the named place' (Stortford, 'ford at the tail of land', Tachbrook, 'boundary stream', Tawton, 'village on river Taw', Teignton 'village on river Teign', Stoke, 'dependent place', and Waltham, 'homestead by a wood'); the bishops concerned are, respectively, those of London, Chester, Exeter and Winchester. **Bishton** Mon, 'bishop's village' is not quite so clear as **Bishopston(e)**, the name of several other places. The Monmouthshire name alludes to the Bishop of Llandaff [1. *Storteford* 1086, 2. *Tacesbroc* 1086, 3. *Tautona* 1086, 4. *Taintona* 1086, 5. *Stoches* 1086, 6. *Waltham* 904, 5. *Bysshopston Lanathelwather* 1440: OE *biscop, steort, ford, *tæcels*, 'boundary mark', *brōc, tūn, stoc, weald, hām*].

†**Blaby** Lei, 'Bla's farm' (*Bladi* 1086, *Blabi* 1175: ON *bý*).

Black Burn *riv* Abd,—*riv* Cu,—*riv* Nb, **Blackwater** *riv* Sr/Brk/Ha,—*riv* Ess—*riv* La: 'stream with dark or muddy water'. For some of the rivers the name indicates peat-stained water. There are other examples of both names. One river Blaekwater (Brk) has a tributary called the White Water [2. *Mikleblakburne* 1479, 3. *Blagkeburn* c 1170, 4. *La Blakewat'e* 1279, 5. *Blackwater* 1576: OE *blæc, burna, wæter*].

†**Blackburn** La, '(place beside) a dark stream'. The river itself is now known as the Blackwater [*Blacheburne* 1086: OE *blæc, burna*].

†**Blackpool** La, '(place beside) a dark pool'. The original pool was a small stretch of peat-stained water about half a mile from the sea, and it is fair to say that a less promising beginning for what was to become a thriving resort can scarcely be imagined. The name has counterparts in Douglas IOM and Dublin (qq v) [*Pul* 1260, *Blacke Pull* 1661: OE *blæc, pōl*].

Black Torrington D. See Great Torrington.

Black Water *riv*. See Black Burn *riv* and Blackburn La.

Blaenau Mon, 'heights, uplands'. Anglicised as Blaina, the full form of the name is †**Blaenau Gwent**, 'uplands of Gwent (q v)' [*Blayne Gwent* 1594: W *blaen* plural *blaenau*].

Blaenau Ffestiniog Mer, 'heights of Ffestiniog (q v)' [W *blaen*, plural *blaenau*].

Blaenavon Mon, 'headwaters of the river' [W *blaen, afon*].

Blaina Mon. See Blaenau.

Blair Atholl Pth, 'plain in Atholl'. The regional name Atholl ('Ireland again' or 'new Ireland') is affixed to the name to distinguish it from Blairgowrie (q v), not far away. Gaelic *Fōtla* was one of several synonyms for Ireland used in place-names by the Goidels in settling into their new homes in Scotland [*Athochlach* c 970, *Athfoithle* c 1050: G *àth, blàr*, 'plain'].

Blairgowrie Pth, 'plain in Gowrie'. Gowrie is the name given to the district, serving to distinguish this place from Blair Atholl (q v), and meaning, '(territory of) Gabrin'. [*Blare* 13c, *Blair in Gowrie* 1604, *Gouerin* 1165: G *blàr*].

Blaisdon Gl, 'Blæcci's hill'. The same personal name is found in the obsolete name for a ford near Whitchurch O—*Blecces ford* 1012—and in Bletchingdon O [1. *Blechedon* 1186, 3. *Blechesdone* 1066: OE *dūn*].

Blanchland Nb. See Whitland Crm.

Bleadon So, 'coloured hill', alluding to the particoloured appearance caused by outcrops of limestone against green herbage [*Bleodun* 956: OE *blēo*, 'colour', *dūn*].

Bletchley Bk,—Sa: 'Blecca's clearing' [1. *Blechelai* c 1107, 2. *Blecheslee* 1222: OE *lēah*].

Blindbeck *riv freq* 'hidden river'. The word *blind* has at least two senses in river-names: (1) 'concealed by vegetation' and (2) 'intermittent, seasonal'.

Blithfield St. See Blyth *riv*.

Bloomsbury Mx, 'Blemond's manor'. The element *burh* occurs in some post-Conquest names in the sense 'estate, manor', and this is frequently the meaning in the London area. The de Blemund or de Blemunt family, who held the manor in the twelfth and thirteenth centuries, took their name from Blémont in France [*Blemondisberi* 1281: OE *burh*].

Bloxham O, **Bloxholm** LLi: 'Blocc's homestead'. OE *hām* is confused with ON *holmr* in the Lincolnshire name, as in some others in Norse-speaking areas [1. *Blockesham* 1067, 2. *Blochesham* 1086, *Bloxeham* 1130: OE *hām*].

Blubberhouses WRY, 'seething houses'. An industrial process is almost certainly alluded to in this name, but it is not known whether it was for the extraction of salt or some other purpose [*Bluberhusum* 1172: ME *blubber*, 'foaming bubbling', OE *hūs*].

Blyth *riv* Nb, — *riv* Nt, — *riv* Sf, — *riv* St: 'cheerful', usually describing the upper parts of the rivers. From the rivers are named **Blyth** Nb, **Blyth** Nt, **Blithfield** St, **Blyford** Sf, **Blythburgh** Sf, and the District, †**Blyth Valley** Nb [1. *Blitha* c 1137, 2. *Blidan* 958, 4. *Blithe* 12c: OE *bliðe*].

Boat of Garten Inv, 'ferry by Garten, i e field of corn'. Other ferries include **Boat of Forbes** Abd and **Boat of Inch** Inv; names compounded with *of* occur frequently in Scotland, as translations of Gaelic names or simply as a naming habit resulting from numerous translations. Boat of Garten is *Coit Ghairtean* in Gaelic, i e the Garten ferrying place.

Bodmin Co, 'house of the monks'. A monastery is said to have been founded by King Athelstan at Bodmin in the early tenth century [*Bodmine* 1086, *Botmenei* 12c: Co *bod*, 'house', *manach* plural *meneich*, 'monk'].

Bognor Regis Sx, 'Bucge's shore'. The affix *Regis* ('of the king') usually refers to medieval royal estates. Here the royal addition is recent, and purely honorific, having been bestowed by King George V to commemorate his recuperation in Bognor after a serious illness in 1929. Curiously enough, this royal acknowledgement of intangible services rendered maintained the distribution pattern of the element *Regis*, which is not found in the North [*Bucganora* 680: OE *ōra*, 'shore, gravelly landing place'].

Bolton *freq*, 'village with buildings, main village'. In England, the numerous instances of this name are confined to the northern counties and there is at least one example in Scotland, in East Lothian (*Botheltune* c 1200). It is thought that places with this name were the residential centres of communities, distinguished by the allusion to 'buildings' from their subsidiary farms with, perhaps, only temporary shelters. Some of the names have affixed additions, sometimes manorial (e g **Bolton Percy** WRY, *Boulton Perci* 1318, alluding to the feudal tenant named in Domesday Book) or descriptive and usually self-explanatory, e g †**Bolton le Moors** La, **Bolton le Sands** La, **Castle Bolton** NRY; other additions refer to location within districts, such as **Bolton in Copeland** Cu, 'in the purchased land', or **Bolton by Bowland** WRY, 'by the district in the bend of the river', and yet others allude to positions by rivers, such as **Bolton upon Swale** NRY and **Bolton upon Dearne** NRY, the additions signifying 'on the winding river' and 'on the secret river' respectively; the latter was probably so called because it runs through a deep ravine. Lastly, **Bolton Lowhouses** Cu actually alludes to the buildings embodied in the name [OE *bōðl-tūn*].

Bo'ness WLo, 'promontory of Borrowstoun, i e Beornweard's farm'. There are other names as long as, or longer than, Borrowstounness, yet this is one which is consciously abbreviated in both speech and print, acknowledging the contraction in writing by means of the apostrophe. The farm name constituting the first part might well have become *Bernardston or *Berardston, but instead was assimilated to the common noun *burrowstown*, 'municipality' [*Berwardeston* c 1335, *Nes* 1494, *Burnstounnes* 1532: OE *tūn, næss*].

Bonvilston Glm, 'Bonville's farm'. The Welsh name **Tresimwn**, 'Simon's farm' alludes to a thirteenth-century de Bonville, Simon. The family held lands in Somerset and Devon in addition to their Welsh estate [*Boleuilston* c 1160, *Bonevillestun* c 1206: OE *tūn*, W *tref*].

†**Boothferry** ERY, 'ferry by Booth', the latter place being named from the Boothby family from Lincolnshire. The ferry has been replaced by a bridge, but the life of the name has been prolonged by its being applied to a District of Humberside (*Booth's Ferry* 1651: ON *ferja*).

Bootle Cu, —La: 'house, dwelling' possibly alluding to an outlying place, rather than the nucleus of a settlement (cf Bolton) [1. *Bodele* 1086, 2. *Boltelai* 1086, *Botle* 1212: OE *bōtl*].

Borth Crd, 'ferry' [W *borth*].

Boscastle Co, 'Boterel's castle', alluding to the de Botereus, lords in the early fourteenth century [*Boterelescastel* 1302: ME *castel*].

Bosherston. See Stackpole Elidor.

†**Boston** LHo, 'Botulf's stone', referring to either a boundary mark or an assembly point for folk gatherings. There is no sound evidence that this Botulf is identical with the missionary who preached to the East Anglians [*Botuluestan* 1130: OE *stān*].

Bosworth. See Husbands Bosworth, Market Bosworth.

Bourn(e) *freq*, '(place by) a stream' [OE *burna*].

†**Bournemouth** Ha, 'mouth of the stream', or 'mouth of the (stream called) Bourne' (q v). The area has now been transferred to Dorset [*La Bournemowthe* 1407: OE *burna, mūð*].

Bournville Wa, 'town on river Bourne', a modern name of an industrial settlement, compounded of the stream-name and *-ville*. See also Coalville.

Bow Mx. See Stratford le Bow.

Bowland Forest La/WRY, 'land in a bend of a river', the river being the Ribble.

Bowland La takes its name from the district, as does Bolton by Bowland WRY (q v) [*Boelanda* 1102: OE *boga, land*].

Bowness Cu, 'rounded headland', site of *Maia* (q v) [*Bounes* c 1225: ON *bogi, nes*].

Boyne *riv freq*, '(stream of the) Cow-white one', alluding to Boand, the goddess whose name is transferred to these rivers in Scotland and Ireland.

Brabstermire Cai, 'marsh at Brabster, i e broad dwelling' [*Brabustare* 1492, *Brabastermyre* 1538: ON *breiðr, bólstaðr, myrr*].

Bracknell Brk, 'Bracca's nook of land' [*Braccan heal* 942: OE *halh* (WS: *healh*)].

Bradford *freq*, 'broad ford'. In addition to the simple form, e g †**Bradford** WRY, affixes occur as in **Bradford Bryan** Do and **Bradford Abbas** Do; the latter, 'abbot's Bradford', was a Sherborne Abbey possession. Early forms for West **Bradford** WRY (*Braford in Bouland* 1251) allude to Bowland Forest (q v) [OE *brād, ford*].

Braemar Abd, 'upper part of Marr', ultimately derived from a personal name [G *braighe*].

†**Braintree** Ess 1490, 'Branuc's tree', alluding to either a prominent tree on the named person's land, or a cross erected by him [*Branchetreu* 1086, *Brantetre* 1274: OE *trēow*]. See also Coventry, Elstree.

Bramhope WRY, 'broom valley' [*Bramhop* 1086: OE *brōm, hop*].

Bramley *freq*, 'clearing overgrown with broom' [OE *brōm, lēah*].

Brampton *freq*, 'village where broom grew' [OE *brōm, tūn*].

Brancaster Nf, 'Roman station at *Branodunon*, i e the raven's fort' [*Bramcestria* 10c: B *bran, dūno-*, OE *ceaster*].

Brant *riv* LLi, 'deep' [*Brant* 1316: OE *brant*].

Branxton Nb. See Flodden Field.

Bravoniacum (Kirkby Thore We), *Bravonium* (Leintwardine He): 'quern place', relating to a locality in which mill-stones were quarried or collected. Querns were the stones used when the grinding of grain was a domestic, rather than a specialised mechanical, operation, and these Romano-British names provide an interesting record of this fact [1. *Bravonacis* 4c, 2. *Bravonium* 4c: B **bravon-*].

Bray Brk, possibly 'muddy place', an interpretation which accords with the topography, though it presents the difficulty of a name derived from OF recorded in Domesday Book [*Brai* 1086: OF *brai*].

Bray Wic, '(place on) rising ground' [*Bree* n d: I *bri*].

Breadalbane Pth, 'upper part of Alban' the upland district of the headwaters of the river Tay [*Bredalban* c 1600: G *bràighad*].

Brechin Ang, '(place of) Brychan' a British personal name occurring also in Brecon or Brecknock Bre (q v) [*Brechin* c 1145].

†**Breckland** Nf -Sf, 'scrub region', a large area of heathland some parts of which are now forest covered and others have with difficulty been brought into cultivation [OE *bræc, land*].

Brecknock Bre. See Brecon.

Brecon Bre, '(territory of) Brychan', the implied words being made explicit in the form *Brycheinioc* 15c, with its territorial suffix. Forms with *-ioc* gave rise to the Anglicised †**Brecknock**. The personal name refers to a prince of the fifth century [*Brecheniauc* 1100, *Bregnok* 1409: W *-ioc*].

Bredon Wo, **Breedon on the Hill** Lei :'hill', more precisely, 'hill hill', with an additional tautological explanation in the Leicestershire name. The redundancy has arisen because the significance of the British name ceased to be understood [1. *Breodun in Huiĉ* 775, 2. *Briudun* c 730: B **brigā*, OE *dūn*].

Bremenion c 150 (High Rochester Nb), **Bremetennacum** (Ribchester La): 'place on a roaring river', names of Romano-British settlements, some evidence for the history of which survives in the modern place-names [B **bremēn*].

Brenchley K, 'Brænci's clearing' [*Braencesle* c 1100: OE *lēah*].

Brenkley Nb, 'Brynca's burial mound' [*Brinchelawa* 1178: OE *hlǣw*].

Brentford Mx, 'ford across the river Brent, i e holy stream' [*Breguntford* 705: B **Brigantiā*, OE *ford*].

†**Brentwood** Ess, ('place by) burnt wood', the meaning being even clearer in the related name **Burntwood** St [1. *Boscus Arsus* 1176, *Bois Ars* 1227, *Brendewode* 1274, 2. *Brendewode* 16c: ME *brende*, OE *wudu*].

Bressay isld Zet, possibly 'island like a breast' [*Bressa* 1654: ON *brjost, ey*].

Bridge K, **Brigg** LLi: '(place at or by) a bridge', a fairly frequent name, some instances of which are distinguished by feudal affixes, e g **Bridge Sollers** He, **Bridgerule** D, and **Bridgwater** So, alluding respectively to the de Solers family, to Ruald Adobat, and to Walter de Dowai. Brigg was formerly Glanford Brigg, 'bridge by ford at which sports were held' [1. *Brygge* 11c, 2. *Glannford Brigg* 1235, 3. *Bricge* 1086, *Bruges Solers* 1291, 4. *Bruge Ruardi* 1242, 5. *Brigewaltier* 1194: OE *brycg, glēam, ford*].

Bridgend Glm, '(place at the) end of the bridge' [*Byrge End* 1535: OE *brycg, ende*].

Bridgerule D, **Bridge Sollers** He, **Bridgwater** So. See Bridge.

†**Bridgnorth** Sa, 'northern bridge', being higher up the Severn than the old bridge at Quatford [*Brug* 1156, *Brugg Norht* 1282: OE *brycg, norð*].

Bridlington ERY, 'farm of Beorhtel's people' [*Bretlinton* 1086: OE *-ingas, tūn*].

Brigg LLi. See Bridge.

†**Brighton** Sx, 'Beorhthelm's farm', the personal name occurring in the extended form used as recently as the early nineteenth century [*Bristelmestune* 1086, *Brighthelmston* 1816: OE *tūn*].

Brims Ness Cai, 'promontory of the surf' [*Brymmis* 1559: ON *brim, nes*].

Bristol So, 'meeting-place at the bridge'. The termination -*stol(l)* for OE -*stōw* occurs as early as 1200 and is essentially a Norman-French feature (cf *bel/beau*). The interpretation 'holy place' for *stōw* need not be entirely rejected, but political and commercial importance possibly takes precedence here [*Brycg stowe* 11c, *Bristou* 1086, *Bristoll* 1200: OE *brycg, stōw*].

Britain, 'land of the Britons i e figured folk', alluding to the practice of pre-Celtic inhabitants of the island of tattooing their bodies. The Celtic settlers seem to have adopted the custom, as the testimony of Caesar and others confirms. The form **Great Britain** distinguishes the island from Brittany in France [*Prettanoi* c 310 BC, *Britannia* c 50 BC, *Brutaine* 1205, *Breteyne* 1297].

Brixham D, 'Brioc's homestead', possibly alluding to the sixth-century saint who gave his name to Saint Brieuc in Brittany. The personal name occurs also in **Brixton** D 1197 [1. *Briseham* 1086, *Brixeham* 1143, 2. *Brisestone* 1086: OE *hām, tūn*]

Brixton D. See Brixham.

Brixton Sr/GL, 'Beorhtsige's stone', referring to an isolated rock serving as a land-mark, to mark a meeting place or sacred spot [*Brixges stan* 1062: OE *stān*].

Broadstairs K, 'wide stairway', referring to a terracing of the shore to gain access to the sea [*Brodsteyr Lynch* c 1435: OE *brād, stæger (hlinc,* 'bank')].

Broadwas Wo, 'wide fen' [*Bradeuuesse* 779: OE *brād, wāse*].

Broadway Wo, '(place by) the broad road' referring not to the main road by which the village is now approached, but the older one running north and south up the valley [*Bradanuuege* 972: OE *brād, weg*].

Brocolitia (Carrawburgh Nb), 'place of many badgers' [B *brocco-, litu-,* 'abundance'].

Brodick (Arran) Arg, 'broad bay', one of the numerous Scandinavian maritime place-names of the Irish Sea area [*Brathwik* 1306, *Bradewik* 1450: ON *breiðr, vik*].

Brodie Nrn, '(settlement) at the muddy place' [*Brothie* 1380: G *brothaich*].

Bromborough Ch, 'Bruna's fortified place', the fortification being possibly at the moated site of the manor house of the abbots of St Werburgh, Chester. Strong arguments have been put forward (PNCh iv 238-40) supporting the identification of this place with *Brunanburh*, near which invading Norsemen and Scots were defeated in 937 by Athelstan [*Brunburg* c 1120, *Bruneburgh* 1153, *Brumbur*' 1153: OE *burh*].

Bromley Ess, —Hrt,—K, **Abbots Bromley** St, **Kings Bromley** St: 'broom clearing'. Abbots Bromley was held by Burton Abbey [1. *Brumleia* 1086, 3. *Bromleag* 862, 4. *Bromlegh Abbatis* 1304, 5. *Bramlea Regis* 1167: OE *brōm, lēah*].

Brompton *freq*, 'farm on which broom grew' [OE *brōm, tūn*].

†**Bromsgrove** Wo, 'Breme's thicket' [*Bremesgrefan* 804: OE *græfe*].

Bromwich Wa. See Castle Bromwich.

Brondesbury Mx, 'Brand's manor', the second element having this post-Conquest sense as elsewhere in the Home Counties. Brand probably alludes to a man of that name who was canon of St Paul's, c 1150 [*Bronnesburie* 1254: OE *burh*].

Broom, Loch *lke* Ros, 'lake of the drizzle' [*Braon* 1227: G *loch, braon*].

Brora Sut, '(place by) river of the bridge', referring to what was once the only bridge in Sutherland [*Strabroray* 1499: ON *brú*, gen. *brúar, á*].

Brough Db,—ERY (x 2),—NRY (x 2),—Nt, **Brough under Stainmore** We: 'fortified place', referring to ancient camps. The Westmorland example has a Norman castle built on the site of the Roman station of *Verterae*, 'place at the summit'. Stainmore, 'moor of the rock', is a mountainous tract of peat with many boulders and exposures of rock. Brough Db is close to the site of the Roman camp, *Navio*, '(place by) running water'. At **Brough on Humber** ERY was the Roman fort of *Petuaria* [1. *Burc* 1195, 2. *Burgh on Humber* 1239, 4. *Burg* 1086, 6. *Burc* 1174: OE *burh*].

†**Broxbourne** Hrt, **Broxburn** WLo: 'badger stream' [1. *Brochesborne* 1086, 2. *Broxburne* 1638: OE *brocc, burna*].

Brumby LLi, 'Bruni's village'. Lincolnshire places with names in -by are so numerous that it has been suggested that nothing less than a Danish migration here can account for their abundance. Many of the names (as this) have a personal name as first element (*Brunebi* 1086: ON *bý*).

Brunanburh. See **Bromborough** Ch.

Bryher *isld* (Scilly) Co, probably 'district of hills', a name given while this island was still part of a larger one, which subsequently sank; the hills of the large island continued to be referred to as such (*Braer* 1319, *Brehar* 1570: OCo *bre, -ier,* 'area of').

Brynbuga Mon 1450, 'hill of Buga', the Welsh name for Usk Mon (q v) [W *bryn*]. See also *Burrium.*

Bryn-mawr Bre 1832, 'great hill', a late name for a modern industrial settlement [W *bryn, mawr*].

Buccleuch Slk, 'buck's glen'. It has been suggested that the name is of Gaelic origin with *baile* as the first element. The scarcity of Gaelic names in Selkirkshire argues against this; only one, Balnakiel, is listed for this county in the most recent study (Nicolaisen: GPNSS 18-19) [(?) *Selbukleche* c 1200, *Bockcleugh* c 1590: OE *bucc, *clōh*].

†**Buchan** Abd, 'cow place', the northern part of Aberdeenshire. The name occurs also in **Buchanhaven,** near Peterhead Abd, **Kirkton of Logie Buchan** Abd ('church village of the hollow place in Buchan', Gaelic *logaigh,* dative of *logach,* 'hollow'), and **Bullers of Buchan** Abd, 'roaring place of Buchan', a recess in the coast, north of Cruden Bay, where the sea boils like a cauldron [*Buchan* c 1150, *Bouwan* c 1295: OW *buwch, -an*].

Buckfast D, 'buck's stronghold or thicket', near which is **Buckfastleigh** D, 'clearing by Buckfast' [1. *on Bucfæsten* 1046, 2. *Legh* 1286, *Leghe Bucfestre* 13c: OE *bucc, fæsten, lēah*].

Buckie Bnf, 'buck (place or river)' [*Buky* 1362: G *boc, -aidh*].

Buckingham Bk, 'riverside pasture of Bucca's people', the final element here probably having the more precise significance of 'land in a river bend' [*Buccingahamme* 918: OE *-ingas, hamm*].

Buckland *freq,* 'land held by charter', as opposed to *folcland,* 'land held under common law', the former being an advantageous form of tenure in that the land was exempt by royal charter from the heavier public burdens. The name is restricted to the south of England, more than a dozen instances occurring in Devon, e g **East and West Buckland, Egg Buckland** (q v), and **Buckland Monachorum,** 'monks' Buckland', commemorating the abbey founded in 1278. **Minchin Buckland,** or **Buckland Sororum** So, alludes to the priory of nuns there [OE *bōcland*].

Bude Co 1400, '(place on) turbid river [B **boutto-*].

Budleigh Salterton D, 'salt works at Budleigh, i e Budda's clearing', the *-ton* ending representing an 'over-correction' of *-ern.* There were salt-pans at the mouth of the river Otter at an early date. In **Woodbury Salterton** D, there is warrant for the *-ton* ending; this name alludes, not to salt works but to a farm or settlement of salters in Woodbury, i e the woodland fortification [1. *Saltre* 1210, *Salterne in the manor of Buddeleghe* 1405: OE *sealt, ærn, lēah*].

Budock Co, 'church of St Budoc', as in St Budeaux D (q v) [*Ecclesie Sancti Budoci* 1208].

Builth Wells Bre, 'cow pasture, with medicinal springs', an English spelling of a Welsh name, with an English suffix added in the eighteenth century when the chalybeate springs attracted ailing visitors from England [*Buelt* 10 c: B **bow, gelt*].

Bure *riv* Nf 1557, back-formation from Burgh (next Aylsham) Nf (q v).

Burgh *freq,* 'fort, stronghold, fortified manor house' [OE *burh*].

name related to Calder (q v) and developing elsewhere to **Callater** Abd and **Cawdor** Nrn. In Wales, the river-names **Calettwr** and **Clettwr** have the same origin [1. *Kalentare* 1504, 2. *Kalenter* c 1150, 3. *Callendar* 1652, 4. *Kaledor* 1280: B *caleto-*, *dubro-*].

Callater Abd. See Callander.

Calleva Atrebatum, 'wooded place of the Atrebates', the Romano-British name for Silchester Ha (q v). The tribal name means 'settlers, people' [*Kalleoua* c 150, *Calleva* 4c: B *celli-*].

Callow Myo, 'riverside land, flood meadows' [I *caladh*].

Calne W 955, '(place by) noisy river' [B *calaun-*].

Calow Db, 'bare nook of land' [*Calehale* 1086: OE *calu, halh*].

Cam riv Bd-C, back-formation from Cambridge (q v). The alternative name for the river, **Granta** 'fen river', has a long history and is the first element of the early spellings of Cambridge and of **Grantchester** C, 'settlers on the Granta' [2. *Gronte fluminis* c 745, *Grantan stream* c 890, 3. *Grantacaestir* c 730, 4. *Granteseta* 1086: B *grant-*, OE *ceaster, sǣte*].

Camberley Sr, adaptation of Cambridge Town 1862, altered 'for postal convenience'. The original name was bestowed in honour of the Duke of Cambridge (1819-1904), Queen Victoria's cousin. As commander-in-chief for many years he put up a splendidly valiant resistance to all proposed reforms and plans for modernising the army. With this name may be compared **York Town** Sr, not far away, commemorating Frederick, Duke of York, who founded Sandhurst College.

Camberwell Sr/GL, 'spring at Camburn, i e crane stream' [*Cambrewelle* 1086: OE *cran, burna, wella*].

Camborne Co, '(place by) curving slope' [*Camberon* 1181: Co *cam, bron*].

Cambria. See Cymry.

†**Cambridge** C, 'bridge over the river Granta', earlier 'Roman station on the Granta'. The earliest form could have developed to modern Grantchester—but did not do so, as forms with OE *brycg* intervened. The place actually called **Grantchester** has the river-name as its first element, but the second is OE *sæte*, 'settlers'. The changes in spelling between *Grontabricc* and Cambridge are explained by Norman influence [*Grontabricc* c 745, *Grentebrige* 1086, *Cantebrigie* 1086: OE *brycg*]. See also Cam *riv*.

Cambuskenneth Stl, 'river-bend of Cinaed', and not, it has been suggested, 'of Cainnech', the Gaelic name to which Kenneth is usually regarded as the Anglicised equivalent [*Cambuskynneth* 1147: G *camas*].

Cambuslang Lnk, 'river-bend of the ship' [*Camboslanc* 1296: G *camas, long*].

Cambus o' May Abd, 'river-bend of the plain' representing the Gaelic *Camas a' Mhuige* [*Cames i maye* 1600: G *camas, magh*].

Camden Town Mx, area developed on land owned by the Earl of Camden. Formerly Lord Chief Justice Pratt, Camden was raised to the peerage in 1765 and was Lord Chancellor 1766-70. At least three of the Camdens in USA are named after him, honouring his support for the colonists during the War of Independence. The present London Borough of Camden covers a much wider area than Camden Town.

Camelford Co 1205, 'ford over the river Camel, i e crooked stream' [1. *flumen Cambula* 1147: B **cambo-, pol*].

Campbeltown Arg, named in honour of Archibald Campbell, Earl of Argyll, to whom the place, then called Lochead, was granted in the seventeenth century.

Campsie Fells Stl, 'hills by the crooked fairy mountain', the range deriving its name from that of a single hill [G *cam, sith*, ON *fjal*]

Camulodunum, 'fortress of Camulos', the Romano-British settlement at Colchester Ess (q v). Camulos was the British god of war [*Camolodounum* 4c: B **dūno-*].

Canbo Rcm, 'headland of Bugh', said to be named after the daughter of the legendary Bodhbh Derg [I *ceann*].

Candover Ha, '(places in the valley of) the pretty stream'; **Preston Candover** (q v), **Chilton Candover** ('village of young noblemen'), and **Brown Candover** (from a family name) are all in the valley of the stream [*Cendefer* c 882, *Chiltone Candevere* c 1270, *Brunkardoure* 1296: OE *cild, tūn*, B **kanjo, *dubro-*].

Canisbay Cai, 'Conan's farm' [*Cananesbi* c 1240: ON *bý*].

Canna *isld* Ros, possibly 'porpoise island' [*Kannay* 1549: G *cana*, ON *ey*].

Cannock St, **Conock** W: 'hill'. †**Cannock Chase** St, 'hunting ground at Cannock '— a forest which, over some centuries, was reduced to a boggy wilderness by the removal of trees for charcoal used by the iron industry of the Black Country. The area has now, of course, been replanted and provides a suitable name for a District in Staffordshire [1. *Canuc* 956, 2. *Kunek* 1242: B **cunăco-*].

Canonbury Mx, 'canons' manor', formerly held by the Augustinian canons of Smithfield [*Canonesbury* 1373: ME *canoun*, OE *burh*].

†**Canterbury** K, 'fortified place of the *Cantware*, i e the men of Kent', replacing the Romano-British name *Durovernon*, 'fort among the alders', which continued in literary use until the reign of Alfred, and was even given an Anglo-Saxon appearance in the form *Dorwitceaster*, 'Roman station at *Durovernon*'. This name might have produced a third Dorchester in England, but when it was being used the name Canterbury was even better established. The inclusion of the county name in that of its principal town no doubt justified the predominance of the English name [*Cantwaraburg* 754: OE *-ware, burh*]. See also Kent.

Capel K,—Sr, **Capel le Ferne** K, **Capel St Andrew** Sf, **Capel St Mary** Sf, **How Caple** He, **Kings Caple** He: '(place with a) chapel', apart from dedications, English examples sometimes having manorial affixes (How Caple having been held by a man called Hugh) but occasionally topographical ones (*le Ferne* meaning 'among the ferns'). Numerous Welsh instances occur also; additions to these are descriptive or topographical. **Capel Coch** Ang is 'red chapel', **Capel Celyn** Mer, 'chapel with holly trees', and **Capel Newydd** Pmb, 'new chapel'. **Capel-y-ffin** Bre is 'boundary chapel', being near borders of both Monmouthshire and Herefordshire. Dedicatory and other personal names are also found; **Capel Trisant** Crd has, like Llantrisant Glm (q v) three patron saints; **Capel Dewi** Crd (x 2) probably alludes to St David [ME *capel*, W *capel*].

†**Caradon** Co, 'tor hill,' a tautologous form which may have arisen from the hill having been called *Carn* and then the area round it being named after it. If

non-Cornish settlers then referred to the hill it would have been as *Carnedun*, 'hill at Carn'. Like Bredon Hill, Caradon Hill, the natural feature which gives the place its name, now has the further unnecessary addition of *Hill* [*Carnedun* 1175: Co **carn*, OE *dūn*].

Cardenden Fif, 'valley near Carden, i e thicket' [P *cardden*, OE *denu*].

†**Cardiff** Glm, 'fort on the river Taf (q v)', the river-name here being in the genitive case. With this the name applied to the cathedral in Cardiff, Llandaf (q v) may be compared [*Kairdiff* 1106: W *caer*].

Cardigan Crd, 'Ceredig's territory', the name being first used for an area surrounding the present town of Cardigan, which was named, unconventionally, from its region instead of *vice versa;* in Welsh, the town is **Aberteifi**, 'mouth of the river Teifi', the meaning of Teifi being unknown. Cardiganshire (†**Ceredigion**) is now a District of Dyfed, the name of which has a very long history, stemming from the tribal name *Demetae*, mentioned by Ptolemy. The tribe's original home was in Pembrokeshire [1. *Cereticiaun* 12c, *Kerdigan* 1194, 2. *Demetai* c 130: W *-ion*].

Carleton *freq*, **Carlton** *freq:* 'farm of the churls or free peasants', a variant of Charlton. Forms with *Carl-* are limited to the northern and midland counties of England, and represent a Scandinavianisation of *OE ceorla-tūn*. Additions are mostly manorial and topographical [OE *ceorl*, *tūn*].

Carlingford Lth, 'sea-inlet of Cairlinn, i e pool fortress' [*Cairlinn* n d: I *cathair*, *linn*, ON *fjórðr*].

†**Carlisle** Cu, 'fort at Luguvalio, i e Luguvallos's place', the personal name meaning 'strong as (Celtic god) Lugus'. The Celtic compound has prevailed over a hybrid *Luercestre* (for *Luelcestre*) introduced in the 11c [*Luguvalio* 4c, *Luel* 9c, *Karlioli* c 1100: OW *cair*].

Carlow Car, '(place by a) quadruple lake', no trace of which is now to be found, however [*Cetherloch*: I *ceither*, *loch*].

†**Carmarthen** Crm, 'fort at *Maridunum* i e seaside fort' [*Maridunum* 4c, *Cair Mirdin* 1130: B **mari-*, **dūno-*, OW *cair*].

Carnew Wic, 'victory cairn', or possibly 'Buaidh's cairn' [*Karnebo* 1247: OI *carn*, *buaidh*].

Carreg Ddu, Crn, **Carrickdubh** Gal: 'black cliff' [W *carreg*, *du*, I *carraig*, *dubh*].

Carrick Ayr, †**Carrick** Co: 'rock, sea cliff'. The District in Cornwall takes its name from Carrick Roads, the Fal Estuary, in which is Black Rock—formerly *n garrak ruen* the rock of seals [1. *karrio* c 1140, 2. '*n garrak ruen* 15c, *Caregrayne* c 1540, 3. *Caryk Rood*, c 1540: OW *carreg*, OG *carrec*].

Carron *riv* Stl, possibly 'stony one', a pre-Celtic name derived (according to W.F.H. Nicolaisen) from the Indo-European root **kar-* [*Cære* c 950, *Caroun* c 1200].

Carse of Forth Stl, 'alluvial plain of river Forth'. Alongside the Tay is **Carse of Gowrie** Pth, ' . . . of the goat place' [2. *Carse de Gowrie* c 1200: (?) ON *kjarr*].

Carshalton Sr/GL, 'cress-growing Alton, i e farm by a spring', alluding to the source of the river Wandle (q v). Watercress has been grown in the place since the Middle Ages [*Æuueltone* 675, *Kersaulton* c 1150: OE *cærse*, *ǣwiell*, *tūn*].

Carstairs Lnk, 'Tarres's castle' [*Casteltarres* 1170: ME *castel*].

Cas-Gwent. See Chepstow.

Cashel Tip, 'circular stone fort' [I *caiseal*].

Castle Bromwich Wa, 'village in broom-grown area, with a castle'. A twelfth-century motte survives north of the church. **West Bromwich** St is a few miles to the west of this place [1. *Bramewice* 1168, *Castelbromwic* 13c, 2. *Westbromwich* 1322: OE *brōm*, *wic*, ME *castel*].

Castle Cary So, 'castle on river Cary, i e favoured stream', but **Castle Cary** Stl is 'castle by the (ancient) fortifications', alluding to a Roman fort on the Antonine Wall [1. *Castelkary* 1237, 2. *Castlecarris* c 1200: ME *castel*, OW *cair*, B **car-*].

Castle Douglas Kcb, 'estate named after Sir William Douglas', who developed the place formerly called Carlinwark towards the end of the eighteenth century.

Castlepollard Wme, 'estate in the possession of the Pollard family' still surviving in 1837.

†**Castlereagh** Dwn,—Rcm: 'grey castle' [*Castel Raie or Graie* c 1570: I *caisleán*, *riabach*].

Castlesteads Cu 'site of a (Roman) fort' referring to that at *Camboglanna*, 'crooked banks' [ME *castel* OE *stede*, **B cambo*, **glanna*].

Castletown IOM, 'village by a castle' [*villa castelli* c 1370: ME *castel*, OE *tūn*].

Castor Nth, 'Roman fort', distinguished in early spellings by the personal name Kyneburga, that of the canonised daughter of Penda, king of Mercia.

She is said to have founded a monastery here in the seventh century. The fort is *Durobrivae* (q v) [*Kyneburga cæstro* 948: OE *ceaster*].

Caterham Sr 1200, 'homestead by *Cateir*, i e throne-like hill', embodying the British hill-name found in, e g, Cader Idris, and derived from Latin *cathedra* [*Catheham* 1179: OW *cateir*, OE *hām*].

Catterick NRY, probably 'river with cataracts', perhaps a river called *Cataractona*, with this meaning. Ptolemy's spelling, if not erroneous, suggests that folk-etymology may have produced the alteration of the first part of the word to B *catu-*, 'war' [*Catouraktonion* c 150, *Cataractone* 4c: Lat *cataracta*].

†**Ceredigion.** See Cardigan.

Cerne *riv* Do, 'stony river', giving its name to a number of places along its course, including **Up Cerne** Do and **Nether Cerne** Do (in the upper reach and lower reach of the river respectively) and **Cerne Abbas** Do (alluding to monastic tenure). **Charminster** Do is 'great church on river Cerne', but Charmouth (q v) refers to another river [*aqua de Cerne* 1244, *Cherne brooke* 1577: B **carn*].

Chagford D, 'ford among broom or gorse' [*Cagefort* 1086, *Chageford* 1238: OE *ceacge, ford*].

Chalfont St Giles Bk, **Chalfont St Peter** Bk: 'calf's spring' [1. *Celfunte* 1086, *Chaufonte Sancti Egidii* 1242, 2. *Chaufunte Sancti Petri* 1242: OE *cealf, funta*].

Chalgrave Bd, **Chalgrove** O: 'chalk digging' [1. *Cealhgræfan* 926, 2. *Celgrave* 1086, *Chealgraue* c 1170: OE *cealc, græf*].

Chalkfoot Cu. See Maryport.

Chancton Sx, 'farm of Ceawa's people', occurring also in **Chanctonbury Ring** Sx, 'circle of stones at the fortification by Chancton' [1. *Cengeltune* 1086, *Changeton* 1249, 2. *Changebury* 1351: OE *-ingas*, *tūn*, *burh*].

Chapel en le Frith Db, 'chapel in the forest', namely, Peak Forest. Apart from this name and that of Stretton en le Field Lei, *en le* in place-names is usually reduced to *le* in modern forms [*Ecclesia de Alto Peccho* 1219, *capellam de Frich'* 1241, *Capellam in le Fryth* 1484: ME *chapel*, OF *en*, *le*, OE *(ge)fyrhð*].

Chard So, 'rough common', an abbreviated form of the earlier *Ceardren*, 'house on rough common', the second element being a form of OE *ærn*, 'house, building' [*Cerdren* 1065: OE *ceart*, *renn*].

Charing Cross Mx, 'cross at a turning place', probably alluding to the sweeping bend in the Thames at this point. The cross stood at the place where the funeral cortège of Eleanor, wife of Edward I, made its last overnight stay in the journey from Harby to London [*Cyrring* c 1000: OE *cierring*, ME *cros*].

Charleton D, **Charlton** *fr q*: 'farm of the free peasants' [OE *ceorl*, *tūn*]. See also Carlton.

Charminster Do. See Cerne *riv* Do.

Charmouth Do, '(place at) mouth of river Char', the river-name being a variant of Cerne (q v) [*Cernemvde* 1086: OE *mūða*].

†**Charnwood** Lei, 'wood in rocky country' [*Charnewode* 1276: OW *carn* OE *wudu*].

Chatham Ess, —K, **Cheetham** La: 'farm by a wood', hybrid names indicating a survival of considerable British populations beside Anglo-Saxon settlers [1. *Cetham* 1086, 2. *Cætham* 10c, *Chetham* 1212: B *ceto-*, OE *hām*].

Cheadle Ch, —St: 'wood', a tautologous hybrid. To the original British name, meaning, 'wood', has been added OE *lēah* by way of explanation when the significance of the early name was lost on English settlers [1. *Cedde* 1086, *Chedle* c 1170, 2. *Chedele* 1197: B *ceto-*, OE *lēah*].

Cheam Sr/GL, 'homestead in an area of tree-stumps' [*Cegeham* 675, *Ceiham* 1086: OE *ceg*, *hām*].

Cheddar So, 'pouch', referring either to the Gorge, or (more probably) to the caverns to be found in the area [*æt Ceodre* c 880, *Cedre* 1086: OE *cēodor*].

Cheddington Bk, 'Cetta's hill' [*Cetendone* 1086: OE *dūn*].

Chelmer *riv* Ess, back-formation from †**Chelmsford** Ess, 'Cēolmær's ford', the personal name in which was taken to be a river-name. Only rarely is OE *ford* found in combination with a river-name; this usually occurs in the vicinity of a second river: **Crayford** K and **Dartford** K are good examples. The places are not far apart, and the Cray is a tributary of the Darent. Other river-names like Chelmer are Wandle, Thet, Bure, and Alde (qq v) [2. *Chelmer* 1576, 2. *Celmeresfort* 1086: OE *ford*].

Chelsea Mx, 'landing-place for chalk or limestone', i e a quay at which building-materials were brought ashore. Despite a common second element, modern names of Thames-side landing places show great variety—Putney, Lambeth, Rotherhithe, Erith, Maidenhead (qq v) [*Celchyth* 789: OE *cealc*, *hȳð*].

†**Cheltenham** Gl, 'pasture by Celt, i e the hill', the hill-name being related to the first element in Chiltern (q v) [*Celtanhomme* 803: OE *hamm*].

Chepstow Mon, 'market place', earlier called *Strigull* 1224, of unknown origin and meaning. The modern Welsh name is **Cas-Gwent**, 'castle in Gwent i e market' [*Chepstowe* 1308, *castell guent* c 1150: OE *cēap*, *stōw*, W *castell*, B **ventā-*] See also Gwent.

†**Cherwell** *riv* Nth-O, possibly 'winding stream' [*Ceruelle* 681: OE *cierr*, *wella*].

Chesham Bk, 'pasture by a heap of stones'. The DB form alters 'heap of stones' (OE *ceastel*) to 'Roman camp' (OE *ceaster*), but the stones referred to are a circle over which the church was built [*Cæstæleshamm* c 970, *Cestreham* 1086: OE *ceastel*, *hamm*].

Cheshire 1442, 'province of the city of Chester (q v)' [*Legeceaster scir* 980, *Ceasterscire* 1085, *Chestershire* 1326, *Cheschire* 1430: OE *scīr*].

Chesil Bank Do, 'shingle ridge' [*The chisil* c 1540: OE *ceosol*].

Chess *riv* Bk, back-formation from Chesham Bk (q v).

†**Chester** Ch, 'Roman fort', the meaning of the abbreviated form given in Domesday Book, the earliest spelling of the modern name. Longer forms were used in Anglo-Saxon times, to be interpreted 'city or fortress of the legions', but earlier still the name was *Deva*, '(place on) river Dee, i e the holy one' [*Deoua* c 150, *Deva* 4c, *Legacæstir* c 730, *Cestre* 1086: OE *ceaster*].

†**Chesterfield** Db, 'open land by a Roman station' [*ad Cesterfelda* 955: OE *ceaster*, *feld*].

†**Chester le Street** Du, 'Roman station on a paved road'. The fort was known as *Conganium* or *Concangium*, of unknown meaning. The Romano-British name is the first element in an 11c form of the name [*Cunceceastre* c 1050, *Cestra* c 1160: OE *ceaster*].

Chesterton C, —Gl, —Hu, —O, — St, —Wa: 'farm by a Roman station' [1,4. *Cestreton* 1086, 2. *Cestertone* 1086, 6. *Cestertun* 1005: OE *ceaster*, *tūn*].

Cheviot. The *mtn* Nb, meaning unknown and origin obscure [*Chiuiet* 1181].

†**Chichester** Sx, 'Cissi's Roman station', the personal name being an alternative form of Cissa. Cissa is on record as one of the sons of Ælle, first king of the South Saxons [*Cissaceaster* 895: OE *ceaster*].

Chigwell Ess, 'shingly stream or spring' [*Cingheuuella* 1086: ME*chingel*, OE *wella*].

Childwall La, **Chilwell** Nt: 'young men's spring', to be compared with **Maidwell** Nth, 'maidens' spring' [1. *Cildeuuelle* 1086, 2. *Cilleuuelle* 1086, 3. *Medewelle* 1086: OE *cild*, *mægden*, *wella*].

Chillingham Nb, 'homestead of Ceofel's people' [*Cheulingeham* 1187: OE *-ingas*, *hām*].

Chiltern Hills Bk, possibly 'high places'. †**Chiltern District** Bk, on the Herts border, is not so extensive as the Chiltern Hundreds (q v) [*Ciltern* 1009: B **celto-*].

Chiltern Hundreds Bk, 'administrative districts in the neighbourhood of the Chiltern Hills (q v)'. In Anglo-Saxon times, shires were divided into large areas known as *hundreds*, so called probably because they were about one hundred hides in extent. Buckinghamshire contained eighteen hundreds; an arrangement peculiar to this county divided them into groups of three, of which the best known are the Chiltern Hundreds (Desborough, Burnham, and Stoke Hundreds) and the Three Hundreds of Aylesbury (Aylesbury, Stone, and Risborough Hundreds).

Chilton *freq*, 'farm held by the young men or retainers' [OE *cild, tūn*].

Chingford Ess/GL, 'shingly ford' [*Cingeford* 1050: ME *chingel* OE *ford*].

Chinley Db, 'clearing by a ravine' [*Chineleia* c 1200: OE *cinu, lēah*].

Chippenham W, 'Cippa's riverside pasture, or land in a river-bend', identical in origin and meaning with **Cippenham** Bk and Sydenham GL (q v) [1. *Cypeham* c 1080, 2. *Sippeham* c 1110. *Chippeham* 1218: OE *hamm*].

Chipperfield Hrt. See Copmanthorpe.

Chirk Den, '(place on river) Ceiriog, i e favoured one' [*Chirke* 1295: B *car-*].

Chisholm Rox, 'cheese meadow' [*Cheseholme* 1254: OE *cēse*, ON *holmr*].

Chiswick Mx, 'cheese farm' [*Cesewican* c 1000: OE *cēse, wic*].

Chorley Ch (x 2), —La, —Sa, —St, **Chorleywood** Hrt: 'clearing or meadow of the free peasants' [1. *Cerlere* 1086, 3. *Cherleg* 1246, 5. *Cherlec* 1231, 6. *Charlewood* 1524: OE *ceorl, lēah, wudu*].

Chorlton *freq*, 'farm of the free peasants' [OE *ceorl, tūn*]. See also Carleton, Charlton.

†**Christchurch** Ha, '(place with) church dedicated to Christ', replacing, probably on the foundation of an Augustinian priory there, the earlier name *Twynham*, 'between the rivers', referring to its situation between the Stour and the Avon. The area has now been transferred to Dorset [*Cristescherche* 1177, *Cristechurch Twynham* 1242: OE *cirice, betwēonan, ēa*].

Churchill *freq*, either 'hill with a church' or 'hill', the second consisting of a Celtic element with that meaning to which OE *hyll* was added tautologically [OE *cirice*, B *crouco-*, OE *hyll*].

Cippenham Bk. See Chippenham.

Cirencester Gl, 'Roman station at *Corinium*, i e place of the Cornovii', the tribal name possibly 'promontory dwellers' [*Corinion* c 150, *Cirenceaster* 891: OE *ceaster*].

†**Clackmannan** Clk, 'stone of Manau', referring to the district about the Forth basin. The stone is a glacial rock in the centre of the town [*Clacmanan* 1147: W *clog*].

Clacton on Sea Ess, 'farm of Clacc's people' [*Claccingtun* c 1000: OE *-ingas, tūn*].

Claddach Kirkibost (North Uist) Inv, 'shore by church homestead' [*Kirkabol* 1654: G *claddach*, ON *kirkja, bólstaðr*].

Clapham Sr/GL, 'homestead on or by a hillock,' the first element being found with other terminations in **Clapton** *freq*, **Clopton** *freq*, and **Clophill** Bd, the last example being apparently tautological. Among the senses of OE *clop, clap*, however is the possible meaning 'lump', and this might well describe a hill, without any redundancy being involved [1. *Cloppaham* c 880, *Clopeham* 1086, 4. *Clopelle* 1086: OE *clop, hām, hyll, tūn*].

Clapton in Gordano So. See Clapham, Easton in Gordano.

Clara Off, **Clare** Cla: 'level place', a metaphorical extension of the literal meaning, 'board, plank' [OI *clāar*].

Clare Sf, '(place on) gentle stream'. **Clarence**, in a title of nobility, is adapted from the Latin form of this name, *Clarentia*, and was first used by Lionel, third son of Edward III, on his marriage to a member of the Clare family [*Clara* 1086: MW *clayar*].

Clarendon W, possibly 'clover hill' [*Clarendona* 1130: OE *clæfren, dūn*].

Cleddyf *riv* Pmb. See Milford Haven.

Cleethorpes LLi, 'dependencies of Clee i e clay place', the hamlets being Hole and Itterby, respectively 'hollow place' and 'outer farm' [*Cleethorpes* 17c: OE *clæg, hol*, ON *þorp, ytri, bý*].

Clerkenwell Mx, 'spring or stream of the clerics' [*fons clericorum* c 1100, *Clerkenewelle* 1182: OE *clerc, wella*].

††**Cleveland** NRY, **Cleveland Hills** *mts* NRY: 'hilly district' [*Clivelanda* c 1110: OE *clif, land*].

Clifden Gal, 'stones', either in the sense of 'stepping stones' across the river or, possibly, 'stone-built dwellings' of ancient origin, said to have been found in the vicinity [*Clochán* n d: OI *cloch*].

Clifford *freq*, 'ford by a slope' [OE *clif, ford*].

Clifton *freq*, 'farm by a slope', often distinguished by manorial or topographical additions, e g **Clifton Campville** St, held in the thirteenth century by Richard de Camvill, whose family originated in Canville in Normandy; **Clifton upon Dunsmore** Wa is situated on the open stretch of land south of Rugby, 'Dunna's waste-land' [OE *clif, tūn*].

Clitheroe La, 'thrush hill' [*Cliderhou* 1102: ON *kliðra, haugr*].

Clogher Tyr, **Clogher Head** Lth: 'stone place' [OI *cloch*].

Cloncrew Lim, 'wild garlic meadow' [I *cluain, creamha*].

Clonmel Dub, —Off, —Tip: 'honey meadow' [I *cluain, meala*].

Clontarf Dub, 'bull meadow' [I *cluain, tarbh*].

Clun *riv* Sa, 'water', the name being found also in **Clun** Sa, **Clunbury** Sa, **Clunton** Sa, and **Clungunford** Sa, and identical with other river-names such as Colne *riv* Ess (q v) [1. *Coluno flumine* 1572, 2. *Cluna* 13c, 3. *Clvneberie* 1086, 4. *Clvtvne* 1086, 5. *Clungonvert* 1272: B **colauno-*, OE *burh, tūn, ford*].

††**Clwyd** *riv* Den, 'hurdle (river)', possibly named from a place actually on the river, such as a ford or causeway constructed with hurdles [*Cloid fluvium* 1191: W *clwyd*].

Clydach *riv* Bre, —*riv* Glm, **Clyde** *riv* Lnk-Rnf: 'cleansing one', referring either to the strength of the current or to the clearness of the water [1. *Cloutac* n d, 2. *Cleudach* 1208, 3. *Clota* c 110: B **cloutā*].

Clyst *riv* D, 'cleansing one', related to the river-names Clydach and Clyde (qq v). The river gives its name to several places along its course, mostly named from church dedications: **Clyst St George** D, **Clyst St Lawrence** D, **Clyst St Mary** D. In **Clyst Hydon** D the addition is manorial; the place was held by Ricard de Hidune in the thirteenth century. **Clyst William** D, 'source of the Clyst', has as its second element OE *æwielm*, 'spring, source'. **Clyst Honiton** D is a *higna-tūn*, i e 'farm belonging to a monastic community' and was once held by Exeter Cathedral. The modern form of the name has been assimilated to **Honiton** D, 'Huna's farm' [1. *Clyst* 937, 4. *Cliste Sancte Marie* 1242, 6. *Clistewelm* 1238; 7. *Hina tune* c 1100, *Clysthynetone* 1281, 8. *Honetona* 1086: B **cloust-*, OE *tūn*].

Coalbrookdale Sa, 'valley of the Colbrook, i e cold stream', erroneously associated with coal. Although Darby established smelting works here in 1709, the name is not connected with the industry in any way [*Caldebrok* 1250: OE *cald, brōc*].

Coalville Lei, 'coal town', a name given about 1830 to a mining settlement in the parish of Whitwick. The termination -*ville* is characteristic of modern names, e g Ironville Db, Waterlooville Ha, and Bournville Wa [MnE *coal*, F *ville*].

Coatbridge Lnk, 'bridge at Coats, i e (place with) cottages', a modern name for the mining settlement here. The bridge was built at Coats about 1800 [*Coittis* 1584: OE *cot*].

Coates, Coatham. See Cotes.

Cóbh Crk, 'bay, sheltered inlet of the sea', an adaptation of the English *cove*; the name Queenstown was used for a time, in honour of Queen Victoria, who visited Cobh in 1850 [*Cove* 1659: ON *cofi*].

Cobham Sr, 'Cofa's homestead', forms in Cob- having developed owing to the influence of Chobham (q v) [*Coveham* 675: OE *hām*].

Cockerham La, 'homestead on river Cocker, i e crooked river', on the sandy bank of which stands **Cockersand** La. At the mouth of a different river Cocker, with the same meaning, is **Cockermouth** Cu. **Cockerton** Du is on the Cocker Beck, another instance of which is in Nottinghamshire [1. *Cocreham* 1086, 2. *Cocur* 930, 3. *Kokersand* 1212, 4. *Coker* 1230, 5. *Kokermue* 1195: B **kukro-*, OE *hām, sand, mūða*].

Colaboll Sut, **Colbost** (Skye) Inv: 'Kol's homestead', the modern terminations being characteristic in the areas concerned ON *bólstaðr*].

†**Colchester** Ess, 'Roman station on the river Colne', replacing the Romano-

British name *Camulodunum* (q v). The river-name is related to Clun (q v) and means simply 'water, stream'; other rivers of the same name occur in Hertfordshire, Gloucestershire, and Huntingdonshire. The supposed association with King Cole dates from chronicles written in the thirteenth century, by which time the -*n*- had been dropped out of the name; more recent theorists have tried to shore up this unfounded mythical structure by identifying Cole with the god Camulos [*Colneceaster* 921: OE *ceaster*].

†**Coleraine** Lon,—Off, **Coolraine** Lim, **Coolrainey** Wex: 'fern nook' [I *cuil, rathain*].

Coll isld Arg, 'hazel place' [G *coll*].

Colne riv Ess, —riv Gl, —riv Hrt, —riv Hu. See Colchester.

Colonsay isld Arg, 'Kolbein's island' [*Coluynsay* 14c: ON *ey*].

Colwich St 1247, 'outlying farm where charcoal was prepared' [*Colewich* 1240: OE *col, wic*].

†**Colwyn** (Bay) Den, '(place by) whelp (river)', *Bay* having been added when the place developed as a seaside resort during the nineteenth century. Numerous river-names occur in Wales, Scotland, and Ireland consisting of animal names without further qualification [*Coloyne* 1334: W *colwyn*].

Combe freq, 'narrow valley', most common in south and south-west England, with a variety of manorial suffixes [OE *cumb*].

Comberbach Ch, '(place by) stream of the Britons', the first element being the OE adaptation of the Britons' own name for themselves, corresponding to Welsh *Cymry*. The term occurs in other names in counties near the Welsh border, e g, **Comberton** He, **Comberhalgh** La ('Britons' nook of land'), and **Comberford** St [1. *Cambrebech* c 1175, *Combrebeche* 1190, 4. *Cumbreford* 1187: OE *bece, tūn. halh, ford*].

Compton *freq*, 'farm in a narrow valley', often with descriptive, topographical, or manorial additions. Among the last-named may be mentioned **Compton Abbas** Do and **Compton Abbas West** Do, respectively, as early forms demonstrate, 'abbess's Compton' and 'abbot's Compton'. **Compton Greenfield** Gl refers to the de Greinvill family and so reverses the process by which names in *-field* have become *-ville* in modern spellings [2. *Cumtun* 871, *Cumpton Abbatisse* 1293, 3. *Cumpton Abbatis* 1291, 4. *Compton Greneville* 1303: OE *cumb, tūn*].

Comrie Pth, '(place) at the confluence', the junction of the river Earn and an important tributary [*Comry* 1268: G *comar*].

Conganium. See Chester le Street.

Congerston Lei. See Coningsby.

†**Congleton** Ch, 'farm at Conkhill, i e steep, round-topped hill' [*Cogletone* 1086, *Congulton* c 1262: OE **canc, hyll, tūn*].

Coningsby LLi, **Conisby** (Islay) Arg, **Conisby** LLi: 'the king's farm or village'. The ON word for 'king' occurs in numerous other place-names, some possibly adapted from OE forms, e g **Conisbrough** WRY and **Congerston** Lei, the latter having been *Kinigston* in the thirteenth century. This may have been a survival of a pure English form, ousted later by forms appropriate to the still living Anglo-Norse dialect [1. *Cuningesbi* 1086, 3. *Cunesbi* 1086, 4. *Cunungesburh* 1002, 5. *Cuningestone* 1086, *Kinigston* c 1220, *Cunigeston* 1247: ON *konungr*,

ODan *kunung* (OE *cyning*), ON *bý*, OE *burh, tūn*].

Coniston Water *lke* La, 'lake by Coniston, i e the king's farm or manor', **Church Coniston** La being at the head of the lake. The place-name occurs in nearby counties also: **Coniston** ERY, **Conistone** WRY, and **Cold Coniston** WRY are examples, all probably Scandinavianised forms of English names [2. *Coningeston* 1160, 3. *Coningesbi* 1086, *Cuningeston* 1190, 4. *Cunestune* 1086: ON *konungr*, (*bý*), OE *tūn*]. See also Coningsby.

Connaught, '(province of) the *Connachta* tribe', the most westerly of the four main divisions of Ireland. See also Leinster, Munster, Ulster, Meath.

Connemara Gal, 'maritime (territory of) Conmac's people', the progenitor of the tribe being Conmac, son of the legendary queen Medb by Fergus MacRoy [*Conmaicne-mara* n d: I *muir*].

Conovium. See Conway.

Contin Ros, 'land in dispute' [*Conten* 1226: G *cointin*].

Conway Crn, '(place on) famous river', the Romano-British name *Conovium* having been first transferred to the river. The town is properly †**Aberconwy**, 'mouth of the Conwy', but the form without *Aber-* is now replacing the Anglicised Conway [*Conovium* 4c, *Conguoy* 12c, *Aberconuy* 12c: B **can-* W *aber*].

Coolrain Lx (near Mountrath), 'Ruan's nook' or 'nook of reddish land'. OI Ruan, earlier Ruadhan, 'reddish person or thing' was used as a personal name but was also applied to land with soil of this colour [OI *cuil, ruadhan*].

Coolraine Lim, **Coolrainey** Wex. See Coleraine.

Copmanthorpe WRY, 'dependent settlement of the chapmen or merchants', a Scandinavian name embodying ON *kaupmaðr* corresponding to OE *ceapere*, 'seller, merchant', found in **Chipperfield** Hrt. The -n- in the Yorkshire name is explained by the fact that the ON word is in the genitive case of the plural, *kaup-manna* [1. *Copemantorp* 1086 2. *Chiperfeld* 1375: ON *kaupmaðr*, *þorp*, OE *ceapere*, *feld*].

Corbridge Nb, 'bridge at *Corstopitum*', the Romano-British name having been reduced to its first syllable and perhaps mistaken for a river-name [*Corstopitum* 4c, *Corebricg* c 1050: OE *brycg*].

Corby LKe,†—Nth: 'Kori's farm or village'. The two places are not far apart and are both mentioned in Domesday Book. They probably both date from the Danish settlement of the East Midlands about the year 870 [1. *Corbi* 1086, 2. *Corbei*, *Corbi* 1086: ON *bý*].

Cork Crk, 'marsh' on *Corcach-mor-Mumhan*, 'great marsh of Munster' [I *corcach*].

Cornwall, '(territory of) Britons of the *Cornovii* tribe, i e the promontory people', though the promontory referred to need not be the Cornish peninsula itself. The Cornovii were to be found in the West Midlands and also in Scotland. The termination is the OE word meaning 'Celtic-speaking strangers' [*Cornubia* 6c, *on Cornwalum* 891: OE *w(e)alh*].

Corstopitum. See Corbridge.

Corstorphine MLo, 'Thorfinn's cross', or, possibly 'Thorfinn's crossing place'. Thorfinn has not been identified [*Crostorfin* c 1140: ON *kros*].

Cotes *freq*, 'cottages', also spelt **Coates**. The forms **Coton**, **Cotton**, and **Coatham** mean 'at the cottages' [OE *cot*, dat. pl. *cotum*].

†**Cotswold(s)** Gl-Wo, 'Cōd's weald or high open ground' [*Codesuualt* 12c: OE *w(e)ald*].

Cottingham ERY, —Nth: 'homestead of Cotta's people' [1. *Cotingeham* 1086, 2. *Cotingeham* 1086: OE *-ingas*, *hām*].

Cotton. See Cotes.

Coulsdon Sr, 'Cuðred's hill', with a replacement of original -r- by -l- under Norman influence, as in Salisbury, in which *Saresburia* became *Salesberia* [*Curedesdone* 675, *Cudredesdone* 933, *Colesdone* 1086: OE *dūn*].

Countesthorpe Lei, 'dependent settlement held by a countess'. The parent village was Blaby [*Torp* c 1220, *Countastorp* 1242: OE *þorp*, OF *contesse*].

Coveney C 1254, 'Cōfa's island, or dry ground amidst fens' [*Covene* 1291: OE *ēg*].

†**Coventry** Wa 1235, 'Cōfa's tree', with a personal name qualifying *tree*, as in Elstree, Braintree, and Oswestry. Such names often denote meeting places of hundreds or other local assemblies; Coventry was not the centre either of Knightlow Hundred or of its sub-division, Stoneleigh Hundred, and so the landmark here must have had some other function [*Couentre* 1043: OE *trēow*].

Cowbridge Ess, **Cowbridge** Glm, —W: '(place by) bridge used by cattle' [1. *Cubrigea* 1086: 2. *Coubrugge* 1263: 3. *Coubrigge* 1409: OE *cū*, *brycg*].

Cowdenbeath Fif, 'Cowden's property in Beath, i e birch place', an interpretation based on fairly late forms of the compound name [*terris de Baithe-*

Moubray alias Cowdounes-baithe 1626: G *beith*].

Cowes Wt, '(place by) The Cows (sandbanks)', fanciful name transferred from the sandbanks to the coastal resort nearby [*the Cowe, betwixt the Isle of Wight and England* 1512: OE *cū*].

Craigie Pth, 'at the crag or rock' [*Cragyn* 1266: G *creag*].

Craigmore Bte, 'large rock' [G *creag, mór*].

Cranwell LKe, 'cranes' spring' [*Craneuulle* 1086: OE *cran, wella*].

Crathie Abd, 'place amidst brushwood' [G *creathach*].

Crawford Lnk, 'ford by which crows were seen' [*Crauford* c 1150: OE *crāwe, ford*].

†**Crawley** Sx, 'crows' clearing or wood' [*Crauleia* 1203: OE *crāwe, lēah*].

Crayford K, 'ford over river Cray, i e clean stream' [*Creiford* 1199: OE *ford*]. See also Chelmer.

Crediton D, 'farm on river Creedy', the river name, 'winding one' having been used also for Crediton and several other places along the course of the stream; these are now differentiated as **Lower Creedy, North Creedy,** and **Upton Hellions,** i e 'Helihun's manor upstream from Crediton' [1. *Cridie* 739, *æt Cridiantune* 930, 2. *on Cridian* 739, 4. *Northcredy* 1604: B *critio-*, OE *tūn, upp*].

Creech Do, **Creech St Michael** So: 'hill', both being by similarly named hills. The Dorset place is beside Creech Barrow, and that in Somerset has an additional redundancy in being called **Creech Barrow Hill,** the British and two Saxon elements each meaning 'hill' [1. *Criz,*

Cric 1086, 2. *Crice* 1086: B *crūc*, OE *beorg, hyll*].

Cremorne Mhn, 'territory of the tribe called Mughdhorna', the descendants of Mughdhorn, son of Colla Meann. Other members of the same tribe settled in the south of county Down, in the area now known as Mourne [*Crioch-Mughdhorn* n d : I *crich*].

†**Crewe** Ch, '(place by) stepping stones' [*Crev* 1086: W *cryw*].

Cricieth Crn, 'mound of the captives [*Cruckeith* 1273: W *crug, caeth*, pl. *caith*].

Crieff Pth, '(place) among the trees' [*Craoibh* n d: G *craobh*].

Criffell *mtn* Kcb, 'split mountain' [*Crefel* 1330: ON *kryfja, fjall*].

Cromarty Ros, 'crooked sea-place', possibly alluding to the irregular coastline of Nigg Bay and Cromarty Firth. In the county-name, Cromarty does not represent a clearly defined area adjoining Ross, but a number of scattered enclaves within Ross territory [*Crumbathyn* 1264: OG *crumb*, OI *bath*].

Crombie Bnf, 'at the crooked place' [G *crombach*, loc. *crombairch*].

Cromer Nf, 'crows' lake' [*Crowemere* 13c: OE *crāwe, mere*].

Crosby *freq*, 'farm near, or village with, a cross' [ON *kros, bý*].

Crospatrick Wic, 'Patrick's cross'. A direct connexion with St Patrick is possible, but doubtful [*Crospatric* c 1220: OI *cros*].

Crowthorne Brk 1607, '(place by) thorn tree on which crows were seen', the tree forming the landmark being represented on a seventeenth-century map, the earliest reference [OE *crāwe*, *born*].

Croxall St, 'Krok's residence', the personal name being Old Norse. The same personal name is found in **Croxden** St, **Croxley** Hrt, **Croxteth** La, and **Croxdale** Du, respectively '... valley', '...clearing', 'landing-place', and 'tail of land', as well as in numerous examples of **Croxton**, 'Krok's farm' [1. *Crokeshalle* 942, 2. *Crochesdene* 1086, 3. *Crokesleya* 1166, 4. *Crocstad* 1257, *Croxtath* 1297, 5. *Crokesteil* 1195, 6. *Crocestona* 1080: OE *hall*, *denu*, *lēah*, *stæð*, *tægl*, *tūn*].

Croydon Sr, 'valley in which saffron grew' [*Crogedena* 809: OE *croh*, *denu*].

Crucadarn Bre, 'mighty mound' [*Kruc kadarn* 1550: W *crug*, *cadarn*].

Cruchfield Brk, 'open land by a hill' [*Kerchesfeld* 1185: B *crouco-*, OE *feld*].

Crucywel Bre, 'Hywel's mound', **Crickhowel** being the Anglicised form of the name [*Crickhoel* 1263: W *crug*].

Crumlin Dub, —Ant: 'winding valley' [I *crumb*, *ghlinn*].

Cumberland, 'region of the Cymry or Welsh', the Celts of the area not being subdued by the English of Northumberland until the late seventh century. The boundaries were uncertain for a long time after then, and the county has now been absorbed into the larger one of Cumbria (q v) [*Cumbra land* 945: OE *Cumbre*, *land*].

Cumbernauld Dnb, 'meeting of streams, confluence' [*Cumbrenald* c 1295, *Cumyrnald* 1417: G *comar-an-allt*].

Cumbrae, Great isld Rnf, **Little Cumbrae** isld Rnf: 'island of the Welsh', alluding to the Britons of Strathclyde, who like others in southern Scotland, were known as Cumbrians [*Cumberays* 1264: W *Cymry*, ON *ey*].

††**Cumbria**, 'territory of the Welsh', a Latinisation of OE *Cumbreland* or of the British ancestor of Welsh *Cymry*, and referring in particular to the British area of north-west England, from Lancashire-North-of-the-Sands to the Scottish border. This area, including part of Lancashire, Westmorland, and Cumberland, has now become a single county [*Cumbria* 8c: W *Cymry*].

Cummister (Yell) Zet, 'the king's shieling or summer pasture' [*Cunnyngsitter* 1639: ON *sǽtr*].

Curragh IOM, **The Curragh** Kld: 'racecourse' [I *cuirreach*].

Currie MLo, 'wet plain, marsh' [*Corry* 1368: G *currach*].

Cwmbran Mon, 'valley of (river) Bran', the river-name meaning 'raven' [*Cwmbran* 1707: W *cwm*].

Cymry, 'fellow-countrymen', modern Welsh development of the name used by Britons of themselves, and now applied to Wales. The Latinised forms *Cambria* and *Cumbria* have been used since the Middle Ages of Wales and North-West England respectively, and the Anglicised *Comber-* and *Cumber-* prefixes are found in a number of place-names indicating areas occupied by Britons after the general English settlement [B *combrogi-*].

†**Dacorum** Hrt, 'belonging to the Danes', originally the name of a Hundred, now of a District [*Danais* 1086: *Daneshdr* 1161, *de hundredo Dacorum* 1196: L *Dacus*, 'a Dane'].

Dagenham Ess/GL, 'Dæcca's homestead' [*Dæccanhaam* 692: OE *hām*].

Dalbeattie Kcb, 'field by the birch trees' [*Dalbaty* 1469: G *dail, beithe*].

Dalbury Db. See Dawley.

Dalgheal Ros. See Dalziel.

Dalgleish Slk, 'green haugh or alluvial valley', the first element having a range of meanings similar to OE *hamm*, varying from 'field, meadow' to 'piece of riverside land' [G *dail, ghlas*].

Dalkeith MLo, 'field by a wood'. The second element of this Brittonic name occurs in Penketh La and Lytchett Do; it is concealed in the modern forms of Lichfield St and Penge Sr, and appears as MnW *coed* in Pencoyd He (qq v). The area around Dalkeith is still well forested [*Dolchet* 1144: B **dol, *cēd*].

Dalkey Dub, 'thorn island' [ON *dalkr, ey*].

Dallas Mor, —Ros: 'homestead by a meadow' [1. *Dolays* 1232, 2. *Dollace* 1574: B **dol, *ais*].

Dalston Mx, 'Deorlaf's village' [*Dorleston* 1338: OE *tūn*] See also Darlaston St.

Dalton Dmf, —La 1212, —Nb (x 2), — NRY (x 2), —We 1228, —WRY (x 2), **Dalton-in-Furness** La, **Dalton-le-Dale** Du, **Dalton Piercy** Du, **Dalton-upon-Tees** NRY, **North & South Dalton** ERY: 'village in a valley'. Dalton-le-Dale is tautological; Dalton Piercy was held by the great Border family of Percy [1. *Delton* c 1280, 7. *Daltun* 1086, 10. *Daltune* 1086: OE *dæl, tūn*].

Dalwhinnie Inv, 'valley of the champions' [G *dail, cuingid*].

Dalziel Inv, —Lnk, —Ros, '(at the) white meadow'. The erroneous *-z-* in this and some other Scots names arose from a

misreading of '3' (= *gh*) in medieval spellings. An alternative form of the Ross-shire name, Dalgheal, indicates the etymology more clearly [G *dail, geal* (dat. *ghil*)].

Danby NRY, **Danby-on-Ure** NRY, **Danby Wiske** NRY, **Denaby** WRY, **Denby** Db, **Denby** WRY (x 2), 'village of the Danes'. Names like Saxton, Walton, and Danby, which have a racial term as first element, are usually explained as being settlements of those people among aliens. The termination *-by* in Danby etc indicates that either the alien neighbours were themselves Scandinavians other than Danes, or that the term was in use also among the whole population. Danby Wiske is on the river Wiske, 'marshy stream', near the source of which is Ingleby Arncliffe [1. *Danebi* 1086, 4. *Denegebi* 1086, *Danebi* 1086: OE *Dena* (gen. pl. *Dena, Deniga*), ON *bý*].

Dane riv Ch-St, 'slow one'. As, at least in its upper reaches, 'this is a fairly brisk water in a steep valley' (PNCh i 20), the name may be ironic [*Dauene* 12c, *Daane* 1295: OW *dafn*, 'drop'].

Dano. See Doncaster

Darent riv K, **Dart** riv D, 'oak stream'. On the Darent are **Darenth** K and **Dartford** K (q v) [1. *Diorente* 822, 2. *Dertan stream* 10c, 3. *Daerintun* 940, *Dærente* c 980: B **deruentiu-*]. See also Dartmoor, Dartmouth, Derwent *riv*.

Darlaston St, **Darliston** Sa, 'Deorlaf's village' [1. *Derlaveston* 1262, 2. *Derloueston* 1199: OE *tūn*].

Darley Db. See Derby.

Darlington Du, 'village associated with Dēornōð'. Substitution of *-l-* for *-n-* is characteristic of Norman and some other French dialects, as in Boulogne (earlier *Bononia*). Unlike some names in which the confusion occurred, e g Avening Gl, spelt *Avelinges* in the twelfth century, Darlington did not revert to its earliest form [*Darthingtun* c 1050, *Dearningtun* c 1106, *Derlintun* 1196: OE *-ingtūn*].

Dart *riv* D. See Darent *riv* K.

†**Dartford** K, 'ford across the river Darent (q v)' [*Tarentefort* 1086, *Derentef'*, *Derteford* 1194: OE *ford*].

Dartington D, **Dartmoor** D, **Dartmouth** D: 'village of the people dwelling by the Dart', 'upland wilderness in the Dart valley', and 'mouth of the river Dart', respectively [1. *Dertrintona* 1086, 2. *Dertemora* 1182, 3. *Dærentamuða, Dertamuða* 1049: OE *-ingtūn, mōr, mūða*].

Darwen La, '(place on the) river Darwen, i e oak river', a variant of Darent, Dart, and Derwent (qq v) [*Derewent* 1208: B *deruentio-*]

Datchett Bk, 'honourable place'. The British name is probably related to OI *dech*, 'best' and L *decus*, 'ornament' [*Deccet* 10c, *Daceta* 1086: B *dek-*].

†**Daventry** Nth, '(place at) Dafa's tree', perhaps a community meeting place (though Daventry was not the meeting place of Fawsley Hundred); it might indeed have been a cross or crucifix erected by the named man [*Daventrei* 1086, *Dauntre* 1205, *Daventre al. Deyntre* 1564: OE *trēow*].

Dawley Sa, 'clearing or pasture of Dealla's people'. The personal name means 'proud, splendid'. Dealla also occurs as the first element of **Dalbury** Db [1. *Daleli* 1086, *Dalilega* 1185, 2 *Dellingeberie* 1086: OE *-ing, lēah, burh*].

Dawlish D, '(place by) the black stream'. The river is now called Dawlish Water; the settlement was intermittently alluded to as Dawlish-ford between the eleventh and the fifteenth centuries, but then, like Usk, Thame, and a good many other places, was designated by the name of its river without further modification [*Doflisc, on doflisc ford* 1044, *Douelisford* c 1200, *Dawlysshe* 1483: B *dubo-, *glassjo*]. See also Douglas IOM.

Deal K, 'valley' is possible, but seems out of place on the coast, so 'low-lying area' may be a more accurate interpretation [*Addelam* 1086, *Dale* 1275: OE *dæl*].

Dean *freq*, **Dean Prior** D, **East Dean** Gl, **East Dean** Ha, **East Dean** Sx (x 2), **Little Dean** D, **West Dean** Gl, **West Dean** Sx (x 2). **Priors Dean** Ha, **Deane** Ha, **Dean Prior** D, **Forest of Dean** Gl: 'valley'. Dean Prior (*Dene Prioris* 1316) was held by Plympton Priory; Priors Dean (*Pryorsden* 1475) by Southwick Priory [OE *denu*].

Dedham Ess, 'Dydda's homestead' [*Delham* 1086, *Dedham* 1185: OE *hām*].

Dee *riv* Mer-Ch 1043, **Dee** *riv* Abd-Knc: 'holy one, goddess'. The Anglo-Welsh river was credited with prophetic gifts, displayed by cutting away the bank on whichever side was to be defeated in an ensuing conflict. The Welsh name **Dyfrdwy** means 'River Dee' [1. *Deova* c 150, *Dubrduiu* 1140, 2. *Deova* c 150: B *dēvā*].

Denaby WRY. See Danby.

Denbigh Den 1534, 'little fortress'. The normal MnW form is identical with the 1269 spelling [*Dinbych* 1269, *Dynbiegh* 1334: W *din, bach*].

Denbury D. See Devon.

Denby Db. See Danby.

Denge K 1292,'valley district'.The second element is found in only a few very early OE names in SE England and is related to Mn German *Gau* 'district'. **Denge Marsh** is 'marsh used by people of Denge': **Dungeness** is 'promontory of Denge or Dunge Marsh' [2. *Dengemerse* 774: OE *denu *gē, mersc, næss* (K *ness*)].

Denny Stl 1601, 'well-watered land in a valley' [*Litill Dany* 1510; OE *denu, ēg*].

Denton freq, 'village in a valley'. A name of wide distribution in England, yet without affixed forms [OE *denu, tūn*]. See also Duddington Nth.

Deptford K/GL, 'deep ford'. The place is at the confluence of the Ravensbourne with the Thames, and the ford is over the tributary [*Depford* 1334: OE *dēop, ford*].

†**Derby** Db 1086, 'village where deer are found'. When Danes settled in the area, they replaced the existing English name, Northworthy, by a Scandinavian one. One reason for this may have been that to the newcomers there were completely different points of reference, so that 'north enclosure' would appear unintelligible if they were not trying to distinguish between the place of that name and some 'south enclosure' (in fact, unidentified) elsewhere. **Darley** Db has an OE name meaning 'deer clearing', indicating that the English inhabitants were also aware of the deer in the neighbourhood [1. *Northworthige* c 1000, *Dyreby* 1009, *Deoraby* c 1050, 2. *Derlega* c 1156: ON *djúr, bý*, OE *dēor, lēah, norð, worðig*].

Derg (Lough) *lke* Cla-Tip, 'lake of the red (place)' [I *loch, dearg*].

Derravarragh (Lough) *lke* Wme, 'lake with abundant oak woods'. The interpretation is confirmed by the botanical history of the area, in which oaks grew in profusion down to the seventeenth century and possibly later. The heavily moralistic meaning proposed in 1682, 'severe judgment', could only be reached by misreading *dairbhreach*, 'abounding in oaks', as the phrase *daoir bhreath* [*Logh Dervaragh* 1412: I *loch, dairbhreach*].

Derry Lon. See Londonderry.

Derwent *riv* Cu, —*riv* Db, —*riv* NRY-ERY,'river abounding in oaks'. From the Cumberland name that of **Derwentwater** *lke* Cu is derived. The fairly frequent occurrence of this and similar river-names (e g Darent, Dart) bears witness to the abundance of upland oak forests in ancient Britain [1. *Deruuentionis* c 730, 2. *Deorwentan* c 1020, 3. *Deruuentionem* c 730: B *deruentā].

Desborough Nth, 'Deor's fortified place' [*Dereburg* 1088, *Deresburc* 1166, *Desburc* 1197: OE *burh*].

Deveron *riv* Bnf, 'little stream' [*Douern* 1273: G *dobharan*].

Devizes W, '(place at) the boundary'. Many important towns in England are on or near Hundred boundaries; this one is noteworthy (and so, name-worthy) in that Potterne Hundred was royal domain, but the adjoining Cannings Hundred was in the hands of the powerful Bishops of Salisbury [*Divisas* 1139: OF *devise*].

Devon, '(place of) the tribe of *Dumnonii*, i e the deep ones'. The tribal name, probably relating to mining, was applied to people in south-west Scotland and in Ireland, doubtless emigrants from Devon. The tribal name also occurs in **Denbury** D, 'fortified place of the Devon men' [1. *Defnascir* c 1000; 2. *Defnasberie* 1086, OE *Defnas, scir, burh*].

Devon *riv* Knr, —*riv* Lei-Nt: 'black river' [1, *Glendovan* c 1210; 2. *Dyvene* 1252: B **dubo-*].

Dewsbury WRY, 'Dewi's fortified place' [*Deusberia* 1086: OE *burh*].

Dibden Ha, 'deep valley' [*Debedene* 1086: OE *dēop, denu*].

Didcot Brk, 'Dudda's cottage'. The same personal name occurs also in **Didley** He, 'Dudda's clearing' [1. *Dudecota* 1206, 2. *Dodelogie* 1086: OE *cot, lēah*].

Diffwys *mtn* Mer, 'precipice' [W *diffwys*].

Dinas Crn, —Crm, —Pmb: 'stronghold, fortified place' [W *din* < B **duno-*].

Dingle Ker, 'fortress (of O'Cush)' [*Daingean-ui-Chuis* 16c: I *daingean*].

Dingwall Ros, 'field where the district assembly took place'. The 'Thing', the Scandinavian assembly of free men for the administration of justice and the discussion of public affairs, took place at regular intervals at a fixed site. The name survives also as Tynwald in IOM. Tingwall in Orkney, and Thingvellir in Iceland [*Dingwell* 1227: ON *þing-völlr*]. See also Peffer.

Ditton Bk. —K, —La 1194, **Fen Ditton** C, **Wood Ditton** C, **Long Ditton** Sr, **Thames Ditton** Sr, 'village by a ditch or dike' [1. *Ditone* 1086, 2. *Dictun* 10c. 4. *Dictun* c. 995, *Fen Dytton* 1286, 5. *Wodedittone* 1228, 7. *Temes Ditton* 1235: OE *dic, tūn*].

Doddington *freq*. See Duddington Nth.

Dolgellau Mer 15c, 'water meadows with monastic cells' [*Dolkelow* 1254, *Dolgethly* 1338: W *dôl, cell* (pl. *cellau*)].

Don *riv* Du 1140, —*riv* La, —*riv* WRY 1180: 'river'. On the WR Don is **Doncaster**, originally *Dano*, 'place on the river Don'; the modern name means 'Roman station on the river Don'

[1. *Doni amnis* c 1106, 3. *Douni* 1161, 4. *Dano* 4c: B *Dānō-*, OE *ceaster*].

Don *riv* Abd 1170, **Doon** *riv* Ayr: '(river of) river goddess'. At the mouth of the Don is Aberdeen (q v) [2. *Don* 1197: B *Dēuonā*].

Donagh Fmn, '(place by) a church'. The Irish word, from L *dominicus*, means 'belonging to the Lord' and so corresponds in sense to Greek *kuriakon*, the ultimate origin of MnE *church*. *Donagh* occurs as a first element in a number of other place-names, e g **Donaghmore** *freq*, 'big church', **Donaghpatrick** Mth, 'church of St Patrick', and **Donaghadee** Dwn, 'church by a rampart' [I *domhnach*].

†**Doncaster** WRY, 'Roman station on the river Don'. The termination -*caster* occurs only within the Danelaw; elsewhere the spelling -*chester* prevails. The *k*- sound is reasonably attributable to ON influence [*Dano* 4c, *Donecastre* 1002: OE *ceaster*]. See also Don *riv* WRY.

Donegal Don, 'fortress of the foreigners'. The foreigners were Danes, who occupied an earthen fortification in the area, in the tenth century [I. *Dun-na-nGall* 12c: I *dūn, gall*].

Donibristle Fif, 'Breasal's fortress'. The personal name means 'warrior' [*Donibrysell* c 1165: G *dùn*].

Donisthorpe Lei. See Mablethorpe.

Doon *riv* Ayr. See Don *riv* Abd.

Dorchester Do, 'Roman station at *Durnovaria*, i e sports place'. There is no reason to think that the contests in the great amphitheatre in Dorchester consisted exclusively of boxing bouts, as the literal meaning of *Durnovaria*, 'fist play', would suggest. The British name was modified by the Anglo-Saxons to

Dornware, 'dwellers at Dorn', replacing the unintelligible Celtic termination by a familiar Germanic word that sounded very similar and made sense in the context, in much the same way as B *Eburacum* was transformed into OE *Eoforwic* (see York). [*Durnovaria* 4c *Dornuuaranaceaster* 847, *Dorecestre* 1086: OE *ceaster*]. See also Dorset.

Dorchester O, 'Roman station at *Dorcic,* i e the splendid place'. [*Dorciccaestræ* c 730, *Dorchecestre* 1086 B* *derk,* OE *ceaster*].

Dorking Sr, '(place of) Deorc's people' [*Dorchinges* 1086: OE *-ingas*].

Dorn *riv* O, 'river on which Dornford stands'. Like Chelmer, Wandle (qq v) and others, this river-name is a back-formation. **Dornford** O, 'hidden ford', is at a ford on the river now called the Dorn but earlier possibly called *Meolce,* 'milky stream', from the whitish colour of the water [2. *Deorneford* 777, *þam stream bæ scyt fram Meolcforda* 958, *Derneford* 1239: OE *derne, meoluc, ford*].

Dornoch Sut, 'place of handstones', alluding to fist-sized pebbles suitable as missiles. **Dornock** Dmf has the same meaning, but may be British rather than Gaelic in origin [1. *Durnach* 1145, 2. *Durnack* 1182: G *dornach,* OW *durnauc*].

Dorset, '(place of) the settlers around *Dorn*'. Like Devon and Somerset, this county also bears a folk-name, and modern usage omits *-shire* though there is historical warrant for its inclusion [*Thornsaeta* c 894, *Dorsæton* 955, *Dorseteschire* c 944: OE *sæte*]. See also Dorchester Do.

Douglas Crk, —IOM, —Lnk: '(place on) the black stream'. As a river-name, Douglas occurs in La and Lx, in Abd

and Slk as **Douglas Burn,** and in Arg and Lnk (x 2) as **Douglas Water** [2. *Dufglas* c 1257, 3. *Duuelglas* c 1150, 4. *Duglas* 1147: B **dubo-, *glassjo-,* OG *dub, glas,* I *dubh, glais*]. See also Dawlish, Dowlas *riv* Mon, Dulais *riv* Crm.

†**Dover** K, '(place at) the waters'. When the Celtic name was adopted by the Anglo-Saxons, the plural number of the original was retained in the OE form *Dofras,* and as elsewhere in Kent, e g Reculver and Richborough, *-ceaster* was not added to the British name [*Dubris* 4c, *Dofras* c 700: B**dubro-*].

Dowlas *riv* Mon, **Dowles** *riv* Wo: 'black stream' [1. *Dyueleys* 1307, 2. *Doules* 1296: B**dubo-, *glassjo-*]. See also Dawlish, Douglas.

†**Down, Downpatrick** Dwn, 'fort (of St Patrick)' [I *dun*].

Draycot(t) *freq,* 'cottage by a passage or porterage'. The first element alludes to places where something can be dragged, e g to a spit of land between two waterways, across which boats would be conveyed, and occurs even more frequently in **Drayton,** which, like Draycot, is often furnished with distinguishing affixes [OE *dræg, cot, tūn*].

Drewsteignton D. See Teign.

Drogheda Lth, 'bridge of the ford' [I *droichead-atha*].

Droitwich Wo, 'muddy place with salt workings'. The second element cannot be taken unambiguously to mean 'brine pit, salt works' but has a general sense of 'industrial settlement' which can be specially modified according to context; the reference here, as in Nantwich Ch and Northwich Ch, is to salt extraction. The grandiose 'princely' sometimes suggested as the meaning of the first element is rejected in view of numerous early spellings and of confirmation from early forms for Higher and Lower Wych in Wigland Ch (PN Ch iv 51). The latter demonstrate the existence of alternative names Fulwich and Droitwich for these places, with numerous spellings identical with those for Droitwich Wo [*Saltwic* 888, *Wich* 1086, *Drihtwych* 1347, *Dertwych* 1396, *Dirtewych* 1460, *Dertwich* vel *Droitwich* 1466: OE *drit, wic*]. See also Northwich Ch.

Dromore Dwn, 'great ridge'. The Gaelic word *druim* signifies 'back (of an animal)' and is regularly used of a long, low hill [I *druim, mór*].

Dronfield Db 1282, 'open land infested by drones' [*Dranefeld* 1086: OE *drān, feld*].

Druim Fada *mtn* Inv (x 2), 'long ridge' [G *druim, fada*]. Cf Dromore Dwn.

Drummond Lx, —Pth: 'ridge' [2. *Droman* 1296: G *dromainn*].

Drumnadrochit Inv, 'ridge by the bridge' [G *druim, drochaid*].

Dryburgh Rox 1150, 'dry fortress' [*Drieburh* c 1160: OE *drȳge, burh*].

Dublin Dub, '(place by) the black pool', the part of the river Liffey on which the settlement was built [*Eblana* c AD 50, *Dyflin* c 1000, *Duibh-linn* 12c: I *dubh, linn*]. See also Baile atha Cliath.

Duddington Nth, 'village of Dudda's people'. **Denton** Nth 1749 and **Doddington** Nth, as well as Doddington in several other counties, have the same meaning [1. *Dodinton* 1086, 2. *Dodintone* 1086, *Denenton* 1483, 3. *Dodintone* 1086: OE -*ingtūn*].

†**Dudley** Wo, 'Dudda's wood'. The extensive forests of this area provided

fuel for the nascent iron industry, and the numerous names in -*ley* in the vicinity bear witness to the former abundance of woodland [*Dudelei* 1086: OE *lēah*].

Dulais *riv* Crm, **Dulas** *riv* Crm, 'black stream' [W *du, glais*]. See also Dawlish, Douglas.

Dulverton So, 'village at Dilver or Dulver, i e hidden ford' [*Dolvertune* 1086: OE *digol, ford, tūn*].

Dulwich Sr/GL 1530, 'marshy meadow on which dill grew'. The uncommon second element has been gradually transformed into the familiar termination -*wich* [*Dilwihs* 967, *Dilewisse* 1212, *Dilewyshe* 1279: OE *dile, wisce*].

†**Dumbarton** Dnb, 'stronghold of the Britons', applied by the neighbouring Gaels to the place the Britons themselves called *Alclut*, 'rock of Clyde'. The spelling of the county name, **Dunbartonshire**, was arbitrarily modified in recent times [*Dumbrethan* c 1290: G *dùn, Breatann*]. See also Bishop Auckland.

††**Dumfries** Dmf, 'woodland stronghold' [*Dunfres* c 1183: G *dùn, preas*].

Dunbar ELo, 'fort on the summit' [*Dynbaer* 709: B *duno-, *barro-*].

Dunblane Pth, 'hill of Blaan', on which the bishop of that name had his principal monastery. He ruled the see of Kingarth in Bute during the sixth century [*Dumblann* c 1200: G *dùn*].

Duncannon Wex, 'Conan's stronghold' [I *dùn*].

Duncansby Cai, 'Donald's farm' [*Dungalsbaer* c 1225: ON *bý*].

Dundalk Lth, 'Delga's stronghold' [I *dùn*].

Dundee Ang, 'Daig's stronghold' [*Dunde* c 1180: G *dùn*].

Dundrum Dwn, —Dub, —Tip: 'fort of the ridge' [I *dùn, druim*].

†Dunfermline Fif 1251, of uncertain meaning.

Dungeness K. See Denge K.

Dunkeld Pth, 'stronghold of the Caledonians', referring to the Picts occupying most of what became Perthshire [*Duncalden* 10c: G *dùn*]. See also Schiehallion.

Dun Laoghaire Dub, 'fort of Laoghaire'. The named man has not been identified with certainty [I *dùn*].

Dunoon Arg 1472, 'fort of the river' [*Dunnon* c 1240, *Dunhoven* 1270: G *dùn, abh*].

Duns Ber 1150, 'hills' [OE *dūn*].

Dunsmore Wa. See Clifton.

Dunstable Bd, 'Dunna's post or pillar', possibly alluding to a landmark at or near the intersection of the Icknield Way and Watling Street, and the site of the Roman posting station of *Durocobrivae* [*Dunestapele* 1123: OE *stapol*].

Dunwich Sf, '(place by) deep water'. The British name *Domnoc* was adapted into Anglo-Saxon in some such form as **Dunnuc*, the second syllable being readily misheard as *wīc* [*Domnoc* c 730: B **dubno-*, 'deep'].

†Durham Du, 'island with a hill'. ON *holmr* usually refers to well-watered riverside land or to an island in a river. Durham is hardly an island, but is within a great bend in the river Wear. The early form *Dunelm* is still used with reference to the university, in the signature of the bishop, and similar contexts; the change from *Dun-* to *Dur-* is a Norman dissimilation, to be compared with the *l/n* substitution in Darlington (q v) [*Dunholm* c 1000, *Dunhelme* 1122, *Durealme* c 1170: OE *dūn*, ON *holmr*].

Durness Sut, 'deer promontory' [*Dyrnes* 1230: ON **djúr, nes*].

Durobrivae, 'bridges by the stronghold': (1) near Castor Nth (q v), (2) Rochester K (q v).

Durocobrivae. See Dunstable.

Durocornouium. See Cirencester.

Durolipons. See Godmanchester.

Durovernon, 'walled town by an alder swamp': Canterbury [B **duro-, *verno*].

Dursley Gl, 'Deorsige's clearing' [*Dersilege* 1086: OE *lēah*].

Dyce Abd, 'in the south' [G *deas*].

†† Dyfed. See Cardigan.

Dysart Fif, 'hermit's cell'. The Gaelic word is derived from L *desertum*, 'wilderness', the usual site of hermitages [*Disard* c 1210: G *diseart*].

Eagle LKe, 'oak wood', OE *āc* having been replaced by its ON equivalent, *eik* [*Aycle* 1086, *Eicla* 1141: OE *āc, lēah*, ON *eik*].

Ealing Mx, '(place of) Gilla's people' [*Gillingas* c 700: OE *-ingas*].

Eardisland He. See Leominster.

Earls Barton Nth 1290, 'corn farm held by the earl', in the tenure of David, Earl of Huntingdon in the twelfth century [*Bartone* 1086; OE *bere-tūn*].

Earlsfield Sr/GL, 'earl's land'. A late name, doubtless alluding to Earl Spencer, who owned land in this area in the eighteenth and nineteenth centuries [MnE *field*].

Earn *riv* Pth 'flowing one' [*Erne* 1190: OC **arā*].

†**Eastbourne** Sx, 'eastern (place by) stream' [*Burne* 1086, *Estburn* 1279: OE *burna*].

East Coker So. See West Coker So.

East Dereham Nf, 'eastern deer pasture', by contrast with **West Dereham** Nf [1. *Derham* 1086, *Estderham* 1428, 2. *Deorham* c 1000 *Westderham* 1203: OE *ēast*, *west*, *dēor*, *hamm*].

Easter Ardross Ros, 'eastern promontory of the height' [OE **ēastor*, G *àird*, *ros*].

Easter Ross. See Ross.

East Garston Brk, 'Esgar's hamlet' [*Esgareston* 1180: OE *tūn*].

East Grimstead W, 'eastern homestead amidst grassland', literally 'green homestead', cf **West Grimstead** W, a little to the SW [*Gremestede* 1086: OE *grēne*, *hæmstyde*].

East Grinstead Sx, 'eastern green place'; there is also **West Grinstead** Sx, about twenty miles away [1. *Grenesteda* 1121, *Estgrenested* 1271, 2. *Westgrenested* 1280: OE *grēne*, *stede*].

East Ham Ess/GL, 'eastern riverside pasture', now combined with West Ham to form the London Borough of Newham [1. *Hamme* 958, *Estham* 1206, 2. *Westhamma* 1186: OE *hamm*].

Easthouses MLo, 'eastern house(s)' [*Esthus* 1261, *Eisthousis* 1590: OE *ēast*, *hūs*].

East Kilbride Lnk, 'eastern (place by) church of Brigid' [*Kellebride* 1180: G *cill*].

†**Eastleigh** Ha, 'eastern wood' [*Estleie* 1086: OE *ēast*, *lēah*].

†**East Lothian**, 'eastern part of the territory of Leudonus'. The former province of Lothian, now much reduced in area and divided into three counties, is thought to have been named after a shadowy hero also called Lleidun, Loth, or Lot. East Lothian was formerly known as Haddingtonshire, from its chief town, Haddington (q v). [*Loonia* c 970, *Loðene* 1095: OE *ēast*]. See also West Lothian, Midlothian.

Easton *freq*, 'eastern farm or village'. Various affixes are found, e g **Easton Maudit** Nth, **Easton Bassett** W, and **Easton Royal** W, all relating to feudal tenure. **Easton in Gordano** So bears the name of a district, derived from OE *gor-denu*, 'dirty valley', disguised and dignified by its Latinised form. **Batheaston** is to the east of Bath So [OE *ēast*, *tūn*].

Easton Neston Nth has a different derivation from other Eastons: this is from *Estanestone* 1086, 'Ēadstān's farm' [OE *tūn*].

East Riding ERY, 'eastern third'. The Scandinavian division of large areas was frequently into thirds (ON *þriðjung*); the practice obtained in both Yorkshire and the Parts of Lindsey, Lincolnshire, which was divided into North, South, and West Ridings. The initial *þ*-(later *t*-) coalesced with the final consonant of *East*-, *West*-, etc, and the form *Riding* emerged [*Est Treding*, *Oustredinc*, *Estreding* 1086: ON *austr*, *þriðjung*, OE *ēast*]. See also West Riding, North Riding, Lindsey (s v Lincoln).

East Riggs Dmf, 'eastern furrows or arable land' [ON *hryggr*].

Eastry K, 'eastern district'. The second, rare, element is found also in Ely and Surrey (qq v) [*Eastorege* c 820: OE **eastor, *gē*].

East Sheen Sr. See Sheen.

East Wemyss Fif, 'eastern (place by) caves'. G *uaim* is made plural here by the addition of E -*s* (ScE -*is*, -*ys*) [*Wemys* 1239, *Easter Weimes* 1639: G *uaim*].

East Wittering Sx, **West Wittering** Sx: '(place of) Wihthere's people' [*Wihttringes* 683: OE -*ingas*].

Eaton *freq*, either 'farm or village on a river' or 'farm or village on an island or riverside land', a subtle distinction based on the difference in meaning between OE *ēa*, 'river', and *ēg*, 'island, well-watered land beside a river'. In the first group are the several examples of **Water Eaton**, in Bucks, Oxon, and Staffs, **Eaton Bishop** and **Eaton Tregose** in Herefordshire, **Eaton Constantine**, **Eaton Mascott**, and **Eaton under Haywood**, all in Shropshire, and a number without a suffix in Berkshire, Herefordshire, Nottinghamshire, and Shropshire. Although **Eaton Socon** Bd belongs to the first group, **Eaton Bray** in the same county is in the second, as the early spellings *Eitone* 1086, *Eitona* 1130, and *Eitun* 1156, indicate. Also in the second group are **Long Eaton** and **Cold Eaton** Db, two of the Cheshire Eatons, and Eaton Lei (*Aitona* c 1125, *Eyton* 1236). **Eton** Bk (*Ettone* 1086, *Eitun* 1156) probably also belongs to the second group [OE *ēa, ēg, tūn*].

Eau *riv freq*, 'river'. This name is applied to a number of artificial watercourses in the Fens, but also to some natural streams as well. Local pronunciations vary from 'ee' to '(h)a' and 'awe'. Some of the names seem to be derived from ON *á*, which would have been rounded to *ō* in Middle English, and so regarded as identical with French *eau* because of similarity of sound. Others are from OE *ēa*, 'river', which is sufficiently near *eau* in spelling to cause confusion.

Eccles Ber, —Dmf, —K, —La, —Nf: 'place with an ancient church', alluding to pre-English villages with places of worship and employing the British loanword meaning 'church'; the term occurs also in **Ecclesall** WRY, **Eccleshall** St, **Exhall** Wa ('nook by an *Eccles*-village'), and **Eccleston** Ch, **Eccleston** La ('farm by an *Eccles*-village') and a number of other names in Scotland and England, including **Ecclefechan** Dmf, 'little church' [1. *Eccles* 1200, 2. *Eklis* 1494, 4. *Eccles* c 1180, 5. *Eccles* 1086, 7. *Ecleshelle* 1086, 10. *Eglestun* 1086: B*eglēs, OE *halh, tūn*, W *bechan*].

†**Eden** *riv* Cu-We 'gushing one' [*Itouna* c 150: B *ituna*].

Edge Ch, —Gl, —Sa: '(place by) a hillside' [1. *Eghe* 1086, 2. *Egge* 1268, 3. *Egge* 1276: OE *ecg*].

Edgware Mx, 'Ecgi's weir' [*Ægces wer* 973: OE *wer*].

Edinburgh MLo, 'fortification at a place called Eidyn'. Although there is no doubt that the site of the present city was called *Eidyn* long before King Edwin's reign, the idea persists that the name means 'Edwin's fortress'. Various linguistic difficulties stand in the way of a firm interpretation of *Eidyn* [*Eidyn, Din Eidyn* c 600, *Edenburge* 1126: OE *burh*].

Edith Weston R, 'Queen Edith's western village'. A large part of what became the

county of Rutland was assigned by
Edward the Confessor as a dower for his
queen, Edith [*Westona* 1167, *Weston
Edith* 1275: OE *west, tūn*].

Edmonton Mx, 'Edhelm's village'
[*Adelmeton* 1086: OE *tūn*].

Eggardon Hill Do, 'Eohhere's hill', a
tautological name, the unnecessary affix
Hill having been added in spite of
the synonymous termination *-don*
[*Giochresdone* 1084: OE *dūn, hyll*].

Egham Sr, 'Ecga's homestead' [*Egeham*
c 950: OE *hām*].

Egloshayle Co, '(place with a) church on
the Hayle, i e the estuary', alluding to the
mouth of the river Camel. **Hayle** is
derived from a British word meaning
'salty (place)' [*Egglosheil* 1201: B *eclēsia*
(Co *eglos*), *saliā* (OCo *seil, heil*)].

Eigg *isld* Inv, '(island with) nick or
indentation' [*Egg* 1654: G *eag*].

Eilean Donnan *isld* Ros, 'St Donan's
island', commemorating St Donan,
martyred in Eigg in 617 [*Elandonan*
c 1425: G *eilean*].

Éire. See Ireland.

Elford Nb, 'Ella's ford' [*Eleford* 1256:
OE *ford*].

Elgin Mor 1136, 'little Ireland'. A number
of places in Scotland have Gaelic names
recalling the Irish homeland, under
various disguises (cf Atholl, Banff)
[G *Ealg*+diminutive *-in*].

Ellen *riv* Cu, 'holy one' or 'mighty one'
[*Alne* 11c: B *alaun-*].

Ellesmere Sa, 'Elli's lake'. **Ellesmere Port**
Ch, formerly Whitby Locks, was so called
from its position at the junction of the

Dee and Mersey branch of the Shropshire
Union (or Ellesmere) Canal, and the river
Mersey [1. *Ellesmeles* 1086, 2. *Ellesmere
Port in Netherpool* 1831: OE *mere*]. See
also Whitby Ch.

Elmet WRY, of unknown meaning. The
British kingdom of Elmet remained
independent until the seventh century,
the name surviving as that of a district
and embodied in **Barwick-in-Elmet** ('corn
farm in Elmet') and Sherburn-in-Elmet
(q v) [1. *Elmete* c 730, 2. *Berewith* 1086,
Berewic 13c: OE *bere, wīc*].

Elstow Bd, 'Ællen's (holy) place' [*Elnestou*
1086: OE *stōw*].

Elstree Hrt, 'Tidwulf's tree'. The settlement would doubtless have first been
designated as being *at* the location of the
tree, and misdivision of the phrase *æt
Tidwulfestreow* gave rise to subsequent
forms such as *Idulfestre* 13c, *Idolvestre*
1254, and *Idelstre* 1331. The tree would
have marked an important boundary
point, at which met no fewer than four
parishes, two in Herts and two (Stanmore
and Edgware) in Middlesex. Furthermore,
although Elstree was in Cashio hundred,
the adjacent Herts parish of Aldenham
was in Dacorum hundred [*Tiðulfes treow*
785, *Tidulvestre* 1188: OE *trēow*].

Eltham K/GL, 'Elta's homestead'
[*Elteham* 1086: OE *hām*].

Ely C, 'eel district'. The archaic suffix *-ge*,
found also in Eastry K, Lyminge K,
Denge K, and Surrey (qq v), was altered
in early times to *-ēg*, 'island, dry land
amid fen', which makes topographical
sense here [*Elge* c 730, *Elig* c 890:
OE *ǣl, gē*].

Emsworth Ha, 'Æmele's enclosure'
[*Emeleswurth* 1224: OE *worð*].

Enderby Lei, **Bag Enderby** L, **Mavis
Enderby** L, **Wood Enderby** L: 'Eindriði's

village'. Wood Enderby is distinguished as being 'in woodland', and *Bag* is probably topographical. *Mavis* is a manorial addition, cf William Malebisse 1212, [1. *Andretesbie, Endrebie* 1086, 2. *Andrebi* 1086, *Bag-enderby* 1291, 3. *Endrebi* 1086, *Enderby Malbys* 1302, 4. *Endrebi* 1086, *Wodenderby* 1198: OE *wudu*, ME *bagge*, ON *bý*].

Enfield Mx, 'Eana's open land' [*Enefelde* 1086: OE *feld*].

England, 'land of the Angles, i e men from the angle-territory', alluding to the Continental homeland in Schleswig [*Englaland* c 890: OE *Engle* (gen.pl. *Engla*), *land*].

Englefield Brk, 'open land of the Angles'. Berkshire was West Saxon territory. Similarly, **Engleton** St, 'Angles' village', alludes to a group of Middle or East Anglians settled in Mercia [1. *Engla Feld* 871, 2. *Engleton* 1242: OE *Engle, feld, tūn*]. See also Inglewood Forest Cu, Exton Ha.

Ennis Cla, 'island' [I *inis*].

Enniskillen Fmn, 'Cethlenn's island'. The personal name is doubtful. Cethlenn was the wife of Balor of the Great Blows, the Fomorian pirate [I *inis*].

Enoch Dmf, 'marsh' [G *eanach*].

Enville St, 'smooth open country' [*Efnefeld* 1086: OE *efn, feld*].

Epping Ess/GL, 'people of the look-out place'. †**Epping Forest** Ess with Hainault Forest make up Waltham Forest, all that remains of the royal forest that in Norman times covered almost the whole of Essex [*Eppinges* 1086: OE *yppe, -ingas*]. See also Uppingham.

†**Epsom** Sr, 'Ebbe's homestead' [*Ebesham* 675: OE *hām*].

†**Erewash** *riv* Db-Nt, 'wandering stream'. The termination -*wash* arose relatively late, probably by confusion with the stream-name Wash [*Irewys* c 1145: OE *irre, wisce*].

Eriboll Sut, 'farm on a gravel bank' [*Eribull* 1499: ON *eyri, ból*].

Ericht, Loch *lke* Pth, **Ericht** *riv* Pth: 'lake/river of assemblies' [G *eireachda*, 'assembly'].

Eriskay *isld* Inv, 'Erik's island'. An interpretation 'island of the goblin' has also been suggested, derived from G *uruisg* [*Eriskeray* 1549: ON *ey*].

Erith K/GL, 'gravel landing place'. A number of Thames-side places have names terminating in OE *hȳð*; some, e g Lambeth and Rotherhithe (qq v), allude to cargoes brought to the landing-place, while others possibly refer to the soil or other materials associated with the area [*Earhyd* 695: OE *ēar, hȳð*].

Ermine Street, 'paved road of Earna's people', the Roman road from London to the Humber [*Earninga stræt* 955: OE *-ingas, strǣt*].

Errigal mtn Don, 'oratory', so called possibly because it served as a site for hermitages [I *aireagal* < L *oraculum*].

Esher Sr, 'ash-tree district' [*Æscæron* 1005, *Esshere* 1062: OE *æsc, scearu*].

Esk *riv* Dmf-Cu, 'water' [*Ask* c 1200: B **iscā*].

Essex, '(territory of) the East Saxons'. The early kingdom included not only the present county but also Middlesex and most of Hertfordshire [*East Seaxe* 894: OE *ēast*].

Etive, Loch *lke* Arg, 'lake of the dreadful one', embodying the name Eite, 'horrid one', goddess of the lake.

Eton Bk. See Eaton.

†**Ettrick** *riv* Slk, meaning uncertain [*Ethric* 1235].

Euston Sf 1242, 'Eof's village', the territorial title of the Earls of Euston, landowners in London, after whom Euston Square and Euston Station are named [*Euestona* 1086: OE *tūn*].

Evanton Ros, 'Evan's town', said to have been named, c 1800, in honour of Evan Fraser of Belcony.

Eversholt Bd 1185, **Eversley** Ha: 'boar's copse or wood', [1. *Eureshot* 1086, 2. *Eureslea* c 1050: OE *eofor, holt, lēah*].

Evesham Wo c 1240, 'Eof's riverside land'. Among the earliest forms of this name are *Homme* 709 and *Ethom* 706, 710, '(at the) land enclosed by a river-loop', *Et-* being a late spelling for OE *æt*. The need to distinguish this *Hamm* from others nearby e g Birlingham and Offenham, gave rise to various alternative forms, among which *Cronuchomme* 706, 'Heron's *hamm*', and *Ecguines hamme* 874, celebrating Bishop Ecgwine, founder of the monastery in Evesham. The eponymous Eof has not been identified [*Eveshomme* 709: OE *hamm*].

Evington Lei 'farm associated with Eafa' [*Avintone* 1086: OE *-ingtūn*].

†**Ewell** Sr, **Temple Ewell** K: 'spring, source of a river'. Temple Ewell was held by the Templars c 1165. Ewelme O, with the same meaning, is from a related element [1. *Euuelle* 675, 2. *Lawelme* 1086, *Eawelma* c 1215: OE *æwielle, æwielm*]. See also Templand.

Ewhurst Ha, —Sr, —Sx: 'yew wood' [1. *Ywyrstæ* 1023, 2. *Iuherst* 1179, 3. *Werst* 1086, *Yuehurst* 1208: OE *iw, hyrst*].

Exbourne D, 'cuckoo stream'. The rather unmelodious OE *gēac*, displaced after the Norman conquest by *cuckoo*, is found in other place-names, e g Exwell D and Yaxley Hu (q v) [*Hechesburne* 1086, *Yekesburn* 1242: OE *gēac, burna*].

Exceat Sx, 'oak nook'. The termination *scēat*, 'projecting angle of land', occurs also in Oxshott Sr, Aldershot Ha, and Mytchett Sr (qq v) [*Essete* 1086, *Exeta* c 1150: OE *āc, scēat*].

Exe *riv* So-D: 'water' [*Iska* c 150: B **Īscā*].

†**Exeter** D 1547, 'Roman station on the river Exe', or 'Roman station at Isca'. OE *ceaster* became -(*c*)*eter* under Norman influence [*Isca Dumnoniorum* 4c, *Exanceaster* 894, *Essecestra* 1086: OE *ceaster*]. See also Devon.

Exhall Wa. See Eccles.

Exton Ha 1182, 'village of the East Saxons', a settlement of aliens in West Saxon territory. **Exton** R 1185 is of different origin and means 'oxen farm' [1. *æt East Seaxnatune* 940, *Essessentune* 1086, 2. *Exentune* 1086: OE *East Seaxe, oxa, tūn*].

Exwell D. See Exbourne.

Eyam Db, '(at the) islands', more accurately 'land between streams', as the place lies between Jumber Brook and Hollow Brook [*Aiune* 1086, *Ayum* 1200: OE *ēg* (dat. pl. *ēgum*)].

Eye *riv* Lei c 1540, 'river' [OE *ēa*].

Eye He, —Mx, —Nth, —Sf: 'island, dry ground in a fen'. **Ebury**, 'manor of Eye', the name of a street and a square in Westminster, alludes to Eye Mx, whose name is not otherwise in use [1. *Eia* c 1175, 2. *Eia* 1086, 3. *Ege* 970, *Eia* 1086: OE *ēg*]

Eynsham O, 'Egon's homestead' [*Egonesham* 571, *Egnesham* 1005: OE *hām*].

Fad, Loch *lke* Bte, **Lough Fad** *lke* Don, **Loch Fada** *lke* (Colonsay) Bte, **Loch Fada** *lke* Ros, **Loch Fada** *lke* (North Uist) Inv: 'long lake' [G *loch, fada*].

Fairford Gl, 'clean ford', referring to an unmuddied river-crossing (cf Fulford) [*Fagranforda* 872: OE *fæger, ford*].

Fair Isle Zet, 'island of sheep'. Variants of the name occur elsewhere in the area of Norse settlement and influence, including the Faeroes, Farø in the Baltic (*Fároy* 1350), **Fara** Ork' and **Faray** Ork [ON *faar, ey*].

Fakenham Nf 1254, **Fakenham Magna** Sf c 1060, **Little Fakenham** Sf: 'homestead of Facca' [1. *Fachenham* 1086, 3. *Litla Fachenham* 1086: OE *hām*].

Fal *riv* Co, meaning uncertain [*Fæle* 969].

Fala MLo, 'variegated hill' [*Faulawe* 1250: OE *fāg, hlāw*].

Falkenham Sf, 'homestead of Falta'. The Domesday Book form, spelt *Faltenham*, occurs in a number of documents until the end of the thirteenth century, but a spelling *Falc-* appeared in 1254, possibly due to the common misreading of *-t-* as *-c-*, perhaps reinforced by the form of Fakenham (q v) [OE *hām*].

†**Falkirk** Stl, '(place with) mottled church' i e one constructed with speckled stone. The interpretation is confirmed by Gaelic, Latin, and French translations of the place-name in medieval documents. *Egglesbreth* 1065 represents G *eaglais breac*, perhaps an adaptation of Cumbrian Welsh **eglés brith*; the Latin version *varia capella* occurs in 1166, and the French *vaire chapelle* in several documents of the late thirteenth century [*Faukirke* 1298: OE *fāg, cirice*].

Falmouth Co, '(place at) mouth of the river Fal' (q v) [*Falemuth* 1235: OE *mūð*].

Fara(y) Ork. See Fair Isle.

Faraid Head Sut, 'headland of the ladder' [G *fáraidh*].

Farcet Hu, '(place of the) bull's head'. Some at least of the names of this type, e g Swineshead Bd, Shepshed Lei, and Gateshead Du (qq v), may commemorate pagan sacrificial sites at which the head of the animal was impaled on a pole [*Fearresheafde* c 957: OE *fearr, hēafod*].

†**Fareham** Ha, 'homestead near which ferns abounded' [*Fernham* 1086: OE *fearn, hām*].

Faringdon Brk, —Do, —Ha, **Little Faringdon** O: 'fern-covered hill'. A similar sound-development is found in **Farington** La, 'village where ferns abounded' [1. *Fearndun* 924, 2. *Ferendone* 1084, 3. *Ferendone* 1086, 4. *Parva Ferendon* 1199, 5. *Farinton* c 1140: OE *fearn, dūn, tūn*].

Farleigh Sr,—W, **East & West Farleigh** K, **Farleigh Wallop** Ha, **Monkton Farleigh** W: 'fern-covered clearing' [1. *Ferlega* 1086, 2. *Farlega* 1086, *Fernelega* c 1115, 3. *Fearnlege* c 880, *East-*, *West-Farlegh* 1291, 4. *Ferlege* 1086, 5. *Farnleghe* 1001, *Farley Monachorum* 1316: OE *fearn, lēah*]. See also Wallop, Faringdon, Zeal Monachorum.

Farmborough So, **Farnborough** Brk, —Ha, —K: 'fern-covered hill'. Forms with -m- are found among early spellings and OE *fearn* has become *Farm-* also in **Farmcote** Gl, **Farmcote** Sa, 'cottages on fern-covered land' [1. *Fearnberngas* 901, *Ferenberge* 1086, 2. *Fearnbeorgan* 916,

3. *Ferneberga* 1086, 4. *Fearnbiorginga mearc* 862 ('boundary of the Farnborough people'), 5. *Fernecote* 1086, 6. *Farnecote* 1209: OE *fearn, beorg, cot*].

Farne Islands Nb, 'fern islands', so called for a reason not completely explained [*Farne* c 730, *Fearne* 9c: OE *fearn*].

Farnham *freq*, 'homestead or meadow where ferns grew' [OE *fearn, hām, hamm*].

Farnham Nb, '(place by) thorn bushes', from the dative plural *þyrnum*, with change of initial consonant. **Thurnham** La has developed normally from the same form [1. *Thirnum* 1242, 2. *Tiernun* 1086: OE *þyrne*].

Fasnakyle Inv, 'level place by a wood'· G *fas* alludes to a 'station' or 'stance', i e a level place suitable for a night's camp in the course of a droving journey [G *fas, coille*].

Faversham K, 'smith's homestead'. Metalworking seems to have existed in this area in Romano-British times, which probably explains the adoption into the OE name of a Latin word *faber* [*Fefresham* 811: OE **fæfer, hām*].

Fawler Brk, —O: '(place with) variegated pavement', i e a Roman tessellated floor [1. *Fagelor* c 1170, 2. *Fauflor* 1205: OE *fāg, flor*].

Fearn Ros, '(place of) alders' [*Ferne* 1529: G *fearna*].

Feeagh, Lough *lke* Myo, 'woody place' [I *fiodagh*].

Felixstowe, Sf, 'Filica's holy place'. The similarity of the personal name with that of the first bishop of East Anglia led to the eventual acceptance of *Felix-* as the first element of the place-name [*Filchestou* 1254: OE *stōw*].

Felsted Ess, 'settlement in the open land'. Very similar to this is **Feltham** Mx, 'homestead in the open land' [1. *Feldstede* 1082, 2. *Feltham* 969: OE *feld, stede, hām*].

Fenham Nb (x 2), '(place) in the fens' [1. *Fenhu'* 1256, 2. *Fennum* c 1085, OE *fen* (dat.pl. *fennum*)].

†**Fenland** C, 'marshy region', now the name of a District approximately corresponding to the area known as The Fens [OE *fen, land*].

Fenton *freq*, 'farm by a fen' [OE *fen, tūn*].

Fenwick Ayr, —Nb (x 2)— WRY: 'dairy farm by a fen' [2. *Fenwic* 1208, 3. *Fenwic* 1242, 4. *Fenwic* 1166: OE *fen, wic*].

Feock Co, '(church of) St Feoc' [(*ecclesia*) *Sancte Feoce* 1264].

†**Fermanagh**, '(place of) men of Monach', a tribe descended from the named hero, driven from Leinster after an assassination [I *fir*].

Fermoy Crk, '(church or monastery of) the *Fir Maighe*, i e men of the plain' [I *Mainistir Fhear Mai*].

Fern Ang, **Lough Fern** *lke* Don, **Ferns** Wex: '(place of) alders' [G *fearn*]. See also Fearn.

Fetlar *isld* Zet, 'bands, girdles' [*Fætilar* c 1250: ON *fetill*].

Fettercairn Knc, 'slope by a thicket' [*Fotherkern* c 970, *Fettercairn* c 1350: G *faithir*, P *carden*].

Fews Arm, —Wat: 'woody places' [I *feadha*].

Ffestiniog Mer, 'place of defence' [*Festynyok* c 1420: *ffestin, -iog*]. See also Blaenau Ffestiniog.

Fforest Fawr Bre, 'great park' [W *fforest, mawr*].

Fife 'territory of (?) Vip'. The derivation of the name from 'Fib, one of the seven sons of Cruithne' is unsatisfactory, since the personal names are almost certainly later than those of the territories to which they correspond; to each of the sons was assigned one of the seven provinces of Pictland (cf Wainwright, *Problem of the Picts* 46-7) [*Fib* c 1150, *Fif* 1165].

Fifehead Magdalen Do, **Fifehead Neville** Do, **Fifield** O (x 2), **Fifield** W, **Fifield Bavant** W: 'estate of five hides of land'. This unit of land-size, regarded as sufficient to support a peasant family, differed in various parts of the country; in Wessex, and certainly in Dorset and Wiltshire, it comprised about forty acres. *Magdalen* records the dedication of the church. *Neville* and *Bavant* are manorial additions [1. *Fifhide* 1086, *Fyfhyde Magdaleyne* 1408, 2. *Fifhide* 1086, *Vyfhyde Nevyle* 1303, 3. *Fifide* 1316, 5. *Fifide* 1230: OE *fif, hid*].

Filey ERY, 'five clearings' [*Fiuelac* 1086: OE *fif, lēah*].

Filton Gl 1187, 'hay farm' [OE *filiðe, tūn*].

Finchampstead Brk, 'homestead frequented by finches' [*Finchamestede* 1086: OE *finc, hāmstede*].

Finchley Mx, 'clearing frequented by finches' or possibly 'clearing of a man called Finch', the surname being on record from the eleventh century [*Fynachesle*' 1243: OE *finc, lēah*].

Findhorn *riv* Inv, —*riv* Mor, —*riv* Nrn, 'white Isarona', celebrating the river-goddess of that name [G *fionn*].

Findlater Bnf, 'white slope' [*Finletter* 1266: G *fionn, leitir*].

Finedon Nth 1685, 'valley in which the folk assembly took place'. In this name, *thing* has become *fine*, and *dene*, 'valley' has been promoted to *don*, 'hill'. The Scandinavian institution is also referred to in **Fingest** Bk, 'wooded hill, on or by which the *thing* assembled' [1. *Tingden(e)* 1086, *Thingdon* 1302, 2. *Tingeherst* 1163: ON *þing*, OE *denu, hyrst*].

Finisk *riv* Wat, 'white or clear water'. The river was also known as the Phoenix, a transformation by popular etymology to be found in the name **Phoenix Park** (Dublin), also derived from a river-name Finisk [I *fionn, uisg*'].

Finnart Pth, 'white headland' [*Fynnard* 1350: G *fionn, àrd*].

Finsbury Mx. 'Finn's manor' [*Finesbury* 1254: OE *burh*].

Fishbourne Sx, **Fishburn** Du: 'stream abounding in fish' [1. *Fiseborne* 1086, 2. *Fisseburn* c 1190: OE *fisc, burna*].

Fishguard Pmb, 'yard (with pool) for fish', one of the numerous Norse names in the coastal areas on both sides of the Irish Sea, and in the Isle of Man. Pembroke is particularly well supplied with names commemorating the Scandinavians, among which are Caldy, Skokholm, Tenby, Skomer, and Grassholm (qq v), [*Fissigart* 1200: ON *fiskr, garðr*]. See also Abergwaun.

Fitzhead So, **Fivehead** So: 'estate of five hides of land' [1. *Fifhida* 1065, 2. *Fifhide* 1086: OE *fif, hid*]. See also Fifehead.

Five Boroughs: centres of military control in the Scandinavian area of England after partition between Saxons and Danes, viz Derby, Leicester, Lincoln, Nottingham, and Stamford. Of these, only Derby was renamed by the Vikings, having previously been *Northworthy*. The territory of the Five Boroughs became a coherent political unit within the region of the Danelaw—which was virtually the whole of England north of Watling Street [OE: *fíf, burh*].

Five Towns: the separate places which together constitute †**Stoke-on-Trent** St. They are: Stoke, Burslem, Hanley, Tunstall (qq v), and **Longton**, 'long village', a variant of the more frequent Langton (q v).

Flamborough ERY, 'Flein's fortified place', the personal name being Scandinavian [*Flaneburg* 1086: OE *burh*].

Flamstead Hrt, 'flight-place, refuge'. The manor, near the Beds border, was held by tenure of protecting travellers [*Fleamstede* 1006: OE *flēam, stede*].

Flannan Isles *islds* Ros, 'islands of St Flannan', commemorating an Irish hermit who died in 680.

Flat Holm *isld* Glm, 'fleet island'. It was used as a Viking naval base [*Les Holmes* 1358, *Flotholm* 1375: ON *floti, holmr*].

Fleckney Lei, 'Fleca's riverside land'. The same personal name is found in **Flecknoe** Wa, 'Fleca's hill-spur' [1. *Flechenie* 1086, 2. *Flechenho* 1086: OE *ēa, hōh*].

Fleet Do, —Ha, —K, —LHo, **Fleet** *riv* Mx: '(place by) stream' [1. *Flete* 1086, 2. *Le Flete* 1506, 3. *Fleote* 798, 4. *Fleot* 1086, 5. *Flieta* 1159: OE *flēot*].

Fleetwood La, 'place named after the Fleetwood family', having been founded by Sir Peter Fleetwood of Rossall Hall in the early nineteenth century.

Flegg Nf 1254, 'iris bed' [*Flec* 1014, *Fleeg* 1196: ME *flegge*].

Flimby Cu, 'Flemings' village' [*Flemingby* c 1174: ON *Flæmingr, bý*].

Flint Flt 1284, '(place of) hard stone'. In early usage, *flint* lacked the special geological sense it has today, and this broader meaning is usually appropriate in place-names, e g Flintham Nt, Flinthill Nth. Among early forms for Flint are some spelt in the Welsh way, e g *Le Fflynt* 1300, as well as French translations, e g *Le Chaylou* 1277 [*Le Flynt prope Basingewerk* 1277: OE *flint* (OF *caillou*)].

Flitwick Bd, 'outlying farm by a stream [*Flicteuuiche* 1086: OE *flēot, wic*].

Flixborough LLi, 'Flik's fortified place'. The Scandinavian personal name occurs also in **Flixton** La 1177, **Flixton** Sf 1254; 'Flik's village' [1. *Flichesburg* 1086. 2. *Fleustone* 1086, 3. *Flixtuna* 1086: OE *burh, tūn*].

Flodden Field Nb, 'battlefield or open country by the hill of slabs'. The earliest records of the name refer to the battle at Branxton ('Branoc's farm'), and so it is difficult to tell whether *Field* is an essential part of the name or merely a reference to the conflict [*Floddoun* 1517: OE *flōh*, 'slab, fragment', *dūn*].

Flotta *isld* Ork, 'flat island' [*Flotey* c 1250: ON *flatr, ey*].

Foleshill Wa, 'people's hill', indicating a place of assembly [*Focheshelle* 1086, *Folkeshull* c 1240: OE *folc, hyll*].

Folkestone K, 'Folca's stone'. Stones marking boundaries of meeting places occasionally bear a personal name, e g Brixton Sr, (q v) [*Folcanstan* 696: OE *stān*].

Follifoot WRY, **Follithwaite** WRY: 'place where horse-fights took place'. Both horse-racing and horse-fighting played an important part in the social activities of the Norse settlers in England as in Scandinavia. The fights were between stallions, provoked by the sight and smell of mares tethered nearby, and were sometimes followed by conflicts between the owners of the animals. As these names are of OE origin, it seems that the practice spread among the native population in the areas of Scandinavian settlement, and the replacement in Follithwaite of the OE termination by a common ON element *þveit*, of quite different meaning, is noteworthy [1. *Fulifet* 1167, 2. *Folifeit* 1180, *Folitwait* 1316: OE *fola, gefeoht*]. See also Hesket.

Fordingbridge Ha, 'bridge of the men of Ford', denoting the meeting place of a hundred centred on the place originally called Ford, which later adopted the longer name [*Forde* 1086, *Fordingebrige* (Hundred) 1086: OE *ford, -ingas, brycg*].

Foreland Wt, **North Foreland** K: 'headland, promontory' [2. *Forland* 1326: OE *fore, land*].

Forfar Ang 1137, perhaps 'wood on a ridge' [*Forfare* c 1200: G *fothir, fàire*].

Formby La, 'Forni's village' [*Forneb* 1086: ON *byʲ*].

Forres Mor, '(place) beneath a copse' [*Forais* c 1195: G *fo, ras*].

Fort Augustus Inv. 1716, 'garrison named in honour of William Augustus, duke of Cumberland'. It was formerly *Cil Chūmein* 'church of Cummen', dedicated to a saint who died in 669 [G *Cill*]. See also Fort George, Fort William.

Forteviot Pth, 'slope of Tobacht', the allusion being, it is thought, to a place in Ireland; references to Irish places occur in other names bestowed by the Scots on first settling this area [*Fothuirtabaicht* c 970: G *fothir*].

Fort George Inv, 'fortress named in honour of King George II'. The last of the Scottish forts to bear royal titles, Fort George was established after the Jacobite rising of 1745 and was first so called in 1748. See also Fort Augustus, Fort William.

Forth *riv* Pth/Stl, 'slow stream' [*Forthin* c 970: OCelt *Voritia*].

Fortrose Ros, 'beneath the promontory' [*Forterose* 1455: G *fo* (comp. *foter*) *rois*].

Fort William Inv 1690, 'fortress named in honour of King William III', though actually established in 1655. See also Fort Augustus, Fort George.

Fotheringhay Nth, 'island of Forðhere's people'. OE Forðhere is on record as a personal name of the early period. The parish has water on three sides, lying between the river Nene and its tributary the Willow Brook [*Fodringeya* c 1060, *Frodigeya* 1075: OE *-ingas, ēg*].

Foula *isld* Zet, 'bird island' [ON *fugl, ey*].

Foulness Ess, —Nf, 'bird promontory' [1. *Fughelnesse* 1215: OE *fugol, næss*].

Foulness *riv* ERY, 'dirty river' [*Fulanea* 959: OE *fūl* (dat. *fūlon*), *ēa*].

Fountains Abbey WRY, '(place with) springs' [*Fontes* 12c: L. *fons*, (pl. *fontes*), OE *fontein*].

Foveran Abd, '(place with) little well' [*Furene* c 1150: G *fuaran*].

Fowey Co, 'place on river Fowey, i e beech river' [*Fawe* c 1200: OCo *fawi*].

Foyers Inv, 'terraced slope' [*Fyers* 1769: G *foithir*].

Framlingham Sf, 'homestead of Framela's people' [*Framalingaham* 1086: OE *-ingas, hām*].

Fraserburgh Abd, 'Fraser's incorporated town'. The name first appears, Latinised as *burgum de Fraser*, in a grant of 1592. Sir William Fraser bought land here in 1504, and the present town was developed from an earlier settlement known as *Faythlie* [*The toun and burghe of Faythlie, now callit Fraserburghe* 1597: OE *burh*].

Frensham Sr, 'Fremi's homestead' [*Fermesham* 10c: OE *hām*].

Freshfield La, **Freshford** Klk: 'clean land'. The Kilkenny name is a mistranslation of I *Achad-ur*, *achad* evidently having been misheard or misread as *ath*, 'ford' [1. OE *fersc, feld*, 2. MnE *fresh, ford*].

Freshford W, 'ford with clear water', as opposed to the several instances of Fulford (qq v) [*Fersceford* c 1000: OE *fersc, ford*].

Freshwater Wt, '(place on) river with clear water', the place retaining the former name of the river Yard [*Frescwatre* 1086: OE *fersc, wæter*].

Friern Barnet Mx. See Barnet.

Frimley Sr, 'Fremi's clearing' [*Fremeley* 933: OE *lēah*].

Frinton Ess, 'Friða's village' [*Frientuna* 1086: OE *tūn*].

Frisby Lei (x 2). **Friston** Sf: 'Frisians' farm or estate', referring to an alien settlement amid Angles or Danes [1. *Frisebi*, 1086, 2. *Frisebie* 1086, *Frisetuna* 1086: OE *Frisa, tūn*, ON *bȳ*].

Frobost (S. Uist) Inv. 'seed homestead' [ON *frjo, bólstaðr*].

Frome *riv freq*, 'fair river' [B **fram-*].

Frome So, 'place on river Frome (q v)', [*Froom* 705].

Fulford D. —ERY, —So, —St: 'dirty or muddy ford' [1. *Voleford* 1310, *Foleford* 1330, 2. *Fuleford* 1086, 3. *Sordidum vadum* 854 (L= 'dirty ford'), *Fuleford* 1327, 4. *Fuleford* 1086: OE *fūl, ford*]. See also Fairford, Freshford.

Fulham Mx. 'Fulla's riverside grassland' [*Fullanhamm* 879: OE *hamm*].

Furness La, 'headland of Futh' i e opposite to Piel Island, originally known as Futh or Fouldray, 'isle of rumps' [*Futhþernessa* c 1150: ON *fuð, nes*]. See also Barrow in Furness.

Fyfield Brk, —Ess, —Gl, —Ha, —W: 'estate of five hides of land' [1. *æt fīf hidum* 956, *Fivehide* 1086, 2. *Fifhida* 1086, 3. *Fishyde* 1086, 4. *æt Fifhidon* 975, 5. *Fiffhide* 1242: *fīf, hid*]. See also Fifehead.

†**Fylde** La, 'plain', a district name occurring in Poulton le Fylde (q v) [*Filde* 1246: OE *gefilde*].

Fylingdales NRY, 'valleys of Fygla's people' [*Fygelinge* 1086: OE *-ingas, dæl*].

Fyne *riv* Arg, 'wine (stream)', the term apparently being used of the water of healing wells etc, and possibly of rivers regarded as particularly sacred [G *fìon*].

Gaddesby Lei, 'Gadd's farm or village', the personal name being ON Gaddr [*Gadesby* 1086: ON *bȳ*].

Gaddesden Hrt, 'Gæte's valley'. The river-name **Gade** is a back-formation from Gaddesden and not a development of the earlier *Gatesee* 1242 [*Gætesdene* c 945: OE *denu*].

Gaick Forest Inv, 'forest in a cleft' [G *gàg* (dat. *gàig*)].

Gaineamhach, Loch *lke* Arg, — — Ros, — — Sut: 'sandy lake' [G *loch, gaineamh*].

GainsboroughLLi, 'Gegn's fortified place'. Gegn is the regular shortened version of such OE personal names as Gænbeald or Geanburh [*Gegnesburh* 1013: OE *burh*].

Gairloch Ros, '(place by) short lake' [*Gerloth* 1275, *Gerloch* 1366: G *gearr, loch*].

Gairsay *isld* Ork, 'Garek's island' [ON *ey*].

Galashiels Slk, 'huts by Gala Water'. The river-name is obscure; it is sometimes interpreted as 'gallows stream', but there are both linguistic and historical difficulties against this. ME *schele* was the term used for a temporary hut, especially one used by shepherds on summer pastures in those areas where transhumance was practised. The term has survived in numerous field-names as well as in some major names [*Galuschel* 1237: ME *schele*].

Gala Water *riv* Slk. See Galashiels.

Gallan Head (Lewis) Ros, 'pillar' headland' [G *gallan*].

††**Galloway** Kcb-Wig, '(territory) among the stranger-Gaels'. The political and linguistic history of this area is complex and controversial, but the settlement of Gaelic-speaking invaders of mixed Irish and Norse descent is undisputed. These were the *Gall-Ghóidhil* who began to arrive during the ninth century. Combined with Dumfries, the name now provides a title for a Region [*Galweya* c 970: G *Gall-Ghóidhil*].

Galston Ayr, 'village of the strangers' [*Gauston* 1260: G *gall*, OE *tūn*].

Galway Gal, '(place on) stony (river)' [I *Galimh* 'stony'].

Gamallt *mtn* Crd, 'crooked hillside' [W *cam, allt*].

Garelochhead Dnb, 'head of the short lake' [*Gerloch* 1272, *Keangerloch* c 1345: G *gearr, loch*, OE *hēafod* (G *ceann*)].

Garrabost (Lewis) Ros, 'farmstead in a gore or triangular plot' [ON *geiri, bólstaðr*],

Garriannus, 'place by noisy stream', Romano-British name for Burgh Castle Nf [*Garrianno* c 425: B **gar-*].

Garroch Head Bte, 'rough headland' [*Garrach* 1449: G *garbh*].

Garron *riv* He, 'crane stream' [*Garran* 1558: B **garan*].

Garstang La, '(place of the) spear shaft', alluding to a boundary pole or a post marking a meeting-place [*Cherestanc* 1086, *Gairstang* c 1195: ON *geirr, stǫng*].

Garve Ros, 'rough place'. **Garvellach** *islds* Arg. 'rough rocks'. **Garvellan** *isld* Sut, 'rough island' [2. *Garbeallach* 1390, 3. *Garvellan* 1580: G *garbh, eilach, eilan*].

Gateholm *island* Pmb, 'goat island' [*Goteholme* 1480: ON *geit, holmr*]. See also Grassholm.

†**Gateshead** Du, either '(holy place where) head of a goat (was displayed)' or 'headland on which goats abounded'. Though the Germanic custom of impaling animals' heads at sacrificial sites is undisputed, there is now some doubt

whether the custom gave rise to these place-names (cf Farcet, Swineshead, Shepshed) [*Ad Capræ Caput* c 730, *Gateshaphed* c 1175, *Gatesheued* 1196: OE *gāt, hēafod*].

Gaunless *riv* Du. See Bishop Auckland.

Gele *riv* Den. See Abergele.

Georgemas Cai, 'place where annual fair took place on St George's Day, 23 April' [OE *mæsse*].

Germansweek D, 'outlying farm, with church dedicated to St Germanus'. Originally called Wick, the place was identified by the addition of *German* in 1458, alluding to the dedication of the church to St Germanus of Auxerre (c 378-448), who twice visited Britain and who is honoured also in the name of St Germans Co (q v) [*Wica* 1086, *Wyke Germyn* 1458, *Germaneswyk* 1468: OE *wīc*].

Gidding, Great Hu, '(place of) Gydda's people', *Great* to distinguish this place from **Little Gidding** and **Steeple Gidding**, though it must be said that both Great Gidding and Steeple Gidding churches now have a tower and spire [*Gedelinge* 1086, *Geddinge* 1086, 1147 etc: OE - *ingas*].

Gigha *isld* Arg, 'rift island' [*Gug* 1309, *Gya* c 1400: ON *gjá, ey*].

Gillingham Do, † —K, —Nf, 'homestead of Gylla's people'. There is no reason to suppose that there should be less than three men of the same name involved in the appellations of these widely separated places [1. *Gillingaham* 1016, 2. *Gillingeham* 1086, 3. *Kildincham* 1086, *Gelingeham* c 1110: OE -*ingas, hām*].

Gilmorton Lei. See Moreton.

Girton C, —Nt; 'village built on gravel' [1. *Gretton, Gryttune* 1060, 2. *Gretone* 1086, *Grettuna* 1145, *Girtone* 1525: OE *grēot, tūn*].

Girvan Ayr, perhaps '(place of the) thicket' [*Girven* 1275: G *gar*].

Glamis Ang, 'open country' [*Glames* 1187: G *glamhus*].

Glamorgan, 'Morgan's shore', commemorating a prince of Gwent [*Glanna Morgan* n d: W *glan*].

Glasbury Rad, 'fortified place by a sanctuary or cloister'. This is a hybrid name; to the W *clas* has been added OE *burh* [*Clastbyrig* 1056, *Glasbiria* 1191: W *clas*, OE *burh*].

Glascoed, Mon, 'green wood' [W *glas, coed*].

Glascote Wa, 'shed where glass was made' [OE *glæs, cot*].

†**Glasgow** Lnk, 'green hollow' [*Glasgu* 1136: B **glasto-, cau*].

Glaston R, 'Glad's village' [*Gladestone* 1086: OE *tūn*].

Glastonbury So, 'fortified place at *Glastonia*, i e woad garden'. The earliest English form of the name means 'island of the Glastings, i e the Glastonia people' alluding to the British settlement and its marshy environs, but it may also be a folk-etymological alteration of *Glastonia* [*Ineswytrin* 601 ('woad island'), *Glastonia* 7c, *Glastingaea* 704, *Glestingaburg* c 740: (OW **inis, gwydrin*), OE -*ingas, burh*].

Glencoe Arg, 'valley of the river *Comhann*', the meaning of the river-name being unknown [*Glenchomure* 1343, *Glencole* 1491: G *gleann*].

Glencolumbkille Don, 'St Columba's valley' [I *gleann*].

Glenrothes Fif, 'valley named in honour of the Earls of Rothes', a recent name applied to a New Town. **Rothes** Mor 1238 is 'lucky station' [G *rath, fas*].

Glevum Gl, 'bright place', the Celtic name for the Romano-British town on the site of which Gloucester (q v) now stands [*Coloniae Glev'* 2c B **glevo-*].

Glooston Lei, 'Glor's village' [*Glorstone* 1086: OE *tūn*].

Glossop Db, 'Glott's little valley'. OE *hop* is found in place-names in the Midlands and North with the sense of 'small enclosed valley, especially one overhanging the main valley' and occurs in the many instances of Hope and Hopton, as well as in Bacup, Bramhope, and Worksop (qq v) [*Glosop* 1086, *Glotsop* 1219: OE *hop*].

Gloucester Gl, 'Roman station at *Glevum*, (q v)'. As in Manchester, Winchester Wroxeter, and some other names, the Saxon form was produced by the addition of OE *ceaster* to the British name, which then underwent various transformations as it was adapted to English ears and tongues, the Celtic word being made to resemble first OE *glēaw*, 'wise', and then, by coincidence, the OE verb *glōwan*, 'to shine' [*Gleawecestre* 804, *Glowcestre* 1086: OE *ceaster*].

Glyme *riv* O, 'shining stream' [*Glim* 958: B **glimo-*].

Glynch Brook *riv* Gl-He-Wo: 'pure stream' [*Glenc* 963: B **glano-*].

Gnossall St, 'nook of land belonging to Gneað', the personal name meaning 'miser' [*Geneshale* 1086: OE *halh*].

Godalming Sr, '(place of) Godhelm's people' (*æt Godelmingum* c 880: OE *-ingas*].

Godmanchester Hu, 'Roman station associated with Godmund or Guðmund'. The several medieval forms spelt with Gurm- or Gorm- are traceable to the probably groundless story that the place was founded by Guthrum. The Roman station was probably *Durolipons* [*Godmundcestre* 1086: OE *ceaster*].

Gola Don, 'river forks' [I *gabhal*].

Golspie Sut, 'farm of a man called Gold' [*Goldespy* 1330: ON *bý*].

Goodwin Sands K, possibly 'sandbank commemorating earl Godwin', though the name may be a placatory euphemism 'good friend' [*Godewynesonde* 1317: OE *sand* (*gōd, wine*)].

Goole WRY, '(place by) channel or sluice' [*Gowle* 1553: ME *goule*].

Goosnargh La, 'Gosan's shieling'. The Irish-Norse settlers in NW England brought with them a number of place-name elements (e g ON *erg* < OI *airigh*, 'shieling') and some personal names, including Gosan or Gusan [*Gusanarghe* 1086: ON *erg*.]

Gordonstoun Mor, 'Sir Robert Gordon's village', a name dating from soon after the purchase of the estate in 1638[OE *tūn*].

Goring O, '(place of) Gora's people' [*Garinges* 1086: OE *-ingas*].

Gorleston Nf, 'Gurl's village' [*Gorlestuna* 1086: OE *tūn*].

Gosford D, —O, —Sf, —So, —Wa, **Gosforth** Cu, **Gosforth** Nb: 'goose ford'. The *-forth* variant of *-ford* occurs in certain places in the North, e g Horsforth

WRY, Cornforth NRY, Ampleforth NRY, and exceptionally elsewhere, e g Garforth Brk. Animal names occur frequently with *ford*, indicating either the suitability of the river-crossing for domestic animals, or its frequent use by wild ones [1. *Goseford* 1249, 2. *Goseforde* 1234, 5. *Gosseford* 1202, 6. *Goseford* 12c, 7. *Goseford* 1166: OE *gōs*, *ford*].

†Gosport Ha, 'market where geese were sold' [*Goseport* 1250: OE *gōs*, *port*].

Gotham Nt 1269, 'homestead where goats were kept' [*Gatham* 1086: OE *gāt*, *hām*].

Gourock Rnf, 'hillock'. The Gaelic word for 'pimple' is used metaphorically here [*Ouir et Nether Gowrockis* 1661: G *guireag*].

Govan Lnk 1275, 'dear rock' [*Gvuan* c 1150: OW *cu*, *faen*].

Gower Glm, 'curved promontory' W *gwyr*].

Grafton Underwood Bk. See Grendon Underwood.

Graiguefrahane Tip, 'whortleberry village' [I *graig*, *freaghan*].

Graiguenamanagh Klk, 'village of the monks' [I *graig*, *manach*]

Grain, Isle of K, 'gravel island' [*Grean* c 1100: OE *grēon*].

††Grampian *mts* Pth, Abd, Bnf, a word of uncertain origin and meaning, but not connected with *Mons Graupius*. The term *The Mounth* was formerly used for the area. Mounth is G *monadh*, 'hilly district'.

Grampound Co, '(place by) great bridge' [*Graundpont* 1373: OF *grand*, *pont*].

Grangemouth Stl, 'mouth of the river Grange'. The river, Grange Burn, is so called from its passing a former monastic establishment called Abbot Grange, 'abbot's granary or corn farm', an outlier of Newbattle Abbey [OF *grange*, OE *mūð*].

Granta *riv* C. See Cam *riv*.

Grantchester C. See Cam.

Grantham LKe 1086, possibly 'village built on gravel' [OE *grand*, *hām*].

Grantown on Spey Mor, 'place settled by Grant' [OE *tūn*].

Grasmere *lke* We, 'grass lake'. The suffixed -*mere* was originally redundant, as early forms indicate that the name was a dithematic one, *Grisse*, from ON *Gres-sær* [*Grissemere* 1375, *Gresmyer* 1570, *Grassmeer-water* 1671: ON *gres*, *sær*, OE *mere*].

Grassholm *isld* Pmb, 'grass island'. Scandinavian names are borne by several islands off the Pembrokeshire coast— Skomer, Gateholm, Grassholm, and Skokholm to the south of St Bride's Bay, Ramsey to the north of it, and Caldy in the Bristol Channel (qq v). The suffixes -*holm* and -*ey* make the word *Island* unnecessary [*Insula Grasholm* 15c: ON *gras*, *holmr*].

Gravesend K, 'at the end of the grove' [*Gravesham* 1086, *Grauessend* 1157: OE *grāf*, *ende*].

Grays Thurrock Ess, 'de Grai's marshland', a metaphorical use of OE *þurruc*, literally 'bilge, sump', neither of which terms would find much favour either as a place-name or its definition. The manorial affix is quite late [*Turruc* 1086, *Turrokgreys* 1248, *Grayes* 1399: OE *þurruc*].

Great Badminton Gl, 'village of Beadumund's people' [*Badimyncgtun* 972: OE *-ingas, tūn*].

Great Barr St, '(place by) a summit'. Barr Beacon, nearby, is a hill of about 700 feet [*æt Bearre* 957, *Barre* 1086, *Little Barre* 1208, *Great Barre* 1322: B **barro-*].

Great Bernera (Lewis) Ros, 'Bjarni's island' [*Bjarnarey* c 1250: ON *ey*].

Great Britain. See Britain.

Great Cumbrae *isld* Bte. See Cumbrae.

Great Malvern Wo. See Malvern.

Great Orme's Head Crn, 'headland resembling a snake's head'. This is a Norse landmark name; the corresponding OE form occurs in Worm's Head Glm (q v) [*Ormeshede insula* 15c: ON *ormr, hǫfuð*].

Great Snoring Nf, '(place of) Snear's people' [*Snaringes* 1086: OE *-ingas*].

Great Torrington D, 'village on river Torridge', distinguished from **Little Torrington** D; Great Torrington was formerly Chipping Torrington, i e 'Torrington with a market'. **Black Torrington**, on the same river, is named from the dark staining of the water here [1. *Torintona* 1086, *Chippingtoriton* 1284, 2. *Liteltrorilanda* 1086, *Parva Toriton*' 1242, 3. *Torintona* 1086, *Blaketorrintun* 1219: OE *grēat, lytel, blæc, tūn*]. See also Torridge *riv* D.

Great Walsingham Nf, 'homestead of the people of Wæls'. In addition to **Little Walsingham** Nf, there was a third Walsingham near East Carleton Nf, but the last name is no longer used [1. *Walsingaham* c 1035, *Walsingeham Magnum* 1086, 2. *Little Walsingham* 1263, 3. *Walsingham* 1046: OE *-ingas, hām*].

†**Great Yarmouth** Nf, '(place at) mouth of river *Gerne*'. The river-name (replaced by Yare, a back-formation from Yarmouth) is derived from a British word meaning 'to shout, to cry', probably on account of the strength of the tide at the seaward end. The prefix distinguishes the town from Little Yarmouth Nf, but Yarmouth Wt (q v) has a different origin and meaning [1. *Gernemwa* 1086, *Gernemuta Magna* 1254, 2. *Gernemutha* 1086, *Parva Gernamuta* 1219: OE *mūð*]. See also Yare *riv* Nf.

Greenford Mx, 'green ford' [*et Grenan forda* 845: OE *grēne, ford*].

Greenhalgh La, 'green hollow' [*Greneholf* 1086: OE *grēne, holh*].

Greenham Brk, 'green riverside meadow', the river being the Kennet. The 1220 form alludes to the Knights Hospitallers, who held the manor from the late 12c [*Greneham* 1086, *Grenham Hospitalium* 1220: OE *grēne, hamm*].

Greenhithe K, 'green landing-place', on the Thames [*Grenethe* 1264: OE *grēne, hȳð*].

Greenlaw Ber, 'green mound' [*Grenlawe* 1250: OE *grēne, hlāw*].

Greenock Rnf, 'sunny hillock' [*Grenok* c 1395: G *grianag*].

Greenwich K/GL, 'green trading place'. The Thames-side places terminating in *-wich* had perhaps a greater importance than the mere *-hithes*, and it is of interest to note the sequence down river of the names on the south bank of the river: Putney, Lambeth, Rotherhithe, Greenwich, Woolwich, Erith, Greenhithe (qq v) [*Grenewic* 964: OE *grēne, wíc*]. See also Ipswich, Norwich, Sandwich.

Greet *riv* Nt, 'gravelly river' [*on Greotan* 956: OE *grēot*].

Greetham LLi, —R: 'homestead on gravel' [1. *Gretham* 1086, 2. *Gretham* 1086: OE *grēot*].

Grenan Bte 1400, 'sunny spot' [G *grianan*].

Grendon Nth 1086, —Wa 1236, **Grendon Underwood** Bk: 'green hill'. The affix in the Bucks name means 'in the shelter of a wood' and occurs also in **Grafton Underwood** Bk, 'grove village' [2. *Grendone* 1086, 3. *Grennedone* 1086: OE *grēne, dūn*].

Greta *riv* Cu 1278, —*riv* WRY, La, —*riv* NRY: 'stony stream' [2. *Gretagila* c 1215, 3. *Gretha* 1279: ON *grjót, ā*].

Gretna Dmf, '(by the) gravelly hill' [*Gretenho* 1223, *Gretenhou* c 1240, *Gratnay* 1576: OE **grēote* (dat. *grēotan*), *hōh*].

†Grimsby LLi, 'Grim's village'. Names in *-by* are very common in Lindsey, bearing witness to a settlement amounting almost to a migration of Danes. Very few of these names are on the coast, or within five miles of it, so that Grimsby is of particular interest [*Grimesbi* 1086: ON *by*].

Grimsetter Ork, **Grimshader** (Lewis) Ros; 'Grim's homestead' [ON *setr*].

Grimston ERY (x 2), —Lei, —Nf, —NRY, —Sf, —WRY: 'Grim's village', a hybrid name which provides the technical description for those of its type, viz, a Scandinavian personal name combined with OE *tūn*. Places of the type (e g Kedleston Db, Wigston Magna Lei, Croxton Lei and LLi, and Thoroton Nt) were almost certainly originally English settlements taken over and renamed by the Danes [1-6 *Grimeston(e)* 1086, 7. *Grimestun* 1086: OE *tūn*].

Groby Lei, 'place by a gully', possibly alluding to the tarn now called Groby Pool [*Grobi* 1086: ON *gróf, by*].

Grudness Zet, 'gravel promontory' [ON *grjót, nes*].

Guay Pth 1457, 'marsh' [G *gaoth*].

†Guildford Sr, 'ford by which golden flowers grew' [*Gyldeforda* c 875: OE **gylde, ford*].

Guisachan Inv, 'pine forests' [*Gulsackyn* 1221, *Guisachane* 1578: G *guithsachan*].

Guisborough NRY, 'Gig's fortified place', the first element being the Scandinavian personal name, Gigr [*Ghigesburg, Gighesborc* 1086: OE *burh*].

Gumley Lei, 'Godmund's clearing' [*Godmundesleah* 779: OE *lēah*].

Gunnersbury Mx, 'Gunnhild's manor' [*Gunnyldesbury* 1348: OE *burh*].

Gwaunysgor Flt, 'meadow by fortification' [*Wenescol* 1086: W *gwaun, ysgor*].

Gweek Co, 'outlying farm' [*Wike* 1337: OE *wīc*].

Gwennap Co, '(church of) St Wenep' [*(ecclesia) Sancte Weneppe* 1269].

††Gwent, 'favoured place', formerly a Welsh kingdom and now, under recent local-government reorganisation, an administrative county [B **ventā*].

Gwerneigron Flt, 'Eigron's alder marsh' [*Gwernigron* 1607: W *gwern*].

††Gwynedd, 'territory of Cunedda', an administrative county of North Wales, formerly a kingdom, named after the fifth-century leader.

Haa, The (Whalsay) Zet, 'high place' [ON *há(r)*].

Habost (Lewis) Ros, 'high farm' [ON *há(r), bólstaðr*].

Hackney Mx, 'Haca's island' [*Hakney* 1231: OE *ēg*].

Haddington ELo, 'farm associated with Hada'. Haddingtonshire, the former name of the county, is on record from the twelfth century [*Hadynton* 1098: OE *-ingtūn*].

Hadleigh Ess, —Sa, —Sf: 'heather-covered clearing' [1. *Hæplege* c 1000, 2. *Hatlege* 1086, 3. *Hetlega* 1086: OE *hǣð, lēah*].

Hadzor Wo, 'Headdi's slope' [*Headdesofre* 11c: OE *ofer*].

Hagley Sa, —So, —St, —Wo 1462: 'hawthorn clearing' [1. *Haggele* 1272, 2. *Haggelegh* 1243, 4. *Hageleia* 1086: OE *hagga, lēah*].

Hainault Ess/GL, 'wood belonging to a religious community'. The forest became the property of Barking Abbey; the name acquired its French appearance owing to a supposed connexion with Philippa of Hainault [*Henehout* 1221: OE *higna, holt*].

Hale *freq*, 'nook, corner, pocket of land', sometimes alludes to a place in an isolated valley, but perhaps more often refers to a piece of low-lying land almost encircled by a river. **Hale** Ch lies in a hollow; **Hale** We is within a former loop in Birk Sike. Plural forms also occur, including Halesowen Wo and Sheriff Hales Sa (qq v), and **Hales** Nf and St. **Halam** Nt is the dative plural 'at or in the nooks' [OE *halh*, dat. pl. *halum*]. See also Hallam.

Halesowen Wo, 'Owen's nooks', commemorating a Welsh prince who held this place in 1204 [*Hales Owayn* 1272: OE *halh*]. See also Hale.

Halesworth Sf. 'Hæle's homestead or enclosure', a name of the same type as Isleworth Mx (q v) [*Healesuurda* 1086: OE *worð*].

Halewood La, 'wood near or beside Hale (q v)' [*Halewode* c 1200: OE *wudu*].

Halifax WRY, 'rough grassland on rocky slopes' [*Halyfax* c 1095: OE *hall*, 'rocky slope', *gefeax*, 'growth of coarse grass'].

Halkyn Flt, 'willow-tree place' [*Helchene* 1086, *Helygen* 1315: W *helygen*].

Hallam WRY, '(place) on the rocky slopes', from which **Hallamshire** WRY derives its name. In addition to denoting counties, -shire is also used for smaller areas enjoying special manorial privileges [*Hallun* 1086: *Halumsira* 1161: OE *hall, scir*].

Halstead Ess, —K, —Lei: 'place of refuge or shelter' [1. *Haltesteda* 1086, 2. *Halsted* 1201, 3. *Elstede* 1086: OE *hald, stede*].

Haltwhistle Nb, 'confluence by a high place', a hybrid name [*Hautwisel* 1240: OF *haut*, OE *twisla*].

Hamble *riv* Ha, 'crooked one' [*Hamele* 901: OE *hamel*].

Hamilton Lnk, 'farm in broken country' [*Hamelton* 1291: OE *hamel, tūn*].

Hammavoe (Yell) Zet, 'inlet of the haven' [*Hafnarvag* 12c: ON *hafn, vágr*].

Hammersmith Mx, 'hammer forge' [*Hameresmithe* 1312: OE *hamor, smiðde*].

Hampshire, 'county based on Southampton (q v)'. Although the ceremonious *County of Southampton* form is frequently used in official documents, the various grades of abbreviation have been employed from the eleventh century. The shortest form, *Hants*, is from the DB forms *Hantescire, Hantescira*, which represent a coming to terms with the difficult group of sounds in the middle of *Hamtunscir*, found in the Anglo-Saxon Chronicle [OE *scīr*].

Hampstead Mx, —Wt, **Hamsted** St, 'homestead, dwelling place'. The OE term seems to have been applied to very small settlements—single dwellings or farms, rather than groups—and thus presents an interesting contrast with the element *hām*. Compounds containing this element are not numerous but include Berkhamsted, Hempstead Gl, and Hemel Hempstead (qq v) [1-3 *Hamsted(e)* 10-13c: OE *hām-stede*].

Hampton He, —Mx, 'farm within a river-bend', accurately describing the sites of these places on the rivers Lugg and Thames respectively [1. *Homtona* 1242 2. *Hamntona* 1086: OE *hamm*, *tūn*]. See also Southampton.

Handa isld Sut, 'sand island'. The initial *S* of this Norse compound name has undergone a sound-change as if it were Gaelic [ON *sandr*, *ey*].

Handley Ch, —Db, —Do, —Nth,'(place) at the high clearing'. [1. *Hanlei* 1086, 4. *Hanlegh* 1220: OE *hēah*, dat, *hēan*, *lēah*]. See also Hanley, Henley.

Hankelow Ch, 'Haneca's mound', probably the tumulus within which the named man is interred [*Honcolawe* 12c: OE *hlāw*].

Hanley St, '(place) at the high clearing'. Though they lack the *-d-* which has crept into the spelling of *Handley*, the names in this group are identical in origin and meaning. **Hanley William** Wo and **Hanley Child** Wo refer to the feudal lords, respectively William de la Mare and the young monks of a neighbouring monastery [1. *Henle* 1212, 2. *Williames Henle* 1275, 3. *Cheldreshanle* 1255: OE *hēah*, dat. *hēan*, *lēah*].

Hanwell Mx, 'spring at which wild birds were found' [*Hanewelle* 959: OE *hana*, *wella*].

Harlech Mer, 'fine slab of rock' [*Hardelagh* c 1290: W *hardd*, *llech*].

†**Harlow** Ess, 'army mound', possibly an assembly point or an administrative centre, and the meeting-place for the Hundred of Harlow [*Herlawe* c 1045: OE *here*, *hlāw*]

Harold Wood Ess, '(King) Harold's wood'. Harold, defeated at Hastings by William the Norman, had held land in this area [*Horalds Wood* c 1237: OE *wudu*].

Harpenden Hrt, 'valley of the military road'. Watling Street runs along the narrow valley here, and was doubtless used by the Anglo-Saxon army and by that of the Danes [*Herpedene* c 1060: OE *here-pæð*, *denu*].

Harringay Mx 'Hæring's hedged enclosure'. There are two current variants of this name—Hornsey, used of the parish from the sixteenth century onwards, and **Haringey**, now the name of the London Borough. The spelling *Harringay* was deliberately revived as the name of a house built in the 1790s, and this form was used for local government purposes in the next century [*Haringeie* 1201, *Harengheye* 1232, *Heringheie* 1274, *Haringesheye* 1243, *Harnsey* 1392, *Hornesey* 1539, *Hornesey* alias *Harynghay* 1549: OE *(ge)hæg*].

Harrington Cu, 'farm of Hæfer's people' [*Haverinton* c 1160: OE *tūn*].

†**Harrogate** WRY, 'pasturage by a cairn [*Harougat* 1333: ON *horg*, 'heap of stones', *gata*, 'way, road, right of pasturage'].

Harrow on the Hill Mx, 'heathen shrine on the hill', the temple of a tribe known as the Gumenings [*Gumeninga hergae* 767, *Harghe* 1299, *Harowe atte Hille* 1398: OE *hearg*, *hyll*].

†**Hartlepool** Du, 'pool by Hart'. *Hart* or *Hart Island* was the headland on which Hartlepool now stands, the pool being the bay which it shelters. The modern name seems to have developed from *Herte-pol* by way of *Herterpol* c 1180 and *Hertelpol* 1195. [*Heruteu* c 730, *Hert* c 1130: OE *heorot*, 'stag', *ēg*, 'island', *pōl*].

Harwich Ess, 'military camp'. There was a considerable Danish force here in 884-5 [*Herwyz* 1238: OE *herewic*].

Haselbech Nth, **Haseley** O, —Wa, —Wt, **Haselor** Wa, **Hasfield** Gl, **Hasland** Db, **Haslemere** Sr, **Haslingden** La, **Haslington** Ch: 'valley, wood, etc, in which hazels grew'. Besides OE *hæsel*, name-forming elements include *hæslen*, 'growing with hazels' and ON *hesli*, 'hazel' [OE *bæce*, 'valley', *lēah*, 'clearing, wood', *ofer*, 'slope', *feld*, 'open land', ON *lundr*, 'wood', OE *mere*, 'lake', *denu*, 'valley', *tūn*, 'farm']. See also Hazelmere, Heslington.

†**Hastings** Sx, '(territory of) Hæsta's people', originally applied to a large area of Sussex [*Hæstingceaster* 1050, *Hastings* 1086: OE -*ingas*].

Hatfield He, —Hrt, —WRY, **Hatfield Broad Oak** Ess, **Hatfield Peverel** Ess: 'open land on which heather grew'. [1. *Hetfelde* 1086, 2. *Haethfelth* c 730, 4. *Hadfelda* 1086: OE *hǣð*, *feld*].

Haughley Sf, 'wood or clearing in which haws were found' [*Hagele* c 1040: OE *haga*, *lēah*]. Cf Hagley.

†**Havant** Ha, 'Hama's spring' [*Hamanfunta* 935; OE *funta*].

Haverfordwest Pmb, 'western goat ford'. As the spelling *Hereford* occurs among the early forms, it was evidently desirable to distinguish this town from the English place of that name, by means of the suffix -*west* [*Haverfordia* 1191: OE *hæfer*, *ford*].

Havering Ess/GL. See Quadring.

Hawarden Flt, 'high enclosure' [*Haordine* 1086, *Haworthyn* 1275: OE *hēah*, *worðign*].

Hawick Nb, —Rox, 'high outlying farm' [1. *Hawic* 1242, 2. *Hawic* c 1167: OE *hēah*, *wic*].

Haworth WRY, prob 'haw enclosure', suggesting a hawthorn hedge [*Hauewrth* 1209: OE *haga*, *worð*].

Hay Bre —He: 'enclosure' [1. *Hagan* 958, *La Haye* 1259: OE (*ge*)*hæg*].

Hayle Co, '(place at an) estuary' [*Heyl* 1265: Co *heyl*].

Hayling Island Ha, 'island of Hægel's people' [*Hailinges island* c 1140: OE -*ingas*].

Hazelmere Bk, **Hazlebadge** Db, **Hazleton** Gl, **Hazlewood** Db, —WRY: 'lake' valley, etc, by or in which hazels grew' [2. *Heselebec* 1086, 3. *Hasedene* 1086, 5. *Heseleuuode* 1086: OE *mere*, *bæce*, *denu*, *wudu*]. See also Haselbech, Heslington.

Headingley WRY, 'clearing of Hedde's people' [*Hedingeleia* 1086: OE *lēah*].

Heaton. See Kirkheaton.

Hebrides, meaning uncertain. Various origins and explanations have been proposed, and interpretations such as 'without corn' or 'without food' make limited sense. The Norse name for the islands was *Suðreyar*, 'southern islands', whence modern *Sodor* in the diocesan title 'Sodor and Man'. The Hebrides were described as 'southern' with reference to the Orkneys [*Hæbudes* 77, *Hebudes* 300].

Hedderwick ELo, 'outlying farm among heather' [*Hatheruuich* 1094: OE **hǣddre*, *wic*].

Helensburgh Dnb, 'town named after Helen'. The lady was the wife of Sir James Colquhoun, who established a new settlement here in 1776 [MnSc *burgh* <OE *burh*].

Helmsdale Sut, 'Hjalmund's valley' [*Hjalmunddal* 1225: ON *dalr*].

Helvellyn *mtn* Cu, meaning unknown [*Helvillon* 1577].

Helvick Head Wat, 'headland by Helvick, i e rock-shelf bay' [ON *hjalli*, *vik*, OE *hēafod*].

Hemel Hempstead Hrt, 'homestead in district called Hamel'. There is early evidence that this part of Hertfordshire was called *Hæmele*, 'broken country', accurately descriptive of the topography. The Domesday Book form *Hamelamestede*, written as one or two words, persisted for more than two centuries with only minor spelling changes. From 1339 contracted forms like *Hemlamsted* began to appear, with a reduction to *Hempsted* in 1544. The modern form of the name then seems to have been reconstructed [OE *hamol*, 'broken', *hāmstede*].

Hempstead Gl, 'high homestead' [*Hechanestede* 1086: OE *hēah*, *hām-stede*].

Hempstead Nf, **Hemsted** K: 'place where hemp was grown' [1. *Henepsteda* 1086, 2. *Empestede* 1240: OE *henep*, *stede*].

Hendon Mx, '(at the) high hill' [*Hendun* 959: OE *hēah*, dat. *hēan*, *dūn*].

Hendygwyn-ar-Daf Crm, 'old white house on river Taf'. The English name, Whitland, (q v) is a parallel name rather than a translation. The place was known simply as *Ty Gwyn* ('white house') in Welsh documents until 1561, when the first reference to its antiquity appears as *Hendygwyn*.

Among the non-Welsh series of names appear L *Alba Landa* 1214, OE *Blaunchelande* 1318, and L *Blancalanda* 1329, inviting comparison with Blanchland Nb (*Blanchelande* 1165, *Alba Landa* 1203). It is worth noting that at the latter place was a foundation of Premonstratensian or White Canons, and at Whitland the Cistercians or White Monks established themselves [*Ty gwyn ar daf* 13c, *Hendygwyn* 1561: W *hen*, 'old', *ty*, 'house', *gwyn*, 'white']. See also Whitland.

Hengoed Gla, —Rad, — Sa, 'old wood' [W *hen*, *coed*].

Henley Sa, —So, —Sr, 'glade in which wild birds were found' [1. *Haneleu* 1086, 2. *Henleighe* 973, *Henlea* 673: OE *henn lēah*].

Henley-in-Arden Wa, **Henley-on-Thames** O: 'high clearing'. The riverside situation of Henley-on-Thames suggests that *High* here may be unconnected with elevation. It is of interest to observe that **High Legh** Ch (although at an altitude of more than two hundred feet) has its counterpart not in Low Leigh but in **Little Leigh,** implying that here too the implication of *High* is 'great, important' rather than 'on high ground' [1. *Hanleye* 1285, 2. *Heanlea* 1186] OE *hēah*, dat. *hēan*, *lēah*]. See also Arden.

Hentland He. See St Devereux.

Herbrandston Pmb, 'Herbrand's farm', alluding to a Fleming who took refuge in the cantref of Rhos about 1107 [*Villa Herbrandi* 13c, *Herbraundistone* 1307: OE *tūn*].

†Hereford He 958, 'army ford' [OE *here*, *ford*]. See also Haverfordwest.

Hermiston MLo, 'herdsman's farm' [*Hirdmannistoun* 1233: OE *hirdman*, *tūn*].

Herne Ha 1086, —K: 'land in an angle' [2. *æt Hyrnan* 11c: OE *hyrne*].

Herringfleet Sf, 'stream of Herela's people' [*Herlingaflet* 1086: OE *flēot*].

Herringthorpe WRY. See Mablethorpe.

Herstmonceux Sx, 'wooded hill in the manor of the Monceux family' [*Herst* 1086: OE *hyrst*].

Hertford Hrt, 'hart ford'. The county name, Hertfordshire, is formed normally [*Herutford* c 750, *Heortfordscir* c 1060: OE *heort, ford, scir*].

Hesket Cu, **Hesketh** La, **Hesketh Grange** NRY: 'race-course' [1. *Heskgeth* 1330, 2. *Hescheth* 1288: ON *hesta-skeið*]. See also Follifoot.

Heslington ERY, 'farm on or near which hazels grew' [*Haslinton* 1086: OE *hæslen, tūn*].

Hestercombe So. See Hexham.

Heston Mx, 'farm among brushwood' [*Hestone* c 1130: OE **hǣs, tūn*].

Hexham Nb, 'bachelor's homestead', like **Hestercombe** So, alluding to land held by a *hagustald*, a younger son not inheriting any part of a noble's estate [1. *Hagustaldes ham* 685, *Hexteldesham* 1188, 2. *Hegsteldescumb* 854: OE *hām, cumb*].

Hi. See Iona.

Hibernia, Latin name for Ireland, replacing *Scotia* when the latter began to be used for Scotland [*Hibernia* c AD 50].

†**High Peak** Db. See Peak.

High Wycombe Bk, 'at the outlying farms', *High* probably alluding to importance rather than elevation, as it was also known as Magna Wycombe.

OE *cumb* is not an element in the name, which is almost certainly from the dative plural of *wic* [*Wicumun* c 970, *Wicumbe* 1086: OE *wic*].

Hillingdon Mx, 'Hilda's hill' [*Hildesdun* c 982: OE *dūn*].

Hillswick Zet, 'battle bay' [*Hildiswik* c 1250: ON *hildr, vík*].

†**Hinckley** Lei, 'Hynca's clearing' [*Hinchelie* 1086: OE *lēah*].

Hitchin Hrt, '(territory of) the Hicce tribe', a relatively small one about which little is known. The present name is from the dative *Hiccum* [*Hiccam* c 945].

Hodder *riv* WRY-La 930, 'pleasant river' [OW **hōd*, B **dūbro-*].

Hoddesdon Hrt, 'Hod's hill', the personal name occurring also in **Hodsock** Nt and **Hodsock** Wo, 'Hod's oak' [1. *Hodesduna* 1086, 2. *Odesach* 1086: OE *dūn, āc*].

Holborn Mx, 'stream in a hollow bed', from which the manor (later a borough) was named. The stream was also known as the Fleet [*Holeburne* 1086: OE *hol, burna*].

†**Holderness** ERY, 'promontory ruled by a *hold*,' i e a high-ranking yeoman in the Danelaw [*Heldernesse* 1086: ON *holdr, nes*].

Hole LLi. See Cleethorpes.

Holland LHo, 'land by or on a hill-spur'. This was one of the three Parts into which Lincolnshire was divided from the eleventh century, the others being Kesteven and Lindsey (qq v). Holland occurs also in Essex and in two places in Lancs—**Up Holland** and **Down Holland**, 'upper' and 'lower' Holland respectively. The several WRY places called **Hoyland** have a similar derivation [1. *Hoiland* 1086, 2. *Hoilanda* 1086, 3. *Upholand* 1226: OE *hōh, land*].

Holyhead Agl, 'holy headland', cf the Welsh form—**Caergybi**, 'fort of (saint) Cybi', alluding to the famous ecclesiastical settlement there. The meaning of the English name is also that of Penzance Co (q v) [*Halihefed* 1315: OE *hālig, hēafod*, W *caer*].

Holywell Flt, —Hu, —K, **East & West Holywell** Nb, 'holy spring'. The Flintshire name alludes to the spring which appeared at the spot where St Winifred's head fell when it was struck off by her rejected suitor, Caradoc of Penarlâg. St Winifred was restored to life by St Beuno, but the spring remains to this day. The holy well in the Hunts place also survives [1. *Haliwel* 1093, 2. *Haliewelle* 1086, 4. *Halewell* 1218: OE *hālig, wella*].

Holywood Dmf, —Dwn: 'holy wood', commemorating a monastic site or a pagan sacred place. The Dumfries-shire place was formerly Dercongal, 'oakwood of Congal', alluding to the saint whose name occurs also in **Kirkconnel** Kcb, 'church of St Congal' [1. *de Sacro Nemore* 1252: OE *hālig, wudu*].

Honiton D. See Clyst *riv* D.

Hope *freq* **Hopton** *freq*: '(place in a) valley', 'farm in a valley' [OE *hop, tūn*]. See also Glossop.

Horncastle. See Bewcastle.

Hornsey Mx. See Harringay.

Horsford Nf 1254, **Horsforth** WRY: 'horse ford' [2. *Horseford* 1086: OE *hors, ford*].

†**Horsham** Sx 947, —Wo 1271, **Horsham St Faith** Nf: 'farm on which horses were kept' [OE *hors, hām*].

Horton *freq*, 'farm on muddy land' [OE *horu, tūn*].

Houghton *freq*, 'farm on a hill-spur' [OE *hōh, tūn*].

Hounslow Mx, 'Hund's mound or barrow' [*Honeslaw* 1086: OE *hlæw*].

Houston Rnf, 'Hugh's village', alluding to Hugo de Paduinan 1160 [*Villa Hugonis* c 1200, *Huston* c 1230: OE *tūn*].

†**Hove** Sx, 'place of shelter', a metaphorical extension of the meaning of an OE word meaning 'hood, head-covering' [*Houue* 1288: OE *hūfe*].

Howe Cai, **The Howe** IOM: 'mound, barrow' [ON *haugr*].

Howth Dub, 'headland' [ON *hofuð*].

Hoxay *isld* Ork, 'island with a mound' [*Haugaheith* c 1390: ON *haugr, ey*].

Hoxton Mx, 'Hoc's farm' [*Hochestone* 1086: OE *tūn*].

Hoy *isld* Ork, 'lofty island' [ON *há(r), ey*].

Hoylake Ch, '(place by) the tidelake within Hile, i e the sandhill'. The seaside resort dates from the end of the eighteenth century, developing around the Royal Hotel at Little Meols. The earliest form, *Highlake* 1766, represents a misdivision of the name *Hile Lake*, the roadstead on the landward side of a sandbank supposedly known as The Hile [OE *hygel*, 'hillock', ME *lake*].

Hoyland Swaine WRY, 'land on or by a hill-spur', alluding to *Suanus de Hoiland* (Swayn of Hoyland) who died in 1129 [*Holandeswayn* 1266: OE *hōh, land*].

Hucknall Torkard Nt, **Hucknall under Huthwaite** Nt, **Ault Hucknall** Db:

'Hucca's angle or nook of land', recording possibly a district on the Db-Nt boundary. Ault Hucknall Db 'high Hucknall' represents one edge of the district, Hucknall Torkard another, and Hucknall under Huthwaite lies between them. Torkard was the name of the family holding the manor in the twelfth century; Huthwaite means 'clearing on a hill-spur' [1. *Hochenhale* 1086, *Hokenhale Torkard* 1287, 2. *Hukenall under Hucthwet alias Dirti Hukenall* 1519, 3. *Hokenhale* 1291, *Haulte Huknall* 1535: OE *halh*, *hōh* ON *þveit*, OF *haut*].

Huddersfield WRY, 'Hudred's open land' [*Oderesfelt* 1086; OE *feld*].

Hugh Town (Scilly) Co, 'town on a ridge' [*Hew Hill* 1593: OE *hōh*].

Huish Champflower So. See Wick Champflower.

Hull *riv* ERY 1025, 'muddy river, fen river'. The argument against a Scandinavian origin for this name is that the spelling occurs in a copy of an early MS which contains no Scandinavian place-names, Derby, for instance, appearing as Northworthy. Apart from *Hol* 1268 and *Howll* 1325 all the early forms are *Hul* or *Hull*, which tells against an English origin in *hol;* moreover, names containing this root relate to rivers running in deeply cut beds, and the course of the Hull is quite different from this, being across flat country. A pre-English origin therefore seems probable [Br **hul-*]. See also Kingston upon Hull ERY.

Humber *riv* ERY, 'good river'. In addition to the estuary of the Ouse and Trent, a number of rivers of varying sizes and in parts of England as far apart as Dorset, Oxfordshire, and Durham, are designated by this name. A British origin is probable, consisting of the element **bro*, 'river', prefixed by an aspirated form of **su-*

'good'. The complimentary title might have a literal sense, indicating that the river was a good place for fishing etc, or it might be a euphemism intended to appease a destructive river-god [*Humbre* 892: Br **humbro-*].

Hume Ber, 'at the ridges or hill spurs' [*Houm* 1127: OE *hōh*, dat.pl. *hōum*].

Huna Cai, 'haven river' [*Hofn* c 1250: ON *hafn*, *á*].

†**Huntingdon** Hu, prob 'huntsman's hill'. The possibility must be mentioned that the first element may be the personal name Hunta. The difficulty is that *huntsman* in the singular does not make very good sense; other Hunting- names (e g **Huntingford** Do, **Huntingford** Gl, and the several **Huntingtons**) have a clear plural first component, making the connexion with hunting far more plausible. The Huntingdon District of Cambridgeshire corresponds to the historic Huntingdonshire, whose name dates from 1011 [*Huntandun* 973. *Huntandunscir* 1011: OE *hunta*, *dūn*, *scir*].

Huntley Gl, **Huntly** Ber: 'huntsman's clearing or wood'. **Huntly** Abd is a transferred name, from the title of a landowner, the Earl of Huntly, who originated in the Berwickshire place [1. *Huntelei* 1086 2. *Huntleie* 1180: OE *hunta*, *lēah*].

Hurstpierpoint Sx, 'wooded hill in the tenure of Pierpoint'. Robert de Pierpoint held the manor at the time of Domesday Book [*Herst* 1086: OE *hyrst*].

Husabost (Skye), Inv, 'house dwelling place' [ON *hús*, *bólstaðr*].

Husbands Bosworth Lei, 'Bār's village, occupied by husbandmen', distinguished from Market Bosworth (q v), in which commercial, rather than agrarian, pursuits would prevail [*Baresworde* 1086: OE *worð*].

Hutton Ber, —Dmf, —*freq* in England: 'farm on or by a ridge' [1. *Hotun* c 1098, 2. *Hotone* 1306, 3. *Hotun(e)* 1086: OE *hōh, tūn*].

Hyle *riv* Ess. See Ilford.

Hynish (Tiree) Arg, 'high headland' Note also **Heanish** on the adjoining promontory [ON *hā(r), nes*].

Hythe Ha, —K: 'landing place'. This element terminates such diverse names as Putney, Erith, Chelsea, Lambeth, and Maidenhead (qq v) [2. *Hyþe* 1052: OE *hȳð*].

I. See Iona.

Iarlshof. See Jarlshof.

Ibstock Lei, 'Ibba's dairy farm' [*Ibestoche* 1086: OE *stoc*].

Icknield Way, of unknown etymology and meaning. The name is probably British, like the trackway itself, and was earlier used without 'Way' or 'Street' being affixed [*Icenhylte* 903, *Ycenilde weg* 973, *Hykenild* c 1090].

Idle *riv* Nt, 'slow river' [*Idlæ* c 730: OE *idel, ēa*].

Idrigill (Skye) Inv, 'outer gulley' [ON *ytri, gil*].

Ierne, Greek name for Ireland. A form *Iris* was also used by ancient writers.

Ilford Ess, 'ford over the river Hyle, i e trickling stream', the river now being called the Roding. But Ilford So is 'ford over river Isle (q v)' [1. *Ilefort* 1086, 2. *Illeford* 1260: OE *ford*, B *sil*].

Ilfracombe D, 'valley of the people of Ielfred', embodying the West Saxon form of Ælfred [*Alfreincombe* 1086, *Ilfridecombe* 1279: OE *cumb*].

Ilkeston Db, 'Ealac's hill'. An abundance of early forms in -*dun* or -*don* overrides the Domesday Book -*ton* ending, though the latter has now prevailed. The *T*- at the beginning of the 1086 form has been detached from a preceding *at* [*Tilchestune* 1086: OE *dūn*].

Ilkley WRY, perhaps 'grove or clearing by place called *Olicana*'. The British name, probably 'place of Ollecnus', has been much discussed and considerable difficulties remain in the identification [*Olikana* c 150, *Hillicleg* c 972: OE *lēah*].

Illogan Co, '(church of) St Illogan' [*Sancti Illogany* 1291].

Ilminster So, **Ilton** So: 'church or farm on the river Isle (q v)' [1. *Illemynister* 995, 2. *Atiltone* 1086: OE *mynster, tūn*].

Immingham LLi, 'homestead of Imma's people' [*Imungeham* 1086: OE *hām*].

Inagh Cla, 'abounding in ivy' [I *eidnach*].

Ince Ch, **Inch** Crk, —Ker, —Tip, —Wex, 'island'. Drainage may sometimes conceal the truth of this interpretation, but places so named will usually be found to have been islands at one time. Other English examples of the name are **Ince in Makerfield** La, which includes the old regional name meaning 'open land by or with a ruin', and **Ince Blundell** La, which was held by the Blundell family about the year 1200 [1. *Inise* 1086, *Ynes* c 1100, 6. *Ynes* 1206, 7. *Ins Blundell* 1332: PrW **inis*, W *ynys*, I *inis*].

Inchcape Rock Ang 'basket-island rock'. The name is said to have been formerly

Inchscape, the Norse termination meaning 'basket' [G *inis*, ON *skeppa*]. See also Arbroath.

Inchcolm Fif, 'St Columba's island' [*Insula Sancti Columbae* c 1123, *St Colmes Ynch* 1605: G *inis*].

Inchkeith *isld* Fif, 'wood island' [*Insula Keð* c 1200: G *inis*, B **ceto-*].

Inchnamuck Tip, 'island of pigs' [I *inis*, *muc*].

Ingatestone Ess, **Ingrave** Ess: 'at the stone in Ing' and 'Ralph's manor in Ing' respectively. Half a dozen names in Essex embody a district name *Ing*, interpreted as a tribal designation 'people of Giga'. It is difficult to accept the *stone* in Ingatestone as 'Roman milestone', since there must have been a number of milestones within the district; moreover the use of the word *petra* suggests a rock which may have marked a meeting place. The tenant of Ingrave in 1086 was a certain Ralf [1. *Ginges ad Petram* 1254, *Gynges Atteston* 1283, 2. *Gingeraufe* 1276: OE *-ingas*, *stān*].

Ingleborough WRY, 'Ingeld's fortified place', the same OE personal name, or ON Ingiald, being found also in **Ingleton** Du and **Ingleton** WRY, 'Ingeld's farm' [1. *Ingelburc* c 1170, 2. *Inglestune* 1086, 3. *Ingeltun* c 1050: OE *burh*, *tūn*].

Ingleby Db 1275, 'farm of the Angles', an English settlement among Scandinavians [*Englaby* 1009: ON *Engle*, *bý*]. See also Normanby.

Inglewood Forest Cu, 'forest of the Angles', indicating an English population among the Cumbrian Welsh [*Englewod* c 1150: OE *Engle*, *wudu*].

Inishargy *isld* Dwn, 'island of the rock' [*Inyscargi* 1306: I *inis*, *carraig*].

Inishbofin *isld* Don, **Inishbofin** *isld* Gal: 'island of the white cow' [I *inis*, *bō*, *fionn*].

Inishdooey Don, 'island of the sandhill' [I *inis*, *dumhach*].

Inisheer *isld* Gal. See Aran Islands.

Inishfree Don, 'heath-covered island'. Other examples occur off the coasts of Ireland, and Yeats's 'lake isle of Inisfree' is in Lough Gill Sli [I *inis*, *fraech*].

Inishmaan *isld* Gal, **Inishmore** *isld* Gal. See Aran Islands.

Inishturk *isld* Myo, 'island of the boars'. There is also **Inchturk** on Lough Ree Wme [I *inis*, *torc*].

Instow D, 'John's holy place', the church being dedicated to St John the Baptist [*Johannesto* 1086: OE *stōw*].

Invergordon Ros, 'Gordon's (place at the) river-mouth', named after Sir Alexander Gordon, landowner here about 1760, before which it was *Inverbreckie*, 'speckled river-mouth' [G *inbhir*, *breac*].

†**Inverness** Inv, '(place at) mouth of the Ness', the river-name possibly means 'roaring one' [*Invernis* 1300: G *inbhir*, OC ** ned-*].

Iona *isld* Arg, 'yew place', regularly called Hi or I in earlier times. The present name may be due to a misunderstanding of a reference to Jonah [*Hiiensis* 634, *Ioua insula* c 700, Hy 730, *Hiona-Columcille* c 1100: OI *eo*].

†**Ipswich** Sf, 'Gip's port or landing-place', the versatile *-wic* here having the same sense as in Greenwich K and Norwich Nf (qq v) [*Gipswic* 993: OE *wīc*].

Irby Ch 1288, —NRY, **Irby in the Marsh** LLi, **Irby on Humber** LLi, **Ireby** Cu, —La: 'Irishmen's village'. *Iri* was the Norse word used of Norwegian settlers from Ireland or of Irishmen who accompanied the Viking invaders. In areas of predominantly Danish settlement the term is thus ambiguous, but in the north-western counties, whose Scandinavian settlers almost all came from Ireland, the term would almost certainly refer to native Irishmen. Other names with a similar reference include **Ireleth** La 'slope of the Irish' and **Kirk Ireton** Db 1450 'Irishmen's village with a church' [1. *Irreby* c 1100, 5. *Yrebi* 1185, 6. *Irebi* 1086, 7. *Irlid* 1190: ON *Iri, by, hliđ*, OE *tūn*].

Ireland, 'land of the Irish, land called "Éire"', the English name for the more westerly of the two major islands of the British Isles. Like any other alien name for a place, it would be regarded as a convenient label rather than a 'significant word'. The earliest examples of the word *Irish*, used of the people or their language, date from about 1205, but *Ireland* occurs in English texts considerably earlier, being found in Ælfric's *Lives of the Saints* in about 966.

Ireland's Eye Dub, 'Eria's island', a hybrid name based on a mistranslation. *Eye* represents ON *ey*, 'island'. In its original form the name was Inish Ereann, the second word being the name of an identified woman, but mistaken for the genitive case of *Éire*.

Ireleth La. See Irby.

Iris. See Ierne.

Irlam La, 'homestead on the river Irwell, i e winding river' [1. *Urwilham* c 1190, 2. *Urwil* c 1200: OE *hām, irre, wella*].

Ironbridge Sa, 'place by an iron bridge'. The earliest cast-iron bridge was built across the Severn here in 1778. See also Coalbrookdale Sa.

Ironville Db 1837, 'town in which iron is worked'. This late name is a good instance of *-ville*, which does not occur in medieval English names. Cf Coalville Lei, and Bournville Wa.

Irthlingborough Nth, 'fortified place used by ploughmen' or '... of the people of Yrtla' [*Yrtlingaburg* 780: OE *yrđling, burh*].

Irwell *riv* La. See Irlam.

Isbister (Whalsay) Zet, 'Ine's dwelling' [ON *bólstađr*].

Isca Dumnoniorum. See Exeter.

Isca Legionum, Isca Silurum. See Caerleon.

Isis *riv* O, the Thames (q v) at Oxford, formed on the supposition that *Tamise* could be analysed into *T(h)ame* and *Ise* or *Isis* [*Ise* 1347, *Isis* 1577].

Islay *isld* Arg, perhaps 'swelling island', the present form being the result of fairly recent alterations; *-s-* was inserted on the analogy of *island*, and *-ay* was added [*Ilea* c 690, *Ile* 800: OC* *ili*].

Isle *riv* So, probably 'swift river'. Ilminster So and Ilton So (qq v) are on the river, and so are **Isle Abbotts** So, formerly held by Muchelney Abbey, and **Isle Brewers** So, in the tenure of the Briwer family in the thirteenth century [1. *Yle* 693, 2. *Yli* 966, *Ile Abbatis* 1291, 3. *Ile Brywer* 1275: B **il-*].

Isleworth Mx, 'Gislhere's enclosure' [*Gislheresuuyrth* 695: OE *worđ*].

Islington Mx, 'Gisla's hill' [*Gislandun* c 1000: OE *dūn*].

Isurium (Aldborough WRY), 'place on the holy river' [*Isourion* c 150: B*isura].

Itchen *riv* Ha, perhaps 'mighty, powerful', but perhaps derived from the name of a Celtic deity [*Icene* 701: B *icenā].

Itterby LLi. See Cleethorpes.

Ivel *riv* Bd-Hrt, **Yeo** *riv* So: 'forked river' [1. *Givle* c 1180, 2. *Gifle* c 950: B*gablo-].

Iver Bk, '(place on a) slope' [*Yfreham* 1086, *Eura* c 1130: OE *yfer*]

Ivinghoe Bk, 'hill-spur of Ifa's people' [*Evingehov* 1086: OE *hōh*].

Ixworth Sf, 'Gicsa's enclosure' [*Gyxeworde* c 1025: OE *worð*].

Jacobstow Co, **Jacobstowe** D: 'James's holy place', alluding to the dedication of the churches [1. *Jacobstowe* 1270, 2. *Jacopstoue* 1331: OE *stōw*].

Jamestown Dmf, —Dnb, —Lx, —Ros, —Wme; 'settlement named after a man called James'; **Johnstown** Kld, —Klk, —Wic (x 4): '. . . called John'. The suffix *-town* occurs in Scotland and Ireland more frequently than in England, where *-ton* or *-by* would be the usual forms suffixing personal names, e g **Johnby** Cu. Some of the Irish examples are relatively recent translations of names such as Ballyshan. See also Johnston.

Jarlshof Zet, 'temple of a *jarl* or Norse nobleman', said to have been bestowed by Sir Walter Scott on the site at the southern extremity of Mainland [ON *jarl, hof*].

Jarrow Du, '(place of) the Gyrwe tribe', the folk-name, meaning possibly 'people of the fen', was also applied to a tribe of the Peterborough district [*Gyruum* c 730: OE *gyr*].

Jedburgh Rox, 'enclosure by the river Jed, i e twisting one' [*Gedwearde* 800: OE *worð*].

Jeffreyston Pmb, a name of the same type as Herbrandston (q v). See also Jamestown.

Jervaulx NRY, 'valley of the river Ure, i e holy one', French adaptation of the British river-name possibly suffixed by an English element such as -*dale* [*Jorvalle* c 1145: OF *val*].

Johnby Cu. See Jamestown.

John o' Groat's Cai, 'place named after John o' Groat', baillie to the earl of Caithness about 1500.

Johnson Hall St, **Johnston** Pmb, **Johnstone** Dmf, —Rnf, 'farm or settlement named after a man called John' [4. *Johannestun* 1227: OE *tūn*]. See also Jamestown.

Jolby NRY, 'Joel's farm' [*Johelby* c 1195: ON *bý*].

Jura *isld* Arg, 'Doirad's (island)' [*Doirad Eilinn* 678: (G *eilean*)].

Jurby IOM, 'Dyri's farm' [*Dureby* 1291: ON *bý*].

Kail Water or **Kale Water** *riv* Rox, 'calling one'. This name, together with *Calneburne*, the former name of Hazelly Burn Rox, may be compared with those of rivers in England—Colne WRY and Colne Water La, which appear to be derived from the same British root [1. *Kalne* c 1200, 3. *Calne* c 1180, 4. *Aqua de Coune* 1292: Br *Calaune].

Kanturk Crk, 'head or hill of the boar' [*Ceann-tuirc* n d : OI *ceann, torc*].

Katrine, Loch *lke* Pth, possibly 'lake of the wood of Eriu' [*Loch Ketyerne* 1463: G *loch*, Br *ceto-].

Keadeen *mtn* Wic; **Keadew** *mtn* Rcm: **Keady** *mtn* Arm: '(little) flat-topped hill'. The Wicklow name is in the diminutive form [1. *Kedi* c 1238, *Kedyn* c 1310: OI *céide* (dim: *céidin*)].

Kedleston Db 1385, 'Ketil's farm', a hybrid name of the type of Grimston (qv). [*Chetelestune* 1086: ON pers. n. *Ketill*, OE *tūn*].

Keele St, 'cow hill' [*Kiel* 1169: OE *cū*, *hyll*].

Keeloges Lim, —Wic, 'narrow ridges' [2. *Byllok* (*sic*, for *Kyllok*) 1619, *Culloges* 1690: I *caológa*].

Keighley WRY, 'Cyhha's clearing or wood'. The modern pronunciation 'Keethly' is a rare instance of an attempt to preserve *-gh-* (OE *-h-*) in speech [*Chichelai* 1086: OE *lēah*].

Keith Bnf, —Ang 1489: 'wood' [1. *Ket*, *Keth* 1203: Br **cēto-*].

Kells Ant, —Klk, —Mth, 'cells', a double plural, English *-s* being added to Irish *ceall*, plural of *kil*.

Kelso Rox, 'chalk hill-spur' [*Calkou* 1126, *Calcehou* c 1128: OE *calc*, *hōh*].

Kemble Gl, possibly 'Camulos's place,' alluding to the Celtic god whose name appears also in *Camulodunum* [*Kemele* 682].

Kempston Bd, 'farm by a bend'. North of Kempston the river Ouse describes three-quarters of an ellipse [*Kemesttone* 1047, *Camestone* 1086: Br **cambo-*, OE *tūn*].

Kendal We, 'valley of the river Kent (q v)', really the affix of the town-name, which was formerly Kirkby Kendal i e 'village with a church in Kendal '. The addition *Kendal* served to distinguish this Kirkby from Kirkby Lonsdale and Kirkby Stephen. Intermittent examples of Kendal used alone can be found from the fifteenth century onwards [*Cherchebi* 1086, *Kircabikendala* c 1095: ON *kirkju-býr, dalr*].

Kenilworth Wa, 'Cynehild's enclosure'. Cynehild is an Anglo-Saxon female personal name [*Chinewrde* 1086: OE *worð*].

Kenmare Ker, **Kinvarra** Gal: 'limit of the tide'. The Irish term *ceann-mara* is literally 'head of the sea' and is applied to the highest point in a river which the tide (regarded as the inflow from the sea) reaches. A similar idea is found in Kinsale Crk, from I *ceannsaile* 'head of the brine'.

†**Kennet** *riv* W-Brk 1574. **Kent** *riv* We-La c 1175: 'noble or holy river'. The literal meaning of the British root word is 'high one', but this is not likely to have a topographical application, as neither of these rivers belongs to a highland area. They are, however, of some importance and it may well be they were both objects of worship in the remote past [1. *Cynetan* 894, *Kinete* c 1200; 2. *Cainton* 1207, *Kenet* 1246: B *Cunetio-*].

Kennington Brk, —Sr/GL: 'farm of Cena's people'. The early forms of **Kennington** K, however, show that it means 'royal farm or manor' [1. *Chenitun* 821, 2. *Chenintune* 1086; OE *-inga-tūn*; 3. *Chintun* 1072, *Kynigtune* 11c: OE *cyning*, *tūn*].

Kensal Green Mx, 'the king's wood' [*Kingisholte* 1253: OE *holt*]. **Kensington** Mx, 'farm of Cynesige's people' [*Chenesitun* 1086; OE *-ingatūn*].

Kent, probably 'borderland, land on the rim'. Various meanings for the county name have been put forward. Some can be rejected for not taking early forms into account, or for proposing irrelevant linguistic explanations. Caesar uses *Cantium*, corresponding to the Greek geographers' form *Kantion*. The most likely Celtic root is **canto-* 'rim, border, periphery', which fits the geography of the county. See also Canterbury.

Kent *riv* We-La. See Kennet.

†Kerrier Co, 'area of rounds', referring to Iron-Age fortified homesteads found in Cornwall and particularly abundant in the Helford River area. The District name was formerly that of the Hundred [*Kerier* 1201: Co **ker*, with a special plural termination *-ier*].

Kerry, 'Ciar's people', a tribal name alluding to the legendary Ciar, son of Fergus and Maev [I *Ciarraidhe*].

Kesteven L, 'wood meeting-place'. Tribal and district meeting-places tended to remain the same for successive populations of Britons, Angles, and Anglo-Scandinavians. This fact explains this unusual hybrid name, containing Celtic and Scandinavian elements. Possibly the meeting-place for the people in this part of Lincolnshire went by the simple name *Chet* ('wood') through the early English period. Danes would have pronounced this *Ket*, to which they must have added the explanatory term *stefna* 'meeting (place)' [*Chostefne* c 100, *Chesteven* 1086, *Ketstevne* 1185: B **cēto* ON *stefna*].

Keswick Cu, —Nf (x2), **East Keswick** WRY: 'cheese farm'. It is to be noted that these places are all areas dominated at one time by Scandinavians, whose influence has affected the initial consonant (cf Kesteven). Elsewhere, the same common OE name became Chiswick (q v) [1. *Kesewik* 1276, 2. *Chesewic, Kesewick* 1086, 3. *Casewic* c 1150: OE *cēse, wic*].

†Kettering Nth, a difficult name for which no explanation can be offered beyond the possibility that it is a folk name of the same type as Reading (q v). The first element does not seem to be topographical, but no personal name can be traced which might have been shortened to *Cytra* [*Cytringan* 956: OE *-ingas*].

Kew Sr, 'wharf promontory' [*Cayho* 1327: OF *kai*, OE *hōh*].

Kidderminster Wo, 'Cyda's monastery'. Before the establishment of the monastery in the eighth century, the town was probably called *At Stour*, from the river on which it stands [*Chideminstre* 1086: OE *mynster*].

Kidwelly Crm, 'Cadwal's territory'. The modern Welsh form is Cedweli [*Cetgueli* 10c: W *-i*].

Kielder *riv* Nb, 'rapid stream' [*Keilder* 1326: B **caled, *dubro-*].

Kilbeg Wic, probably 'little wood', an interpretation based partly on the traditional pronunciation 'Kylebeg' [*Kilbege* 1562: I *coill* 'wood', *bheag* 'small'].

Kilbride *freq in Scotland and Ireland*: 'holy place or church of St Bridget'. More than a dozen saints called Bridget are on record, and there was an ancient Celtic goddess of the same name [G *cill*].

Kilchattan Bte, 'church of St Catan', commemorating the friend of St Columba who worked in Bute and the neighbouring islands [*Killecatan* 1449: G *cill*].

Kilchenzie Arg. See Kilkenny.

Kildare Kld, 'church of the oak', alluding to the traditional site of the cell of St Bridget (452-523), who may well have established herself in a pagan sacred grove [I *cill, dara*].

Kildonan Sut, 'church of St Donan', commemorating the Irish monk, active in the seventh century on the island of Eigg, where he and his companions were burnt alive by a party of marauding Vikings [*Kelduninach* c 1230: G *cill*].

Kilham ERY,—Nb. See Millom.

Kilkenny Klk, 'church of St Kenneth', commemorating Canice or Kenneth, the sixth-century Irish monk who worked in the Hebrides and western Scotland (cf **Kilchenzie** and **Kilkenneth** in Argyllshire). On returning to Ireland he is said to have founded monasteries at Kilkenny and at Kilkenny West in Westmeath [I *cill*].

Killarney Ker, 'church of the sloes', and so for places of the same name in Kilkenny and Roscommon, but **Killarney** Wic seems to be 'church of Bishop Sarain' (*cill easpuig Sáráin*) [4. *Kilescosather* 1207, *Killosarn* c 1280: 1-3 I *cill, airneadbh*].

Kilmalcolm Rnf. See Kilmarnock.

Kilmarnock Ayr, 'church of St Ernan', the saint being designated by the familiar *mo-* 'my' and the diminutive suffix *-oc*, affectionate additions found in other place-names embodying the names of saints; in **Kilmalcolm** Rnf the practice has brought an erroneous form into existence, the name having been *Kilmacolme* in 1205, 'church of my little Colm' [*Kelmernoke* 1299: G *cill*].

Kimbolton He, —Hu 1330: 'Cynebald's farm' [1. *Kimbalton* c 1245 2. *Chenebaltone* 1086: OE *tūn*].

Kimmeridge Do, 'place on a useful stream' [*Cammerich* 1086, *Kimerich* 1212: OE *cyme*, 'convenient', **ric* 'stream'].

Kincardine Fif, —Pth, —Ros, **Kincardine O' Neil** Abd: 'head or end of the copse'.

†**Kincardine(shire)** takes its name from a small place in Fordoun Knc. The second element in these names is a Pictish word related to W *cardden* 'thicket'. The Aberdeenshire parish was one of the possessions of the great Uí Néill family of Northern Ireland [1. *Kincaocann* 1195, 2. *Kincarden* 1172, 4. *Kyncardyn O Nelee* 1337: G *ceann*].

Kincraig Inv, 'head or end of the rock' [G *ceann, creag*].

Kinder Scout Db, of uncertain meaning. The *Scout* component presents no difficulty; this is from a Scandinavian word meaning 'projecting cliff, overhanging rock' and is found elsewhere, e g in the Westmorland names **Scout Crag**, **Scout Scar**, and **Ravenscout** [ON *skúti*].

Kinglassie Fif, possibly 'church of the brook', though some early forms suggest '(church at the) head of the brook', the latter being *ecclesia de Kinglassin* 1224 against other thirteenth-century forms *Kilglassi, Kilglassin*. It was evidently a holy place, probably incorporating pre-Christian associations, as there are references to the holy stream and to a holy hill nearby. A fictitious saint was brought into existence by misinterpreting *Kilglassi*, and St Glass was even provided with a feast-day, which is more than was ever bestowed on the equally spurious St Kilda (q v) [G *ceann, glais*].

Kingsbridge D, 'the king's bridge'. Though the monarch cannot be identified, he must have been an Anglo-Saxon king [*Cinges Bricge* 962: OE *cyning, brycg*].

King's Cliffe Nth, 'the king's hill-slope'. The place was often visited by the Norman kings, and was a royal manor in 1086 [*Clive* 1086, *Kyngesclive* 1305: OE *cyning, clif*].

Kingsland He. See Leominster.

Kings Langley Hrt, 'the king's manor in *Langley*, i e long wood or grove'. From the manor granted to the abbot of St Albans, the king's manor was extracted in the early 12th century, leaving **Abbots Langley** in monastic tenure. Other similar pairs include **Abbots Bromley** and **Kings Bromley** St, and **Abbot's Ripton** and **King's Ripton** Hu, the abbots being respectively those of Burton and Ramsey [1. *Langalege* c 1060, *Lengele Regis* 1428, *Kyngeslangeley* 1436: OE *cyning*, *lang*, *lēah*]. See also Shendish.

King's Lynn Nf, 'the king's manor in *Lynn*, i e (place by) the pool' [*Lun* 1086, *Lynna* c 1105: B *lindo*-].

Kingston *freq*, usually 'royal farm', but some, e g **Kingston upon Soar** Nt, are 'royal stone'. Affixed forms include **Kingston Lacy** Do, **Kingston Russel** Do, **Kingston Pitney** So, **Kingston Seymour** So, **Kingston Bagpuize** Brk, and **Kingston Lisle** Brk. Between **Kingston Deverell** W and **Monkton Deverell** W the distinction is made by Kingston and Monkton, differentiating the royal possession from the monastic one, cf Kings Langley. In †**Kingston upon Hull** ERY and **Kingston upon Thames** Sr/GL, identity is established by the addition of a river-name. **Kingston-by-Sea** Sx seems appropriate near Portslade-by-Sea and Shoreham-by-Sea, but the addition is in fact manorial, the place having been held by Robert de Busci in the twelfth century [OE *cyning*, *cyne*, *tūn*, *stān*].

Kingstown Dub, 'town named in honour of the king', commemorating a visit of George IV in 1821. The present name is Dun Laoghaire (q v).

Kingswinford St, 'king's (place by) pig ford' [*Svinesford* 1086, *Kyngesswynford* 1322: OE *cyning*, *swin*, *ford*]. See also Stourport.

Kingussie Inv, 'head of the pinewood' [*Kinguscy* c 1210: G *ceann*, *giuthseach*].

Kinlet Sa. See Shirlet.

Kinloch *freq*, 'head of the loch' [G *ceann*, *loch*].

Kinnerton Ch, —Flt, —Rad: 'Cyneheard's farm' [1. *Kynarton* 1240, 2. *Kinarton* 1285, 3. *Kynardton* 1303: OE *tūn*].

Kinross Knr 1214, 'tip of the promontory', at the point of a peninsula projecting into Loch Leven [*Kynros* c 1144: G *ceann*, *ros*].

Kinsale Crk, Kintail Inv, Kintale Don, 'head of the salt water', i e the highest point in a river reached by the tide [2. *Keantalle* 1509: G *ceann t' saile*].

Kintyre Arg 1266, 'end of the land'. **Mull of Kintyre** is 'headland at the end of the land' [*Ciunntire* 807, *Mael Chinn Tire* c 1200: G *ceann*, *tire*, ON *múli*].

Kinvarra Gal. See Kenmare.

Kippure *mtn* Wic, 'great place of rough grass' [*Kippoore* 1604: I *ciop* 'coarse grass', *mhór*].

Kirby *freq* 'village with a church'. Apart from **West Kirby** Ch, all the places bearing this name are distinguished by additions usually of the manorial type. One or two, however, are of the same kind as **Kirby Knowle** NRY, 'Kirby beside the hill called Knowle' or **Kirby Grindalythe** ERY, 'Kirby on the slope (ON *hlið*) of Crandale or crane valley' **Kirby Misperton** NRY combines Kirby with the name of the adjacent village, meaning possibly 'farm with a dung hill' (OE *mistbeorg*) and **Kirby Underdale** ERY is 'Kirby in Hundulf's valley' [ON *kirkju-bý(r)*]. See also Kirkby.

Kirkabister (Bressay) Zet, **Kirkibost** Inv: 'church homestead' [1. *Kirkabuster* 1654: ON *kirkju-bólstaðr*].

Kirkandreas IOM, **Kirkandrers** Kcb. See Llanandras, St Andrews.

Kirkby *freq* 'village with a church'. Like Kirby (q v), Kirkby also receives manorial additions in order to distinguish places within the same county. Thus, there are **Kirkby Stephen** We and **Kirkby Thore** We. But rather more affixes are of the geographical type, e g **Kirkby Lonsdale** We ('in the valley of the river Lune'), **Kirkby Wharfe** WRY ('in the valley of the river Wharfe'), and **Kirkby Moorside** NRY ('at the top of the moor'— *Moresheved*). The addition in **Kirkby Overblow** WRY represents OE **oreblā-were* 'smelter', and alludes to early iron working there [ON *kirkju-bý*]. See also Ashfield.

†Kirkcaldy Fif, 'fort at Caledin'. *Caledin* itself means 'hard fort', but was not significant to those who added W *caer*, which in turn was transformed into *kirk* [*Kircalethyn* 12c: W *caer*, *caled din*].

Kirk Christ Lezayre IOM, 'Christ church near The Ayres, i e the gravel banks', the connective *-lez-* (F *les*), functioning in the same way as *-le-* in Newton le Willows, i e replacing an original *en le*. The addition distinguishes this place from **Kirk Christ Rushen** IOM, 'Christ church on the little moor' [1. *kyrkecrist* c 1370, *Leay-* 1231: ON *kirkja*, *eyrr*, G *ros*, *-an*].

Kirkconnel Kcb. See Holywood.

Kirkcudbright Kcb, 'church of St Cuthbert', celebrating the seventh-century Northumbrian monk who made arduous missionary journeys in Galloway. The personal name is English, the first element Norse, and the order of elements Celtic. It is therefore possible that the name replaces an earlier Celtic dedication in *Cil-*. **Kirkcudbrightshire** is also known as †**Stewartry**, alluding to the grant to the Earl of Douglas of the stewardship of Crown lands between Nith and Cree [*Kircuthbright* 1296: ON *kirkja*].

Kirk Hallam Db, '(place with a) church in the nooks', the prefixed element distinguishing the place from West Hallam. *Kirk* is here a Scandinavianised form of *Church* [*Kirkehalum* 1234: OE *cirice*, *halh* (da.pl. *halum*)].

Kirkheaton Nb, —WRY, 'high farm with a church'. The Yorkshire name distinguishes the place from a number of other Heatons in the same Riding, e g **Cleckheaton**, **Earls Heaton**, and **Hanging Heaton**. Kirkheaton Nb was formerly *Little Heton*, its larger counterpart being now **Capheaton** or 'chief Heaton' [2. *Heptone* 1086, *Hetun* c 1190: OE *hēah*, *tūn*, OE *cirice*, ON *kirkja*].

Kirkibost Inv. See Kirkabister.

Kirkintilloch Dnb, 'fort at the head of the eminences'. Just as Kirkcaldy has to be divided Kir-caldy in order to separate the elements, so this name must be analysed as Kir-kintilloch, separating the British first element from the Gaelic compound which seems to have replaced an earlier British **Pen-bryn* 'head of the heights'. A third transformation is in process in the earliest spelling *Cair Pentalochh*, which elucidates *Kir-* and preserves *Pen-* [*Cair Pentalochh* c 1000, *Kirkintulach* c 1200: OW *cair*, *penn*, G *ceann*, *tulaich*].

Kirk Ireton Db. See Irby.

Kirk Michael IOM, 'St Michael's church' [ON *kirkja*].

Kirkness Ork, 'promontory with a church' [ON *kirkja*, *nes*].

Kirkoswald Ayr, —Cu 1235: 'St Oswald's church'. Like Kirkcudbright and Kirk Michael, this name also shows Celtic word order. Oswald was a Northumbrian king killed in action against the pagan Penda of Mercia, and regarded as a saint and martyr [2. *Carcoswald* 1167: ON *kirkja*].

Kirkton, Kirktown *freq* in Scotland: 'village with a church' [OE *cirice, tūn*].

Kirkwall Ork 1488, 'church bay'. The present form of the name, nearly 500 years old, is evidently the result of folk etymology. ON *vágr* has survived in the Orkneys and elsewhere as Voe [*Kirkiuvagr* c 1225: ON *kirkja, vágr*].

Kirriemuir Ang, 'great quarter'. Fractions of this kind in Scottish names usually refer to areas of land expressed in parts of a *davoch*, a variable amount of land representing what was required to support a household [*Kerimor* 1250: G *ceathramh, mór*].

Knighton *freq*, 'farm or village of the knights'. In place-name contexts, *knight* will usually have a feudal sense, and the land would have been that held by the personal followers of a baron or other lord. Knighton (as distinct from Knightston or Knightstone) is always from the plural form *cnihta* 'of the knights', as the early spellings demonstrate; **Knighton** Do was *Knicteton* 1212, and **Knighton** So *Knytteton* in 1372. The spellings *Nisteton* 1086 and *Knysteton* 1285 for **Knighton** Brk and **East Knighton** Do respectively represent Norman attempts to come to terms with the sound represented by OE *-h-*, and the spelling *Chenistetone* 1086 for **West Knighton** Do exemplifies the effort made by the Domesday Book clerk to cope with OE *Cn-* as well [OE *cniht*, gen. pl. *cnihta, tūn*].

Knock *freq* in Ireland and Scotland, 'hill' [G *cnoc*].

Knoidart Inv, 'Knut's inlet'. The Knut referred to may be King Canute, who invaded Scotland in 1031. By the time of the earliest records of the name, three centuries later, ON *fjord* had been transformed into *-worath* or *-worth*, analogous to the spellings of the terminations in Moidart (*-ward, -worth*) and Loch Sunart (*-wort*) of about the same period [*Knodworath* 1309: ON *fjórðr*].

Knutsford Ch, 'Knut's ford'. There is no question of a fjord here, and the location of the ford is not certain. M. Gelling (NTC 120) has suggested that the name may have been applied to a causeway across the marshy ground south of Tatton Mere. Like Knoidart, this place also has been traditionally associated with King Canute. The street name, Canute Place, is quite modern; this was Market Place in 1860, probably identical with *Le Markethsted* 1377. [*Cunetesford* 1086: OE *ford*].

Kyle Ayr 1173, '(territory of) Coel Hen'. There were two branches of the ruling line of the Britons of south-west Scotland. The Strathclyde Britons' royal house derived from Riderch Hael; the rulers of Ayrshire and Galloway descended from Coel Hen, sometimes identified with the legendary 'old King Cole' [*Cyil* 750, *Chul* c 1150: OW pers. n. *Coel*].

Kyleakin (Skye) Inv, 'Hakon's strait'. A hybrid name, combining a Gaelic topographical element with a Scandinavian personal name, said to be that of Haakon IV of Norway, who sailed through this strait after his disastrous defeat at Largs in 1263 [G *caol*].

Kyle of Durness Sut, **Kyle of Lochalsh** Ros, **Kyles of Bute** Bte: 'straits in or by the named places' (qq v) [G *caol*].

Kyle *riv* NRY, 'narrow (stream)', [Kiil 1220: B *cūlio-*].

Kyo Du,'cowridge or hill' (*Kyhow* c 1240: OE *cū, hōh*].

Lactodoron. See Towcester (s v Tove *riv*).

Lagg Ayr, — (Arran) Bte, — (Jura) Arg: '(place by) a cave or hollow', the diminutive form being found in **Laggan** Ayr, — Inv, — (Islay) Arg [G *lag*].

Lagnamuck Myo, **Lugnamuck** Wic: 'hollow of the pigs' [I *lag, muc*].

Lairg Sut, 'shank', possibly from the shape of the valley in which it lies. The same element occurs in **Pitlurg** Abd, —Bnf: 'shank portion' [1. *Larg* c 1230, 2. *Petnalurge* 1232: G *lorg*, P **pett*].

Lake Country 1842, **Lake District** 1835, **Lakeland** 1829: synonymous terms for the area of part of Lancs, Westmorland, and Cumberland (now all in ††Cumbria), in which are found the English Lakes (Windermere, Grasmere, Ullswater etc) only one of which—Bassenthwaite Lake— has the word *lake* appended to its name.

Lakenheath Sf, 'landing place of Laca's people'. Spellings with *-e-* occur as early as the eleventh century, and so the confusion with *-heath* names is of long standing [*Lacingahið* 945, *Lakinghethe* 1086: OE *hyð*].

Laleston Glm 1514, 'farm of a man called Lawless'. Thomas and Walter Legeles are named in a number of 13c documents and this Anglo-Scandinavian family had probably been in the area since the eleventh century or earlier. Although the present spelling arose in 1514, forms in Law- are found in 1606, indicating the survival of this element in the local pronunciation of the name [*Lagelestun* c 1165, *Laweleston* 1268: OE *tūn*].

Lambay *isld* Dub, 'lamb island'. The island was probably a pasture reserved for yeaning ewes [ON *lamb, ey*].

Lambeth Sr-GL, 'landing place for lambs' [*Lambhyð* 1041: OE *lamb, hyð*].

Lammermuir Ber, **Lammermuir Hills** ELo, 'waste land on which lambs grazed' [2. *Lombormore* 800: OE *lamb* (gen. pl. *lambra*), *mōr*].

Lamorran Co, 'church of St Moren' [*Lannmoren* 969: OCo **lann*].

Lampeter Crd 1301, 'church of St Peter'. The Welsh *Llanbedr Pont Steffan* is 'St Peter's church at Stephen's bridge', the affix distinguishing it from Llanbedr elsewhere (e g in Breconshire, Radnorshire, and Merionethshire). The maintenance of bridges was a serious public duty in the Middle Ages, and the personal name attached was more for the apportioning of responsibility than to bestow honour on the bearer of the name [*Lanpeder* 1284, *Lampeter Pount Steune* 1301: W *llan, pont*].

Lanark Lnk 1289, 'glade'. The same element is found in **Lanercost** Cu and **Lendrick Hill** Knr; **Lendrick** Pth is in the Pictish area, which suggests that the word was present in the vocabulary of the Picts as well. The corresponding Cornish form is found in **Landrake** Co [1. *Lannarc* 1188, 2. *Lanercost* 1169, 4. *Lennerick* 1669, 5.. *Landrei* 1086: OW *lannerch*, Co *lanherch*].

†**Lancaster** La, 'Roman military station on the river Lune'. The name of the county has been shortened from its fourteenth-century form to the present Lancashire (cf Cheshire). The Roman fort may have been the cavalry station *Olenacum* (perh. 'wool place') [1. *Loncastre* 1086, 2. *Lancastreshire* 14c: OE *ceaster, scir*]. See also Lune.

Lancing Sx, '(territory of) Wlenca's people' [*Lancinges* 1086: OE *-ingas*].

Landore Glm, 'river bank' [W *glan*, *dŵr*].

Landrake Co. See Lanark.

Land's End Co, 'extremity of the mainland', a name analogous to Finistère Brittany and Finisterre, Spain. The present name dates from the fourteenth century; earlier it was *Penwihtsteort*, 'tail of Penwith' (q v) [*The Londis End* 14c: OE *land*, *ende*].

Lanercost Cu. See Lanark.

Langdales We 1597, 'long valleys'. There are two valleys; one is Great Langdale— a name of quite recent origin; the other is Little Langdale, which was *Langdenelittle* c 1160. In this and other early spellings the second element was OE *denu*; forms like *Longdon* and *Longdene* are occasionally found in records as late as the seventeenth century. But *-dale* forms, derived from ON *dalr*, prevailed [*Langdene* 1179: OE *lang*, *denu*, ON *dalr*].

Langham *freq*, 'long homestead or village' [OE *lang*, *hām*].

Langley *freq*, 'long wood or grove', occasionally with manorial additions, e g **Kings Langley** Hrt (q v), **Langley Burrell** W (in the tenure of Peter Burel 1242), or **Langley Marish** Bk (held by Christiana de Mariscis in 1285) [OE *lang*, *lēah*].

Langton *freq*, 'long farm or village', sometimes occurring with a manorial or descriptive addition, e g **East Langton** Lei, **Church Langton** Lei, **Langton Herring** Do (in the tenure of the Harang family 13c), and **Great Langton** NRY. **Tur Langton** Lei, although near the other Langtons in that county, has a different origin, being 'village associated with Tyrhtel'; it might have developed to *Turlington* from *Tirlingeton* 1206 if it had not been for the influence of the Langton names nearby [OE *lang*, *tūn*].

Lanteglos Co. See Llandaf.

Lanthony Gl, 'dependency of Llanthony' (q v).

Laois. See Leix.

Larbert Stl 1251, 'farm by a thicket'. In the modern name Gaelic *làrach* seems to have replaced *leth*, 'portion', found in early forms [*Lethberth* 1195: G *leth*, *làrach*, P *pert*].

Largs Ayr, 'slopes'. The Gaelic element has been changed to the plural by the addition of *-s*, as though it were English [*Larghes* c 1140: G *learg*].

†**Larne** Ant, (territory of) people of Lathair'. This name was formerly applied to an extensive area, the Latharna being the descendants of one of the twenty-five children of the legendary Hugony. He distributed approximately equal shares of the country to each child but only Lathair's portion has survived into the modern nomenclature. The town was formerly *Inver-an-Latharna* 'river mouth of Lathair's people' [I *inver*].

Latheron Cai, probably 'miry place'. The extended form of the name, **Latheron Wheel**, represents the Gaelic addition *a' Phuill* 'of the pool' [*Lagheryn* 1287: G *láthach*, 'mire'].

Lauder *riv* Ber, perhaps 'wash-place river'. This name is related to Lowther We (q v) and also to a lost British name *Lavatres* NRY. The valley of this river contributes to the District name †**Ettrick and Lauderdale**, Borders Region [*Louueder* 1208: B *lou-*, *dubro-*].

Laugharne Crm, 'end of the place at the mouth of the Corran'. The river-name is an affectionate diminutive, *corran* 'little one' [*Talacharn* 1191, *Abercoran* 1191: W *tal* 'end', *aber* 'river mouth'].

Launceston Co, 'farm at the elder copse enclosure'. This hybrid name has an English suffix attached to a Cornish compound (cf Landrake) [*Lanscavetone* 1086: OCo *lann*, 'enclosure', *scawet* 'elder copse', OE *tūn*].

Lavenham Sf, 'Lafa's homestead' [*Lauanham* c 995: OE *hām*].

Lavernock Glm 1425, probably 'lark hill' [*Lawernach* 13c: OE *lāwerce*, *cnocc*].

Laxa Zet, **Laxay** (Islay) Arg, — (Lewis) Ros, **Laxey** IOM: ('place by) salmon river' [ON *lax*, *á*].

Laxton ERY, — Nt c1190, — Nth 1166: 'Leaxa's farm', a hybrid compound, the first element being a Scandinavian personal name and the second the English *-ingtūn*. [1. *Laxinton* 1086, 2. *Laxintune* 1086, 3. *Lastone* 1086, *Laxintona* 12c: OE (*ing*) *tūn*].

Lea *riv* Bd-Ess/GL: possibly 'bright river'. The root-word may, however, be the name of a deity, in which case the meaning may be rendered, 'river under the protection of Lugus'. As it forms an extensive county boundary, separating Essex from Middlesex and Hertfordshire, the river is alluded to in numerous documents from the ninth century onwards. That the river served also as a dialect boundary is indicated by distinct spellings found in documents from the different counties through which it flows. The general Essex spelling is *Leye*, preserved in Leyton (q v); Bedfordshire documents between about 1120 and 1400 have *Luy(e)*, so clarifying the connexion between the river-name and Luton (q v) [*Ligan* 880, *Luye* c 1130, *Leye* 1274: B **lug-*].

Leach *riv* Gl-O, 'muddy stream' [*Lec* c 730: OE **læcc*].

Leamington Hastings Wa, 'farm by the river Leam, held by the Hastings family'.

The river-name belongs to a group (including Lemon, Lymn, and Lympne) with the meaning 'elm river' The tree became known as 'the Warwickshire weed', giving this interpretation some support. There was also said to be an abundance of elms along the course of the Lympne. The manorial name Hastings distinguishes this Leamington from **Leamington Priors**, which was held by Kenilworth Priory and which is now **Royal Leamington Spa**. The honorific title was granted by Queen Victoria after a visit in 1838 [1. *Lunnitone* 1086, *Lemyngton Hasting* 1285, 2. *Lamintone* 1086, *Lemynton Prioris* 1325: OE *tūn*].

Leatherhead Sr 1630, 'people's ford' [*Leodridan* c 880: OE *lēode*, **rida*].

Lechlade Gl. 'ferry near river Leach' (q v)'. The ferry would have been across the Thames. The second element here is OE (*ge*)*lād*, 'water-course, passage over a river', narrowed to the sense 'ferry' in WCy dialects and usually appearing in place-names as *-lode* (cf Evenlode) [*Lecelade* 1086: OE (*ge*)*lād*].

Leckwith Glm, '(place of) Helygwydd', possibly commemorating a saint associated in some way with the area. This is an instance of an uncommon type of name, found both in Wales and elsewhere, in which a personal name is used unmodified by a prefix or suffix such as W *Llan-* or E *-ton* [*Leocwtha* c 1170].

†**Leeds** WRY 1518, 'people of the region of the river', probably alluding to the river Aire under its former name of *Lat-*. The origin of the name Aire (q v) is in a British root, and so an alternative British name (meaning 'hard-flowing one') for the same river is worthy of note. Leeds was in the British kingdom of Elmet, which continued to exist for two hundred years after the arrival of the Anglo-Saxons in Yorkshire [*Loidis* c 730]

†**Leicester** Lei, 'Roman station of the Ligoran folk'. This difficult name has suffered much at the hands of myth-makers, but some serious suggestions have also been made and deserve consideration. The interpretation given above still requires elucidation: how did the *Ligore* get their name? A possible answer is that the basis is a river-name, an earlier or alternative name for the Soar (q v). The Celtic origin of the latter does not preclude a British alternative (cf Leeds). In Roman times the place was known as *Ratae Coritanorum* 'fortress of the Coritani' [*Ligera Ceaster* 917, *Ledecestre* 1086: OE *ceaster,* B**rat*].

Leigh *freq* in England, 'clearing, wood' [OE *lēah*, dat. *lēage*].

Leighton Ch, —La, —Sa: 'vegetable farm', literally 'leek farm'. As a common noun, OE *lēactūn* meant 'kitchen garden', suggesting that Leighton (and also Laughton) names were applied to market-garden places. Affixes occur in **Leighton Buzzard** Bd, which commemorates the first prebendary, Theobald de Busar (cf J. Godber, *Hist. of Bedfordshire* 38), and **Leighton Bromswold** Hu, in which Bromswold ('Brun's wood') was originally a separate settlement [1. *Lecton* 13c, 2. *Lecton* 1255, 3. *Lestone* 1086, 4. *Letton Busard* 1254, 5. *Letton super Bromeswald* 1254: OE *lēac-tūn*].

Leinster, 'place of the Lagin people', alluding to Celtic tribes who entered Ireland probably in the third century BC. The Irish form of the name, *Laighin*, is simply the folk name which is said to be derived from that of a broad-bladed spear. The Scandinavian suffix, meaning 'place', was added also to the Irish names of two other provinces—Munster and Ulster [*Laynster* 1515: ON *staðr*].

Leith MLo, 'moist place'. Unless the name is tautological, it seems likely to have been primarily of a place beside a river, rather than of the river itself [*Inverlet* c 1130, *Inverlethe* c 1315: W *llaith*, 'moist'].

Leitrim Ltm,—Wic: 'grey ridge' [2. *Leetrim* 1310: *liath, druim*].

Leix, Anglicised form of **Laois,** '(place of) the Laeighis tribe'. The founder of this tribe, Lughaidh Laeighseach, was granted land in the kingdom of Leinster in recognition of his having expelled invaders from Munster. The -*x* of the English form represents an -*s*- sound as in Wexford (q v). The county name occurs also in **Abbeyleix** and in **Port Laoise.**

Leixlip Kld, 'salmon leap', by the river Liffey, on which the salmon-leap can be seen. The name is sometimes said to be of ON origin, but a derivation from ME is equally possible [*Lexlepe* 1328: ON *leax, hlaup* (ME *lex*, OE **hlēp*)].

Len *riv* K, back-formation from **Lenham** K, 'Leana's homestead' [2. *Leanham* 850: OE *hām*].

Lendrick Pth. See Lanark.

Lennox Forest Stl, 'place abounding in elms' [*Leuenaichs* 1174, *Lenox* 1234: G *leamhanach* < *leamh* (*an*), 'elm'].

†**Leominster** He, 'monastery in the district of Leon'. Leon or Lene ('district of the streams') is a wedge of land with Leominster at its point and the rivers Arrow and Lugg as its converging boundaries. Within the district lie **Monkland, Kingsland, Eardisland** and, higher up the Arrow, **Lyonshall.** The last named is 'Leon nook', and the district name occurs as a termination in the other three, all of which allude to feudal lords. Eardisland is 'Earl's holding in Leon' [1. *Leomynster* 10c, 2. *Lionhina gemære*

958, 3. *Munkelen* c 1180, 4. *Kingeslan* 1213, 5. *Erlesl en* 1230, 6. *Lenehalle* 1086: OW **llion*, OE*mynster*, *munuc*, *eorl*, *halh*].

Lerwick Zet 1625, 'mud inlet' [ON *leirr*, *vik*].

Leslie Abd, 'court of hollies' [*Lesslyn* c 1180, *Lescelin* c 1232: W *llys*, *celyn*].

Lesmahagow Lnk, 'enclosure of beloved Fechin'. The saint's name here is in the diminutive form of affection, Mo-Fhegu. St Fechin died about the year 666; his feast day was celebrated on 20 January [*Lesmahagu* c 1130: G *leas*].

Letchworth Hrt, 'enclosure settlement' [*Leceworde* 1086: OE **lycce*, 'locked place, enclosure', *worð*].

Letterbrick Don. See Letterfearn.

Letterfearn Ros 1509, 'alder-grown hill slope'. The first element, found in both Scottish and Irish place-names, is usually taken to mean not merely a slope but one which is well supplied with springs and streams. A number of names of this type have personal names as specifying elements, e g **Letterkenny** Don, 'O' Kenny's hill slope'; others, e g **Letterbrick** Don, allude to animals, in this instance the badger; another group contains descriptive terms such as 'beautiful', in two places called **Letterkeen,** one in Mayo and the other in Fermanagh [G *leitir*, I *leitar*].

Letterkeen, Letterkenny. See Letterfearn.

Leuchars Fif, '(place of) rushes' [*Locres* 1300: G *luachair*].

Leven Fif, 'elm (place)' or 'elm-river (place)', since this name, applied also to more than one loch in Scotland, is related to the river-names Leam, Lemon, Lymn etc—all of which mean 'elm river'.

Gaelic *Leamhain* is also found in Lennox (q v) [*Levin* c 1535: G *leamhain*].

Lew *riv* D, 'brilliant or coloured stream' [*Lyu* 1282: OW *lliw*, 'colour'].

†**Lewes** Sx 1086, 'burial mounds', alluding to the many tumuli in the area. Singular spellings occur among the early forms, and the name may have originally referred to one notable burial mound at which the local community met, or near which they settled; the present plural may have developed quite accidentally, or may have seemed more appropriate because of the numerous tumuli [*Læwe, Læwes* c 959: OE *hlǣw*].

Lewis *isld* Ros, possibly 'marshy place' [*Leodus* c 1100, *Leoghuis* 1449: G *leoghuis*].

Lewisham K/GL, 'Lēofsa's homestead' [*Levesham* 1086: OE *hām*].

Leyton Ess/GL 1226, 'farm on the river Lea'. Dialect differences probably account for the variation between this name and Luton Bd (q v) [*Lugetune* c 1050: OE *tūn*]. See also Lea *riv*.

Lezant Co, 'saint's enclosure' [*Lansant* 1276: Co *lan*, *sant*].

Lezayre IOM. See Kirk Christ Lezayre.

Libberton Lnk, **Liberton** MLo, probably 'barley farm on a hillside' [1. *Libertun* c 1186, 2. *Libertun* 1128: OE *hlið*, *bere-tūn*].

†**Lichfield** St, 'open country by the wood called *Licced*'. OE *Licced* has a history going back to the fourth-century Antonine Itinerary, in which it appears as *Letoceto*, a British name meaning 'grey

wood' [*Liccidfeld* c 730: B *lēto-*, *cēd*, OE *feld*]. See also Lytchett Matravers Do.

Liddisdale Rox, 'valley of river Liddel'. This is a tautological name, as Liddel itself means 'valley of river *Hlyde*, i e noisy stream' [*Lidelesdale* 1179: OE *hlȳde, dæl*].

Limbury Bd, 'fortified place on river Lea' [*Lygeanburgh* 571: OE *burh*]. See also Leyton, Luton.

Limerick Lim, 'bare patch of ground' [*Luimneach* 11c: OI *luimne*, dim. of *lom*, 'bare', *-ach*].

†**Lincoln** LLi, 'Roman colony at *Lindo*, i e lake place'. There was probably a settlement called *Lindo* before the establishment of the colony of veterans at the end of the first century AD. The county name **Lincolnshire** dates from the eleventh century, but **Lindsey**, 'island about Lindon' is mentioned by Bede in the eighth century. Lindsey, an Anglo-Saxon kingdom in early times, preserved its identity as an administrative unit for a millennium and a half. As the **Parts of Lindsey** it was a county until 1974 (the other Parts in Lincolnshire being Holland and Kesteven) and was subdivided into North, South, and West Ridings, Riding being for ON *þriðjung* 'third part' [1. *Lindon* c 150, *Lindocolina* c 730, *Lincolnescire* 1016, 3. *Lindissi* c 730: Lat *colonia*, B *lindo-*, OE *scir*, *ēg*].

Lindisfarne Nb, 'island of the Lindsey travellers'. The name suggests either a migration of Lindsey folk to the island, or regular traffic, possibly by sea [*Lindisfarena Ea* c 890: OE *faran*, *ēg*].

†**Lindsey (Parts of)**. See Lincoln.

Linlithgow WLo, 'lake by Lithgow, i e moist hollow'. Increasing precision in place-names is often only attained by the addition of components. Here, Lithgow seems to have been the original name of a somewhat damp area; within this area was a lake, to which the name Llyn-Lithgow ('Lake Lithgow') was applied. When a settlement was established by the lake it might have been possible to add yet another element, but evidently the name was regarded as by then quite long enough [*Linlidcu* c 1138: OW *linn*, W *llaith, cau*].

Liscard Ch 1558, 'hall by a rock'. The rock mentioned was probably that later known as Stonebank Hill. The syllable *-ne-* in some early forms is the OW definite article [*Lisnekarke* 13c: OW *lis*, 'court, hall', *carreg*, 'rock'].

Liscolman Wic, 'fort of the sons of Colman'. Colman is said to have been a king in south Leinster in the fifth century [*Lismacluman* c 1200: OI *lios*, 'fort'].

Liskeard Co, 'court of Carrud' — or 'court of the free stronghold'. Cornish *lys-* is often followed by a personal name, indicating ownership of the important residence or fortified place; in this name it is not clear whether the second component is a compound (*car-ruid*) meaning 'free stronghold or town' or a personal name. The town was the most important in the hundred of West Wivelshire [*Lyscerruyt* 11c: Co *lys, car, ruid*].

Lismore Wat, 'great enclosure or fortification' [OI *lias, mor*].

Liss Ha, 'court' [*Lis* 1086: OW *lis*].

Listowel Ker, 'Tuathal's fort' [*Lios-Tuathail* n d: OI *lias*].

Littlehampton Sx, 'small homestead', designated *Little-* in order to distinguish it from Southampton [*Hantone* 1086, *Lyttelhampton* 1482: OE *lytel, hām-tūn*].

†Liverpool La, 'clotted pool'. Water may be so described if it is exceptionally weedy or heavily polluted, and the Red Sea was called the Liversea in the sixteenth century. The pool, beside which the town grew, was a tidal creek [*Liuerpul* c 1190: OE *lifer*, *pōl*].

Liza *riv* Cu, 'bright river'. Names of the same derivation — *Ljosa* and *Lysa* — occur in Iceland and Norway [*Lesagh* 1294: ON *lióss*, 'bright', *á*].

Lizard Co, 'high court' [*Lisart* 1086: OCo *lis*, *art*].

Llanandras Rad, 'church of St Andrew', the Welsh name for Presteigne (q v) and the equivalent of Kirkandrers Kcb and Kirkandreas IOM [*Llanandras* 1566: W *llan*, 'enclosure, church'].

Llanasa Flt, 'church of St Asaph'. This sixth-century saint was almost certainly the founder of the monastery at Llanelwy (q v) [*Llanassa* 1254: W *llan*].

Llanbedr Pont Steffan Crd. See Lampeter.

Llandaf Glm, 'church on the river Taf'. As may be seen from this name, W *llan*- is not always followed by a personal name though when the specifying element is a river-name there is always a suspicion that the first component was originally *nant*- 'valley' as in Llanthony Mon (q v) or Lanteglos Co ('valley of the church': *Nanseglos* 1309). There is no evidence of this in Llandaf, however, which was *Lanntaf* in the twelfth century. The river-name means 'stream' [*Lanntaf* c 1150, *Landaph* 1191: W *llan*].

Llanddyfri Crm (properly Llanymddyfri), 'church near the stream'. The Anglicised form, Llandovery, attempts to represent

the pronunciation—with -*dove* rhyming with *love* [*Llanamdewri* 12c, *Llanymddyvri* c 1470: W *llan*, *am*, *dwfr*].

Llandeilo Crm, 'church of Teilo'. The Anglicised spelling, Llandilo, corresponds to the local pronunciation. This name is found elsewhere in Wales, and the Carmarthenshire place was distinguished by the addition *Mawr* 'great' from the Middle Ages until as late as the seventeenth century [*Lanteliau Maur* 1130 : W *llan*, *mawr*].

Llandough Glm, 'church of Docco' [*Landochan* 1106, *Landough* 1427: W *llan*].

Llandrindod Wells Rad, 'Trinity church by the springs'. The reference to the chalybeate springs here occurs only in late forms of the name, which has itself been changed from an earlier *Llanddwy*, 'God's church', as *Lando* 1291 testifies [*Llandynddod* 1535, *Llandrindod* c 1555: W *llan*, *trindod*].

Llandudno Crn 1291, 'church of Tudno'. Like many other saints immortalised in place-names, Tudno is a shadowy figure of whom only legendary stories are told [W *llan*].

†Llanelli Crm 1553, 'church of Elli'. Elli is said to have been one of the daughters of the legendary king Brychan [*Lan Elli* c 1173: W *llan*].

Llanelwy Flt, 'church on river Elwy, i e driving river' [*Lanhelwy* 1345: W *llan*].

Llanfair Mer, 'Mary's church'. This name occurs so frequently in Wales that it is not surprising that it has to be qualified by various additions. These may be local, e g Llanfair Caereinion Mgm, 'Llanfair by Einion's fort', or descriptive, eg Llanfairfechan Crn, 'little Llanfair'. It has been said that the dedication became common when Anglo-Norman ecclesiastical pressure brought about the replacement of many obscure Welsh saints' names by that of the Blessed Virgin—*Mair*, becoming *Fair* in compounds [W *llan*].

Llanfairpwllgwyngyllgogerychwyrndrobwllllandysiliogogogoch Agl, 'St Mary's church by Pwllgwyngyll, i e the white hazel pool'. Clearly this is the meaning of only part of the name, but it should be stated that only this portion is an authentic designation for the place. The remainder of the name was added by way of a joke in the nineteenth century. The additions can be explained as follows: *goger y chwyrn drobwll* means 'near the fierce whirlpool', referring to Pwll Ceris in the Menai Strait; Llandysilio is a parish adjacent to Llanfair, but it is not identical with Llandysilio-Gogo ('Tysilio's church by the cave'), which is in Cardiganshire; the termination -*goch* has no significance as part of a place-name, and seems to have been added as a derisive echo to the (and preceding inappropriate) -*gogo*. The superfluous syllables doubtless occasioned great hilarity when they were first proposed, but possibly the practical joker was somewhat dismayed when they were regarded as genuine, and little harm is done to (or by) those who regularly visit this place for the sake of its record-breaking name [W *llan*].

Llanfair-ym-Muallt Bre, 'Marychurch in the cow pasture'. Only the second part of this name is used in the Anglicised **Builth Wells**. The Welsh *buellt* is a compound of *bu* 'cow' and *gwelt* 'pasture', the modern spelling being due to a confusion with *allt* 'hill' [*Lanveir in Bueld* 1271: W *llan*, B **bow-gelt*].

Llanfihangel *freq*, 'Michael's church'. W *Mihangel* (mutated in compounds to -*fihangel*) is derived from the Latin impacted compound *Michangelus* (*Michael* + *angelus*) 'Michael the angel'.

For several places with this name the English form used is Michaelston, e g Michaelston-le-pit Glm (q v) [W *llan*]. See also Michaelston-le-Pit (s v Michaelchurch).

Llanfyllin Mgm, 'Myllin's church' [*Llanvelig* 1254: W *llan*].

Llangarren He, **Llangefni** Agl 1566: 'church by river Garren', 'church by river Cefni' respectively. Garren means 'crane stream'; Cefni is possibly 'stream from the ridge' [*Lan Garan* c 1150, *Llangevni* 1254: W *llan*, *garan*, *cefn*].

Llangollen Den 1391, 'Collen's church' [*Lancollien* 1234: W *llan*].

Llangrove He, 'long grove'. The spelling of the first element in this entirely English name has been affected by that of the common Welsh *llan-* [*Longe grove* 1372: OE *lang*, *grāf*].

Llangstone Mon, '(place at) the long stone', probably alluding to a standing stone. Like Llangrove, this purely English name is spelt as though it were a compound of *llan-* [*Langeston* c 1280: OE *lang*, *stān*].

Llangwathan Pmb. See Roberton.

Llanidloes Mgm 1603, 'church of Idloes' [*Lanidloes* 1254: W *llan*].

Llanrothal He, 'Rethal's church'. The identity of the saint is as uncertain as the exact spelling of his or her name. Forms with Ri-, Re-, and Ro- occur among early spellings [*Lan Ridol* c 1150: W *llan*].

Llanrwst Den 1560, 'church of Grwst' [*Lhannruste* 1254: W *llan*].

Llansantffraed Bre, 'church of St Bride'. Only Bride receives the title of *saint* in

Welsh place-names; in other counties are **Llansantffraed-in-Elvel** Rad, **Llansantffraid** Crd, **Llansantffraid-Glan-Conwy** Den, and **Llansantffraid-ym-Mechain** Mgm [W *llan*].

Llanthony Mon, 'valley of the river Honddu'. In this, as in other *Llan-* names compounded with river-names, *Llan-* has replaced *Nant-* ('valley'). Lanthony Gl, was the site of a daughter priory of the monastery at Llanthony [1. *Lanthotheni* 12c, 2. *Lantoeni* 1130: W *nant*].

Llantriddyd Glm, 'Rhirid's valley'. Despite the presence of *Llan-* spellings among the early forms of this name, it has been strongly argued (by Gwynedd Pierce, PNDPH 123-4) that *Nant-* was the original first element, and the connexion of 'Trithyd, a pupil of St Illtud' with the place and its name is entirely fanciful. Nevertheless, Rhirid has not been identified [*Landrirede* c 1126, *Nantririd* 1545: W *nant*].

Llantrisant Glm, 'church of the three saints', viz Gwynno, Dyfodwg, and Illtud [*Landtrissen* 1246: W *llan*].

Llanvair Waterdine Sa, 'St Mary's church in the river valley'. The place is beside the river Teme. Although Waterdine appears to be a mere distinguishing element, evidence for this part of the name antedates that for the Llanvair component by about two centuries [*Watredene* 1086, *Thlanveyr* 1284: W *llan*, OE *wæter, denu*].

Llanwarne He, 'church by the alder swamp' [*Ladvwern* 1086: W *llan, gwern*].

Llanwrtyd Wells Bre, 'church of Gwrtud'. The addition of *Wells* took place in the nineteenth century, the heyday of the watering places possessing chalybeate springs [*Llanwrtid* 1553: W *llan*].

Llanymynech Sa, 'monks' church' [*Llanemeneych* 1254: W *llan, mynach*].

Llyfni *riv* Crn, **Llynfi** *riv* Bre, —*riv* Glm: 'smooth-flowing one' [1. *Lleueni* 1578, 2. *Lyfni* c 1150; 3. *Thleweny* 1314: W *llyfn*].

Loanend Nb, **Loanhead** MLo: '(place at) the end of a lane'. *Loan* is currently used in northern dialects for StdE *lane* [2. *Loneheid* 1618: OE *lane, ende, hēafod*].

†**Lochaber** Inv, '(place by) lake at the confluence' [G *loch*, P *aber*].

Lochalsh *lke* Inv, possibly 'foaming lake' [*Lochalche* 1449 : G *loch, aillseach*].

Lochgelly Fif, '(place by) the shining lake' [*Lochgellie* 1606: G *loch, geal*].

Lochgilphead Arg, '(place at) the head of Loch Gilp, i e the chisel-shaped lake' [*Lochgilpshead* 1650: G *loch, gilb*].

Lochinvar Kcb 1540, '(place at) the loch on the height' [G *loch an bharra*].

Lochy *riv* Inv, 'the dark one' [*Locha* 1472: G *lochaidh*].

Lockerbie Dmf, 'Locard's farm' [*Lokardebi* 1306: ON *bý*].

Loddon *riv* Brk-Ha, 'muddy one' [*Lodena* c 1220: B **lutá*, 'mud'].

Lofthouse WRY (x 2), **Loftsome** ERY, **Loftus** NRY: '(place by) a house or houses with an upper floor'. When most dwellings had only ground-floor rooms, a two-floored house was sufficiently unusual to be a landmark. Early spellings vary between singular and plural forms, the latter surviving in Loftsome [1. *Lofthose* 1086, 2. *Lofthus* 1086, *Lofthusum* c 1145, 3. *Lofthus* 1208, 4. *Loctehusum* 1086, *Lofthus* c 1175: ON *lopthús*].

Logie Buchan Abd. See Buchan.

Lomond, Ben *mtn* Dnb, **Lomond Hills** Fif: 'beacon hill'. Loch Lomond derives its name from the adjoining mountain [3. *Lochlomond* c 1340: G *beinn, loch,* OW *loimon*].

Londesborough ERY, 'Lothen's fortified place' [*Lodenesburg* 1086: OE *burh*].

London, meaning uncertain. Traditional theories of the etymology of the original name are no longer accepted. Its obscurity may in fact result from the very antiquity of the settlement itself—possibly antedating the Celtic language which provides the earliest recorded forms. Terminations, such as *-burh* and *-ceaster*, were added by the Anglo-Saxons, but the name soon settled down to a spelling differing little from that of today and remarkably similar to the one used in Roman times [*Londinium* c 115, *Lundenne, Lundenceaster* c 890].

†**Londonderry** Lon, originally **Derry,** 'oak wood'. The wood itself survived for six or more centuries after the name was first recorded. Like other fairly common names, Derry required distinguishing additions, the first being *Calgagh,* a personal name meaning 'fierce warrior'. In 546 Columba established a monastery there, and the name was changed to Derry-Columcille at some time between that date and the tenth century. When James I granted a charter authorising a plantation by merchants of London, in 1609, that name was prefixed [*Daire-Calgaich* 7c: I *doire*].

Longford Lfd, 'fortified place' [I *longphort*].

Longhirst Nb, **Longhope** Gl, **Longleat** W: 'long wooded hill', 'long valley', 'long stream' respectively [*Langherst* 1200, 2. *Hope* 1086, 3. *Langlete* 1235: OE *lang, hyrst, hop,* (*ge*)*læt*].

Longmynd Sa, 'the long hill'. A hybrid name, as is to be expected in border country, this combines OE *lang,* 'long', with W *mynydd,* 'hill' [*Longameneda* 12c].

Looe *riv* Co, 'inlet' [*Looe* 1301: Co *lo*].

Loop Head Cla, 'headland of the leap'. About twenty-five feet beyond this promontory is a small rock. According to legend, the hero Cuchullin leaped on to the rock in order to escape from a furious woman called Mal. When the woman made the same leap, Cuchullin sprang back to the mainland; his pursuer was less agile and fell into the sea. From this exploit the place was called *Leim-Chonchuillin,* 'Cuchullin's leap'. The hero's name was less important to the Danes, however, who were satisfied with the simple term *Hlaup,* 'leap', from which the present name is derived [ON *hlaup*].

Lorne Arg, '(territory of) Loarn's tribe'. Loarn Mór, 'the great fox' son of Erc, flourished about the year 500 [*Lorne* 1304].

Lossiemouth Mor, 'mouth of the Lossie, i e river rich in plants' [G *Uisge Lossa,* 'water of herbs'].

Lostwithiel Co, 'tail of Withiel, i e upland wood'. Withiel was evidently the name of the whole district terminating at Lostwithiel [*Lostwetell* 1194: Co *lost,* 'tail', *gwydh,* 'trees' *iâl,* 'upland region'].

††**Lothian,** 'territory of Leudonus'. The identity and ethnic origin of the founder have been much debated. Lothian is now a Region comprising four Districts —†**East Lothian,** †**Midlothian,** †**West Lothian,** and †Edinburgh City [*Loonia* c 970, *Lodoneó* 1098, *Louthion* c 1200].

Loughborough Lei, 'Luhhede's fortified place'. The DB spelling in *-burne* is probably a misreading of -*burue* in a draft of the survey [*Lucteburne* 1086, *Lucteburga* c 1175: OE *burh*].

Loughrea Gal, 'grey lake' [I *Lochriabach*].

Loughton Ess, 'Luca's village' [*Lukintone* 1062: OE *tūn*].

Louth LLi, '(place on) river Lud'. The river-name means 'loud one' [*Hludensis monasterium* c 790: OE *hlūd*, 'loud'].

Louth Lth, '*Lugh* plain', the meaning of the first element being unknown [*Lughmhaigh* n d: I *magh*].

Lovat Inv, 'swampy place'. The Gaelic *lobh* means 'putrefy', suggesting the formation of peat [*Loveth* c 1235: G *lobh*, -*aid*].

Lower Bebington Ch, '(lower) farm associated with Bebba'. Like many such names, this was qualified by a great variety of terms through its 700 years or so of history: *Inferior* (13c), *Subterior* (13c), *Nether* (13-19c), *Church* (13-17c), and *Kirk* (15c) [*Bebinton* c 1100: OE -*ingtūn*].

Lowestoft Sf, 'Hloðver's dwelling-place' [*Lothu Wistoft* 1086, *Lowistoft* 1219: ON *topt*].

Lowis Slk. See Yarrow.

Low Peak. See Peak Db.

Lowther Hills Dmf, meaning uncertain.

Lowther *riv* We, possibly 'foaming river' [*Lauther* c 1170: ON *lauðn* 'foam', *á*, 'river'].

Lud *riv* LLi. See Louth.

Ludgarshall Gl, **Ludgershall** Bk, **Ludgershall** W, **Luggashall** Sx: 'secluded place

with a trapping spear'. A remote spot or nook would be suitable for such a purpose. For a long time a much-debated problem, the interpretation of these names is now generally agreed on [1. *Lutegareshale* 1220, 2. *Lutegasheale* 1015, 3. *Litlegarsele* 1086, *Lutegareshala* 1190, 4. *Lutesgareshale* 12c: OE *lūtegār*, *healh*].

Ludlow Sa, 'mound by a rapid' [*Ludelawe* 1138: OE *hlūde* 'loud one', *hlāw*].

Lugnaquillia *mtn* Wic, 'hollow of the cocks'. The mountain seems to have been named from a small area which was doubtless much frequented by hunters of grouse [*Logney O Nill* 1617, *Lugnaquilla* 1760: I *lug-na-geoilleach*].

Luguvallium. See Carlisle.

Lundy *isld* D, 'puffin island'. Though rare on the mainland, puffins frequently visit the island. The name is Scandinavian, as are those of other islands across the Bristol Channel [*Lundey* c 1145: ON *lundi*, *ey*].

Lune *riv* (1) La-We, (2) NRY: 'health-giving river', perhaps alluding to a deity invoked on behalf of the sick. Lonsdale is 'valley of the Lune (1)', and Lancaster is 'Roman military station on the Lune' [1. *Loin* c 1158, 2. *Loon* 1201, 3. *Lanesdale* 1086: OW **lon*, 'health-giving'].

Lurgan Dwn, 'shin', a term applied to a long, low hill [I *lurgan*].

Luss Dnb, '(place of) plants' [*Lus* 1225: G *lus*].

Luton Bd 1195, 'farm on the river Lea'. Early forms show numerous spelling variations (*Lygetun* 792, *Lygtun* 917, *Ligtun* 914, *Loitone* 1086, *Lytone* c 1290, *Lowton* 1291, *Leuton* 1293) and yet the name seems never to have coincided with Leyton (q v) of the same origin and meaning, though there seems to have been, briefly, some danger of confusion with Loughton (q v) in the spelling L(o)ughton 1376. [OE tūn]. See also Lea riv.

Lutterworth Lei, perhaps 'enclosure by *Hlūtre*, i e clean one'. It is suggested that the river Swift may have been earlier known as Hlūtre, from OE hlūttor, 'pure, clean' [Lutresurde 1086: OE worð].

Luxulian Co, 'Sulian's monastery' [Lauxsolian 1329: Co loc].

Lybster Cai, 'dwelling place by sheltered spot' [Libister 1538: ON hlýe (hlý), bólstaðr].

Lyme Forest. See Newcastle-under-Lyme.

Lyme Regis D, 1285, 'royal borough on river Lyme'. The river-name means 'flood' [Lim 774, Lime 1086: L regis 'of the king'].

Lyndon R, 'lime-tree hill' [Lindon 1167: OE lind, dūn].

Lyn riv 1282, D, So, 'torrent' [OE hlynn].

Lynmouth D, **Lynton** D: '(place at) mouth of river Lyn' and 'farm on river Lyn' respectively [Lymmouth 1330, Linton(a) 1086: OE mūða, tūn].

Lynn. See King's Lynn.

Lyonshall He. See Leominster.

Lytchett Matravers Do, **Lytchett Minster** Do: Lytchett is almost certainly from B Lētocēto-, 'grey wood', as in Lichfield St (q v). Matravers alludes to the family of Hugh Maltravers, who held the manor in 1086. Minster means '(with a) church' [Lichet 1086, Luchet Mautravers 1291, Lyceminstr' 1253: OE mynster].

Lyth We, **Lytham** La, **Lythe** NRY: 'place on slope(s)'. The Westmorland and North Riding names are probably from the ON word hlið; the Lancs name is from the dative plural hliðum, OE hlið [1. Le Lyth 1247, 2. Lidun 1086, Lithum 1201, 3. Lid 1086, Lith 1194: OE hlið, ON hlið].

Mablethorpe LLi, 'Malbert's secondary settlement', the OF personal name indicating a post-Conquest formation as are also Countesthorpe Lei (q v), **Donisthorpe** Lei ('Durand's thorp'), and **Herringthorpe** WRY ('thorp in tenure of Jordanus Heryng'). Coastal settlements such as Mablethorpe would often be dependencies of larger places inland [Malbertorp 1086: ON þorp].

†**Macclesfield** Ch, 'Maccel's open land', [Maclesfeld 1086: OE feld].

Macduff Bnf, 'place named in honour of the earls of Fife' and said to have been named by James Duff, earl of Fife in 1783.

Machers, The Wig, 'plains' [G machair].

Machynlleth Mgm, 'Cynllaith's plain' [Machenleyd 1254: B *magos].

Macosquin Lon, 'Cosgran's plain' [Magh-Cosgrain n d: I magh].

Maentwrog Mer, 'stone of Twrog' [W maen].

Maesteg Glm, 'fine field'. Although a fairly recent settlement, this place has preserved the name of the farm on which it is sited; 'Lower Fine Field' is on record from the sixteenth century [Maes tege issa 1543: W maes, teg].

†**Maghera** Lon, 'plain' [I machaire].

Maia, 'larger (place)', the Romano-British name for the settlement at

Bowness Cu (q v) [*Maio, Maia* c 670: B **māios* comparative of **māros*, 'great'].

†**Maidenhead** Brk, 'landing-place of the maidens'. The OE termination *-hȳð* takes on a great variety of modern forms, as Chelsea, Rotherhithe, Putney, Erith, Lambeth, and Riverhead (qq v) bear witness; this variety is reflected in the early spellings of Maidenhead, the terminations of which between the thirteenth and fifteenth centuries include *-heg, -huth, -heth, -hee, -hus, -hith,* and *-hethe. Maid-* or *Maiden-* constantly appears, though the exact significance is obscure [*Maidenhee* 1202, *Maydenhith* 1262: OE *mægden, hȳð*].

Maidstone K, 'stone of the maidens', probably alluding to a place of assembly for ritual or superstitious purposes [*Medestan* 1086: OE *mægden, stān*].

Maidwell Nth. See Childwall La.

Mainland *isld* Ork,—*isld* Zet: 'principal country or district', applied in these instances to the largest islands in the groups [*Meginland* c 1150: ON *megin, land*].

Makerfield La. See Ince.

Malborough D. See Marlborough.

Malden Sr, †**Maldon** Ess: 'hill surmounted by a cross', [1. *Meldone* 1086, 2. *Mældun* 913: OE *mæl, dūn*].

Maldwyn. See Montgomery.

Mallaig Inv, 'gull bay' [ON *mar,* NG *aig* < ON *vík*].

†**Malling** K, 'Mealla's people' [*Meallingas* c 950: OE *-ingas*]. See also Tonbridge.

Mallow Crk, 'plain of the river Allow', the meaning of the river-name being uncertain [I *magh*].

Malmesbury W, 'Mailduf's fortress', the personal name here being reasonably certain despite a number of different medieval spellings. The name of abbot Ealdhelm has become involved and accounts for the medial *-m-. Mailduf* or *Maldulf* can be seen as Anglo-Saxon attempts to render the original OI personal name Maeldub or Maelduib [*Maildufi urbs* c 730, *Maldulfes burgh* c 890: OE *burh*].

Malpas Brk,—Ch,—Co,—Mon: '(place of) difficult passage', the widespread use of this OF term suggesting that it was early adopted into the English vocabulary. Most of the names allude to marshy ground or muddy roads; the Cheshire name replaced a former one meaning 'at the deep valley containing a stream' (*Depenbech*) and the Monmouthshire place is by wet ground through which the old road passed [1. *Maupas* 14c, 2. *Malpas* c 1125, 4. (*de*) *Malo Passu* 1291: OF *mal, pas*].

Maltby LLi,—NRY,—WRY, **Maltby le Marsh** LLi: 'Malti's farm' [1-5, *Maltebi* 1086: ON *bȳ*].

Malton NRY, 'middle farm', the OE name having been Scandinavianised, as in the more usual Melton (q v) [*Maltune* 1086: OE *middel* (ON *meðal*), OE *tūn*].

Malvern Wo, 'bare hill', in full is **Great Malvern,** to distinguish the place from **Little Malvern** Wo. A related name is **Malvern Link** Wo, 'hill-slope of Malvern' [1. *Malferna* 1086, 2. *Parve Malvernie* 1232, 3. *Link* 1215; W *moel, bryn*, OE *hlinc*].

Mamble Wo, perhaps '(place of) Momele tribe, i e dwellers in the breast-shaped hills' [*Momelagemæra* c 957]. See also Mam Tor, Manchester.

Mam Tor *mtn* Db, possibly 'breast,

(-shaped) hill', [*Manhill* 1577, *Mantaur* 1630, *Mam Tor* 1668: B *mammā, OE *torr*].

Man, Isle of, said to be 'land of Manannan', from the Irish god Manannan mac Lir, king of the Land of Promise. The adjective *Manx* is derived from ON *mansk* and thus reflects the great Scandinavian influence on the language and names of the island, the Celtic vernacular of which, Manx, is related to the Gaelic formerly spoken in south-west Scotland. Manx Gaelic is no longer a living language [OI *Manu, Inis Manann*, MxG *Ellan Vannin*].

Manacles, The Co, 'church rock' [Co *men, eglos*].

Mancetter Wa, 'Roman station at *Manduessedum*', a name formed, like Manchester, Richborough, and Lichfield, by the addition of an OE termination to all or part of the Celtic name. *Manduessedum* seems to mean 'horse chariot'; though the precise significance of this seems obscure, a parallel can be cited in *Tarvessedum*, 'ox chariot or waggon', the name of a hill-feature in Switzerland, presumably alluding to its shape. This name may perhaps be similarly explained. [*Manduessedum* 4c, *Manecestre* 1195: B **mandu-*, Gaulish *essedum*, OE *ceaster*].

Manchester La, 'Roman fort at *Mamucium*', the meaning of the Romano-British name being obscure; the first element may be B *mammā, as in Mamble (q v) [*Mamucio* 4c, *Mameceaster* 923: OE *ceaster*].

††Manchester, Greater (Metropolitan county): the county includes, in addition to Manchester and Salford, the Lancs towns of Bolton, Bury, Rochdale, and Wigan, and the Altrincham and Stockport areas of Cheshire.

Manduessedum. See Mancetter.

Mangotsfield Gl, 'Mangod's open land' [*Mangodesfelle* 1086: OE *feld*].

Manningtree Ess, 'Manning's tree' [*Manitre* 1274, *Manyngtre* 14c: OE *trēow*].

†Mansfield Nt, 'open land by the river Maun', the river-name being perhaps an adaptation of a former name of a hill, *Mammesheud*, '*Mam* headland', possibly misread as 'source of (river) *Mam*'. **Mansfield Woodhouse** Nt is 'woodland hamlet settled from Mansfield' [1. *Mamesfelde* 1086, *Mamesfeld* 1202, 2. *Wodehuse* 1230, *Mamesfeud Wodehus* 1280: OE *feld, wudu, hūs*].

Mar Abd, '(land of the) Mar tribe', a name which is itself derived from a personal name Marsos.

Marazion Co, 'little market', the alternative name, **Market Jew,** 'south market', having a separate history and not being, as was once thought, a mere alteration of Marazion [1. *Marghasbighan* 1372, 2. *Marchadion* 1291: Co *marchas, bichan, dyow*].

March C, '(place on a) boundary' [*Merce* 1086: OE *mearc*].

Margate K, 'gap in cliffs at The Mare', rather than, as has been proposed, 'gap leading to the sea'. Coastal names are frequently named from off-shore features such as rocks, and the suggestion here is that a mare-shaped rock near the site of the present town has provided the name [*Meregate* 1254: OE *mere, geat*].

Margidunum. See Newark.

Market †Bosworth Lei, **Market Deeping** LKe, **Market Drayton** Sa, **Market †Harborough** Lei, **Market Lavington** W, **Market Overton** R, **Market Rasen** LLi, **Market Weighton** ERY: 'place with a market', the prefixed term serving to distinguish some names from places with similar appellations. Market Bosworth, 'Bosa's enclosure' is thus set off against Husbands Bosworth (q v), Market Deeping, 'deep fen' against other Kesteven Deepings, and Market Lavington, 'farm of Lava's people', against Bishop's Lavington. Market Harborough is 'market place on hill where oats were grown'; Overton occurs fairly frequently and means 'upper village'; Market Rasen is by a 'plank bridge', and Market Weighton is 'market place at an outlying homestead' [1. *Boseworde* 1086, 3. *Draitune* 1086, 4. *Hauerberga* 1177, 5. *Laventone* 1086, 6. *Marketesoverton* 1200, 7. *Resne* 1086, 8. *Wicstun* 1086: ME *merket*, OE *worð*, *dræg*, **haefera*, *beorg*, *uferra*, *ræsn*, *wic*, *tūn*].

Market Jew. See Marazion.

Markinch Fif, 'horse meadow' [*Marchinke* 1055, *Markynchs* c 1290: G *marc*, *innis*].

Markyate Hrt, '(place by) boundary gate', on the Beds-Herts border [*Mark ate* c 1130: OE *mearc*, *geat*].

Marlborough W, 'Marl's hill' or possibly 'gentian hill', the name being identical in origin with **Malborough** D [1. *Merleberge* 1086, 2. *Malleberge* 1270: OE *mergelle*, *beorg*].

Marlow Bk, '(place on or by) bed of a former lake', the second element meaning 'remnant, what is left' [*Merelafan* 1015: OE *mere*, *lāf*].

Marple Ch, '(place on) boundary stream', viz the river Goyt, the county boundary [*Merpille* 13c, *Merpel* 13c, *Marpell* 13c: OE (*ge*)*mǣre*, *pyll*].

Marscow (Skye) Inv, 'sea-mews' wood' [ON *már*, *skgór*].

Marshfield Gl, 'open land by a marsh' [*Meresfeld* 1086: OE *mersc*, *feld*].

Marston *freq*, 'farm by a marsh', distinguished in some counties by manorial and other suffixes [OE *mersc*, *tūn*].

Martock So, '(holy) place by a lake', with OE *stoc* as second element, the *s*-omitted owing to Norman influence [*Mertoch* 1086: OE *mere*, *stoc*].

Marylebone Mx, 'stream by St Mary's church', replacing **Tyburn** owing to the opprobrious associations of the latter. Because of the church dedication the form St Marylebone is also used, *le-bone* being an alteration due to popular etymology, the phrase presumably being taken to mean 'blessed' [*Tyborne al Maryborne* 1490: OE *burna*].

Maryport Cu 1762, 'port named in honour of Mary Senhouse'. This was a renaming of the former *Elnefoot*, 'land at the mouth of river Ellen', to commemorate the wife of Humphrey Senhouse, who constructed the harbour here in the middle of the eighteenth century. The element *foot* in the older name means 'land at an estuary' in a few other names in northern England and in Scotland, e g Chalkfoot Cu, near the mouth of Chalk Beck [2. *Aylnfoote* 1656, *Elnefoot* c 1745: OE *port*, *fōt*].

Marytavy D. See Tavistock.

Masham NRY, 'Mæssa's homestead' [*Massan* 1086: OE *hām*].

Matlask Nf, 'assembly ash', i e ash-tree at which meetings were held; the second element has been modified under Scandinavian influence [*Matelasc* 1086: OE *mæþl*, *æsc*].

Matlock Db, 'assembly oak' (cf Matlask) [*Meslach* 1086, *Matlac* 1196: OE *mæþl*, *āc*].

Maughold IOM, 'place (with church) dedicated to St Maccul', celebrating the fifth-century missionary who is credited with the division of the Isle of Man into parishes. According to legend Maccul was a robber converted by St Patrick. This name really belongs to the numerous group of hybrid compound names in *Kirk-* to be found in IOM. Dr Gelling (PN IOM 168) observes that this is the earliest *Kirk-* name appearing in vernacular form [*Ecclesia Sancti Maugholdi* 13c, *Kirkemahald* 1302: ON *kirkja*].

Mawddach *riv* Mer, 'little (river of) Mawdd'. See Barmouth.

Maxwelltown Kcb, 'village at Maxwell, i e pool of Maccus' [*Mackeswel* 1144, *Maxwell* 1190: OE *wella, tūn*].

May, Island of *isld* Fif 1165, 'sea-mew island' [*Mai* 1143, *Maeyar* 1250: ON *már, ey*].

Maybole Ayr, 'plain or moor of danger' [*Mayboill* 1275: G *magh, baoghail*].

Mayfield St, 'open land on which madder grew', alluding to *Rubia peregrina*, associated with limestone areas in the wetter western parts of Britain [*Medeveld*, 1086: OE *mæddre, feld*].

Mayfield Sx, 'open land where mayweed grew'. Other references to this plant (*Anthemis cotula*) occur in **Mayford** Sr, **Maytham** K and in the lost names *Mægþeford* in Abingdon Brk and *Maȝþeford* in Norton Gl [1. *Magefeud* c 1200, 2. *Maiford* 1212: OE *mægðe feld, ford, hamm*].

Maynooth Kld, 'Nuet's plain' [*Magh Nuaddhat* n d: I *magh*].

Mayo Myo, 'plain of the yew' [I *magh, eo*].

Maytham K. See Mayfield Sx.

Meall Dearg *mtn* Pth, 'red mountain' [G *meall*, 'lump, round hill', *dearg*].

Meall Dubh *mtn* Arg,——*mtn* Inv,—— *mtn* Ros: 'black mountain' [G *meall, dubh*].

Meall Garbh *mtn* Arg,——*mtn* Pth: 'rough mountain' [G *meall, garbh*].

Meall Geal *mtn* (Lewis) Ros, 'white mountain' [G *meall, geal*].

Meall Gorm *mtn* Abd,——*mtn* Ros: 'blue mountain' [G *meall, gorm*].

Meall Meadhonach *mtn* Sut, 'middle mountain' [G *meall, meadhon*].

Mealrigg Cu 1576, 'middle ridge', possibly a Scandinavianised form of OE *Midelhrycg* [*Midelrig*' 1189, *Melderige* 1439; OE *midel, hrycg*, cf ON *meðal, hryggr*].

Mearns Ang, 'land of the steward', a sub-area of Angus; together they made of old the province of *Cirech*, from a personal name meaning 'crested' [*Moerne* 12c: G *maor*].

Mease *riv* St-Lei, 'mossy (river)'. **Measham** Lei, 'homestead on river Mease' stands on the river [1. *Meys* 1247, 2. *Messeham* 1086: OE *mēos, hām*].

Meath, 'middle (place)', the fifth province of Ireland in the early Middle Ages, the others being Connaught, Leinster, Munster, and Ulster (qq v); Meath was almost certainly an addition—probably in the fifth century AD—representing a large settlement by invaders from the north [*Mide* 9c: I *mide*].

Meaux ERY, 'lake with sandy shores', the French appearance of the modern form being due to an early confusion between -*el*- and -*eu*- spellings (cf -*feud* in the early forms of some names in -field) [*Melse* 1086: ON *melr, sær*].

Meden riv Nt, 'middle one', being the middle of the three rivers (the others being Poulter and Maun) which together form the Idle. The modern form is due to misreading of spellings in -me or -ime, a similar confusion being found in the river †**Medina** Wt, which divides that island into two approximately equal parts [1. *Medine* 1227, *Medme* c 1250, *Medom* 1393, 2. *Medine* 1196, *Medeme* 13c, *Medme* c 1279: OE *medume*].

Mediolanum, 'in the middle of the plain', a Roman station near Whitchurch Sa [*Mediolano* 4c: B *medi-*, **landā*].

†**Medway** riv Sx-K, 'sweet river', the second element possibly having some general meaning such as 'that which carries', as in the river-names Wey and Wye (qq v). The first element is the Celtic term for 'mead' [*Meduuuæian* 764, *Medeuuæge* c 780, *Medwæg* 894: B *medu*, OW **weg*].

Meesden Hrt, 'mossy hill' [*Mesdone* 1086; OE *mēos*, *dūn*].

Megdale Dmf, **Meigle** Pth: 'boggy meadow'. The first element is found also in Strathmiglo Fif (q v) [2. *Migdele* c 1200, *Mygghil* 1378: OW *mig-*, W *dol*].

Melbourn C, 'orach stream', referring to *Atriplex patula*, a plant of the beetroot family [*Meldeburna* 970: OE *melde*, *burna*].

Melbourne Db, 'mill stream' [*Mileburne* 1086, *Mel(e)burna* 1163: OE *myln*, *burna*].

Melbourne ERY, 'middle stream' [*Middelburne* 1086, *Medelbornn* 1285: OE *middel*/ON *meðal*, OE *burna*].

Melchet Ha, possibly '(place by) bare wood' [*Milchete* 1086: B **maol*, **cēd-*].

Meldreth C, '(place by) mill stream' [*Melreda* c 1080: OE *myln*, *rið*].

Mellor Db, 'bare hill' [*Melver* 1283, *Moluer* 1330: B *mailo-*, *brigā*].

Melrose Rox, 'bare moor' [*Mailros* c 700: B *mailo-*, *ros*].

Melton Mowbray Lei, 'middle farm, in the tenure of de Moubray', showing a replacement of OE *middel* by ON *meðal*, a substitution found also in **Melton Ross** LLi, **High Melton** WRY, **West Melton** WRY, and **Great & Little Melton** Nf [1. *Medeltone* 1086, *Melton Moubray* 1284, 2. *Medeltone* 1086, *Melton Roos* 1402, 3. *Middeltun* 1086, *Medeltone* 1086, *Melton le Heyg* 1285, 4. *Middeltun* 1086, 5. *Middilton* c 1060, *Methelton* c 1060: OE *middel*/ON *meðal*, OE *tūn*]. See also Malton.

Menai Strait Agl-Crn, 'narrow stretch of water called "stream" ', the suggested meaning being based on the supposed connexion with a root meaning 'go' giving the sense here of 'flowing water'. A feature of the strait is the swiftness of the current [*Mene* 11c, *Menei* 13c: W *men-*].

†**Mendip (Hills)** So, 'hill valley', a curious hybrid name with a seemingly paradoxical combination of elements. To the Welsh 'hill', doubtless the first designation, was added OE *hop*, 'valley', possibly because the English settlers established themselves in the valley which bisects the Mendips; the compound name was then applied to the whole area, which of course includes both hills and valleys [*Menedepe* 1185, *Menedup* 1225: W *mynydd*, OE *hop*].

Menevia, 'grove', the Latinised form of W *mynyw*, an alternative name for St Davids Pmb (q v) [*Miniu* 12c: W *mynyw*].

Meopham K, 'Meopa's homestead', the personal name being found also in **Mepal** C, 'Meopa's nook of land'

[1. *Meapaham* 788, 2. *Maphal* 1254: OE *hām, halh*].

Mercaston Db, 'Merchiaun's farm' [*Merchenestune* 1086: OE *tūn*].

Merevale Wa, 'splendid valley', an interpretation that attempts to compromise between the original form and its later development. The earliest spellings indicate that the name was then either Latin *Mira Vallis*, 'wonderful valley', or its Norman-French equivalent. Spellings in thirteenth-century documents show that the name might have developed to something like **Mirevaulx*, the termination of which may be compared with Jervaulx and Rievaulx (qq v). The existence of an OE word of similar spelling and related meaning caused the adoption of *myrig* in place of *mira*, with the result that Merevale was identified in sound and meaning with **Merryvale** He. Other names with the meaning 'pleasant valley' include **Meriden** Wa and **Merridale** St [1. *Miravall* 1148, *Mirevallis* 1154, *Mirevaus* 1232, *Murival* 1316, *Merivale* 1462, 3. *Mereden* 1230, *Murydene* 1400: L *mira, vallis*/OF *val*, OE *myrig, denu*].

Mersea Island Ess, 'island in the sea' [*Meresig* 895: OE *mere, ēg*].

Mersey *riv* Ch-La, 'river of the boundary', namely the border between Northumbria and Mercia from about 600, and subsequently that between Cheshire and Lancashire. The new Metropolitan County of ††**Merseyside** consists of Liverpool and its neighbours, including Birkenhead, St Helens, and Southport [*Mærse* 1002: OE *(ge)mǣre, ēa*].

Merther Co (x 2), 'place of martyrdom, saint's death-place, grave of a saint' [1. *Merder* 1302, *Mether* 1327, *Merthyr* 1523: Co *merther*].

Merthyr Tydfil Glm, 'Tudful's burial place' [*Merthir* 1254, *Merthyr Tutuil* 13c: W *merthyr*].

Merton D,—Nf,—O,—Sr: 'farm by a lake' [1. *Mertone* 1086, 2. *Meretuna* 1086, 3. *Meretone* 1086, 4. *Merantune* 755, *Mertone* 967: OE *mere, tūn*].

Methven Pth, 'mead stone', a British name of rather obscure significance [*Methfen* 1211: W *medd, maen*].

Methwold Nf, 'middle woodland', occupying a central position between **Hockwold** Nf, 'woodland where mallow grew', and Northwold Nf (q v) [1. *Medelwolde* c 1050, 2. *Hocuuella* 1086, *Hocwood* 1198:OE *wald, hocc, middel*/ON *meðal*]. See also Southwold Sf.

Mevagissey Co, '(church dedicated to) Mewa and Ida', the two names being joined by the Cornish conjunction *ag*, an unusual place-name element [*Mevagisi* 1410].

Mexborough WRY, 'Mēoc's fortified place' [*Mechesburg* 1086: OE *burh*].

Mey Cai, '(place) in the plain' [G *magh*].

Michaelchurch He, '(place with) church dedicated to St Michael', a dedication found also in *Michaelchurch Escley* He, on a stream called the Escley, and in *Michaelstow* Co. In Wales the characteristic form is Llanfihangel (q v), which occurs among the early forms of **Michaelston-le-pit** Glm, in which *-ton* has replaced a former *-stow*. There are places called **St Michael(s)** in Lancashire, Cornwall, and Hertfordshire [1. *Lann mihacgel cil luch* c 1150, 2. *Michaeleschirche* c 1275, 3. *Mighelestowe* 1302, 4. *Michelstowe* c 1291, *Ll. fihangel or pwll* c 1566, *Michaelston le Pitte* 1657: OE *circe, stōw, pytt, tūn*, W *llan, pwll*].

Micheldever Ha, possibly 'stream in a bog', taking both elements to be Celtic. The second is the frequently occurring British word for 'stream', found in Dover,

Andover, Candover, Calder, and Conder. The first seems to have been transformed by popular etymology owing to its similarity to OE *micel*, 'great' [*Mycendefr* 862, *Myceldefer* 901: B *micn, dubro*-].

Middle Sa, 'wood by a confluence' [*Mulleht* 1086, *Muthla* 1121: OE (*ge*) *mȳðe, lēah*].

Middleney So, '(by the) middle island' [*Midelneia* 1086: OE *middel, ēg*].

†**Middlesbrough** NRY, 'middlemost fortified place', a superlative for which not much use can be found in modern English. It is suggested that there was a district called *Middle* in the centre of which Middlesbrough was sited [*Midelesburc* c 1165: OE *midleste* (superlative of *middel*), *burh*].

Middlesex, '(territory of) the Middle Saxons', i e those between the East Saxons of Essex and the West Saxons of Berkshire and beyond. The Middle Saxons included a number of tribes whose names are embodied in those of places, e g Ealing, Mimms, and Yeading (qq v), and probably their territory extended beyond the historic county, doubtless at one time including Surrey and a part at least of Hertfordshire. It is paradoxical that the area including within its bounds such an important settlement as London and such an impressive sacred site as Harrow should have so obscure a history [*Middelseaxan* 704: OE *middel*].

Middleton *freq*, 'middle farm', distinguished in some counties by manorial, descriptive, and topographical affixes [OE *middel, tūn*].

Middlewich Ch, 'middlemost (salt-) works', i e between Northwich Ch and Nantwich Ch (qq v). In these names OE *wic* has the general sense of 'farm or premises associated with a particular activity or trade', but coincidentally specialised in Cheshire to 'salt-works' [*Wic* c 1003, *Wich* 1086, *Mildestuich* 1086, *Le Mydlestwych* 1394: OE *midleste, wic*]. See also *Salinis*.

Midhurst Sx, 'middle wooded hill' [*Middeherst* 1186: OE *middel, hyrst*].

†**Midlothian**, 'middle Lothian (q v)', the county in which Edinburgh is situated, and formerly bearing the name of the city as an alternative appellation.

Mile End Brk,—Ess,—Mx: '(place) at the end of a mile' respectively from Lambourn, Colchester, and Aldgate [1. *Mile Ende* c 1220, 2. *La Milende* 1200, 3. *La Mileende* 1441: OE *mil, ende*].

Milford Haven Pmb 1394, 'harbour at Milford, i e sandy inlet', essentially an ON name, one of many in the Irish Sea area, English *haven* being added when the Norse forms were no longer intelligible. In Welsh the estuary is **Aberdaugleddyf**, 'mouth of the two (rivers) Cleddyf'; the river-name means 'sword', the two branches being the Eastern Cleddau and the Western Cleddau [*de Milverdico portu* c 1191, *Mellferth* 1207, *Aber Dav Gleddef* 15c: ON *melr, fjorþr*, W *aber, dau*].

Millom Cu, 'at the mills', from *mylnum*, dative plural of OE *myln*, analogous to **Kilham** Nb and **Kilham** ERY, 'at the kilns', from OE *cylnum*. Millom seems to be a late name, possibly replacing the former *Hougenai*, 'fen-island by a mound', perhaps to be identified with Millom Castle [1. *Millum* c 1180, *Milnum* c 1205 2. *Killum* 1177, *Kylnom* 1323, 3. *Chillun* 1086: OE *myln, cylen, ēg*, ON *haugr*].

Milton *freq*, usually 'middle farm', though occasionally 'farm or village with a mill'. The first meaning applies to the following, as the early spellings attest: **Milton Brk** (*Middeltun* 956), **Milton C** (*Mideltune* c 1050), **Milton** Ha (x 2: 1. *Middelton in Portesia* 1188, 2. *Mildeltune* 1086), **Milton** O (x 2: 1. *Midelton* 1240, 2. *Mideltone* 1086), **Milton under Wychwood** O (*Middelton* 1199), **Milton** So (x 3: 1. *Midelton* 1285, 2. *Middeltun* 1065, 3. *Middeltone* 1086), also **Milton Bryant** and **Milton Ernest** Bd, **Milton Keynes** Bk, **Milton Abbot** D, **West Milton** Do, **Milton Abbas** Do, **Milton on Stour** Do, **Milton Malzor** Nth, **Podimore Milton** So, and **Milton Lilbourne** W. **Milton** Db, near Repton, is certainly a 'middle farm', but here ON *meðal* has been substituted for OE *middel* (*Middeltune* 1086, *Meelton* c 1162, *Meauton*' 1219). Other Derbyshire instances of the name, however, **Chapel Milton** and **Tunstead Milton**, near Chapel en le Frith, are clearly both 'mill farm' (1. *la Mulneton* 1290, *Chappell Mylnetowne* 1586, 2. *Tounstedemylne* 1330, *Tunstead Milnton* 1625). Though **Milton next Sittingbourne** K is 'middle farm' (*Middeltun* 893), **Milton next Canterbury** K (*Melentun* 1044) is 'mill farm', and so are **Milton** Nb, **Milton** Nt, and **Milton** St [OE *middel, myln*].

Milngavie Dnb, 'hill of the wind' [*Mylngavie* 1669: G *meall* (*na*) *gaoithe*].

Mimms, North Hrt, **South Mimms** Mx: possibly '(territory of) tribe called Mimms', though this takes but a short step towards explaining the name [1. *Mimmine* 1086, *Nordmimmes* 1190, 2. *Mimes* 1086, *Suthmimes* 1253: OE *norð, sūð*].

Minch, Little Inv, **North Minch** Ros: perhaps '(sea of the) great headland(s)' [ON *megin, nes*].

Minchin Buckland So. See Buckland.

Minchinhampton Gl, 'nuns' Hanton, i e high farm', an instance of a name in *-hampton* from *hēan-tūn* rather than *hām-tūn*, and certainly justified by the site

here. The nuns who held this place were those of Caen [*Hantone* 1086, *Minchenhamtone* 1221: OE *hēah, tūn, myncen*].

Minehead So, 'headland(s) by or of a hill', the first element also providing the names for **East** and **West Myne** So [1. *Mynheafdon* 1046, 2. *Mene* 1086: W *mynydd*, OE *hēafod*].

Minginish (Skye) Inv, 'great headland', in Gaelic *rubha mór* [ON *megin, nes*].

Mingulay *isld* Inv, 'great island' [*Megala* 1580: ON *mikil, ey*].

Minto Rox, 'mountain', strictly 'mountain hill', the OE termination being added at a time when the Celtic first element was no longer intelligible to the users of the name [*Myntowe* 1296: OW *minid*, OE *hōh*].

Misbourne *riv* Bk, 'stream called *Mysse*, i e mossy one', the suffix here perhaps serving as an explanatory title in much the same way as today both 'Thames' and 'River Thames' are used indifferently [*Misseburne* 1407: OE **mysse, burna*].

Missenden Bk, '(place in) valley of Mysse', referring to the river now called Misbourne (q v) [*Missedene* 1086: OE *denu*].

Misterton Lei,—Nt: 'village with a large church'. In neither place is there any record of a monastery, the primary sense of OE *mynster* [1. *Minstretone* 1086, 2. *Ministretone* 1086: OE *mynster, tūn*].

Mitcham Sr/GL, 'great homestead' [*Micham* 675: OE *mycel, hām*].

Mitton St,—Wo, **Great Mitton** WRY **Little Mitton** La, **Lower Mitton** Wo, **Upper Mitton** Wo: 'farm at a confluence'. Mitton Wo is at the junction of the Avon and the Carrant Brook; Upper and Lower Mitton at that of the Stour and the Severn; Little and Great Mitton are distinguished from each other by their prefixes, both being near the confluence of the Hodder and the Ribble [2. *Myttun* 841, 3. *Mitune* 1086, *Magna Mitton* 1241, 4. *Parva Mitton* 1242, 5. *Myttun* 841, *Nethere Mutton* 1340, 6. *Ouermutton* 1359: OE (*ge*)*mȳðe*, *tūn*]. See also Myton.

Moate Wme, either '(place with a) mound' or 'plain of the caves', from the ancient designation of the plain between Athlone and Moate, *Magh n-uatha* [I *mota*, *magh*, *uath*].

Mobberley Ch, 'clearing at *Mōt-burh*, i e fortified place where assemblies were held', the fortification being possibly at Grimsditch Farm within the parish. A related name, **Modbury**, occurs twice in Devon: one example is a parish in Ermington Hundred; the other is in Buckland Filleigh, in Shebbear Hundred, and it may be relevant that the petty sessions were formerly held here. A related name, Mutley 'assembly clearing', occurs in Plymouth; this may have been the meeting-place of Roborough Hundred, [1. *Motburlege* 1086, *Moberleche* 1170, 2. *Motberia* 1086, *Modberia* c 1180 4. *Modleia* 1086, *Motlegh* 1311: OE (*ge*)*mōt*, *burh*, *lēah*].

Moccas He, 'moor used for swine-pasture' [*Mochros* c 1150: W *moch*, *rhos*]. See also St Devereux.

Moffat Dmf, '(place in the) long plain' [G *magh* (locative *mo*), *fada*].

Moidart Inv, 'Mundi's inlet', a Norse name much affected by Gaelic influence (cf Knoidart) [*Muddeward* 1292: ON *fjorðr*].

Mold Flt, 'high hill'. The present mono-syllabic form developed from the coalescence of two words containing quite similar sounds, aided by the nasalisation of the vowel in *mont*. The sequence of early spellings clearly indicates how the modern form arose [*Montem Altum* 1278, *Moald* 1284, *Mohaut* 1297, *Mold*(*e*) 1297: OF *mont*, *hault*].

Mole *riv* Sr, back-formation from **Molesey** Sr, 'Mūl's island', provides the District name †**Mole Valley** Sr [*Muleseg* c 670: OE *ēg*].

Mollendinar Burn *riv* Lnk, 'stream from *Mellendonor*, i e hill of the stranger', and not 'miller's stream', which is based on the modern form. *Rivus Molendinarius* is a fanciful distortion, possibly stemming from the idea that any ancient name was 'really' Latin. It has been suggested that the 'green hollow' which is Glasgow (q v) was beside this stream [*Mellindonor* 1185: G *meall* (*an*) *dhonar*].

Monadhliath *mts* Inv, 'grey-blue moors' [G *monadh*, *liath*].

Monabraher Lim, **Monambraher** Gal, **Monamraher** Wat: 'bog of the friars' [I *Moin-na-mbrathar*].

Monaghan, 'little shrubbery' [I *muineachan*, diminutive of *muine*].

Mondrum Ch, 'pleasure-ground', literally, 'happiness, bliss', a rare instance of an abstract noun being used as a place-name. Mondrum or Mondrem was an area within the Forest of Delamere; the name is not current in its simple form, but occurs in **Aston Juxta Mondrum**, 'east farm beside Mondrum' [1. *Mondreym* 13c, *Mondrem* 1284, *Mondrun* 1313, *Mundrum* 1356, 2. *Estone* 1086, *Aston subtus Mondrem* 1290, *Aston iuxta Mondrem* 1347: OE *man-drēam*, *ēast*, *tūn*].

Moness Pth, '(place) near the waterfalls' [G *i mbun eas*].

Monfod Ayr, **Monifieth** Ang: 'moor of the peats' [1. *Monfoit* 1150, 2. *Munifod* 1178: G *moine, foide*].

Monkland He. See Leominster.

Monkseaton Nb. See Seaton.

Monks Risborough Bk, 'Risborough, i e brushwood hill, held by monks', namely those of Canterbury [*Hrisanbyrge* 903, *Monks Ryseberge* 1290: OE *hrisen, beorg*]. See also Princes Risborough.

Monkton D,—Du,—K, **Bishop Monkton** WRY, **Nun Monkton** WRY, **West Monkton** So, **Monkton Deverill** W, **Monkton Farleigh** W: 'place in monastic tenure'. Some of the affixes show that changes took place during the Middle Ages; Bishop Monkton, for instance, was so called because it was owned by the archbishop of York, and the land in Nun Monkton passed from monks to nuns. Glastonbury Abbey owned Monkton Deverill W and West Monkton So, but monastic ownership of Monkton D had ceased long before the Conquest, since it was already within a royal demesne in the time of Edward the Confessor [1. *Muneketon* 1244, 2. *Munecatun* c 1106, 4. *Monucheton* 1086, 5. *Nun Monketon* 1303, 7. *Devrel* 1086, *Deverel Monketon* 1275: OE *munuc, tūn*].

†Monmouth 1267, '(place at) estuary of river Mynwy'. The river-name means 'fast-flowing'. It is interesting to note how soon the river-name lost its second syllable in the English forms of the name [*Munwi Muþa* 11c, *Monenmvde* 1086, *Munemuda* 1190: OE *mūða*].

Montacute So, '(place by) pointed hill', originally a transferred OF name, its Latin translation, *Mons acutus*, providing the English form (cf Pontefract) [*Montagud* 1086, *Monte acuto* 1160: (OF *mont, aigu*)].

Montford Sa, 'common ford' [*Maneford* 1086: OE *(ge)mǣne, ford*].

†Montgomery Mgm, '(place) held by Montgomery', a name which is simultaneously a feudal addition to, possibly, *castle*, and a transferred place-name, since Roger de Montgomery took his name from Montgommery in Calvados. In Welsh, Montgomery is **Trefaldwyn**, 'Baldwin's town', from Baldwin de Bollers, to whom the castle was granted in the early twelfth century. Maldwyn has been used occasionally, but incorrectly, for the county name, the regular form of which is Sir Drefaldwyn. [*Montgomeri* 1086, *Trefaldwyn* 1440: OF *mont*, W *tref*].

Montrose Ang, 'moor of or on the promontory' [*Munros* c 1178: G *moine, ros*].

Monzievaird Pth, 'enclosed meadow by a moor' [*Muithauard* c 1200, *Moneward* 1203: G *moine, bard*].

Moorfoot Hills MLo, 'hills by Moorfoot, i e moorland clearing' a repetitive name; probably the clearing was first called *morþveit*, 'clearing by the moor', alluding to the hills as *mor;* the hills were then named from the clearing [*Morthwait* c 1142: ON *mōr, þveit*, OE *hyll*].

Moorton. See Moreton.

Morar Inv, 'big water', from the stream draining into Loch Morar. Though short, this stream justifies the name by its volume. A British origin is probable, early spellings indicating the connexion with names in -dover, -dever, -der [*Morderer* 1292, *Mordhowar* 14c: G *mor, dobhar* (B **dubrā*)].

†Moray (-shire), 'sea settlement' [*Moreb* c 970, *Morauia* 1124, *Murewe* c 1185: OC**mori-, *treb*].

Morden Do,—Sr, **Guilden Morden** C, **Steeple Morden** C, **Mordon** Du: 'hill by a boggy waste' [1. *Mordone* 1086, 2. *Mordune* 969, 3. *Gildene Mordon* 1204, 4. *Stepelmordun* 1242, *Mordun* c 1050: OE *mōr, dūn, gylden,* 'splendid'].

Morecambe La, 'curving inlet of the sea', a revival of Ptolemy's name for the Lune estuary, *Morikambe.* The English seaside holiday was more or less an invention of the eighteenth century, so that it is not surprising to find that many coastal names date from that period. There seems little to complain about in this name; it is a fair version of the Celtic name as rendered by the Greek geographer, it pleasantly recalls other coastal names that happen to end in *-combe*, and it has all that a publicity man might desire in its punning suggestion of large numbers of visitors (*Morikambe* c 150: B *mor,* **cambo*-].

Moreton *freq*, 'farm on or by a boggy waste', with spelling variants **Moorton** Gl, **Moorton** O, and **Morton** *freq.* Additions of all kinds are found, occasionally impacted e g **Britsmorton** Wo (naming the family of Le Bret, who held the manor in the twelfth century) and **Gilmorton** Lei (prefixing the adjective *gylden*, 'splendid') [OE *mōr, tūn*].

Morfa Crd, 'plain beside the sea' [W *morfa*].

Morfe St, 'big village' [*Moerheb* 736: B *mor, dreb*].

Morpeth Nb, 'murder path', evidently indicating a dangerous neighbourhood. Uncomplimentary names are more common among minor places than elsewhere; **Ardnimort**, near Kirkcowan Wig, for instance, is 'plain of the murder'. Other names, such as Ardnaree, refer to executions [*Morthpath* c 1200: OE *morð, pæð*].

Mortlake Sr, perhaps 'salmon stream' [*Mortelace* 11c: OE *mort, lacu*].

Morton. See Moreton.

Motherwell Lnk, possibly 'our Lady's well' [*Matervelle* c 1250, *Moydirwal* 1265: OE *mōdor, wella*].

Mound, The Cai, — Sut: 'low hill, embankment'. The first name refers to the Ord of Caithness, originally the boundary between the two divisions of the old province; the second is an embankment or causeway at the head of Loch Fleet, overlooked by Mound Rock [Etymology obscure].

Mountain Ash Glm. See Aberpennarth.

Mounth, The Pth, 'the mountain', the former name of the Grampians (q v) [*Moneth, Muneth* 1198: G *monadh*].

Mourne Mountains *mtns* Dwn, 'mountains of the Mughdhorna tribe', Mughdhorn's people, who gave their name also to Cremorne (q v).

Mousa *isld* Zet, 'moss island' [*Mosey* c 1150: ON *mosi, ey*].

Mousehole Co, possibly 'mouse hole' or perhaps 'mouse nook', said to allude to a cave in the cliff [*Mushal* 1284, *Musehole* 1347: OE *mūs, hol, halh*].

Mowsley Lei, 'mouse infested clearing' [*Muselai* 1086: OE *mūs, lēah*].

Moy Inv (x 2), **Moy** *riv* Sli, **Muie** Sut, **Mye** Stl: '(place) in the plain' [1. *Muy* 1235, 5. *Mye* 1510: G *magh*, locative *maigh*].

†**Moyle** Ant. See Mull of Deerness.

Moyness Nrn, 'meadow in the plain' [G *magh, inis*].

Muck *isld* Inv, '(island of) pigs' [*Helantmok* 1370: G *eilean, muc*].

Muckle Flugga (Unst) Zet, 'great precipices' [ON *mikill, flugi*].

Mudford So, 'muddy ford' [*Mudiford* 1086: OE **muddig, ford*].

Muir of Ord Ros, 'moorland of the rounded hill' [OE *mōr*, G *ọrd*].

Mull *isld* Arg, possibly 'highly-favoured place', like most interpretations an tttempt to be consistent with modern Gaelic forms and Ptolemy's version of ahe old Celtic name, *Malaios*. 'Pre-eminence' or 'prominence' has been taken to refer to the topography, but this leans heavily on an epithet rather than the name itself; too much reliance can be placed on such a phrase as *Muile nam Mor-bheann*, 'Mull of the great peaks' [*Malaios* c 150: G *muileach*, 'dear, beloved'].

Mull of Deerness Ork, **Mull of Galloway** Wig, **Mull of Kintyre** Arg: 'cape of... (the respective places)', Gaelic *maol*, 'bald', being used of a bare, sharp promontory, alternatively, the root may be ON *muli*, 'snout'. †**Moyle** Ant is named from *Sruth na Maoile*, 'Straits of Moyle', between NE Antrim and the Mull of Kintyre [G *maol*, ON *muli*].

Mullagh Cav, 'summit' [I *mullach*].

Mullaghareirk *mtns* Lim, 'summit(s) of the prospect' [I *mullach, radharc*].

Mullaghcarn *mtns* Tyr, 'summit with a mound or cairn' [I *mullach, carn*].

Mullingar Wme, said to be 'lefthand-wise turning mill' [*Muilinn Cirr* 1305, *Muilenn Cearr* 1450: I *muillen, cearr*].

Mumbles, The Glm, meaning uncertain, but the second element is probably ON

múli, as in Mull of Deerness etc (q v) [*Mommulls* 1549: ON *múli*].

Munster, 'place of the Mumu tribe' [I *Mumu*, gen *Muman*, ON *staðr*].

Musbury D, — La: 'fortified place infested by mice' [1. *Musberie* 1086, 2. *Musbiri* 1311: OE *mūs, burh*].

Musselburgh MLo, 'mussel town', a place whose fame for this sea-food goes back to the eleventh century and was probably established before the earliest records [*Muselburge* c 1100: OE *musele, burh*].

Mutley D. See Mobberley.

Mutlow Ch, 'mound on which assemblies were held' [*Motlowe* 1354: OE *(ge)mōt, hlāw*].

Mybster Cai, 'boggy farmstead' [ON *mýrr, bólstaðr*].

Mynwy *riv* Mon. See Monmouth.

Mynydd Bach *mtn* Crd, 'little mountain' [W *mynydd, bach*].

Mynydd Du *mtn* Crm, 'black mountain' [W *mynydd, du*].

Mytchett Sr, 'large projecting piece of land' [OE *micel, scēat*]. See also Exceat Sx.

Mytham Bridge Db. See Mytholmroyd.

Mytholmroyd WRY, 'clearing at *Mythum* i e the junction of streams', the ending of the dative plural, *-um*, here (as in Moorsholm NRY) being taken as the frequent element *-holm*. Elsewhere, as at **Mytham Bridge** Db, the ending is confused with *-hām*. The termination *-royd* is frequent in Lancs and West Riding names; it survives in the dialect of the area [1. *Mithomrode* 1307, 2. *Mithomford* 1285: OE *(ge)mȳðe, *rodu, ford*].

Myton Wa, Myton on Swale NRY, **Mytton** Sa: 'farm at the junction of streams'. Myton Wa is near the junction of the Leam and the Avon, Myton NRY is a mile or so from the point where the Swale joins the Ure to become the Ouse [1. *Mytun* 1033, 2. *Mitune* 1086, 3. *Mutone* 1086: OE *(ge)mȳðe, tūn*]. See also Mitton.

Naas Kld, 'place of meeting', the residence of the kings of Leinster until the tenth century [OI *nás*].

Nadder *riv* W, 'flowing one' [*Noodr* 705: OW **nōtr*].

Nailsworth Gl, 'Nægl's enclosure' [*Nailleswurd* 1196: OE *worð*].

†**Nairn** Nrn, '(mouth of the) penetrating one', like Ayr (q v), the name of the town is strictly an estuary name which has been eroded to that of the river. At the end of the twelfth century *Invernaren* was the regular form, but this had been shortened by the fifteenth century to *Narne* [*Inuernaren* c 1195, *Narne* 1382: OC **na-*].

†**Nantwich** Ch 1257, 'renowned salt-works', the fame being due to the excellence of its salt. Like a number of other similarly named places, this seems to have begun simply as *Wich*, a manorial suffix being added in the twelfth century, Malbana, alluding to the post-Conquest barons of Nantwich. The complimentary epithet dates from the late twelfth century, the earliest spellings clearly demonstrating that this is not the Welsh word *nant*, 'stream' [*Wich* 1086, *Wike Malb'* c 1130, *Wico Maubanc* c 1150, *Nametwich* 1194, *Namptwich* 1322: OE *wīc*, ME *named*].

Narberth Pmb, '(place) near the hedge', an original *Arberth* taking over the *n* from a preceding *yn*, 'in' (cf Nash). The second element is that found also in

Perth [*Nethebert* 1220, *Arberth* c 1310: W *ar, perth*].

Naseby Nth, 'Hnæf's fortified place', a name commemorating a legendary hero who was evidently supposed to have built the earthworks found by English settlers on their arrival. OE *burh* was subsequently replaced by ON *bȳ* (cf Rugby) [*Navesberie* 1086: OE *burh*].

Nash Bk, — Glm, — He, — Mon, — Pmb: '(place) at the ash tree', the *N*- being derived from a preceding definite article in ME [1. *Esse* 1231, 2. *Ecclesia de Fraxino* 1291, *le Nasshe* 1431, 3. *Nasse* 1291, 4. *Capella de Fraxino* 1289, *Assh* 1322, *Nasse* 1348, 5. *esse* 1291, *Nasshe* 1377: OE *æsc*, ME *atten*].

Naunton Gl (x 2), — Wo, **Naunton Beauchamp** Wo: '(at the) new farm or village', a local variant of Newington, Newnton (qq v), derived from the oblique form after a preposition such as OE *æt*. Another variant, **Neenton** Sa, might have developed otherwise but for the accident of its being on the river Neen [1. *Niwetone* 1086, 2. *æt Niwantune* 1004, 3. *Newentone* c 1120, 4. *in Niuuantune* 972, *Newenton Beauchamp* 1370: OE *niwe, tūn*].

Naver *riv* Sut, 'foggy one' [OC *nav-*].

Navio. See Brough.

Nayland Sf, '(place on) the island', with *N*- transferred from *atten* as in Nash (q v). **Stoke by Nayland** Sf takes its name from Nayland [1. *Eilanda* 1086, *Neiland* 1227, 2. *Stoc* 970, *Stokneylond* 1272, *Stoke atte Neylaunde* 1303; OE *ēgland, stoc*, ME *atten*].

Naze, The Ess, 'promontory' though now unspecified, was once *Eadwulf's Ness*. **Nazeing** Ess is '(dwelling place of) people of The Naze', and **Walton on the Naze** Ess, 'serfs' farm on The Naze', is at the tip of the promontory [1. *Eadulfes næsse* 1052, 2. *Nasinga* 1086, 3. *Edulvesnasse by Waleton* 1320: OE *næs, -ingas, w(e)alh, tūn*].

Neagh, Lough *lke* Ant, 'lake of Eochaidh', alluding to the legendary king of Ulster [I *loch*].

Neasden Mx, 'hill on or by a promontory', one of several hills in this part of Middlesex (cf Hendon, Willesden) [*Neasdune* 939: OE **nēs, dūn*].

Neenton Sa. See Naunton.

Nelson La, 'place by the Lord Nelson inn', a nineteenth-century name for an industrial settlement.

Nene *riv* Nth-LLi, 'bright river' [*Nyn* 948, *Nen* 972: B **nēnā*].

Ness (Lewis) Ros, 'promontory' [ON *nes*].

Ness *riv* Inv. See Inverness.

Nether Wallop Ha, 'lower Wallop, i e stream valley' distinguished by its locative prefix from **Over Wallop** [1. *Wallope* 1086, *Wallop inferior* c 1270, 2. *Wallop superior* 1283: OE *wælla, hop, neoðera, uferra*]. See also Farleigh Wallop Ha.

Nevis, Ben *mtn*, Inv, 'mountain of (river) Nevis, i e the venomous one', an interpretation of the river-name which is borne out in a number of uncomplimentary references in Gaelic literature [*Nibheis* 1532: OI *nem*].

Newark Nth, — Sr, †**Newark (on Trent)** Nt: 'new fortifications' or 'new building-work', in contrast, in some instances, to some old fortification in the neighbourhood. *Margidunum*, the Romano-British fort at East Bridgford and not far from Newark Nt, was known as

Aldewerke in the Middle Ages. The early spellings of Newark Nth suggest a Scandinavian origin, and no doubt allude to the occupation of Peterborough by the Danes [1. *Nieuyrk* 1189 2. *Newerk* 1414, 3. *Newarcha* c 1060: OE *niwe, (ge)weorc*, ON *nýr, virki*].

Newbegin NRY, **Newbiggin** Cu, — Du (x 2), — La, — Nb (x 3), — NRY, — We (x 3), **Newbigging** Ang, — Lnk: 'new building' [1. *Neubiggin* 1310, 3. *Newbigin* c 1208, 9. *Neubigging* 1223: OE *niwe*, ME *bigging*].

Newbold *freq*, **Newbottle** *freq*: 'new building' [OE *niwe, bōðl, bōtl, bold*].

Newborough Agl, — St, **Newbrough** Nb, **Newburgh** La, — NRY, †**Newbury** Brk: 'new fort, new chartered market town', the second meaning being relevant to Newburgh La and Newbury Brk. The latter lay in the DB manor of *Ulvritun* ('estate of Wulf's people'), but this name went out of use as the market town grew [2. *Neuboreg* 1280, 3. *Nieweburc* 1203, 4. *Neweburgh* 1431: OE *niwe, burh*].

New Brighton Ch 1841, a seaside resort established during the nineteenth century and named after Brighton Sx.

Newcastle Dwn, — Gal, — Glm 1349, — Lim, — Mon, — Sa, **Newcastle Emlyn** Crm, †**Newcastle under Lyme** St, †**Newcastle upon Tyne** Nb: 'newly-built castle', with additions to some examples. Emlyn ('around the glen') was the cantref or district of which the Carmarthenshire Newcastle was the administrative centre. Lyme Forest ('elm place') is alluded to in the Staffs example, which lies near the southern boundary of the ancient forest [3. *Ecclesia de Novo Castello* 1106, 4. *de Castro Novo* 1362, *Noef Chastel* 1361, 7. *Novum Castrum de Emlyn* c 1240, 8. *Nouum Oppidum sub Lima* 1168, 'new town ...', *Novum* *castellum subtus Lymam* 1173, 9. *Novum Castellum* 1130: OE *niwe, castel*]. See also Ashton under Lyne La.

†**New Forest** Ha, 'new (game) forest', created by William the Conqueror in the area previously known as the Forest of Andred [*Nova Foresta* 1086: OE *niwe*, ME *forest*].

Newham GL, a recent name applied to the Greater London Borough amalgamating East Ham (q v) and West Ham.

Newham Nb (x 2), — NRY, **Newholm** NRY: 'new homestead' [1, 2 *Neuham* 1242, 3. *Neuham* 1086, 4. *Neueham* 1086: OE *niwe, hām*].

Newhaven ELo, — Sx: 'newly built harbour', both late names.

Newington *freq*, 'at the new farm', derived from the oblique case of the elements after a preposition, as spellings such as *Niwantune* 1050 indicate [OE *niwe, tūn*].

Newmarket Sf. See Newport.

Newnham *freq*, 'at the new enclosure', bearing the same relationship to Newham as Newington (q v) does to Newton [OE *niwe hām*]. See also Nuneham Courtenay O.

Newnton W, a variant of Newington (q v).

Newport D, — Ess,† — Mon, — Pmb, — Sa, — Wt, **Newport Pagnell** Bk: 'new (market) town'. Newport Pagnell was in the tenure of Fulc Paganel in the twelfth century. The second element here has the sense of 'town with market rights', a meaning which can be seen also in Newmarket Sf 1418 [1. *Neuport by Barnstaple* 1295, 2. *Neueport* c 1080, 3. *Novus Burgus* 1138, *Neuborh* 1291, *Neuporte*

1322, 4. *Nuport* 1282, 5. *Niweport* c 1050, 7. *Neuport* 1086, *Neuport Paynell* 1220, 8. *Novum Forum* 1200: OE *niwe, port*, ME *market*].

†**Newry** Dwn, '(place by) the yew tree'. In early documents the name appears as *Iobhar Chind Tráchta*, 'yew tree at the head of the strand' [I *an tIúr*].

Newton freq, 'new farm or village', is, almost certainly, the most numerous place-name of OE origin occurring in all parts of the British Isles. The simple forms Newton and Newtown are very frequent, but there are many affixed forms as well, from **Newtownmountkennedy** in County Wicklow, †**Newtownabbey** in Antrim, and **Newtonferry** in North Uist to **Newton Burgoland** in Leicestershire and **Newton on the Moor** in Northumberland. There are two examples of **Newton le Willows**, one in NRY and the other in Lancashire, where also there is **Newton in Makerfield**; **Makerfield**, an old district name meaning 'open land by a ruin', occurs also in Ashton in Makerfield and Ince in Makerfield (qq v). With **Newton Stewart** in Wigtownshire may be compared **Newtownstewart** in County Tyrone [OE *niwe, tūn*]. See also Naunton, Newington.

Neyland Pmb, '(place at) the island', with initial *N-* from ME *atten*, 'at the' [*Nailand* 1596: OE *ēg, land*, ME *atten*].

Nidd *riv* WRY, 'brilliant river' [*fluvium Nid* c 715, *Nide stream* c 890: B **nido-*].

Nigg Knc, — Ros: 'the bay', the initial *N-* being carried over from the Gaelic definite article, *an* [1. *Nig* c 1250, 2. *Nig* 1257: G *uig*].

Nith *riv* Dmf-Ayr, 'new (one)', perhaps with reference to a change of course or to freshness or greenness along its banks [*Noouios* c 150, *Nud* 1181: B **nouio-*].

Noctorum Ch, 'dry hill', an interpretation entirely consistent with the topography; the settlement is on a slight elevation amid marshy land [*Chenoterie* 1086, *Cnoctyrum* 1119: OI *cnocc, tīrim*].

Noe *riv* Arg, 'new (one)', probably as Nith (q v) [G *nodha*].

Noe riv Db, 'flowing one' [*Noue* c 1290: B *nāuion-*].

Norbiton Sr/GL, 'northern corn farm', being the more northerly of the two ·outlying farms east of the royal manor of Kingston. The other is Surbiton (q v) [*Norberton* 1205: OE *norð, bēre-tūn*].

Norbury Ch (x 2), — Db — Sa, — Sr, — St: 'northern manor-house or fortified place'. One of the Cheshire examples was at the northern extremity of Macclesfield Hundred; the other was the most northerly part of Whitchurch Sa, of which it was an outlying corn-farm. Norbury Db is north of Rocester St. The Surrey Norbury is north of Croydon [1. *Norberie* 1086, 3. *Nortberie* 1086, 5. *Le Northbury* 1314: OE *norð, burh*].

Norfolk, 'the northern people' i e of the East Angles, in contrast to the southern people, Suffolk. These names of peoples, others of which include Devon, Dorset, and Wales (qq v), were transferred to their territories without the addition of *land* (as in Northumberland and Westmorland) or any similar element [*Nordfolc* 1086: OE *norð, folc*].

Normanby LLi (x 4), — NRY (x 3): 'farm of the Norsemen or Norwegians', a name characteristic of alien enclaves; the termination indicates that the name was given by other Scandinavians, viz Danes. Three of the Lincolnshire examples have affixes: Normanby by Spital is two or three miles south-east of Spital in the Street (q v);

the second is Normanby by Stow, near which is another name of the same type, Ingleby (q v). Normanby le Wold is in the Lincoln Wolds [1-4. *Normanebi* 1086, 5. *Northmannabi* c 1050, 6, 7. *Normanebi* 1086: ON *Norð-maðr, bý*].

Normanton Db, — Lei, — LKe, — Nt (x 2), — R, — WRY, Normanton le Heath Lei, Normanton Turville Lei, Normanton on the Wolds Nt, Normanton upon Soar Nt, Normanton upon Trent Nt, South Normanton Db, Temple Normanton Db: 'farm of the Norsemen', a name bestowed by English neighbours on Scandinavians within their territory (cf Normanby). The first element here is late OE *Norðman*, rather than the Scandinavian word from which it was derived. South Normanton Db is south of Temple Normanton ('... in the tenure of the Knights Templars') which was also known as North Normanton. It will be noted how much more widely distributed this name is than Normanby [1. *Normantun(e)* 1086, 3. *Normenton* 1086, 5. *Normanton* 1183, 13. *Normanton Templer* 1330: OE *Norðman*, OE *tūn*].

Northallerton NRY, 'northern Allerton, i e Ælfhere's farm', the prefix indicating that there are other Allertons, though it should be observed that their origin and meaning are quite different, viz OE *alra-tūn*, 'alder farm' [*Aluretune* 1086, *North Alverton* 1293: OE *tūn*].

†Northampton Nth, 'northern Hampton, i e home farm', distinguished from Southampton probably as early as the eleventh century (cf Southampton). The shire name also bore the prefix very early [*Hamtun* 917, *Norðhamtun* 1065 (12c copy), *Hamtunscir* 1011, *Norðhamtunscir* 1114: OE *norð, hām, tūn, scir*].

North Coker So. See West Coker.

Northfield Wo, 'open land lying to the

north', relative to King's Norton (v Norton). Both places are now within the boundaries of Birmingham [*Nordfeld* 1086: OE *norð, feld*].

North Foreland K, 'northern headland', distinguished from South Foreland, near Dover [*Forland* 1326: OE *forð, land*].

Northolt Mx. See Southall Mx.

North Riding LLi, — NRY: 'northerly third part'. The Scandinavian practice of dividing large areas into three parts is reflected in the Ridings of Yorkshire and in the Parts of Lindsey in Lincolnshire. For the phonetic development see East Riding ERY [1. *Nortreding, Nort Treding* 1086, *Nortriding* c 1115, 2. *Nort Treding* 1086, *Nortrithing* 1198: ON *norð, þriðjung*].

North Shields Nb. See Shields, North.

Northumberland Nb, 'land of those dwelling north of the Humber', a development of the tribal name *Norðhymbre*, early used of the territory, then much more extensive than the present county, to which the name has been applied since the early twelfth century {*Norðhymbre* 867, *Norðhymbralond* 895: OE *norð, land*]. See also Humber *riv*.

Northwich Ch 1119, 'salt-works lying to the north', relative to Nantwich (q v), with Middlewich (q v) between them. Northwich was originally a few acres within the township of Witton ('dwelling place attached to a specialised estate', OE *wic-tūn*). A similar relationship existed between Witton Wo and Droitwich Wo [*Wich* 1086, *Norwich* 1086, *Northwich* 1119: OE *norð, wic*].

Northwold Nf, 'north wood', located in relation to Hockwold and Methwold Nf (q v). †**North Wolds**, District in Humberside, is named from the Yorkshire Wolds

[1. *Northuuold* 970: OE *norð, wald*]. See also The Wolds.

Norton *freq*, 'northern farm', relative to a place of some importance: **King's Norton** Wo is north of Bromsgrove, **Norton Nth** north of Dodford Nth, **Norton Rad** north of Presteigne, and so on. Often the relationship is with a place called Sutton, 'south farm'; **Norton Ch** was separated from Sutton Ch by an assart—**Stockham** 'at the tree stumps' (OE *stoccum*). Numerous manorial affixes occur, e g **Norton Canon** He, held by the Dean and Chapter of Hereford Cathedral, **Norton Hawkfield** So, held by the de Hautevilles, and **Norton Conyers** NRY, held by Roger de Koiners in 1196. **Cold Norton** occurs in Essex, Oxfordshire, and Staffordshire, and **Blo Norton** Nf ('bleak Norton') also refers to the chilly implications of a northern site [OE *norð, tūn*].

Norwell Nt. See Southwell Nt.

†**Norwich** Nf, 'north specialised farm', OE *wic* here implying 'town' or possibly 'port', north in relation to Ipswich [*Norðwic* c 930, *Noruic* 1086: OE *norð, wic*].

Norwick (Unst) Zet, 'northern inlet' [ON *norð, vík*].

Noss Head Cai, **Noss of Bressay** Zet: 'promontory' [ON *nós*].

†**Nottingham** Nt 1172, 'homestead of Snot's people', the personal name, Snot, having undergone permanent mutilation by Norman speakers of English in this name but not in **Sneinton** Nt 1194, 'farm of Snot's people', which suffered the loss of *S-* only temporarily [1. *Snotengham* c 895, *Snotingeham* 1086, *Notingeham* 1130, 2. *Notintone* 1086, *Snotintone* 1165, *Snottinton* 1174: OE *-ingas, hām, tūn*].

†**Nuneaton** Wa, 'nuns' Eaton, i e river

farm', the prefix alluding to the Benedictine nunnery founded here in the reign of Stephen. After the Dissolution, the manor was granted to Sir Marmaduke Constable, but his surname was soon replaced by the older addition. The river is the Anker [*Etone* 1086, *Nonne Eton* 1247, *Constables Eyton* 1548: OE *nunne, ēa, tūn*].

Nuneham Courtenay O, '(at the) new homestead, held by the Courtenay family' [*Newnham* 1227: OE *nīwe, hām*].

Nybster Cai, 'new farm' [ON *nýr, bólstaðr*].

Nympsfield Gl, 'open land by a holy place'. The first element is a British word meaning 'grove, sacred place', and by coincidence Nymphsfield, an occasional form found in the eighteenth and nineteenth centuries, seems to place this interpretation within a classical context [*Nymdesfeld* 872: B **nemeto-, feld*].

Oa, The (Islay) Arg, 'mound' [ON *haugr*].

†**Oadby** Lei, 'Auði's homestead' [*Outheby* 1199: ON *bý*].

Oakham R, 'Oca's or Occa's homestead' [*Ocham* 1067: OE *hām*].

Oaksey W. See Odiham.

Oban Arg, 'little bay'. The modern Gaelic name means 'little bay of Lorne (q v)' [G *An t-Òban Latharnach*].

Ochill Hills *mtns* Pth/Stl: 'high ones'. From the same word is derived **Ochiltree** Ayr, 'high homestead' [2. *Ouchiltre* 1232: B *uxello--*, W *tref*].

Ockendon Ess. See Odiham.

Odell Bd. See Odiham.

Odiham Ha, 'wooded homestead'. The loss of initial *W-* in this name, probably due to Norman influence, is paralleled in such names as **Odell** Bd, 'woad hill' and **Oaksey** W and **Ockendon** Ess, respectively 'Wocca's island' and 'Wocca's hill' [1. *Wudiham* 1116, 2. *Wadehelle* 1086, 3. *Wochesie* 1086, 4. *Wokendune* 1067: OE *wudiga, hām, wād, hyll, ēg, dūn*].

Offaly, 'people of Failghe'. Ros Failghe (Ros of the Rings) was the eldest of the thirty sons of Cahirmore, King of Ireland AD 120-3. The present boundaries were established during the reign of Mary I of England, commemorated in the now obsolete name *Queen's County*.

Offa's Dyke, '(King) Offa's earthwork'. Strong traditions, both Welsh and Saxon, attribute the building of this linear rampart to King Offa, the eighth-century ruler of Mercia, to define the boundary with Wales. The name of this ruler, who in some of his charters grandiloquently claimed the kingship 'of the entire fatherland of the English', occurs in other place-names, e g **Offley** Hrt ('Offa's wood') where he is said to have died. Not all the places whose names embody the personal name, however, necessarily refer to the king. **Offchurch** Wa is 'Offa's church', **Offham** K, 'Offa's homestead', and both **Offington** Sx and **Offton** Sf, 'village of Offa's people'. **Offham** Sx, however, is 'Weohha's homestead', showing the same loss of *W-* as that noted under Odiham Ha (q v) [1. *Offan dīc* 854, 2. *Offanlege* 945, 3. *Ofechirch* 1043, 4. *Offaham* c 1130, 5. *Ofintune* 1086, 6. *Offetuna* 1086, 7. *Wocham* c 1092: OE *dīc, lēah, cirice, hām, tūn*].

Oich *riv* Inv, 'stream place' [*Obhaich*: G *abh, -aich*].

Okehampton D, 'village on river Okement'. Lower down the same river is

Monk Okehampton D, so called from its having been possessed in former times by Glastonbury Abbey. **Okement** is a British river-name probably meaning 'swift mover' [1. *Ocmundtun* c 970, 2. *Monacohamentona* 1086: OE *tūn*, B*āku-].

Oldbury *freq*, 'old fortification'. Most instances of the name are in West Midland counties, apart from one in Kent [OE *eald, burh*].

Old Sarum W, 'old Salisbury (q v)'. The form *Sarum* arose from a misreading of the abbreviated spelling of *Sarisberie* in MSS. The name was conventionally contracted by writing the first two letters followed by a symbol resembling the figure 4. As this sign was regularly used for the frequent termination -*rum*, it can be seen that a misreading could easily occur [*Sarum* 1091].

Olenacum. See Lancaster.

†**Omagh** Tyr, 'plain', specified by the first element, the meaning of which is unknown [*Oghmaigh* c 1450: I *magh*].

Ongar Ess, 'pasture land' [*Aungre* 1045: OE *anger].

Ord. See Muir of Ord.

Ore *riv* Sf. See Orford.

Orford Sf, 'ford at the sea-shore'. The ford is across the river Ore, which for some distance flows parallel to the coastline. The river-name is a back-formation from Orford, i e it is supposed that Orford is compounded of a river-name followed by -*ford*, whereas in fact the first element is OE *ōra*, 'shore' (cf Chelmsford) [*Oreford* 1164: OE *ōra, ford*].

††**Orkney**, perhaps 'whale island'. An alternative suggestion is that the Celtic word *Orcos* is a tribal name, possibly meaning 'boar', a favourite Celtic totem. In the earliest literary references, the Greek form *Orcades* is used, from which the adjective *Orcadian* is derived in current usage [*Orkas* 330 BC, *Orkaneya* 970: ON *ey*].

Ormskirk La, 'Orm's church'. Orm is on record as the feudal tenant in 1203, but he is not necessarily identical with the man referred to in the place-name [*Ormeschirche* c 1190: OE *cirice*, ON *kirkja*].

Oronsay *isld* Arg, — *isld* Inv: 'island of St Oran'. The Argyllshire island has an abbey site and a chapel with this dedication [1. *Orvansay* 1549, 2. *Oransay* 1549: ON *ey*].

Orphir *isld* Ork, 'tidal island' —one which is uncovered only at low water [*Örfura, Jorfiara* c 1225: ON *örfiris-ey*].

Orpington K/GL, 'village of Orped's people'. The personal name is a nickname meaning 'energetic'; it survived as a surname: William Orpede is named in a Warwickshire document of 1230, and Walter le Orpede in a Buckinghamshire deed dated 1255 [*Orpedingtun* 1001: OE -*ingtūn*].

Osterley Mx, 'meadow by a sheepfold' [*Osterlye* 1294: OE *eowestre, lēah*].

†**Oswestry** Sa, 'Oswald's tree or cross'. The place is traditionally associated with St Oswald, the king of Northumbria, whose death at an unidentified place called *Maserfelth* is recorded by Bede. It has been long and widely held that *Maserfelth* was near Oswestry. Yet the present·name is not documented before the thirteenth century—half a millennium and more after the events it purports to commemorate [*Oswaldestre* 1272: OE *trēow*].

Oundle Nth, '(place of) the Undalas',

a tribal name (cf Devon) used to denote a region. The meaning of OE *un-dal*, 'without share', suggests that the area consisted of residual land after a division of territory, or (if the word is strictly tribal) those who received such land [*in Undolum* c 725, *in provincia Undalum* c 750, *Undele* 1086].

Ouse *riv* Nth-N,—*riv* NRY-ERY, 'water'. Like many famous river-names, this one is disappointingly trite in its interpretation. Many questions remain when it has been established that a river-name means something like 'river' or 'water'. One is that if the early peoples were so circumscribed that it was necessary only to refer to the local river as 'the river', why are not more rivers called Avon or Ouse? Following from that it may be asked whether at least the larger rivers may have had two names, one used by the local population, the other by strangers travelling through the area. Ouse is a Celtic name, from a root **usso*. related to Greek *hudor* and OI *usce*. A third example, in Sussex, must be mentioned. This is first recorded as *aqua de Lewes* c 1200, and the name was probably read erroneously as 'de l'Ouse'. A Bedfordshire stream, the Ouzel, is thought to be named from the weasel; for part of its length it is known as Whizzle Brook (*wizzle* is a dialect form of *weasel*), but its proximity to the Ouse has brought about the present form of the name [1. *on Usan* 880, *Use* 937, 2. *on Usan* 959, *Usa* c 1110, *House* c 1300, *Ouse* 1268: B **usso*-].

Over Wallop Ha. See Nether Wallop Ha.

Owstwick ERY, 'eastern outlying farm'. This is almost certainly a Scandinavian adaptation of an English name. The OE element *wic* had no Scandinavian equivalent of a similar form, and so when it occurs in combination with a Norse element, it can be concluded that what has happened is Scandinavianisation rather than the replacement of an English name by a Norse one [*Osteuuic* 1086, *Austwick* 1177: OE *wic* + OE *ēast* affected by ON *austr*].

†**Oxford** O, 'ford used by oxen'. Fords used by other animals are alluded to in Shefford Bd, Hertford Hrt, Horsford Nf, and Gateford Nt. The importance of fords at a time when bridges were few and far between is illustrated in the number and variety of such names, of which these are an inconsiderable sample. Like four other places in *-ford*, Oxford became a county centre, and Oxfordshire is referred to from the eleventh century onwards [*Oxnaforda* c 925, *Oxeneford* 1086, *Oxenafordscir* 1010: [OE *oxa*, gen.pl. *oxna*, *ford*, *scir*].

Ox Mountains *mtns* Sli: the Irish name (Sliabh Ghamh) has been translated as if it were Sliabh Dhamh, 'mountain of the oxen'; the original name means 'stormy mountain' [I *sliabh*, *ghamh*].

Oxnam Rox, 'oxen village' [*Oxanaham* 1152: OE *oxa*, genitive plural *oxna*, *hām*].

Oxshott Sr, 'Ocga's patch of land' [*Okesseta* 1180: OE *scēat*].

Oykel *riv* Sut, 'high one'. This name is related to Ochill (q v) [*Okel* 1365: B *uxello*-].

Pabay *isld* Inv (x 2), 'hermit island' [*Paba* 1580: ON *papi*, *ey*].

Pabcastle Cu. See Bewcastle.

Padbury Bk. See Padiham.

Paddington Mx 998, 'village of Padda's people' [*Padintun* 959: OE *-ingas*, *tūn*]. See also Padiham.

Paddock Wood K, 'wood by a grass

enclosure' [*Parrok* 1346 : OE *pearroc, wudu.*]

Padiham La, 'homestead of Padda's people'. The personal name occurs also in Paddington (q v) and **Padbury** Bk, 'Padda's fortified place' [1. *Padingham* 1292, 2. *Pateberie* 1086: OE *-ingas, hām*].

Paignton D, 'farm or village of Pæga's people'. The modern spelling with *-gn-* seems to have been introduced by the Great Western Railway; the spelling Paington was usual until about 1850 [*Peinton* 1086, *Peington* 1267: OE *-ingas, tūn*].

Paisley Rnf, '(place with) church' [*Passeleth* 1161, *Passelek* 1298: MI *baslec*].

Pant *riv* Ess, 'valley (stream)' [*Pentæ* c 730: B **panto-*].

Parret *riv* Do-So, of unknown meaning [*Pedredistrem* 725].

Partick Lnk, 'bushy place' [*Perdeyc* c 1136: OW *perthog*].

Paul Co, '(church of) St Paulinus' [*St Paulinus* 1266, *Pawle* 1435].

Paulerspury Nth, 'pear tree (place), in the tenure of de Pavelli'. The affix distinguishes this place from the adjoining **Potterspury**, 'pear-tree place with a pottery'; they were formerly West and East Pury respectively [1. *Perie* 1086, *West Pyria* 12c, *Pirye Pavely* c 1280, 2. *Perie* 1086, *Estpirie* 1229, *Potterispirye* 1287: OE *pyrige, west, ēast, pottere*].

Peak Db, 'summit, pointed hill'. The Peak designates not a particular hill but a whole region in north Derbyshire. A local government District centred on Buxton is now called †**High Peak**, the name of the Hundred contrasted with that of Wirksworth, or Low Peak,

Hundred [1. *Pecsætna lond* 7c, *Peac lond* 924, 2. *Alto Pech* 1196, *Hye Peake* 1490: OE *pēac*].

Peckham Sr/GL, 'homestead by a hill'. Peckham Rye 1589 is 'brook at Peckham' [*Pecheham* 1086: OE *pēac, hām, riðe*].

Peebles Pbl, '(places with) shelters', possibly alluding to shielings or temporary huts used on summer pastures (cf Galashiels) [*Pebles* c 1125: W *pabell* (pl *pebyll*)].

Peel IOM, '(town by a) castle', replacing the name *Holmetown* in the sixteenth century, though *Peel* had earlier been applied to the castle itself [*Pelam* 1399: ME *pēl*].

Peffer *riv* ELo, **Peffery** Ros, **Peover** *riv* Ch, **Perry** *riv* Sa: 'radiant (stream)'. In *Perry* the OE element *ēa* 'river' has survived, but it has disappeared from *Peover*, though it occurs in forms recorded down to the sixteenth century. An Aberdeenshire stream recorded as *Peferyn* in 1247 is now known as the Silverburn, which is a fair translation of the Celtic name. Among the derived place-names are **Peover Superior** Ch, **Peover Inferior** Ch, and **Nether Peover** Ch, **Strathpeffer** Ros ('valley of the Peffer'), and Inbhir Pheofharan, the Gaelic name of Dingwall Ros. **Inverpeffer** Ang and **Peffer Mill** MLo point to former appellations of renamed streams [1. *Pefferham* c 1125, 3. *Peuerhee* 13c, 4. *Peueree* 12c, 5. *Pevre* 1086, *Peure Superior* 1287, 6. *Parva Pefria* c 1200, 7. *Pevre* 1086, *Nether Pevre* 1288, 8. *Strathpefir* 1350: P *pevr*, OW *pefr*].

Pelaw Du, 'Peola's mound' [*Pellowe* 1242: OE *hlāw*].

Pembridge He, 'Pægna's bridge' [*Penebruge* 1086: OE *brycg*].

Pembroke Pmb, 'land at the end'. It is of

interest to note that names of this type (cf Land's End and Finisterre) imply a westward movement [*Pennbro* c 1150, *Pembroch* 1191: B **penno-*, **brog-*, 'land'].

Penarth Glm 1254, 'headland of the promontory' [W *pen*, *garth*].

Pencoyd He. See Penge.

Pendennis Co, 'fortress hill' [Co *pen*, *dinas*].

Pendlebury La, 'fortified place by or on Penhill', the hill name being tautologous as it stands; it developed further to *Pendle*, whereupon *Hill* was added to explain the topography of a place whose name already meant 'hill' in each of its elements, the one Celtic, the other Germanic. **Pendle Hill** La can therefore be rendered only 'hill-hill-hill' [1. *Penelbiri* 1202, 2. *Pennul* 1258, *Penhul* 1305: W *pen*, OE *hyll*].

Penge Sr, 'end of the wood', of the same origin as **Pencoyd** He and **Penketh** La, viz a British name *Pencēt*, which occurs also in **Penkhull** St, 'hill by *Pencēt*' [1. *Penceat* 1067, 2. *Pencoyt* 1291, 3. *Penket* 1242, 4. *Pinchetel* 1086: B*penno-*, **cēd*, OE *hyll*].

Penicuik MLo, 'hill of the cuckoo' [*Penikok* 1250: OW *penn y cog*].

Penistone WRY, 'Penning's village' [*Pengestone* 1086: OE *tūn*].

Penk *riv* St, derived by back-formation from Penkridge (q v).

Penketh La. See Penge.

Penkhull St. See Penge.

Penkridge St, 'mound on a hill', representing a barely altered British name, originally applied to a Roman military

station. The river-name Penk is a rather inept back-formation from Penkridge, apparently regarded as composed of *Penk + ridge* [*Pennocrucio* 4c, *Pencric* 958: B*penno-*,*crūcā*].

Pennines *mtns*, a late name, the earliest record being of eighteenth-century date and almost certainly a deliberate invention of one William Bertram (1723-65).

Penrhyndeudraeth Crn, 'promontory with two beaches' [*Penrryn Devdraeth* 1457: W *penrhyn*, *dau*, *traeth*].

Penrith Cu c 1100, 'ford by a hill', the ford being probably near Brougham Castle [B **penno-*, **ritu-*].

Penryn Co 1275, 'promontory' [*Penrin* 1259: Co *penryn*].

Pentland Firth Cai, 'inlet in the land of the Picts', the designation *Pictland* being used at first by the sea-borne Vikings for the north of Scotland generally [*Pettaland fjorðr* c 1085: ON *land*, *fjorðr*].

Pentrich Db 1229, **Pentridge** Do, **Pentyrch** Glm: 'hill of the boar' [1. *Pentric* 1086, 2. *Pentric* 762, 3. *Penntirch* 12c: B **penno-*, OW **tyrch*].

Pentyrch Glm. See Pentrich.

†**Penwith** Co, possibly 'extremity, end (of the land)', accepting the suggestion that the name is derived from a Cornish common noun with this meaning. This former Hundred-name is now that of a county district [*Penwid* 1186, *Penawyth* 1336: Co *penwyth*].

Penzance Co, 'holy headland' [*Pensans* 1284: Co *pen*, *sans*].

Peover *riv* Ch. See Peffer.

Perivale Mx, 'pear-tree valley' [*Pyryvale* 1508: OE *pyrige*, ME *vale*].

Perranarworthal Co, **Perranporth** Co, **Parran Uthnoe** Co, **Perranzabuloe** Co: 'St Perran's (place)', modified by affixes—respectively 'in the marshland', 'port', '(formerly) St Judno', and 'in the sand' [1. *Harewithel* 1187, 2. *Peran Uthnoe* 1202, 4. *S. Pierani* 1086: Co *ar, gothal, porth*, L *in, sabulum*].

Pershore Wo, 'osier-bank'. ME *persche* (on which the postulated OE form is based) is the source of the dialect word *persh*, current in Gloucestershire with the meaning 'osier, twig'; the addition of OE *ōra* makes good sense both linguistically and topographically [*Perscoran* 972: OE **persc, ōra*].

Perth Pth, '(place by a) thicket', a name of Pictish origin, alongside which must be placed St Johnstoun, whose antecedents are, of course, English. The parish church is dedicated to St John the Baptist [*Pert* c 1128, *St Johnstoun or Perth* 1220: P **perta-*, OE *tūn*].

†**Peterborough** Nth, '(St) Peter's fortified town', a name replacing the earlier *Medeshamstede*, when the monastery and its dependent settlement were rebuilt after destruction by Danish invaders. The early name implies an agrarian centre; the substitution of a name terminating in *-burh* suggests both an affirmation of the importance of the place and a realisation of its liability to attack. The abbey attained such wealth that its territory in the immediate vicinity enjoyed the status of Soke (OE *sōcn*), was for a time an independent county, then amalgamated with Huntingdonshire, and is now incorporated into the reorganised county of Cambridgeshire [*Medeshamstedi* c 750, *Burg* 1086, *Petreburgh* 1333: OE *hām-stede, burh*].

Peterhead Abd, '(St) Peter's headland', formerly Inverugie, the place is now called by a name alluding to the dedica-tion of the church [*Petyrheid* 1544: OE *hēafod*].

Peterlee Du, '(New Town named in honour of) Peter Lee', the fortuitous appropriateness of the personal name obviates the need of any terminal such as *-town* or *-ville* that might have seemed inevitable to misguided authorities. Peter Lee (d. 1935) was a prominent and much loved trade union leader in County Durham.

Petersfield Ha, 'open land of (place dedicated to) St Peter' [*Peteresfeld* c 1170: OE *feld*].

Petuaria. See Brough.

Pevensey Sx, '(place by) Pefen's river' [*Pefenesea* 947: OE *ēa*].

Phepson Wo, 'farm of the Fepsǣte, i e settlers from the Fepping folk'. The unusual spelling of the name is matched by the complexity of its structure and the obscurity of its history. It was first spelt with initial *Ph-* in the thirteenth century, but the name had been several times transformed by then. The territory of the Feppings was further east, in the land of the Middle Angles; emigrants from there seem to have established a dependency in Worcestershire [*Fepsetnatun* 956, *Phepsynton* 1302, *Fepson* 1583: OE *-ingas, tūn, sǣte*].

Phillack Co, '(place with church of) St Felicity' [(*Ecclesia*) *Sancte Felicitatis* 1259].

Pinchbeck LLi, 'finch stream'. If not ON *bekkr*, the second element is the Scandinavianised form of OE *bæce* [*Pyncebek* 1051: OE *pinc(a)*, OE *bæce*, ON *bekkr*].

Pitcairn Pth, 'portion with or by a mound'. Place-names in *Pit-*, with the small number spelt with the variant *Pet-*, have been very closely studied by Celtic scholars, who have concluded that the term—corresponding to W *peth*, 'thing'— was a Celtic contribution to the vocabulary of Pictish, the linguistic affiliations of which are very uncertain. It is inferred that the distribution of *Pit-* names bears witness to the settlement-pattern of the Picts. The names extend in a band of varying thickness and density down the east coast of Scotland from **Pittentrail** in Sutherland to **Pitcox** ('portion of the fifth part') in East Lothian, with extensions inland along river valleys, especially in Aberdeenshire and Perthshire, Pitlochry (q v) being one of the furthest west and most remote from the sea [*Peticarne* 1247: P **pett*, G *càirn*]. See also Urquhart Fif.

Pitcaple Abd, 'portion of the mare' [P **pett*, G *capuill*]. See also Pitcairn.

Pitchcombe Gl, 'valley from which pitch was got' [*Pichencumbe* c 1212: OE *picen*, *cumb*].

Pitcorthy Fif, 'portion with or by a pillar-stone' [*Pittecorthin* 1093: P **pett*, G *coirthe*]. See also Pitcairn.

Pitcox ELo. See Pitcairn.

Pitcruive Pth, **Pitcruvie** Fif: 'tree portion' [P **pett*, G *chraoibhe*]. See also Pitcairn.

Pitelpie Ang, **Pitewan** Ang, **Pitkennedy** Ang, **Pitkenny** Fif, **Pitkerrald** Inv, **Pitmaduthy** Ros, **Pitmurchie** Abd: 'portion of . . . ', the second element in each being a personal name, respectively Alpin, Eoghan, Cennéitigh, Kenneth, Cairell, Macduff, and Murchadh. Many *Pit-* names have, like Pitcairn (q v) a topographical element as their second component, but personal names are quite numerous, and a substantial number allude to occupations, such as **Pitgersie**

Abd, 'portion of the craftsman' (G *ghréasaighe*), and the several instances of **Pitskelly**, 'portion of the tale-teller' (G *sgéalaighe*).

Pitforthie Ang, — Knc: 'portion with or by a pillar-stone' (cf Pitcorthy) [P **pett*, G *coirthe*].

Pitfoskie Abd, 'portion by a shelter' [P **pett*, G *fosgadh*]. See also Pitcairn.

Pitgersie Abd. See Pitelpie.

Pitglassie Ros, 'meadow portion' [P **pett*, G *ghlasaich*]. See also Pitcairn.

Pitgorno Fif. See Strathmiglo.

Pitkennedy Ang, **Pitkenny** Fif, **Pitkerrald** Inv. See Pitelpie.

Pitliver Fif, 'portion of the book', perhaps because it was church property [*Petlyver* 1450: P **pett*, G *lebar* (gen. *libhair*)]. See also Pitcairn.

Pitlochrye Ang, **Pitlochry** Pth; 'portion of the stones', the first name almost certainly alluding to stepping-stones [P **pett*, G *cloichreach*]. See also Pitcairn.

Pitlurg Abd,—Bnf. See Lairg.

Pitmaduthy Ros. See Pitelpie.

Pitmain Inv, **Pitmedden** Abd: 'middle portion' [P **pett*, G *medon*].

Pitmillan Abd, 'mill portion' [*Pitmulen* c 1315: P **pett*, G *muileann*]. See also Pitcairn.

Pitmurchie Abd. See Pitelpie.

Pitney So, 'Pytta's island', the personal name being a variant of that in Putney (q v). Pytta occurs also in **Pittington** Du, 'hill of Pytta's people' [1. *Peteneie* 1086,

2. *duo Pittindunas* c 1085: OE *ēg, dūn, -ingas*].

Pitsford Nth, 'Peoht's ford' [*Pedesford, Pitesford* 1086: OE ford]. See also Pytchley.

Pitskelly Ang, — Knc, — Pth. See Pitelpie.

Pitsligo Abd, 'shelly portion' [*Petslegach* 1426: P **pett*, G *sligeach*]. See also Pitcairn, Sligo.

Pitstone Bk, 'Picel's ، thorn-tree' [*Pincelestorne* 1086, *Pichelesþorne* 1220: OE *þorn*].

Pittendreich, Pittendreigh, Pittendriech *freq*: 'portion on the hill-face'. The early spellings indicate an origin in G *drech*, 'slope facing the sun, sunny aspect' [P **pett*, G *drech*]. See also Pitcairn.

Pittenweem Fif, 'cave portion' [*Petnaweme* c 1150: P **pett*, G *na h-uamha*]. See also Pitcairn.

Pittington Du. See Pitney.

Plaistow D, —Db, —Ess/GL, —K, —Sx: 'place where people gathered to play'. It has been suggested that such places were sites of more serious assemblies as well [1. *Pleiestou* 1086, *Plegestoue* 1167, 2. *Plagestoue* c 1190, 3. *Playstowe* 1414: OE *pleg-stōw*].

Plumpton La,—Nth,—Sx,—WRY, **Woodplumpton** La: 'plum-tree village'. Plumpton La was also known as **Fieldplumpton**, to distinguish it from Woodplumpton [1. *Pluntun* 1086, *Fildeplumpton* 1323, 2. *Pluntune* 1086, 3. *Pluntune* 1086, 4. *Plontone* 1086, 5. *Pluntun* 1086, *Wodeplumpton* 1327: OE *plūme, tūn, feld, wudu*].

Plumstead K/GL,—Nf, **Great & Little Plumstead** Nf: 'plum-tree place'

[1. *Plumstede* c 965, 2. *Plumestede* 1086, 3. *Plumstede* 1086, 4. *Parva Plumbsted* 1254: OE *plūme, stede*].

Plym *riv* D, back-formation from village name, see Plympton (sv Plymouth).

†**Plymouth** D, '(place at) mouth of the river Plym'. This is a development in the normal order, viz river-name > settlement-name. The river-name, Plym, is a back-formation from the name of the mother-settlement here, **Plympton**, 'plum-tree village', the priory of which held the manor of Sutton Prior, as Plymouth was called until about 1450; the present name was originally applied only to the harbour. **Plymstock** D is probably 'outlying enclosed farm belonging to Plympton' [1. *Plymmue* 1230, *Sutton Prior vulgariter Plymmouth nuncupatur* c 1450, 2. *Plympton Comitis* 1299, 3. *Plemestocha* 1086: OE *plūme, mūð, tūn, stoc, sūð*]. See also Sutton.

Podimore Milton So. See Milton.

Poldhu Co, '(place by) black pool' [Co *pol, du*].

Pollagh Off, 'land full of pits or holes' [I *pollach*].

Pollokshaws Lnk, '(place by) little pool', 'in the woods' added to distinguish it from **Pollokshields**, 'Pollok with the shielings' [*Pullock* 1158: B *poll*, OE *sceaga*, ME *schele*].

Polmadie Lnk 1617, 'pool of sons of Daigh' [*Polmacde* c 1185: B *poll*].

Polperro Co, 'port by a river' or 'port by a river called *Pira*' [*Portpira* 1303: Co *porth*].

Polruan Co. See Romansleigh D.

Pontefract WRY, '(place by) broken bridge'. The present written form of the name is no less than nine-tenths of the Latin form in the ablative case, whereas the spoken form heard until recently represented the Norman-French form, *Pont-Freit* [*Pontefracto* 1090, *Pumfrate* c 1190: OF *pont, freit*].

Pontop Du, 'side valley of the Pont Burn" the stream-name meaning 'valley river, [*Ponthope* 1245: W *pant*, OE *hop, burna*].

Pontypool Mon, 'bridge by a pool'. The name is quite late, and the final element is English *pool*, preceded by the Welsh definite article [*Pont y Poole* 1617: W *pont*].

Pont-y-Pridd Glm, 'bridge by the earthen house'. The significant element *Ty*, 'house' has been lost from the modern form of the name [*Pont y Ty Pridd* c 1700: W *pont, ty, pridd*].

Poole Do, 'pool', alluding to a harbour, just as **North Pool** D and **South Pool** D refer to tidal arms of Kingsbridge harbour [1. *Pole* 1194, 2. *Pola* 1086, 3. *Pola* 1086, *Suthpole* 1284: OE *pōl*].

Poplar Mx, '(place with) poplar tree' [*Popeler* 1350: OF *poplier*].

Porin Ros, 'pasture' [G *pórainn*].

Porlock So, 'fold or enclosure by a harbour' [*Portloca* 918: OE *port, loca*].

Portchester Ha, 'Roman station by Port, i e the harbour'. *Portus Adurni*, the recorded Latin name of Portsmouth Harbour, was probably reduced to *Port* colloquially [*Porteceaster* c 960: OE *ceaster*].

Portgate Nb, 'opening', originally Latin *porta*, 'gate', referring to a gap in Hadrian's Wall, through which Watling Street passes. **Portgate** D, also situated on a main road—that from Exeter to Launceston—seems to be the site of a toll gate on the *portway*, i e 'road to a market' [1. *Portyate* 1269, 2. *Porteyetepark* c 1445: OE *port, geat*].

Porthcawl Glm, 'harbour where sea-kale grew' [*Portcall* 1632: W *porth, cawl*].

Porthkerry Glm, 'port of Curig', possibly referring to the Welsh saint of that name [*Portciri* 1254: W *porth*].

Portinscale Cu, 'harlots' shelters' [*Portquenescales* nd: OE *portcwēn*, ON *skáli*].

†**Portland** Do, 'estate by Port, i e the harbour', cf Porchester *supra*, though of course the name is applied to different places [*Port* 837, *Portlande* 872: OE *land*].

Portmadoc 1838 Crn, 'port founded by Madocks', an industrial port named after its founder in the early nineteenth century. The word-order is Welsh, but the English word *port* is used instead of Welsh *porth*.

Portmahomack Ros, 'harbour of Machalmac', the personal name being in the reverential-familiar form, usually rendered by 'my little . . . ', the saint here being Colman [*Portmachalmok* 1678: G *port*].

Portobello MLo, a transferred name from the place in Central America. A settlement grew from a single dwelling called Portobello Hut, said to have been built by a sailor who had served under Vernon at the battle of Portobello in 1739.

Portpatrick Wig 1630, 'harbour named in honour of St Patrick', and probably so designated because of a chapel nearby dedicated to the saint.

Portree (Skye) Inv, 'harbour of the slope',

though sometimes explained as 'king's harbour', commemorating a visit of James V of Scotland in 1540. The second element (literally 'fore-arm') is used in place-names to mean 'hill-grazing, summer pasture, shieling' [*Portri* 1549: G *port, ruighe*].

Portrush Ant, 'landing-place of the promontory', alluding to the point of basaltic rock projecting into the sea here [I *port, ros*].

Portsdown Ha, 'hill by *Port*', *Port* being probably the earlier name for what is now Portsmouth Harbour (cf Portchester). **Portsea** is 'island by *Port*', and **Portsmouth** 'harbour-entrance of *Port*' [1. *Portesdon* 1086, 2. *Porteseia* c 1125, 3. *Portesmuþa* c 900: OE *dūn, ēg, mūða*].

Portsea Ha. See Portsdown.

Portslade Sx, 'river-crossing by a harbour' [*Porteslage* 1086, *Porteslad'* c 1180: OE *port, (ge)lād*].

Portsmouth Ha. See Portsdown.

Port Sunlight Ch, a modern name for a model village in Lower Bebington Ch (q v), alluding to the brand-name of a type of soap manufactured there.

Port Talbot Glm, nineteenth-century name for docks built at Aberavon. The Talbots were owners of much of the land here.

Portumna Gal, 'landing-place of the oak' [I *port, omna*].

Portus Adurni. See Adur *riv*.

Potters Bar Hrt (formerly Mx), 'gate kept by a man named Potter'. Other places in this area including *Bar* in their names are Swanleybar Farm in North Mimms and the obsolete *Sternesbarre* and *Nevilesbarre*, recorded in the fifteenth

century. These were probably entrances to Enfield Chase [*Potterys Barre* 1509: ME *barre*].

Potter Somersal Db. See Somersal Herbert.

Potterspury Nth. See Paulerspury.

Poulton-le-Fylde La, 'village by a pool'—the affix *le Fylde* distinguishing this place from **Poulton-le-Sands** La. Note the use of *le* as a connective, owing to the loss of a preposition such as French *en*; it is not, as is sometimes suggested, a form of the OF preposition *lès*, 'near', which has not been found in place-names on the British side of the Channel [1. *Poltun* 1086, 2. *Poltune* 1086: OE *pōl, tūn*]. See also Fylde.

††**Powys** Mgm, 'provincial place', rather difficult to translate, since the Latin word from which it is derived is in fact an adjective, *pagensis*, from *pagus*, 'district, region, province'. Powys is the name now applied to the new county consisting of the former Montgomeryshire, Radnor-shire, and Breconshire (qq v), an area approximating to that of the old Welsh kingdom of Powys [L *pagus* > *pagensis*].

Prestatyn Flt, 'village of the priests', a name identical in origin and meaning with the numerous instances of Preston in England (q v). Welsh influence brought about two separate changes: OE *tūn* has become -*tyn* and the stress was shifted from the first syllable of *prēosta* to the second, when that became the penultimate of the compound *prēosta-tūn*, Welsh words being normally accented on the penultimate syllable [*Prestetone* 1086: OE *prēost, tūn*].

Presteigne Rad, 'priests' household', the exact significance of which in a place-name is somewhat obscure. It may indicate a community [*Prestehemede* c 1250: OE *prēost, hǣmed*].

Preston *freq*, 'village of the priests', occurring in Berwickshire and in a number of counties in England. Numerous affixes are found, most of them manorial additions, i e the family names of feudal tenants, e g **Preston Bagot** Wa, **Preston Bisset** Bk, and **Preston Gubbals** Sa. **Preston Candover** Ha and **Preston Crowmarsh** O have a different origin from other Prestons, viz OE *prēostena*, 'priests' —a weak form of the genitive plural—instead of *prēosta-tūn* [OE *prēost*, *tūn*]. See also Candover, Crowmarsh, Prestatyn.

Prestonpans ELo, 'salt pans by Preston, i e priests' village', the priests being the monks of Newbattle Abbey, who laid out the salt pans in the early thirteenth century [*Saltprestoun* 1587, *Prestonpans* 1654, OE *salt*, *prēost*, *tūn*, *panne*].

Prestwich La 1194, **Prestwick** Ayr,—Bk, —Nb: 'outlying farm belonging to priest(s)' [2. *Prestwic* c 1170, *Prestwik* 1330, *Prestwic* 1242: OE *prēost*, *wic*].

Princes Risborough Bk, 'brushwood hills in the tenure of the prince', the prince being none other than the Black Prince; the prefix distinguishes this from Monks Risborough (q v) [*Risenbeorgas* 1004, *Pryns Rysburgh* 1433: OE **hrisen*, *beorg*, ME *prince*].

Princetown D, 'settlement named in honour of the prince', established in 1808 or soon after, at the time of the building of what is now usually known as Dartmoor Prison; the name celebrates the Prince Regent, afterwards King George IV.

Prittlewell Ess, 'babbling brook' [*Pritteuuella* 1086: OE **pritol*, *wella*]. See also Southend-on-Sea.

Pudsey WRY, 'Pudoc's riverside land' [*Podechesaie* 1086: OE *ēg*].

Puffin Island Agl — Ker: 'island on which puffins were seen' [Mn E *puffin, island*].

Putney Sr/GL, 'Putta's landing place', like Rotherhithe, Chelsea, and Lambeth (qq v), a Thames-side haven [*Putelei* 1086, *Potenhiþe* c 1327: OE *hȳð*].

Pwllheli Crn, 'brine pool' [*Pwllhely* c 1292: W *pwll, heli*].

Pytchley Nth, 'Peoht's wood' [*Pihteslea* 956: OE *lēah*].

Quadring LHo, 'muddy place of the Haverings', a tribe, 'Hæfer's people', which gave its name to Havering-atte-Bower Ess [*Quadheueringe*: OE *cwēad*, *-ingas*].

Quaich *riv* Pth, '(stream with) holes'. Numerous potholes are said to occur in the bed of the river [G *cuach*, 'cup'].

Quantock Hills So, 'rim', the name not necessarily referring to the entire chain, but originally doubtless an important ridge within the group [*Cantucuudu* 682: B **canto-*, OE *wudu*].

Quarff Zet, 'bend, nook, corner' [*Quharf* 1569: ON *hvarf*]. Cf Cape Wrath.

Quarles Nf, '(place by) circles', alluding to circles of standing stones [*Huerueles* 1086: OE *hwerfel*].

Quarr Wt, '(place by) quarry'. The earliest references to the place are in Latin [*Quarraria* c 1150, *Quadraria* c 1170, *Quarrer* 1289: ME *quarrere* (< L *quadraria*)].

Queenborough K, 'chartered town named in honour of the queen'. Philippa of Hainault, wife of Edward III, died just after the town received its charter [*Queneburgh* 1376: OE *cwēn*, *burh*].

Queensbury WRY, a village formerly known by the name of an inn, *Queen's Head*, but the name was changed to Queensbury at a public meeting held on 8 May 1863.

Queen's County. See Offaly.

Queensferry WLo, 'river-crossing named in honour of the queen', to celebrate the passage here of Margaret of England, wife of Malcolm Canmore in the eleventh century [*Passagium S. Marg. Regine* 1183, *Queneferie* c 1295: OE *cwēn*, ON *ferja*].

Queen's Town. See Cobh.

Quenby Lei 1242, 'queen's manor', the second element having been originally OE *burh*, but replaced in the twelfth century by ON *bý* [*Qveneberie* 1086, *Qvenbia* c 1125: OE *cwēn, burh*, (ON *bý*)].

Quinag *mtn* Sut, 'churn', from its shape [G *cuinneag*].

Quorndon Lei, 'hill where mill-stones were obtained'. The contracted form, **Quorn**, is also quite regularly used of this place [*Querendon* c 1225: OE *cweorn, dūn*].

Quy C, 'cow island' [*Choeie* c 1080, *Coeia* 1086, *Cueye* 1212: OE *cū, ēg*].

Raasay (Skye) Inv, 'roe ridge island' [*Raasa* 1263: ON *rár, áss, ey*].

Raby Ch, 'village at a boundary', possibly on the edge of a group of Scandinavian settlements in Wirral [*Rabie* 1086: ON *rá, bý*].

Rackham Sx, 'rick homestead', or 'homestead by the hill called Rick'— the latter being more probable in view of the proximity of Rackham Hill [*Recham* 1166: OE *hrēac, hām*].

Radcliffe La, **Radcliffe on Trent** Nt, **Radclive** Bk: 'red cliff', names referring to soil-colour that frequently finds record in place-names. The Lancs place is named from a red sandstone cliff beside the river Irwell, the Notts name being derived from the steep slope of red clay by the Trent, the mention of which in the affix distinguishes this place from Ratcliffe on Soar (q v) [*Radcliue* 1086, 2. *Radeclive* 1086, 3. *Radeclive* 1086: OE *rēad, clif*]. See also Redcliff, Rawcliffe, Rockcliff.

Raddiford D, **Radford** D (x 2), — Nt (x 2), — Wa, — Wo, **Radford Semele** Wa, **Redford** Ang, — Pmb: '(place by) red ford'. Radford Semele was held by the de Simily family from the eleventh century [1. *Radeford* 1323, 2. *Radeford* 1202, 3. *Radeford* 1275, 4. *Redeford* 1086, 6. *Raddeford* 1354, 7. *Radeford* c 1230, 8. *Redeford* 1086, *Radeford Semely* 1325; OE *rēad, ford*]. See also Retford.

Radlett Hrt, 'road junction' [*Radelett* 1453: OE *rād-gelǣte*].

†Radnor Rad, '(at the) red bank or slope', the present name retaining the -*n* of the inflexional ending of the adjective. The former county of Radnorshire is now part of Powys (q v). The form occurs in English place-names, e g Somerford-cum-Radnor Ch (*Radenoure* 1188), and Red Hill near Worcester was alluded to in a document of 969 as *readan ofre* (PN Wo 163) [*Raddrenoue* 1086, *Radenoura* c 1191: OE *rēad, ofer*].

Radwinter Ess, 'Rædwynn's tree', like other names in -*tree*, this has a personal name as first element [*Redeuuintra* 1086: OE *trēow*].

Raglan Mon 1550, 'rampart' [*Raghelan* 1254: W *rhag, glan*].

Rame Co, 'post, barrier', appropriate enough to a place near the Devon border [*Rame* 1086: OE **hrama*].

Ramoan Ant, 'Modan's fort' [*Rath-Modhain* n d: I *ràth*].

Ramornie Fif, 'fort of a man of Clan Morgan' [*Ramorgany* 1512: G *ràth*].

Ramsbottom La, 'wild garlic valley' or 'ram's valley', the second being slightly more probable. Animal names occasionally refer to rocks resembling the animal in some way [*Romesbothum* 1324: OE *hramsa/ramm, botm*].

Ramsdale Ha, — NRY, **Ramsden Bellhouse** Ess, **Ramsden Crays** Ess, **Ramsden** O: 'wild garlic valley' or 'ram's valley'. The affixes in the Essex names are both manorial: Ricardus de Belhous is named in a document of 1208, Simon de Craye in one of 1252 [1. *Ramesdela* 1170, 2. *Ram(m)esdal* 1240, 3. *Ramesdana* 1086, *Ramesden Belhous* 1254, 4. *Ramesden Crei* 1274, 5. *Ramesdon* 1179, *Rammesden* 1279: OE *hramsa/ramm, dæl, denu*].

Ramsden. See Ramsdale.

Ramsey Ess, — Hu, — Wig: 'wild-garlic island', but **Ramsey** IOM is '(place by) wild-garlic river'. **Ramsey Island** Pmb was noted in the nineteenth century for the abundance of the plant, *Allium ursinum* [1. *Rameseia* 1086, 2. *Hramesege* c 1000, 4. *Ramsa* 1257, 5. *Ramesey* 1326: OE/ON *hramsa*, OE *ēg*, ON *á, ey*].

Ramsgate K, 'Hræfn's gap', alluding to a break in the cliffs [*Ramisgate* 1279: OE *geat*].

Randown Rcm, 'promontory of the fortress', a small peninsula on the western side of Lough Ree [*Rinnduin* 1250: I *rinn, dun*].

Rannoch Moor Pth, 'bracken place' [*Rannach* 1505: G *raineach*].

Ranza, Loch *lke* (Arran) Bte, 'lake of the rowan-tree river' [*Lockransay* 1433: G *loch*, ON **raun, á*].

Raphoe Don, 'fort of the huts' [*Rathboth* c 1250: I *rath, both*].

Ratæ Coritanorum, 'fortress of the Coritani', the conventional form of the Romano-British name for Leicester (q v), appearing as *Ratecorion* in the Ravenna Cosmography [B **rate-*].

Ratby Lei, 'Rota's farm', the personal name being identical with that in Rutland (q v) and not impossibly that of the same individual [*Rotebie* 1086: ON *bȳ*].

Ratcliff Mx, **Ratcliffe Culey** Lei, **Ratcliffe-on-the-Wreak** Lei, **Ratcliffe-on-Soar** Nt: '(place by) red cliff', a variant of Radcliffe (q v) [1. *Radclif* 1422, 2. *Redeclive* 1086, 3. *Radeclive* 1086, 4. *Radeclive* 1086, *Radecliva super Soram* c 1195: OE *rēad, clif*].

Rath Off, 'fort' [I *ràth*].

Rathbarna Rcm, 'gapped or dilapidated fort' [I *ràth, bearnach*].

Rathen Abd, 'ferny place' [*Rathyn* 1300: G *ràthain*].

Rathillet Fif, 'fort of the Ulsterman', the second element being the name of the tribe, Ulad [*Radhulit* c 1195: G *ràth*].

Rathlackan Myo, 'fort of the hillside' [I *ràth, leacán*].

Rathmell WRY, 'red sandbank' [*Rodemele* 1086: ON *rauðr, melr*].

Rathmore Ker, — Kld: 'big fort' [G *ràth, mór*].

Rathnew Wic, 'fort of Noe' [*Rath-Naoi n d*: I *ràth*].

Rathnure Wex, 'fort of the yew tree', the infixed -*n*- being the remnant of the article *an* preceding the second element [I *ràth, iubhar*]. See also Newry.

Rattray Pth, 'farm by the fort', a hybrid name, the second element being the British word which became Welsh *tref*, 'farm' [*Rotrefe* 1291: G *ràth*, B **treb*].

Ravenser Odd ERY, 'point of Ravenser, i e Hrafn's gravel bank'. The Norse personal name occurs in *Ravenspur* or *Ravensburgh*, early forms of the name of Spurn Head (q v); Odd is now under the waters of the Humber, near Spurn Head. It was for a short time in the fourteenth century 'a fair town for merchants and shipping' [*burgo del Odd juxta Ravenserre* c 1240, *Odrauenser* 1260: ON *eyrr, oddr*].

Rawcliffe NRY, — WRY, **Rawcliffe Bank** NRY, **Out Rawcliffe, Upper Rawcliffe** La: 'red cliff': Scandinavianised forms of a name which appears elsewhere as Redcliff [1. *Roudeclif* 1086, 3. *Readclive* 1106, 4. *Outroutheclif* 1324: OE *rēad* ON *rauðr*, OE *clif*].

Rawtenstall La, 'rough (outlying) cowpasture'. OE *tūn-stall* was evidently used to denote places where rough grazing was seasonally available on the moors. **Rawtonstall** occurs nearby in WRY, where also are found **Saltonstall** and **Wittonstall** [1. *Routonstall* 1294: OE *rūh*, **tūn-stall*].

Rawtonstall WRY. See Rawtenstall La.

Ray *riv* Bk, —*riv* W, **Rea** *riv* C, —*riv* Sa-Wo, —*riv* Wa: 'river', a name arrived at by the wrong analysis of place-names in the form ME *atter ee* 'at the river', but misheard or misread as *atte ree*, the second word being taken to be a rivername [1. *La Ree* 1363, 3. *Le Ee* 1447, *Le Ree* 1455, 4. *in þære ea* c 957, *Ree* 1310: OE *ēa*].

Rayleigh Ess, 'doe clearing' [*Ragheleia* 1086: OE *rǣge, lēah*].

Rea *riv*. See Ray *riv*.

Read La, 'headland on which female roe-deer was seen', though it should be noted that the first element may also refer to a she-goat [*Revet* 1202, *Rieheved* 1418: OE *rǣge, hēafod*].

†**Reading** Brk, '(place of) people of Rēad or Reada', the personal name Read(a) meaning 'red one' [(*to*) *Readingum* c 900, *Red(d)inges* 1086: OE -*ingas*].

Reculver K, 'great headland', an unusual instance of a name surviving from Romano-British times hardly altered in form [*Regulbium* c 425, *Reculf* 669, *Roculf* 1086, *Raculvre* 1276: B **ro-, gulbiā*].

Redcar NRY, 'ready marshland', a hybrid name, the first element being English, the second Norse [*Redker* c 1170: OE *hrēod*, ON *kjarr*].

Redcliff So, 'red cliff', the name of the feature at Bristol, a variant of Radcliffe or Ratcliff (qq v) [*Radeclive* c 1180: OE *rēad, clif*].

Reddish La, 'reed ditch' or possibly 'red ditch.' The latter is probably the interpretation of **Redditch** Wo, a Latin version of which, (*de*) *Rubeo Fossato* c 1200, seems to remove all doubt [1. *Rediche* 1212, 2. *La Rededich* 1247, 1300, 1348, *The Redde Dych* 1536: OE *hrēod/rēad, dic*].

Redgorton Pth, 'fort by the little enclosure' [*Rothgortanan* c 1250: G *ràth, gortain*].

Redhill Sr, 'red slope', in which the less familiar *hield* has been replaced by the more usual *hill*—probably with some 'over-correction' involved as well, *-ld* frequently occurring in dialect forms for *-ll* in standard spelling, and so likely to be regarded as 'erroneous' even where it is historically justified, as here [*Redehelde* 1301: OE *rēad, helde*].

Redruth Co, 'red ford', the adjective and noun being here in Celtic order [*Ridruthe* 1259: Co *rid* 'ford', *rudh* 'red'].

Reelick Inv, **Ruillick** Inv: 'churchyard' [G *rèilig*].

Reepham LLi, — Nf: 'farm held by a reeve'. It is interesting to note that in each of these names *-fh-* in the early forms has been replaced by *-ph-*, this unnecessary exoticism being due no doubt to learned scribes accustomed to Greek spellings [1. *Refam* 1086, *Refham* c 1115, 2. *Refham* 1086: OE *(ge)refa, hām*].

Reeth NRY, '(place by a) stream' [*Rie* 1086, *Ryth* 1224: OE *rið*].

†**Reigate** Sr, 'doe gate', possibly indicating either an entrance to a deer-park, or a gap in a boundary passable by a doe with her young. A similar interpretation applies to **Rogate** Sx, the first element of which refers to the male roe-deer, instead of the female as in Reigate [1. *Reigata* 1170, 2. *La Rogata* 1196: OE *rǣge/rā, geat*].

Reiss Cai, '(place by a) cairn' [ON *hreysi*].

Renfrew Rnf, 'point of current', alluding to the confluence of the rivers Gryfe and Clyde. About twenty other names in Renfrewshire are of British origin, their present form owing much to Gaelic influence [*Reinfry* c 1128, *Renfriu* c 1150: OW *rhyn, frwd*].

Repton D 1443, 'hill of the Hrype (tribe)', the folk-name occurring also in Ripon WRY, '(among the) Hrype' [1. (*on*) *Hreopandune* 755, *Rep(p)enduna* 1086, 2. (*in*) *Hrypis* c 715, *Ripum* 1086: OE *dūn*].

†**Restormel** Co, 'moorland by Tormel, i e the bare hill' [*Rostormel* 1310: Co *ros, tor, moel*].

Retford Nt 1219, 'red ford', a variant of the frequent Radford (q v). East and West Retford is *Retheford* in Leland's *Itinerary* c 1540, in which the comment occurs '... of sum soundid Redford', and earlier spellings suggest other pronunciations as well [*Redford(e)* 1086, *Radford* 1177, *Rethford* 13c, *Rafford* 1202, *Ratford* 1227: OE *rēad, ford*].

Rhaeadr Rad, 'waterfall'. The Anglicised spelling Rhayader is often seen [*Raidergoe* 1191, *Rayadyr Gwy* 14c ('... on the river Gwy'): W *rhaeadr*].

Rhaglan Mon. See Raglan.

Rhiston Sa, 'rushy farm'. The present spelling is due to Welsh influence [*Ristune* 1086: OE *risc, tūn*].

Rhiwabon Den, 'Mabon's hill', the initial sound of Mabon being modified in the compound, and subsequently lost. The Anglicised spelling Ruabon is occasionally found [*Rywuabon* 1291: W *rhiw*].

Rhobell Fawr *mtn* Mer, 'great saddle' [W *rhobell, mawr*].

†**Rhondda** *riv* Glm,' noisy one', the name passing from the river to its valley and then to the settlement [*Rotheni* 12c, *Glenrotheny* 1268: W *glyn, rhoddni*].

†**Rhuddlan** Flt, 'red bank', alluding to the position of the place on the river Clwyd (q v) [*Roelend* 1086: W *rhudd, glan*].

Rhum *isld* Inv, 'space, room' [*Ruim* 677 G *ruim*].

Rhuthun Den, 'red fort', referring to the colour of the rock. The name is sometimes Anglicised as Ruthin [*Ruthun* 1253: W *rhudd, din*].

Rhyl Flt, 'the hill', a name of mixed origin, English *hill* being prefixed by the Welsh definite article [*Ryhull* 1301, *Hull* 1351: OE *hyll*, W *yr*].

Rhymni Mon, '(place on) the auger (river)', alluding to the powerful stream on which the town stands—indeed, being primarily the name of the river itself. The Anglicised spelling Rumney is occasionally found [*Rempney* 1291: W *rhwmp, -ni*].

Rhynd Pth, 'promontory' [G *rinn*].

Rhynie Abd, 'promontory', but the Rossshire **Rhynie**, near Fearn, is probably 'little fort' [1. *Rhynyn* c 1230, 2. *Rathne* 1529, G *rinn, roinn* 'point of land', *ràthan*, 'small *ràth* or fort'].

Ribble *riv* La-WRY, 'tearing one', alluding to the scouring action of the river (cf Rhymni) [*Rippel* c 715: OE **ripel*].

Ribbleton La, 'farm on (river) Ribble' (q v) [*Ribleton* 1201: OE *tūn*].

Ribchester La, 'Roman station on (river) Ribble (q v)', the great Roman fort of *Bremetennacum*, near which Sarmatian veterans of the Roman army were given land to cultivate. The Romano-British name may be derived from the old name of the river Ribble, **Bremaua*, 'roaring river', with the name-forming suffix *-acum* [*Ribelcastre* 1086: OE *ceaster*]. See also Ribbleton.

Ribigill Cai, 'farm on a ridge', inland from

the Kyle of Tongue, which may account for the persistence of the *-gill* termination, though the present form is due to a transposition of the middle consonants of the original name [*Regeboll*: ON *hryggr, ból*].

Richborough K, possibly 'entrenched place, fortress', the main component here being the Romano-British name *Rutupiae*, the stem of which is B **rut-* meaning 'spade'. The existence here of notable barrows, dating from the second or third century AD, may be relevant to the interpretation of the name [*Routoupiae* c 150, *Ratteburg* 1197: OE *burh*].

Richmond NRY, 'strong hill', a name either bestowed spontaneously by Frenchspeaking feudal tenants or transferred from France, where there are several places called Richemont [*Richemund* c 1112: OF *riche, mont*].

Richmondhill IOM. A name transferred from Richmond NRY (q v).

Richmond-upon-Thames Sr/GL, transferred from Richmond NRY. The previous name was **Sheen**, surviving in East Sheen and North Sheen, meaning 'shelters', doubtless felt by Henry VII to be not sufficiently dignified for the site of a royal palace [*Richemount* 1502: OF *riche, mont*].

Rickmansworth Hrt, 'Ricmār's enclosure'. The Domesday Book spelling with *Pr-* was evidently an error; *-man-* began to replace *-mar-* during the thirteenth century [*Prichemareworde* 1086, *Rykemarwurthe* c 1130: OE *worð*].

Riddings Db, **Riding** Nb, 'clearing(s)' [1. *Rydynges* 1296, 2. *Ryding* 1262: OE **ryding*].

Ridgmont Bd, — ERY: 'red hill', less obvious than **Rougemont** D, the name applied to the castle at Exeter. That Shakespeare's Richard III should have misheard the Exeter name as 'Richmond' suggests that Ridgmont is not so much of a distortion of the original as might be thought [1. *Rugemund* 1227, *Richemond* 1287, *Rougemont* 1349, 2. *Rugemunt* 1166: OF *rouge, mont*].

Riding Nb. See Riddings.

Riding (East, West, North). See East Riding.

Rievaulx NRY, 'valley of the river Rye', the British river-name meaning 'stream'. The OF termination occurs also in Jervaulx NRY (q v) [*Rieuall.* c 1149: OF *val(s)*].

Rigmaiden We, 'maiden's ridge', a hybrid name compounded in the order associated with Norse settlers from Ireland, viz with the qualifying element following the main component (cf Aspatria) [*Rig(g) maiden* 1255: ON *hryggr*, OE *mægden*].

Rinaston Pbl, 'Reyner's farm', alluding to the tenure of the family of John Reyner, mentioned in a document of 1315 [*Villa Reyneri* c 1300, *Reynerhiston* 1315: OE *tūn*].

Ringmer Sx, 'round lake' [*Ryngemere* 1276: OE *hring, mere*].

Rinns of Galloway Wig, 'points, headlands of Galloway' [*Le Rynnys* 1460: G *roinn*].

Rinns of Islay (Islay) Arg, 'divisions of Islay', one of the three districts into which the island was formerly divided [G *rann*].

Ripley *freq*, 'strip shaped clearing' [OE *ripel*, 'strip', *lēah*].

Ripon WRY, '(in the territory of) the Hrype people', the folk name being identical with that found in Repton Db (q v) [*(in) Hrypis* c 715, *Rypum* c 1030].

Rippingale LKe, 'nook of land occupied by the Hreppings, i e Hreppa's people' [*Hrepingas* 675, *Repingale* 806: OE *-ingas, halh*].

Risborough Bk. See Prince's Risborough.

Risca Mon, 'bank' [W *rhisga*].

River K, 'bank of a stream', this being the sense of OF *rivere* < Popular Latin *riparia*, corresponding to Classical Latin *ripa* [*Rip'ia* (=*Riperia, Riparia*) 1199, *La Ryvere* 1228: OF *rivere*].

River Sx, — W: '(place on the) brow of a hill', the initial consonant arising from a wrong division of the phrase *æt þære yfre*, 'at the brow', or its ME equivalent (cf Rock Wo, Rye Sx, and the analogous Nash Bk, Noke O, and Mapleton K) [1. *Euere* 1279, *Rivere* 1396, 2. *on ða yfre* 931: OE *yfer*].

Riverhead K, 'landing-place for cattle' [*Reddride* 1278: OE *hryðer, hȳð*].

Roberton Lnk, **Robeston Wathen** Pmb: 'Robert's village'. As there are two Robestons in Pembrokeshire, identification is ensured by means of affixes; Wathen is a manorial addition, the personal name Gwarthan being found also in **Llangwathan** Pmb; the other place is **Robeston West**, from its location [1. *Villa Roberti* c 1155, *Robertstun* 1229, 2. *Villa Roberti* 1282, *Roberdeston* 1366, 3. *Villa Roberti* 1343, *Robertiston* 1453: OE *tūn*].

Robertsbridge Sx, 'Robert's bridge', alluding to Robert de St Martin [*Pons Roberti* 1199: OE *brycg*].

Robeston Pmb. See Roberton.

Roborough D, 'rough hill'. The name occurs elsewhere in Devon, **Roborough Down** in Buckland Monachorum being one instance. Variants include **Rowberrow** So and **Rowborough** Wt [1. *Rawberga* 1086, 2. *Rueberge* c 1115, 3. *Rugebera* 1177, 4. *Rodeberge* 1086: OE *rūh, beorg*].

Rocester St, 'Hroðwulf's Roman station' [*Rowescestre* 1086: OE *ceaster*].

Roch Pb, **Roche** Co, — WRY, **Rock** Nb: 'rock'. The Nb example is from OE*rocc, derived from OF *roke*; the remainder are ME *roche*, derived from the alternative OF form, *roche* [1. *(de)Rupe* 1259, *(la) Roche* 1271, 2. *La Roche* 1233, 3. *(de) Rupe* 1199, *La Roche* 1251, 4. *Rok* 1242: OE *rocc, ME *roche*].

†**Rochdale** La, 'homestead by a hall', interpreting the earlier form of the name, *Rachedham*. The river-name, now Roch, seems to have been formed from this as *Rached* 13c. The river-valley then became known as *Rached-dale*, which supplanted *Rachedham* as the designation for the settlement. The strict interpretation of the modern name is therefore 'valley of the river flowing by *Rachedham*' [*Recedham* 1086, *Rachedham* c 1190, *Rachedal* c 1200: OE *reced, ræced, dāl*].

Rochester K, '*Durobrivæ* Roman station,' the first element being an eroded form of the Romano-British name. *Durobrivæ*, 'bridges by the stronghold', was accented on the second syllable; this led to the loss of the first syllable on alien lips, with heavy aspiration of the new initial *R-*, *Hrofi* being the outcome of this process [*Hrofæscæstræ* c 730, *Hrofescester* 811, *Rovescestre* 1086: B **duro-, brivā*, OE *ceaster*].

Rock Nb. See Roch.

Rock Wo, 'at the oak', a name of the same type as River Sx (q v) [1. *Ak* 1224, *Roke* 1259: OE *āc*].

Rockcliff Cu, 'red cliff', the first syllable

modified under Scandinavian influence, as in Rawcliffe (q v) [*Roudecliva* 1185, *Redeclive* 1202: OE *rēad, clif*]. See also Radcliffe, Roecliffe.

Rockingham Nth, 'homestead of Hrōc's people' [*Rochingeham* 1086: OE *-ingas hām*].

Rodings Ess, 'people of Hroða'. This family occupied a large area, and the modern villages are differentiated by additions. Some affixes are personal names — **Aythorpe Roding** was held by Aeitrop, son of Hugh, in the twelfth century; **Berners Roding** was in the tenure of Hugh de Berners in 1086. Others refer to such things as the lead of the church roof (**Leaden Roding**) or the rubble of the walls (**White Roding**). The church in **Margaret Roding** is dedicated to St Margaret [*duæ Rotinges* c 1050, *Roinges* 1086, *Rothinge* 1248: OE *-ingas*]. See also Abbess Roding, Beauchamp Roding.

Roecliffe WRY, 'red cliff' (cf Rockcliff Cu) [*Routhecliva* 1170: OE *rēad, clif*].

Rogart Sut, 'red enclosure' [*Rothegorth* c 1230: ON *rauðr, garðr*].

Rogate Sx. See Reigate.

Rogerstone Mon, **Rogeston** Pb: 'Roger's farm' [1. *Rogerston* 1535, 2. *Villa Rogeri* 14c, *Rogeriston* 1370: OE *tūn*].

Rohallion Pth, 'fort of the Caledonians' [G *ràth*].

Romansleigh D, 'Rumon's clearing', in reference to the saint venerated in this area. The church here is dedicated to this Celtic saint, whose name occurs also in **Polruan** Co 1292, 'Rumon's pool', **Ruan Lanihorne** Co, 'St Rumon's in Haiarn's glade', and **Ruan Major & Minor** Co. Tavistock Abbey was under the patronage of the saint, and the minor name Rumonsleigh occurs in that parish [1. *Liega* 1086, *Romundeylegh*' 1242, 3. *Lanrihorn* 1318, *Sti Rumoni de Lanryhorn* 1350, 4. *Sancto Rumono Parvo* 1277, *Sancti Rumoni Magni* 1315; 5. *Rumonslegh* 1349: OE *lēah*, Co *pol, lanerch*].

Romford Ess/GL, 'broad ford' [*Romfort* 1177: OE *rūm, ford*].

Romiley Ch, 'broad clearing' [*Rumelie* 1086: OE *rūm, lēah*].

Rona *isld* Ros, 'rough island' [ON *hraun, á*].

Ronaldsay, North *isld* Ork, 'Ringan's or Ninian's island' [*Rinarsey* c 1150: ON *ey*]. See also Ronaldsay, South.

Ronaldsay, South *isld* Ork, 'Rognvald's island'. The two Ronaldsays are widely separated, so that the differing origins are completely credible. The form *Ringan* for Ninian is hard to explain and seems to stem from Norse and/or vernacular Scots rather than from Gaelic; the customary form is from the Latin *Ninianus*, representing the British name *Nynnyaw*. The Ronald alluded to in South Ronaldsay was the brother of Sigurd, first Jarl of Orkney in the late ninth century [*Rögnvalsey* c 1150: ON *ey*].

Ronaldsway IOM, 'Rognvald's ford' [*Rakenaldwath* 1246: ON *vað*].

Roos ERY, **Roose** La: 'moor' [1. *Rosse* 1086, 2. *Rosse* 1086, *Roos* 1336: OW *ros*]. See also Ross.

Roscommon Rcm, 'grove or wood of Coman', celebrating St Coman, who founded a monastery in the place, and died in 747 [I *ros*].

Roscrea Tip, 'Cre's wood' [I *ros*].

Roseberry Topping NRY, 'hill-top of Oðinsberg, i e Oðin's hill', the initial *R-* remaining from a preposition or prepositional phrase, as in Rock Wo or River Sx (qq v) [*Othenesberg* 1119: ON *berg*, OE *topping*].

Rosemarkie Ros, 'point of land by Marcnidh, i e horse stream' [*Rosmarkensis* 1128: G *ros, marc, -nidh*].

Ross He, — Keb, — Nb, — Pth: 'moor', with the possibility of the secondary senses 'promontory' and 'upland wood' in appropriate instances. The sense is likewise uncertain in the Scottish county name† **Ross and Cromarty** [1. *Rosse* 1086, 3. *Rosse* c 1209: OW *ros*, G *ros*]. See also Cromarty.

Rossington WRY, 'village of the moorland people' [*Rosington* c 1190: OW *ros*, OE *-ingas, tūn*].

Rossinver Ltm, 'upland wood by the estuary' [I *ros, inbher*].

Rosslare Wex, 'middle headland' [I *ros, láir*].

Rostherne Ch, 'Rauð's thorn-tree', alluding doubtless to a tree serving as a landmark, or to a group of such trees, the ON term having occasionally this collective sense [*Rodestorne* 1086: ON *þorn*].

Rothbury Nb, 'Hroða's fortified place' [*Routhebiria* c 1125: OE *burh*].

Rother *riv* Db-WRY: 'principal river', the prefix being an intensive [*Roder* c 1200: B **ro-, dubro-*].

Rotherham WRY, 'homestead on (river) Rother' [*Rodreham* 1086: OE *hām*].

Rothesay Bte, 'Rother's island', the personal name alluding to Roderick, a son of the original grantee of Bute [*Rothersay* 1321: ON *ey*].

Rousay *isld* Ork, 'Rolf's island' [*Hrolfsey* c 1260: ON *ey*].

Rowberrow So, **Rowborough** Wt. See Roborough.

†Roxburgh Rox, 'Hroc's fortress' [*Rokisburc* 1127: OE *burh*].

Roy *riv* Inv, 'red (river)' [G *ruadh*].

Royston Hrt, 'village at Rohesia's cross', the suffix -*ton* being added to the earlier name Roys at a relatively late date. Roys was contracted from *Cruceroys*, referring to a cross which stood at the junction of Icknield Way and Ermine Street [*Crux Roaisie* 1184, *Roiston* 1286: (L *crux*) ME *cros*, OE *tūn*].

Royston WRY, 'Hrōr's village' [*Rorestone* 1086: OE *tūn*].

Royton La, **Ruyton** Sa, **Ryton** Du, **Ryton** Sa (x 2), **Ryton** Wa, **Ryton on Dunsmore** Wa: 'rye farm', only the last example of this fairly common name being distinguished by an affix, meaning 'on Dunn's waste upland' [1. *Ritton* 1226, 2. *Ruitone* 1086, 3. *Ritona* 1183, 4. *Ruitone* 1086, 5. *Rutton* 1250, 7. *Rietone* 1086: OE *rȳge*, *tūn*].

Ruabon Den. See Rhiwabon.

Ruan Lanihorne Co. See Romansleigh D.

Ruardean Gl, 'hill enclosure' [*Rwirdin* 1086: W *rhiw*, OE *worðign*].

Rue Point IOM, 'promontory', the second element being tautologous [G *rudha*].

†Rugby Wa, 'Hrōca's fortified place', the present termination really going back to

an original -*burh*, replaced perhaps only during the eleventh century by the Scandinavian termination [*Rocheberie* 1086: OE *burh*, ON *bỹ*].

Rugeley St, 'ridge clearing' [*Rugelie* 1086: OE *rycg*, *lēah*].

Ruillick Inv. See Reelick.

Ruislip Mx, 'muddy rush-bed', the second element indicating primarily 'slippery place', but in the context of a habitat for rushes being reasonably taken to refer to mud [*Rislepe* 1086: OE *rysc*, *slæp*].

Rumney Mon. See Rhymni.

Runcorn Ch, '(at the) spacious cove', describing the bay between Widnes and Castle Rock, now removed [*æt Rum.cofan* c 1000: OE *rūm*, *cofa*].

†Runnymede Sr, 'meadow on *Runieg*, i e council island', the island being doubtless originally called Runieg from its being a regular meeting place of royal or other assemblies [*Ronimede* 1215: OE *rūn*, *mǣd*].

Rush Dub, 'yew-tree promontory' [*Roseo* n d: I *ros*, *eó*].

Rushden Nth, 'rushy valley' [*Risden* 1086, *Rissenden* c 1115: OE *riscen*, *denu*].

Rutherglen Lnk, 'red valley' is on balance more likely than any meaning supposing a derivation from OE *hryðer* [*Ruthirglen* c 1160: G *ruadh*, *gleann*].

Ruthin Den. See Rhuthun Den.

Ruthven Pth, 'red place' [G *ruadh*, *mhaighin*].

Ruthwell Dmf, possibly 'spring by a cross', a famous Saxon cross preserved there doubtless constituting a sufficient reason for the name [OE *rōd*, *wella*].

†**Rutland** R, 'Rota's estate', the second element here having a special sense, not found, for instance, in other county-names such as Cumberland or Northumberland, in which the element undoubtedly means 'tract of land of considerable extent' [*Roteland* c 1060: OE *land*].

Rutupiæ. See Richborough K.

Ruyton. See Royton.

Ruyton-Eleven-Towns Sa, i e Ruyton of the eleven villages, viz Ruyton, Coton, Wykey, Shotatton, Shelvock, Eardiston, West Felton, Sutton, Rednal, Haughton, and Tedsmore.

Rydal We 1240, 'rye valley' [OE *rȳge*, *dæl*].

Rydal Water We, 'lake in rye valley', a recent name for a lake formerly known as Routhmere, 'lake of the river Rothay', the river-name signifying 'trout stream' [*Rydal Water* 1576—*Routhemere* 13c: ON *rauði, OE *mere*]. See also Rydal We.

Ryde Wt, '(place by) stream' [*La Ride* 1257: OE *rið*].

Rye Sx, '(place) at the island', the *R-* being a remnant of a prepositional phrase, as in Rock Wo (q v) [*Ria* 1130: OE *ieg*].

†**Ryedale** NRY, 'valley of river Rye', cf Rievaulx.

Ryhope Du, possibly 'rough valley' [*Reofhoppas* c 1050: OE *hrēof*, *hop*].

Ryton Du, — Sa, — Wa. See Royton.

Ryton NRY, 'village on river Rye', the river-name being possibly 'hill stream' [*Ritun* 1086: OE *tūn*].

Sabden La, 'fir tree valley' [*Sapeden* c 1140: OE *sæppe*, *denu*].

Sadberge Du, 'flat-topped hill', cf Setbergh [*Satberga* 12c: ON *setberg*].

Saddleworth WRY, 'enclosure on a saddle-shaped ridge'; the first element is found as a topographical term in Anglo-Saxon charters [*Sadelword* c 1230: OE *sadol*, *word*].

Saffron Walden Ess, 'Britons' valley, in which saffron is grown', the addition distinguishing this place from other Waldens in Essex and the neighbouring county of Hertfordshire. Numerous field-names occur in this area which testify to the growing of the saffron crocus (*Crocus sativus*) from about 1340 (cf EFN 189) [*Waledana* 1086, *Saffornewalden* 1582: ME *safron*, *walh*, *denu*]. See also Walcot.

†**St Albans** Hrt, '(place by) shrine of St Alban'. Alban was executed in AD 209, but it is the abbey dedicated to his honour which provided the present place-name, first recorded in the eighth century. Earlier names were *Verulamium* (q v) and *Wæclingaceaster*, 'Roman station of the Wæclings', referring to the people who gave their name to Watling Street (q v) [*Wæclingaceaster* c 900, *æcclesia Sancti Albani* 792, (*æt*) *Sancte Albane* 957: OE *-ingas*. *ceaster*].

St Andrews Fif, '(place with) (shrine of) St Andrew', the final *-s* of the name surviving from *Androis*, the Scots form of Andrew; it is not, as might be supposed, a possessive. An earlier name, Kilrimont or Kinrimont, means 'church (headland) at Rimont, i e royal hill' [*Cind righ monaigh* 747, *Chilrimunt* c 1139, *Sancti Andree* c 1158: G *ceann*, *cil*, OG *rig*, *monad*].

St Asaph Flt, '(church of) St Asaff' a renaming of the earlier Llanelwy, 'church on river Elwy, i e driving river', on its becoming a Norman bishopric. The saint lived during the sixth century [*de Sco Assaph* 1254]. See also Llanasa.

St Austell Co, '(church of) St Austol', alluding to the godson and companion of St Méen or Mewan (commemorated in Brittany under the former name and in Cornwall under the latter) [*Austol* c 1145]. See also St Mewan.

St Bees Cu, 'village with the church of St Bega', evidently originally called Kirkby, to which the saint's name was added, and this alone survives in the modern place-name. St Bega, an obscure Irish female saint of the seventh century, is not to be identified with *Begu* mentioned by Bede [*Cherchebi* c 1125, *Sancta Bega* 12c, *Kirkebibeccoch* c 1195: ON *kirkja-býr*].

St Breock Co, 'church of St Brioc', the dedication being to the sixth-century abbot who was born in Cardiganshire, preached in Cornwall, and then emigrated to Brittany where he founded the monastery near the place now called St Brieuc [*Sancti Brioci* 1309].

St Budeaux D, '(church of) St Budoc', earlier Budshead, 'Budoc's hide of land', the personal name being the male counterpart of Boudicca. The numerous aliases in a deed of 1671 are worth recording: *Butshead al. Boxhead al. Budocoshide al. St Budeax* [*Seynt Bodokkys* 1520, *Bucheside* 1086: OE *hid*].

St Buryan Co, 'church of St Byrian', referring to an obscure saint whose name seems to occur also in Lan-Verrien in Brittany [*Eglosberrie* 1086, *St Beriane* 1220: Co *eglos*].

St Clears Crm, **St Cleer** Co, '(church of) Saint Clear', both names presumably alluding to the same St Clarus [1. *Ecclesia de Sancto Claro* 1291, *Seint Cler* 1331, 2. *Sancto Claro* 1212, *Seintcler* 1230].

St Columb Major & Minor Co, 'greater/ lesser (place with church dedicated to)

St Columba', alluding possibly to the obscure virgin-martyr St Columba of Sens [*Sancte Columbe* 1266, *Sancte Columbe majoris* 1291, *Sancte Columbe Minoris* 1284].

St Davids Pmb, '(church of) St David', the Welsh name for the place being explicitly 'David's church' [*Yn hy Ddewi* 15 c: W: *ty*]. See also *Menevia*.

St Decumans So, '(church of) St Decuman' referring to a Welsh hermit who died at Dunster [*Sancti Decimi* 1203, *St Decuman* 1243].

St Denys Ha, '(place with church dedicated to) St Denis', alluding to the third century bishop and martyr who preached in Gaul and was eventually beheaded in Paris at the place now called Montmartre ('martyrs' hill'). Dedications to St Denis in England are often in the form *Denys* or occasionally (as at Market Harborough Lei) *Dionysius* [*Sancti Dionisii* 1192].

St Devereux He, '(church of) St Dyfrig', the saint commemorated in the early forms of Hentland He, *Hennlann Dibric* 1150, 'old church of St Dyfrig', where was situated one of his foundations; another was at Moccas He (q v) [(*Ecclesia*) *Sancti Dubricii* 1291].

†**St Edmundsbury** Sf. See Bury.

St Florence Pmb, '(church of) St Florentius', alluding to a male saint, either a Roman martyr of the third century or the somewhat later Gaulish saint venerated at Saumur [*Church of St Florentius* 1295].

St George Glm. See St Michael(s).

† **St Helens** La, — (Scilly) Co, — Wt: '(place with church or chapel dedicated to) St Helen' [3. *Selins* 1086, *S. Elena* c 1175].

St Ive Co, **St Ives** Hu: '(church of) St Ivo', referring to the saint whose bones were discovered at the Huntingdonshire place at the end of the tenth century, then known as Slepe (*Slæpi* 672, 'slippery place' <OE *slæp*) [1. (*Ecclesia*) *Sancti Ivonis* 1291, 2. *S. Ivo de Selepe* 1110].

St Ives Co, '(church of) St Ia', formerly Porthia, 'Ia's landing place', being the spot at which the Irish maiden came ashore after her leaf-borne voyage across the Irish Sea [*St Ya* 1283, *Porthya* 1284: Co *porth*].

St Ives Ha, 'ivy-grown place' [*Iuez* 1167: OE **ifet*].

St Ives Hu. See St Ive Co.

St Johnstone Pth. See Perth.

St Just in Penwith Co, **St Just in Roseland** Co: 'church of St Just', the place-name occurring also in France. Justus of Beauvais is said to have been martyred under Diocletian. The local affixes serve to distinguish the two Cornish places; Penwith (q v) is the peninsula in which Land's End is found; Roseland ('heath land') is by the Fal estuary [1. *Sancti Justi in Penwithe* 1334, 2. *Sancti Justi in Roslonde* 1282].

St Kilda *isld* Ros, 'shields'. A misreading of the name on charts led to the bringing of a spurious saint into existence. It is possible that the name was not originally applied to St Kilda itself but to a neighbouring group of islands, the outline of which resembled shields lying upon the surface of the sea [ON *skildar*].

St Lawrence Pmb, '(church of) St Lawrence' [*Rectoria Sancti Laurentii* 1535].

St Martin's Down Wt, 'butter hill, i e hill providing rich pasturage' [*Smeredone* 1313: OE *smeoru, dūn*].

St Marychurch D, 'church of St Mary' [(*æt*) *Sce Maria circean* c 1060: OE *cirice*].

St Marylebone Mx. See Marylebone.

St Mawes Co, 'church of St Mawdeth', alluding to a rather shadowy Celtic monk and missionary, a companion of St Budoc, and probably, like him, of Welsh origin [*Sanctus Maudetus* 1345].

St Mewan Co, 'church of St Mewan', alluding to the disciple of St Samson, whom he accompanied to Brittany with St Austol [*Sanctus Mewanus* 1305]. See also St Austell.

St Michael(s) *freq*, **St Michael Caerhays** Co, **St Michael Penkevil** Co, **St Michael(s) on Wyre** La, **St Michael's Mount** Co: 'place (with church or chapel) dedicated to St Michael', the allusion being to St Michael the Archangel, the veneration of whom dates from the earliest period of Christianity—a legacy, indeed, from Judaism. He was regarded as the patron saint of England probably before St George, the latter being commemorated by no major place-names in England (though he is named in the designation of a small place near Cardiff). In St Michael Caerhays the addition means 'fortified place where barley was grown'; Pencekevil is 'horse hill' [2. *Karihays* c 1300, *S. Mich. Karyheys* 1400, 3. *Sancti Michaelis de Penkevel* 1264: Co *caer, haiz, pen, cevil*]. See also Kirk Michael, Llanfihangel, Michaelston, Wyre *riv*.

St Neot Co, **St Neots** Hu: 'church of St Neot', alluding to a legendary hermit whose bones were translated in the tenth century to Huntingdonshire. Among the recent pronunciations of the Hunts name 'sneeds' and 'snouts' are recorded in PN Hu [1. *Nietestov, S. Neoti* 1086, 2. *S'Neod* 1132, *Villa S. Neoti* 1203: OE *stōw*].

St Osyth Ess, '(priory of) St Osgith', honouring a granddaughter of Penda and wife of Sighere, king of the East Saxons. She is said to have been buried here, and her local fame brought about a change of the name of the place from its former designation *Chich* ('place at a bend') [*Cicc* c 1000, *Cheche* 1280, *Sce Oside* 1205: OE **cicc*].

St Patrick's Isle IOM, 'islet of St Patrick', one of a number of places in the British Isles, especially in the Irish Sea area, honouring the fourth-century Romano-Briton who preached Christianity to the pagan Irish. See also Aspatria, Downpatrick, Kirkpatrick.

St Quivox Ayr, '(church of) St Caemhan', commemorated here in the affectionate-diminutive form, *Mochaemhoc*.

St Weonards He, 'church of St Gwennarth', honouring an obscure saint of the Welsh border. The word 'church' is included in the early forms of the name [*Lan Sant Guainerth* c 1150: W *llan*].

Salcey Forest Bk/Nth, 'forest of the willow wood' [*Boscus de Salceto* 1212: OF *salceie*, ME *forest*].

Salcombe D, **Salcombe Regis** D: 'salt valley'. *Regis*, 'belonging to the king' serves as a distinguishing addition; although it was granted by Æthelstan to the Dean and Chapter of Exeter, the former royal ownership is not recorded in place-name forms until the eighteenth century, and it may be an error arising from the proximity of the place to the road from Exeter to Lyme Regis [1. *Saltecumbe* 1244, 2. *æt sealt cumbe* c 1060, *Saltecumba* 1175: OE *sealt*, *cumb*].

Salcott Ess, **Saltcoats** Ayr: 'building in which salt was prepared or stored' [1. *Saltcot* c 1200, 2. *Saltcoates* 1548: OE *sealt*, *cot*]. See also Salt, Budleigh Salterton.

Sale Ch c 1205, '(place) at the willow-tree', the name being derived from the dative singular of the OE word [*Sala* c 1205: OE *salh*].

Salford Bd,† — La 1086: 'willow ford' [1. *Saleford* 1086; OE *salh*, *ford*].

Salford O, **Abbots Salford** Wa, **Salford Priors** Wa: 'ford over which salt was carried', instances of the numerous names recording the importance of the medieval salt trade. Other examples are **Saltford** So 1291, **Salterford** Nt 1241, and **Salterforth** WRY—the last two including the element *saltere*, 'seller of salt'. The additions in the Warwickshire names allude respectively to the Abbot of Evesham and the Prior of Kenilworth [1. *Saltford* 777, 2. *Saltforde Major* 714, *Salford* 1086, *Saltford Abbotes* 1316, 3. *Saltforde Minor* 714, *Saltford Prior* 1316, 5. *Saltreford* 1086, 6. *Salterford* c 1250: OE *ford*, *sealt*, *saltere*].

Salinis, 'at the salt-pans', Roman stations near Droitwich Wo and Middlewich Ch [2. *Salinis* 7c: L *salinae*].

†**Salisbury** W, 'fortified place at Sorvio', the termination of the British name having been apparently translated by the Saxons, who retained the first element. The Romano-British *Sorbiodunum* or *Sorviodunum* is certainly the name of a fort (B *duno-*), but the significance of the first element is obscure. *Sorbio*, or a form such as **Saruo*, suggested the OE *searu*, 'trick', so that the new formation *Searobyrg*, found in the Anglo-Saxon chronicle, was meaningful. Later a medial *-s-* was introduced, and the Domesday Book *Sarisberie* resulted. In an abbreviated form *Sarisberie* was misread as *Sarum*, which provided an alternative name and, in the form Old Sarum,

was particularly used for the original site of the settlement [*Searobyrg* (552) c 900, *Sarisberie* 1086, *Salesbury* 1227: OE *burh*].

Salkeld Cu, 'willow spring' [*Salchild* c 1100: OE *salh, celde*/ ON *kelda*].

Sall Nf, 'willow clearing or wood' [*Salla* 1086, *Salle* 1196: OE *salh, lēah*].

††**Salop.** See ††**Shropshire** (q v).

Salt St, 'salt-pit' [*Selte* 1086: OE *selte*].

Saltcoats. See Salcott.

Salter Cu, 'summer pasture by a salt-hole' [*Salterghe* 12c: OE *salt*, ON *erg*].

Salterford Nt, **Salterforth** WRY, See Salford O.

Salterton D. See Budleigh Salterton.

Saltford So. See Salford O.

Salton NRY, 'village by willows' [*Saletun* 1086: OE *sealh, tūn*].

Saltonstall WRY. See Rawtenstall.

Sampford Arundel So, **Sampford Brett** So, **Sampford Courtenay** D, **Sampford Peverel** D, **Sampford Spiney** D: 'sand ford'. The affixes all refer to feudal tenants. Besides these west of England examples **Great** and **Little Sampford** Ess may also be noted [1. *Sanford* 1086, *Samford Arundel* 1240, 2. *Saunford Bret* 1306, 3. *Sandfort* 1093, *Saunforde Curtenay* 1262, 4. *Sanforda* 1086, *Saunford Peverel* 1275, 5. *Saunford Gerardi de Spineto* 1234: OE *sand, ford*].

Sancreed Co, '(church of) St Faith', the early form being tautologous in that Cornish *sant* has been taken as part of the name [*Sancti Sancredi* 1291].

Sancton ERY, **Santon** Cu,—Nf, **Santon Downham** Sf: 'village with sandy soil' the term being strictly a distinguishing affix in the Suffolk example (quite near Santon Nf), whose basic name means 'hill homestead'. The spelling of the ERY name supposes a spoken form *Sangton* having developed (perhaps by 'over-correction') from *Santon* [1. *Santun* 1086, 2. *Santon* 13c, 3. *Santuna* 1086 4. *Dunham* 1086: OE *sand, tūn, dūn, hām*].

Sand Zet, 'sand (place), [ON *sand*].

Sand isld Arg, **Sanday** isld Inv, **Sanday** isld Ork: 'sand island' [ON *sand, ey*].

Sandbach Ch, 'sandy valley-stream' [*Sandbec* 1086: OE *sand, bæce*].

Sanderstead Sr, 'sand homestead' [*Sondemstyde* c 880: OE *hæmstyde*].

Sandford D, **Sandford Orcas** Do, **Sandford St Martin** O, **Sandford on Thames** O, **Sandford** Sa, **Sandford** We, **Dry Sandford** Brk: 'sandy ford.' The Berkshire place, distinguished by its affix from Sandford on Thames about four miles away, was the meeting-place of Hormer Hundred; it was a boggy area, and the sandy ford played an important part in providing a safe passage for those attending meetings of the Hundred. The affix in the Dorset name is manorial, representing the name of the Oriescuilz family, recorded in 1177 [1. *æt Sandforda* 930, 2. *Sandford-Orskuys* 1348, 3. *Sanford* 1086, 4. *æt Sandforda* 1050, 5. *Sanford* 1086, 6. *Sanfford* c 1245, 7. *fft Sandforda* 811: OE *sand, ford*]. See also Sampford Courtenay.

Sandhurst Brk, — Gl, — K: 'sandy wooded hill' [1. *Sandherst* 1175, 2. *Sanher* 1086, *Sandherst* 1167, 3. *Sandhyrste* 11c: OE *sand, hyrst*].

Sandown Wt, 'sandy riverside pasture'

[*Sande* 1086, *Sandham* 1271: OE *sand, hamm*].

Sandringham Nf, 'sandy (part of) Dersingham, i e the home of Deorsige's folk' [*Santdersincham* 1086: OE *sand, -ingas, hām*].

Sandwich K, 'sand landing-place' [*Sondwic* 851: OE *sand, wīc*].

Sandwick Zet, 'sandy inlet' [*Sandvik* 1360: ON *sand, vik*].

Sandy Bd, 'sandy island' [*Sandeia* 1086: OE *sand, ēg*].

Sanquhar Dmf, 'old fort' [*Sanchar* 1150: G *sean, cathair*].

Sansaw Sa, 'sandy patch of woodland' [*Sondsawe* 1327: OE *sand, sceaga*].

Santon Cu, — Nf, **Santon Downham** Sf. See Sancton.

Sapley Hu, 'fir-tree wood or clearing', the early spellings providing evidence for the growth of fir-trees in England well before the date normally suggested [*Sappele* 1227, *Sappeleye* 1275: OE *sæppe, lēah*].

Sarclet Cai, 'gull cliff' [ON *skari, klettr*].

Sarn Glm, — Mgm, **Sarnau** Crd, — Crm, — Mer: 'causeway(s)' [W *sarn*].

Sarnesfield He, 'open land by the road or causeway' [*Sarnesfelde* 1086: W *sarn*, OE *feld*].

Sarratt Hrt, 'dry place', an interpretation which tallies well with the location of the place high on the chalk in the sub-Chiltern area. Not far away lies Seer Green Bk, with a similar meaning [1. *Syreth* c 1085, *Sareth* 1094, 2. *La Sere* 1223: OE *sēar -ett*].

Satterthwaite La, 'wood by a summer pasture' [*Saterthwayt* 1336: ON *sætr, þveit*].

Saundersfoot Pmb, 'land at base of hill, held by Saunders'. *Foot* is not very often found in this topographical sense in England, but occasionally occurs in Scotland and Wales [*Sannders foot* 1602: MnE *foot*].

Savernake Forest W, 'district of a river called Sabrinā', alluding not to the Severn, but to another river bearing the same British name—probably the Bedwyn or the easterly branch of the East Avon. The meaning of *Sabrinā* is not known [*Safernoc* 934: B *Sabrinā, -āco-*].

Sawbridgeworth Hrt, 'enclosure of Sæbeorht' [*Sabrixteworde* 1086: OE *worð*].

Saxmundham Sf 1213, 'Seaxmund's homestead' [*Sasmundesham* 1086: OE *hām*].

Sca Fell *mtn* Cu, 'hill with a shieling' [ON *skáli, fjall*].

Scalloway Zet, 'bay by the shielings [ON *skáli, vàgr*].

Scalpay *isld* Inv (x 2), 'Boat (-shaped) island' [ON *skalpr, ey*].

Scapa Bay Ork, 'boat isthmus' [ON *skalpr, eið*].

†**Scarborough** NRY, possibly 'hill by a gap', an interpretation that tallies with the topography, supposing that the first element is the ON noun *skarð* and the second ON *berg*. The tradition of the foundation of the place by Þorgils Skarði goes back to a time before the earliest forms of the name on record, and his connexion with Scarborough is not necessarily being called in question, but the similarity between his nickname and

the *Scar-* component of the place-name may be coincidence; there is no doubt that surviving spellings point to ON *borg* as the second element, though an alteration from *berg* due to popular etymology would satisfactorily explain this [*Scardeburg* 1158: ON *skarð, berg* (or pers. n. *Skarði + borg*)]. See also Flamborough.

Scetis. See Skye.

Schiehallion *mtn* Pth, 'fairy hill of the Caledonians' [G *sidh*].

††Scilly, Isles of *islds* Co, of unknown meaning. The fifth-century Roman author refers to the group as if they were a single island, and uses a recognisable form of the name, which demonstrates a pre-English origin. None of the earliest spellings supports the *Sc-* spelling [*Sylinancim* c 400, *Sully* c 1120, *Sullia* 1186].

Scone Pth, 'lump, mass of rock' doubtless referring particularly to the Mote Hill, the ritual centre of Scottish kingship [*Sgoinde* 1020: G *sgonn*].

Scotland, 'land of the Scots', alluding to the Gaelic-speaking immigrants who invaded Caledonia from the west. By 500 a substantial number of them had reached the mainland by way of the Hebrides. Their small kingdoms were united in the face of opposition by the Picts, until, about 850, *Scotia* was regarded as an appropriate name for the whole country, replacing *Caledonia* and *Pictavia* in Latin texts. Previously, *Scotia* was the literary term for 'Ireland' (q v). See also Alba.

Scrabster Cai, 'rocky homestead, [*Skarabolstad* 1201: ON *skjære' bólstaðr*].

†Scunthorpe LLi, 'Skuma's dependent settlement' [*Escumetorp* 1086: ON *þorp*].

Seaborough Do, '(place by or on) seven hills' [*Seveberge* 1086: OE *seofon, beorg*].

Seaford Sx, 'ford by the sea' [*Saford* c 1150: OE *sæ, ford*].

Seaforth (Lewis) Ros, 'inlet of the sea' [ON *fjorðr, sǽr*].

Seaham Du, 'home settlement by the sea' [*Sǽham* c 1050: OE *sǽ, hām*].

Seasalter K, 'salt-works by the sea' [*Sealtern* 858, *Seseltre* 1086: OE *sǽ, sealtærn*].

Seathwaite La, 'clearing by a lake' [*Seathwhot* 1592: ON *sǽr, þveit*].

Seaton *freq*, **Seaton Carew** Du, **Seaton Delaval** Nb, **Seaton Ross** ERY, **Monkseaton** Nb, **North Seaton** Nb: mostly 'village by the sea', but **Seaton** ERY and **Seaton Ross** ERY are 'village by a lake'. Monkseaton Nb was owned by the monks of Tynemouth [OE *sǽ, tūn*].

Sedbergh WRY, **Sedbury** NRY: 'flat-topped hill' [1. *Sedbergt* 1086, 2. *Sadberge* 1157: ON *setberg*].

Seer Green Bk. See Sarratt.

Segontium. See Caernarvon.

Selattyn Sa, 'Acton, i e oak village, by a gully'. Welsh influence accounts for the change from -*ct*- to -*tt*- and for the retraction of -*u* to -*y*- , analogous to the modification seen in the last syllable of Prestatyn (q v) [*Sulatun* 1254: OE *sulh, āc, tūn*].

†Selby WRY, 'village by a willow copse', a hybrid name pointing to an original *Seletūn*, for which there is some independent evidence [*Seleby* c 1030: OE *sele, ON *bý*].

Selkirk Slk, 'church by a hall' [*Selechirche* c 1120: OE *sele, cirice*].

Selly Oak Wa, 'clearing on a ledge', with *Oak* as a recent addition, commemorating a prominent tree said to have stood in the village at one time [*Escelie* 1086: OE *scelf, lēah*].

Selsdon Sr, 'hill with or by a willow copse' [*Selesdun* c 880: OE **sele, dūn*].

Selsey Sx, 'seal island' [*Seolesiae* c 710: OE *seolh, ēg*].

Selwood So, 'sallow wood' [*Sealwyda* 878: OE *salh, wudu*].

Sence *riv* Lei, 'drinking cup, i e river of pure water' [*Sheynch* 1307: OE *scenc*].

Send Sr, 'sandy place' [*æt Sendan* c 960: OE **sende*].

Severn *riv* Mgm-So, of unknown meaning [*Sabrina* c 116, (*on*) *Sæfyrne* 706].

Severn Sea, 'estuary of the river Severn', also known as the Bristol Channel or Celtic Sea.

Shandwick Ros, 'sandy bay', a name of Norse origin modified by Gaelic influence [ON *sand, vík*].

Shanklin Wt, 'drinking-cup ridge', the first element being that found in the river-name Sence (q v), perhaps alluding to a waterfall from the ridge [*Sencliz* 1086: OE *scenc, hlinc*].

Shannon *riv* Lim-Cla, 'old one, primeval divinity' [*Senos* c 150, *Sinand* nd: OI *sen*].

Shap We 1279, 'heap (of stones)', alluding to the remains of an ancient stone circle by the main road up Shap Fell south of the town. [*Hep* 12c, *Yhep* 1241, *Yhap* 1292, *Shep* 1256: OE *hēap*].

Shapinsay *isld* Ork, 'Hjalpand's island,' with a development of the initial consonants as in Shetland (q v) [*Hjalpandisay* c 1250: ON *ey*].

Sharpness Gl 1349, 'abrupt or pointed headland' [*Nesse* 1086: OE *scearp, næss*].

Sheaf *riv* WRY. See Sheffield.

Sheen Sr, 'the sheds', as the name of the principal settlement changed to Richmond (q v), but surviving in East Sheen, the district between Putney and Richmond [*Sceon* c 950; OE **scēo*].

Sheepstor D, '(place by) bolt-shaped hill' [*Sitelestorra* 1186: OE *scyttels, torr*].

Sheerness K, 'bright headland' [*Shernesse* 1221: OE *scir, næss*].

Sheffield Sx, 'open land on which sheep grazed' [*Sifelle* 1086, *Shipfeud* 1275: OE *scēap, feld*].

†**Sheffield** WRY, 'open land on river Sheaf', the river-name meaning 'boundary', viz that between Derbyshire and the West Riding [1. *Scafeld* 1086, 2. *Scheve* 1183: OE *feld, scēað*].

Shefford Bd, 'sheep ford', being on the river Ivel at the point at which a Roman road crosses, but the ford was probably earlier than the road [*Sepford* 1220: OE *scēap, ford*].

Shehy (Sheehy) Mountains Crk, 'fairy hills' [I *sidh*]. See also Schiehallion.

Shendish Hrt, '(manor held by) Chaineduit'; in full the early forms show the name to have been Langley Chaineduit, so that this, like Virley Ess (q v), is one of the rare instances of a feudal affix surviving as the sole component [*Langleleye Chendut* 1262,

Shenduch 1561: OE *lang, lēah*]. See also Kings Langley, Stratfield Mortimer.

Shenley Hrt, 'bright clearing' [*Scenlai* 1086: OE *sciene, lēah*].

Shepperton Mx, 'shepherds' village' [*Scepertun* 959: OE *scēaphierde, tūn*].

Sheppey, Isle of K, 'sheep island' [*Scepeig* 696: OE *scēap, ēg*].

Shepshed Lei, 'sheep headland'. Though the possibility of an interpretation alluding to animal-head impalements cannot be ruled out, there is no evidence that this was a sacrificial site [*Scepeshefde* 1086: OE *scēap, hēafod*]. See also Gateshead.

Shepton Beauchamp So, **Shepton Mallet** So, **Shepton Montague** So: 'sheep farm', the distinguishing affixes being manorial [1. *Sceptone* 1086, *Septon Belli Campi* 1266, 2. *Sheopton Malet* c 1227, 3. *Schuptone Montagu* 1285: OE *scēap, tūn*].

Sherborne Do, — Gl, — Wa, **Sherborne St John** Ha, **Monk Sherborne** Ha, **Sherburn** Du, — ERY, **Sherburn in Elmet** WRY: '(place by) bright stream'. A tributary of the river Sowe in Warwickshire is called the Sherbourne, but the stream which gives its name to Sherborne Wa is the Sherborne Brook, which empties into the Avon. The first element in some of the examples may be OE *scīr*, 'shire'. There was formerly a priory at Monk Sherborne Ha [1. (*æt*) *Scireburnan* 864, 3. *Scireburne* 1086, 5. *Schireburne Monachorum* c 1270, 7. *Schireburn* 1086: OE *scīr, burna*]. See also Elmet.

Sheriff Hales Sa, 'nooks of land held by the reeve of the shire', the tenant in 1086 being Rainald Bailgiole, sheriff of Shropshire [(*æt*) *Halen* 1002, *Shiruehales* 1301: OE *scīrgerēfa, halh*]. See also Hale.

Sheringham Nf, 'homestead of Scira's people', the same personal name occurring in **Sherington** Bk, 'farm of Scira's people' [1. *Silingeham* 1086, *Siringeham* 1174, 2. *Serintone* 1086: OE *hām, tūn*].

Sherwood Forest Nt, 'wood belonging to the shire', a forest name resembling that of Shirlet Forest Sa (q v). The reference to the county may indicate common pasturage for swine, in much the same way as the Weald served the men of Kent. Alternatively, it may have been a hunting-ground over which the great landowners of the county had rights [(*of*) *Scirwuda* 955, *Shirewuda* 1163, *Sherewode* 1325: OE *scir, wudu*].

††**Shetland** 1289. See Zetland.

Shiant Islands *islds* Ros, 'sacred islands' [G *seunta*].

Shields, North Nb, **South Shields** Du, 'huts', respectively on the north and south of the river Tyne, fishermen's shelters each of which grew into a town [1. *Chelis* 1268, *Nortscheles* 1275, 2. *Scheles* 1235: ME *schele*].

Shifnal Sa, 'Scuffa's nook of land' [*Souffanhalch* 664: OE *halh*].

Shillelagh Wic, '(place of) descendants of Elathach', alluding to a hero of about the ninth century. Cudgels were made from pieces of an ancient oak tree here, known as 'The Sprig of Shillelagh', and the term *shillelagh* was applied to a cudgel of this kind [*Sil nElathaig* 11c, *Shilleylle* 1549: I *siol*].

Shipley Db, — Du, — Nb, — Sa, — Sx, WRY: 'woodland pasture for sheep' [1. *Scipelie* 1086, 3. *Schepley* 1236, 5. *Scapeleia* 1073: OE *scēap, lēah*].

Shipston on Stour Wo, 'farm by *Sheep-*

wash, i e the sheep-dipping place', the topographical feature being independently named in the earliest source, as *vadum nomine Scepesuuasce* c 770 [*Scepuuæisctune* c 770, *Scepwestun* 1086, *Chepeston* 1355: OE *scēap, wæsce, tūn*].

Shipton *freq*, 'sheep farm', a name attracting various feudal affixes including **Shipton Bellinger** Ha, **Shipton Moyne** Gl, and **Shipton Gorge** Do. Local additions include **Shipton under Wychwood** O, ' . . . below the forest of the Hwicce tribe' [OE *scēap, tūn*].

Shirburn O. See Sherborne.

Shire Oak St, **Shireoaks** Nt: 'oak tree(s) marking site of shire assembly'. Such a site is also referred to in **Shirland** Db, 'shire grove' [2. *Scirakes* c 1170, 3. *Sirelunt* 1086: OE *scīr, āc*, ON *lundr*].

Shireshead La 1577, 'head or upper portion of the shire' [OE *scīr, hēafod*].

Shirland Db. See Shire Oak.

Shirlet Sa, 1235, 'shire portion', i e, the territory of the county landowners as opposed to that of the king, represented in **Kinlet** Sa, 'royal portion', held in 1066 by Queen Edith, widow of Edward the Confessor. This apportionment of Wyre Forest land is paralleled by Sherwood Nt (q v) and instances of Kingswood in other counties [1. *Schirlet* 1172, 2. *Chinlete* 1086: OE *scīr, cyne-, hlēt*].

Shirley *freq*, either 'bright clearing' or 'shire clearing', the latter being an assembly-place or land held in common by landowners of the county [OE *scīr, lēah*].

Shoeburyness Ess, 'promontory by Shoebury, i e sheltering fortification', the first element being probably that found in Sheen Sr (q v), though used in a more general sense of topographical features rather than of buildings [*Sceobyrig* 894: OE **scēo, burh, næss*].

Shoreditch Mx 1235, '(place by) ditch of a bank', suggesting a channel draining a steep slope [*Schoresdich* 1221: OE **scora, dīc*].

Shoreham K, **Shoreham-by-Sea** Sx; 'homestead by a bank' [1. *Scorham* 822, 2. *Sorham* 1073: OE **scora, hām*].

Shotts Lnk, 'slopes' [*Bertrum Schottis* 1552: OE **scēot*].

†**Shrewsbury** Sa, 'fortified place of the *Scrob* region', embodying what was almost certainly the district name (meaning 'scrubland') and forming the core of the county name Shropshire (q v) [*Scropesbyri* 1006, *Scrobbesbyrig* 1016: OE **scrubb, burh*].

Shrivenham Brk 1217, 'riverside meadow allotted by decree', perhaps, as recently suggested (PN Brk 376), because the ownership was disputed. There is some evidence that the manor was once held by Abingdon Abbey [*Scriuenham* 821: OE *scrifen, hamm*].

††**Shropshire**, 'the shire headed by Shrewsbury (q v)', the modern form not surprisingly condensed from the very lengthy earliest spelling. The further contraction to ††**Salop** is due to the Normans, who resolved their difficulties with the consonants by changing the *-r-* to *-l-* (as they did also in *Salisbury*, q v), modifying the initial consonant, and breaking up the cluster by inserting *-a-*. The contracted form is no longer used as the official county name [*Scrobbesbyrigscir* 1006, *Sciropescire* 1086, *Salopescira* c 1096: OE *scīr*].

Shuckburgh Wa, **Shugborough** St: 'goblin-haunted hill', a meaning to be found in names with different second elements, e g **Shucknall** He (*Shokenhulle* 1377) [1. *Socheberge* 1086: OE *scucca, beorg* (*hyll*)].

Shuna *isld* Arg, 'look-out island' [ON *sjón*, 'view', *ey*].

Shunner Howe NRY, 'look-out hill' [*Senerhou* 1223, *Shonerhowes* c 1475: ON *sjón, haugr*].

Sidcup K, 'flat-topped hill', the place actually sitting on top of such a hill. The corresponding ON element is found in Sedbergh WRY (q v), Sedbury NRY, and Sadberge Du (q v). For several instances of field-names embodying the OE element, see EFN 196 [*Cetecopp* 1254: OE **set-copp*].

Sidlaw Hills Ang-Pth, perhaps 'seat hills' [*Seedlaws* 1799: G *suidhe*, OE *hlāw*].

Sidmouth D, '(place at) mouth of river Sid, i e the broad river' [*Sidemuða* c 1085: OE *sid, mūða*].

Silchester Ha, 'Roman station by a willow copse'. The Romano-British settlement here was *Calleva Atrebatum* (q v). As some forms in medieval documents relating to Silchester have the spelling *Cil-*, it has been suggested that this may be a survival from the Celtic name [*Silcestre* 1086: OE **siele, ceaster*].

Silloth Cu, 'barn by the sea' [*Selathe* 1299: OE *sǣ, hlaþa*].

Silverburn *riv* Abd. See Peffer.

Simonsbath So. See Bath.

Sion Mills Tyr, 'mills by fairy hills' [I *sidhean*].

Sissinghurst K, 'wooded hill of Seaxa's people' [*Saxinherste* c 1180: OE *hyrst*].

Sittingbourne K, 'stream of the Sidings, i e the slope-dwellers' [*Sidingeburn* 1200: OE *side, -ingas, burna*].

Skail Sut, **Skaill** Ork: 'shieling' [ON *skáli*].

Skeabost (Skye) Inv, 'Skith's farm' [ON *bólstaðr*].

Skegness LLi 1256, 'Skeggi's promontory' [*Shegenesse* 1166: ON *nes*].

Skelbo Sut, 'shell farm', in which the second element has been reduced to one quarter of its original size, as elsewhere in Sutherland [ON *bólstaðr*].

Skelmanthorpe WRY, 'Skelmer's outlying farmstead', containing the same personal name as in **Skelmergh** We, 'Skelmer's shieling', and **Skelmersdale** La, 'Skelmer's valley' [1. *Scelmertorp* 1086, 2. *Scelmeresherhe* c 1190, 3. *Schelmeresdele* 1086: ON *þorp, erg, dalr*].

Skelpick Sut, 'shelly place' [G *sgealbach*].

Skelton *freq*, 'farm on a ledge or bank' the OE first element being Scandinavianised by the change of *sc-* to *sk-*. There are several Skeltons in each of the Ridings of Yorkshire [OE *scylf, tūn*].

Skerray *isld* Sut, 'island by a reef' [ON *sker, ey*].

Skerries Dub, **Skerries** *isld* Ang, 'island by a reef' [2. *insula ... vocata le Skerrys* 15c: ON *sker, ey*].

Sketty Glm, 'island of Ceti' [W *ynys*].

Skibo Sut, 'Skithi's farm' [*Schythebol* 1275: ON *bólstaðr*].

Skiddaw *mtn* Cu, perhaps 'projecting crag', though 'snowshoe or ski mound' is possible [*Skithoc* 1230: ON *haugr*, **skyti/skið*].

Skipton WRY, **Skipton on Swale** NRY: 'sheep farm', the Scandinavianised form of Shipton (q v). A greater transformation has taken place in **Skipwith** ERY, in which not only has the initial consonant group been modified but the second element has been replaced as well, OE *wic*, 'specialised farm' giving way to ON *viðr*, 'wood' [1. *Scipton* 1086, 2. *Schipetune* 1086, 3. *Schipewic* 1086: OE *scēap*, *tūn*, *wīc*].

Skirwith Cu, 'shire wood', a Scandinavianised form of Sherwood (q v), with replaced second element [*Skirewit* 1205: OE *scir*, ON *viðr*].

Skokholm *isld* Pmb, possibly 'island in a channel'. Though many early forms have *Sc-* or *Sk-*, it is possible that spellings in *St-* represent the original name, *Sk-* having prevailed owing to the proximity of Skomer [*Scogholm* c 1225, *Stokholm* 1275: ON *stokkr*, *holmr*].

Skomer *isld* Pmb, 'cloven island' [*Skalmey* 1324: ON *skálm*, *ey*].

†Skye *isld* Inv, 'divided or winged island' [*Skitis* c 150, *Scia* c 700, *Skið* c 1250, *Scy* 1266: G *sgiath*, 'wing'].

Sky Hill IOM, 'wood-covered hill' [*Scacafel* 1257: ON *skógr*, *fjall*].

Slamannan St, 'hill-face of Manau' [*Slethmanin* 1250: G *sliabh*].

Slapton Bk, — D 1244, — Nth: 'farm by a slippery place' [1. *Slapetone* 1086, 3. *Slaptone* 1086: OE *slæpe*, *tūn*].

Slea Head Ker, 'mountain headland' [I *sliabh*, OE *heafod*].

Sleat (Skye) Inv, 'level place' [*Slate* c 1400: ON *slétta*].

Sleatygraigue Lx, 'village by a mountain' [I *sliabh*, *graig*].

Slieau Doo *mtn* IOM, 'black mountain' [G *sliabh*, *dhubh*].

Slieau Roy *mtn* IOM, 'red mountain' [G *sliabh*, *ruadh*].

Slieveardagh Hills *mts* Klk-Tip, 'mountain of the high field' [I *sliabh*, *ard*, *achadh*].

Slieveroe *mtn* Klk, 'red mountain' [I *sliabh*, *ruadh*].

Slieve Snaght *mtn* Don, 'snow mountain' [I *sliabh*, *sneacht*].

Sligo Sli, '(place by) shelly river' [I *sligeach*].

Slimbridge Gl, 'bridge at a slippery place' [*Heslinbruge* 1086, *Slimbrugia* 1153: OE *slim*, 'slime, mud', *brycg*].

†Slough Bk 1443, '(place in) mire', a name confirmed by the topography, a low-lying riverside landscape. The article *le* occurs with several early forms, including that of 1443, indicating that the name was being consciously used of the natural feature rather than as the designation of a settlement [*Slo* 1195: OE *slōh*].

Smailholm Rox, 'narrow village' [*Smalham* 1246: OE *smæl*, *hām*].

Small Heath Wa, 'narrow heath or moor' [*Smallehethe* 1461: OE *smæl*, *hæð*].

Smethwick Ch, — St 1221: 'smiths' place of work', *wic*, 'outlying farm' having here its extended sense of 'specialised premises, including industrial places of work' [1. *Smethewyk* 1331, 2. *Smedeuuich* 1086: OE *smið*, **smeoða* gen. pl. (Angl), *wic*].

Smithfield Mx, 'smooth open land' [*Smethefelda* c 1145: OE *smēðe, feld*].

Snaefell *mtn* IOM, 'snow mountain' [ON *snær, fjall*].

Snape *freq*, of doubtful meaning. Two possible sources have been suggested: OE *snæp*, probably 'boggy patch of land' and ON *snap* 'poor pasturage, patch of scanty grass for sheep to nibble at in snow-covered fields'.

Snead Mgm, 'detached piece of land' [*Sned* 1201: OE *snæd*].

Sneinton Nt 1194, 'village of Snot's people', retaining the *S-* of the personal name which Nottingham, nearby, has lost [*Notintone* 1086, *Snotintone* 1165: OE *-ingas, tūn*].

Snowdon *mtn* Crn, 'snow hill', in Welsh *Yr Wyddfa*, 'cairn place'. It is interesting to note the long history of the English name, compared with the scanty information available of some mountain-names in England itself [*Snawdune* 1095, *Snoudon* 1283: OE *snāw, dūn*, W *gwydd, ma*].

Soa *isld* Arg, **Soay** *isld* Inv, — *isld* Ros, **Soay Mor** *isld* Inv: 'sheep island', the last example being 'great sheep island' [ON *sauða, ey*, G *mór*].

Soar *riv* Wa-Lei-Nt, 'flowing one' [*Sora* 1147: B **sar-*].

Sodor. See Hebrides. See also Sutherland.

Soham C, **Earl Soham** Sf, **Monk Soham** Sf: 'homestead by a lake'. Drainage during medieval times has removed the lakes, but there is Domesday Book evidence of the existence of such a feature in Soham C. The earl alluded to was the Earl of Norfolk; Monk Soham was held by the abbey of Bury St Edmunds [1. *Sægham* c 1195, 2. *Saham*

1086, *Earl Saham* 1235, 3. *Monks Saham* 1235: OE *sæ, hām, eorl, munuc*].

Solent Ha, of uncertain meaning, but the second element is probably a British word signifying 'stream' [*Soluente* c 730].

†Solihull Wa, probably 'muddy hill', confirmed by the existence of thick red clay on the hill to the south of the church [*Sulihull* 1242: OE **sylig, hyll*].

Solway Firth, 'inlet of the pillar ford', probably alluding to the Lochmaben Stone, marking the ford [*Sulewad* 1229: ON *sūl, vað, fjorðr*].

Somerby Lei, — L (x 3). See Somerleyton.

Somerleyton Sf, 'Sumarliði's farm', the ON personal name, meaning 'summer warrior', being found also in the several instances of **Somerby** and in **Somerton** Sf [1. *Sumerledetuna* 1086: OE *tūn*].

Somersal Herbert Db, **Hill Somersal** Db, **Potter Somersal** Db: 'Sumor's nook of land', the additions being respectively 'held by Fitzherbert family', 'on the hill', and 'occupied by potter(s)'. Somersal Herbert was also known as Church Somersal; Hill Somersal, formerly Upper Somersal, is on higher ground than Somersal Herbert [1. *Summersale* 1086, *Somersale Herbert* c 1300, *Chirchesomersale* 1278, 2. *Oversomersale* 1318, *Somersale super montem* 1485, 3. *Alia Summersale* 1086, *Potter Somersall* 1415: OE *halh, hyll, cirice, potere*].

Somerset, '(district of) dependent settlers around Somerton, i e the summer dwelling'. This county name is strictly a 'folkname', i e the designation of the people rather than of the area in which they lived. The termination *-shire* is conventionally omitted from the modern form, though there is historical warrant for its use (*Sumersetescir* 1122) [*Summurtunensis* *paga* c 894, *Sumersæton* 1015: OE *sæte, sumor, tūn*].

Somersham Hu, — Sf: 'Sumor's homestead' [1. *Summeresham* c 1000, 2. *Sumersham* 1086: OE *hām*].

Somerton LKe, — Nf, — O, — So: 'summer dwelling', indicating a pasturage usable only in summer because of marshy conditions, elevation, or other features. Seasonal migration of people with their cattle, known as transhumance, is recorded in various place-names, such as those referring to 'shielings' as well as names that specifically allude to summer. Interpretations are complicated by the existence of OE and ON personal names like *Sumor* and *Sumarliði* [1. *Summertune* 1086, 2. *Sumerton* c 1045, 3. *Sumertone* 1086, 4. *Sumertone* 1086: OE *sumor, tūn*] See also Somerset.

Somerton Sf. See Somerleyton.

Sonning Brk. See Sunningdale.

Sorbioduum, Sorviodunum. See Salisbury.

Sorn Ayr, '(place with a) kiln' [G *sorn*].

Sosgill Cu, 'huts by swampy ground' [*Saurescalls* 1208: ON *saurr, skáli*].

Southall Mx, 'southern nook of land', correlating with Northolt Mx [1. *Sudhale* 1204, 2. (*æt*) *Norðhealum* c 960: OE *sūð, norð, halh*].

Southampton Ha, 'farm by waterside land—in the south', contrasted with Northampton, though it must be noted that despite the similarity of forms, both early and modern, the two names are of different origin. Southampton was originally *Hammtūn*, whereas Northampton was *Hāmtūn*. Because of the great distance between them, the additions are to be taken as 'in the south' and 'in the north',

rather than as 'south of' or 'north of' some named place. The two towns were connected by one of the great medieval trunk routes, via Winchester, Whitchurch, Newbury, Abingdon, Oxford, and Brackley, and it is noteworthy that the form *Suðhamtun* first occurs in a MS of the Anglo-Saxon Chronicle written at Abingdon [1. *Homtun* 825, *Hamtun* 837, *Suðhamtun* 962, 2. *Hamtun* 917, *Norðhamtun* 1065: OE *sūð, hamm, tūn*].

Southease Sx, 'south brushwood (place)' [*Sueise* 966: OE *sūð, hæs*].

Southend-on-Sea Ess, 'southern extremity of the parish', viz of Prittlewell Ess (q v) [*Southende* 1481: OE *sūð, ende*].

†South Hams D, 'southern riverside land', the district between Plymouth and the Dart estuary, bounded on the north by Dartmoor. The area was divided into two, each part being called *Hamme*. Stokenham D was earlier *Stok in Hamme* (1276) from its location in the easterly half of the peninsula between Kingsbridge and the sea [*Southammes* 1396: OE *sūð, hamm*].

South Mimms Mx. See Mimms, North.

South Pool D. See Poole.

Southport La, 'haven in the south', though it is uncertain what the reference is precisely, although (or perhaps because) the name is of quite recent origin. The place developed as a seaside resort, and possibly *port* signified little more than this to the man who devised the name.

South Ronaldsay. See Ronaldsay.

South Shields Du. See Shields, South.

South Uist. See Uist.

Southwaite Cu, 'clay clearing', the first consonant modified by dissimilation [*Thougthuayth* 1380: OE *þōh*, ON *þveit*].

Southwark Sr, 'fortification of the men of Surrey', the sense of the earliest spelling, though forms of a little later can be rendered 'southern fortification', i e south of the city of London. The district has borne the alternative designation of **The Borough** for at least three centuries [*Suþriganaweorc* 10c, *Suðgeweorc* 1023: OE *sūð, geweorc*].

Southwell Nt, '(place at) the southern spring', in contrast to Norwell Nt, some miles to the north-east. The 'spring' is the Lady Well by the church [*at Suðwellan* 958: OE *sūð, wella*].

Southwick Du, — Gl, — Ha, — Nth, — Sx, — W: 'southern dependent or specialised farm' [1. *Suthewich* c 1170, 2. *Sudwicha* 1086, 3. *Sudwic* 12c, 4. (*æt*) *Suthwycan* c 980, 5. *Sudewic* 1073, 6. *Sothewyke* 1322: OE *sūð, wīc*].

Southwick Kcb, 'clearing in a boggy place' [*Suchayt* c 1280: ME *sogh*, ON *þveit*].

Southwold Sf, **Southwood** Nf: 'southern wood'. Although there is a Northwold in Norfolk, Southwold is not named in relation to it. Southwold's point of reference is likely to have been Lowestoft [1. *Sudwolda* 1086, 2. *Suthuuide* 1086: OE *sūð, wald, wudu*].

Sowerby La, — NRY, — WRY, **Sowerby Bridge** WRY, **Sowerby Hall** La, **Sowerby under Cotcliffe** NRY, **Brough Sowerby** We, **Castle Sowerby** Cu, **Temple Sowerby** We: 'settlement in a boggy place', the first element evidently alluding to waterlogged, acid soil of moorland places. The addition *Temple* here, as elsewhere, indicates ownership by the Knights Templars [1. *Sorbi* 1086, 2. *Sorebi* 1086, 3. *Sorebi* 1086, 4. *Soureby Brygge* 1478,

7. *Soureby by Burgh* 1478: ON *saurr, býs*, OE *brycg*].

Spalding LHo, '(place of) the people of Spald', alluding possibly to a place of origin on the continent. Another possibility is that *Spaldas* was the name or title of a small group and the Spaldings were 'people of the Spaldas'. The tribal name is found also in **Spalding Moor** ERY, **Spaldington** ERY, **Spaldwick** Hu, and **Spalford** Nt. There is no reason to think that these names represent the extent of the tribal territory; it is more likely that these were local pockets of colonists from the territory around Spalding itself [1. *Spaldyng* 1051, 2. *Spaldinghemore* 1172, 3. *Spellinton* 1086, 4. *Spaldwic* c 1050, 5. *Spaldesford* 1086: OE -*ingas, ford, tūn, wic, mōr*].

Spanish Head IOM, alluding to the disastrous voyage of the Spanish Armada in 1588. **Spanish Point** Cla commemorates the same event.

Sparkbrook Wo, '(place by a) stream named after the Spark family' referred to in records of Yardley in the thirteenth and fourteenth centuries [*A torrent called Sparkbroke* 1511: OE *brōc*].

Speen Brk 1751, '(place which was source of) shavings, where shingles were made', affected by—but hardly derived from—a Latin form meaning 'at the thornbushes'. *Spene*, the name of a wood referred to in a charter dated 821, has the same relationship with OE *spōn*, 'chip, shaving', as OE *sende* has with *sand*. So just as Send Sr is 'place where sand was obtained', so *Speen* may be interpreted 'place where small pieces of wood were obtained'. The connexion with the Latin word may be one of folk etymology [*Spinis* 4c, *Spene* 821, *Spone* 1086: Lat *spina*, OE *spōn*].

Speke La 1252, '(place among) brushwood' [*Spec* 1086: OE *spæc*].

Spink Lx, '(place by a) pinnacle, point of rock' [I *spinc*].

Spithead Ha, 'headland facing the sandspit', a name for which records go back only to the seventeenth century and applied to the channel within which is a sandbank called Spit Sand.

Spital Cai, **Spital in the Street** LLi, **Spittal** ELo, — Nb, — Pmb, **Spittaltown** Wme: 'place with a poor-house or an asylum for the sick' [2. *Hospitale* 1204, *Spitelenthestrete* 1322, 5. (*de*) *Ospitali* 1259, *Spital* 1319: ME *spitel*].

Sprint *riv* We, 'spirting river', a mountain stream with a swift current [*Spritt* c 1190: OE (*ge*)*sprintan*].

Spurn Head ERY, 'sharply projecting headland', connected etymologically and topographically with Ravenser Odd (q v) [*Ravenserespourne* 1399: ME **spurn*, OE *hēafod*].

Stackpole Elidor Pmb, 'pool by the stack, i e precipitous rock off the coast, held by Elyder'. **Bosherston** Pmb was formerly Stakpole Bosher, and the feudal addition *Elidor* served to clarify the distinction [*Stakepol* 1230, *Stakepoll Elyder* c 1200: ON *stakkr*, OE *pōl*].

Stacks of Duncansby Cai, 'steep coastal rocks off Duncansby Head' [ON *stakkr*].

Staffa *isld* Arg, 'pillar island', from the columns of basalt characteristic of the scenery of the island [ON *stafr, ey*].

†**Stafford** St, 'ford beside a landing-place', the ford being perhaps the limit of navigation on that part of the river Sow, which would account for the growth of a settlement at this point. The earliest form for this name is an abbreviation on tenth-century coins [*Stæþ* 10c, *Stæfford* 913: OE *stæð, ford*].

Stain LLi, **Staines** Mx, **Steane** Nth: '(place by or at) a stone', the feature being either an isolated boulder or a Roman milestone. The first example is derived from the ON element; the others are from OE [1. *Stein* c 1115, 2. *Stana* 969, *Stanes* 1086, 3. *Stane* 1086: OE *stān*, ON *steinn*].

Stainforth WRY. See Stanford.

Stainton *freq.* See Stanton.

Stair Ayr, '(place by) stepping stones' [G *stair*].

Staithes NRY, 'landing place' near, and for the benefit of, Seaton NRY (q v) [*Setonstathes* 1415: OE *stæð*].

Stalbridge So, '(place at a) bridge built on piles' [*Stapulbreicge* 998: OE *stapul, brycg*].

Stalybridge Ch 1687, 'bridge by Stayley', the longer name having been originally that of a small place in Lancashire across the river Tame from **Stayley** Ch, 'clearing where staves were got', and subsequently superseding Stayley as the name of the Cheshire township [1. *Stayley Bridge* 1788, 2. *Stauelegh* c 1220: OE *brycg, stæf, lēah*].

Stamford LKe, — Nb, **Stamford Bridge** ERY: 'stony ford or ford of stones', a modified form of Stanford (q v). Stamford LKe was established where Ermine Street and other ancient roads converged at this crossing of the river Welland, and its strategic as well as commercial importance was recognised by the Danish army in making it an important military centre and one of the Five Boroughs (q v). Stamford Bridge was also originally a ford, situated where a number of roads from all parts of the East Riding converge at the river Derwent; in the battle in September 1066 the bridge was heroically defended by a single Norwegian

[1. *Steanford* 922, 2. *Staunford* 1242, 3. *Stanford* c 730, *Stanfordbrycg* 1066, *Pundelabataille* 1251: OE *stān, ford, brycg* (OF *pont, bataile*)]. See also Stanton.

Stamford Mx, 'sandy ford' [*Sandford* 1236: OE *sand, ford*].

Stamfordham Nb, 'homestead at Stamford, i e stony ford' [*Stanfordham* 1188: OE *stān, ford, hām*].

Stanbridge Bd, — Ha: '(place at a) stone bridge', the Bedfordshire place being about a mile from its bridge [1. *Stanbrugge* 1165, 2. *Stanbrig* 1242: OE *stān, brycg*].

Standen Brk, — Wt: 'stony hill', the meaning concealed by the *-den* spelling of the modern forms, due of course to the lack of stress on the second syllable [1. *Standone* 1086, 2. *Standone* 1086: OE *stān, dūn*].

Standen K, 'a stony woodland pasture', [*Stanehtenden* 858: OE *stæniht, denn*]. See also Benenden.

Standen La, — W: 'stony valley' [1. *Standen* 1258, 2. *Standene* 1086: OE *stān, denu*].

Standish Gl, — La: 'stony pasture' [1. *Stanedis* 872, 2. *Stanesdis* 1178: OE *stān, edisc*].

Stane Street. See Streatham.

Stanford Bd 1086, — K 1035, — Nf, **Stanford Bishop** He, **Stanford Dingley** Brk, **Stanford in the Vale** Brk, **Stanford le Hope** Ess, **Stanford Regis** He, **Stanford Rivers** Ess, **Stanford on Avon** Nth, **Stanford upon Soar** Nt: '(place at) a stony ford or ford made of stones', the more frequent and unmodified form of the name a variant of which is Stamford (q v). A Scandinavianised version is found in Stainforth WRY (x 2). Stanford Bishop and Stanford Dingley are manorial, being respectively

in the tenure of the Bishop of Hereford and of the Dyngley family; Stanford Regis was of course a royal holding; Stanford Rivers was held by Richard Rivers in the early thirteenth century. The Vale referred to in the second Berkshire name is the Vale of the White Horse (q v). Stanford le Hope is near Broad Hope Ess [3. *Stanforda* 1086, 4. *Stanford Episcopi* 1316, 5. *Stanworde* 1086, *Staneford Deanly* 1535, 8. *Kingestanforde* 1242, 10. *Stanford super Hauene* c 1150, 12. *Steinforde* 1086: OE *stān, ford*].

Stanley freq, 'stony clearing' [OE *stān, lēah*].

Stanstead Sf, — Sx, **Stanstead Abbots** Hrt, **Stanstead St Margarets** Hrt, **Stansted** K, **Stansted Mountfitchet** Ess: possibly 'site of a stone building'. Stanstead Abbots was held by the Abbot of Waltham in 1212; it was situated across the river Lea from Stanstead St Margarets, which was originally called Thele or *Pont de Thele*, 'tile bridge', probably indicating that the bridge was constructed from Romano-British tiles or bricks; later names include St Margaret Thele (from the dedication of the church) and Stanstead Thele (from Stanstead Abbots). Richard de Muntfichet held the Essex place in 1190 [1. *Stanesteda* 1086, 2. *Stansted* 1203, 3. *Stanstede Abbots* c 1322, 4. *Thele* 1296, 5. *Stansted* 1231, 6. *Stanesteda* 1086: OE *stān, stede* (OF *tuile*)].

Stanton *freq*, 'stony farm'. Numerous manorial, descriptive, and topographical affixes occur, and the Scandinavianised Stainton is frequent in northern counties of England. Another variant is Staunton, which preserves the AN spelling of the first element [OE *stān, tūn*]. See also Stenton.

Stanwix Cu, 'stone walls', viz those of the Roman fort of *Uxellodunum* 'high fort' [*Steynweuga* c 1160: ON *steinn, veggr*].

Stapenhill St, 'at the steep hill' [OE *æt steapan hylle*].

Stapleford *freq*, 'ford marked by post(s)'. possibly because of hazardous crossings or because the ford was at some distance from the road [OE *stapol, ford*].

Stapleton *freq*, 'farm by a post', except possibly for Stapleton He and Stapleton Sa, 'farm by, or village with, a steeple' [2. *Stepeltone* 1286, 3. *Stepleton* 1242: OE *stapol, stēpel, tūn*].

Start Point D, 'promontory headland' [OE *steort*].

Stathe So 1233, 'landing place' [OE *stæð*]. See also Staithes.

Staughton. See Stockton.

Staunton. See Stanton.

Steane. See Stain.

Stemster Cai, — Ork: 'farmstead with a gable' [1. *Stambustar* 1557, 2. *Stembister* 1559: ON *stafn, bólstaðr*].

Stenhousemuir Stl, 'moorland by the stone house' [*de Stan house* c 1200, *Stenhous* 1601: OE *stān, hūs, mōr*].

Stenness Zet, 'stone promontory' [*Steinsness* c 970: ON *steinn, nes*].

Stenton ELo, 'stone village', a Scandinavianised variant of Stanton (q v) [*Steinton* 1150: OE *stān, tūn*].

Stepney Mx, 'Stybba's landing-place' [*Stybbanhyþ* c 1000: OE *hȳð*].

Stevenage Hrt, '(place at) the firm oak', the first element, rare in place-names, meaning 'stiff, strong' and perhaps alluding to the foliage of the particular tree. OE *hæcc* has been suggested as the

second element; this would indicate a meaning 'firm gate', but it is difficult to accept in view of a general scarcity of forms with -*h*- [*Stithenæce* c 1060: OE *stið, āc*].

Stewarton Ayr, 'Steward's estate', named from Walter, High Steward to King David I [*Stewartoun* 1201: OE *tūn*].

Stichill Rox c 1200, '(place by) sticky or muddy hill' [*Stichehill* c 1270: OE *sticce, hyll*].

Stillorgan Dub, 'Lorcan's church', founded by Lawrence O'Toole (Lorcan ua Tuathail) in the twelfth century. St Lorcan was deeply revered by his flock in his archbishopric of Dublin and defended the rights of the church against Henry II of England. *St*- for *T*- occurs as a dialectal peculiarity in the east of Ireland [*Tigh-Lorcain* n d: I *tigh*].

Stilton Hu 1219, 'farm by or on a steep ascent' [*Sticiltone* 1086: OE *stigel, tūn*].

Stinchcombe Gl, 'dunlin valley', the first element being *stint*, the dialect word for the dunlin or sandpiper (*Calidris alpina*) in current use in parts of Britain [*Stintescombe* c 1155: OE **stint, cumb*].

†**Stirling** Stl, of unknown meaning. Suggestions include the name of the river on which Stirling stands [*Strevelin* 1124, *Sterling* c 1470].

Stob Dubh *mtn* Arg, 'black stump' [G *stob, dubh*].

Stockbridge Ha, — MLo, **Stockbriggs** Lnk: 'bridge of tree-trunks' [1. *Stoccbrigge* 1227: OE *stocc, brycg*].

Stockham Ch. See Norton.

†**Stockport** Ch, 'market-place at a dependent settlement', the first element being

stoc, 'holy place, monastery or monastic cell, secondary settlement', often found in modern names as *Stoke*, a spelling found very early in the medieval forms of Stockport [*Stokeport* c 1165: OE *stoc, port*].

Stockton *freq*, 'farm at a dependent settlement', sometimes with topographical affixes, e g †**Stockton on Tees** Du, **Stockton on Teme** Wo, and **Stockton on the Forest** NRY. Variant forms include **Little Staughton** Bd, **Great Staughton** Hu and the several instances of **Stoughton** [OE *stoc, tūn*].

Stockwell Sr, 'spring by a tree-trunk', possibly alluding to a bridge or other structure [*Stokewell* 1197: OE *stocc, wella*].

Stogumber So, **Stogursey** So: 'secondary settlement', with manorial additions fused with the name. The feudal tenants were Gunmer and de Curci [1. *Stoke Gunner* 1225, 2. *Stoche* 1086, *Stok Curcy* 1212: OE *stoc*].

Stoke *freq*, 'place, religious place, monastery, monastic cell, secondary settlement, hamlet', found with a great variety of additions. Many affixes are surnames, e g **Stoke d'Abernon** Sr, **Stoke Doyle** Nth (d'Oilli), **Stoke Farthing** W (de Verdun), **Stoke Orchard** Gl (Archer), and **Stoke Poges** Bk (le Pugeis). **Stoke Edith** He refers to Queen Edith, who held the manor in 1066. Manors in church hands include **Stoke Prior** Wo (Worcester Priory), **Stoke Prior** He (Prior of Leominster), **Stoke Canon** D (Exeter Cathedral) and **Stoke Bishop** Gl (Bishop of Worcester). Other additions are geographical; †**Stoke on Trent** St is the best known, and **Stoke upon Tern** Sa and **Severn Stoke** Wo are likewise on rivers. Dedications and descriptive terms are also found [OE *stoc*]. See also South Hams.

Stoke by Nayland Sf. See Nayland.

Stokeham Nt, 'at the hamlets' [*Estoches* 1086, *Stokum* 1242: OE *stoc* (dat. pl. *stocum*)].

Stokeinteignhead D, 'Stoke in the ten hides', the second part of the name being probably the designation of a manor and alluding to its extent. The term occurs in a number of other place-names, e g Fifehead and Fyfield (qq v). In this name, the numeral has been confused with the river-name *Teign* (q v) [*Stoches* 1086, *Stokes in Tynhide* 1279: OE *stoc, tēn, hĭd*].

Stokenham D. See South Hams.

Stone *freq*, '(place at or by) a stone', some isolated boulder or even hewn stone serving as a mark of a place of assembly, a boundary, a ford or sea-crossing, or some other site [OE *stān*]. See also Staines.

Stonehenge W, 'stone gallows, from a supposed resemblance of the monument to a series of gallows. The name **Woodhenge** is modern, imitating that of Stonehenge [*Stanenges* c 1130: OE *stān, hengen*.]

Stonehouse D, — Gl: '(place by) a stone house' [1. *Stanehus* 1086, 2. *Stanhus* 1086: OE *stān, hūs*]. See also Stenhousemuir.

Stornoway (Lewis) Ros, 'steerage bay' or 'rudder bay', the precise significance of which is difficult to grasp. An alternative meaning 'star bay' is not really clearer [*Stornochway* 1511: ON *stjórn/stjarna, vágr*].

Stort *riv* Ess-Hrt, back-formation from Bishop's Stortford (q v).

Stoughton. See Stockton.

Stour *riv freq*: 'strong, powerful one'. The name is so common in the Midlands and south of England that some older writers detected the name in rivers which certainly did not bear it; one such suggestion produced a spurious Devon Stour, derived from Sheepstor (q v) [B *stūr-].

Stourbridge Wo, 'bridge over river Stour (q v)', a name first recorded in the thirteenth century in the parish of Old Swinford, the name of which indicates the way the river had been previously crossed. Kingswinford St (q v) was possibly a newer settlement rather than a new ford [1. *Sturbrug* 1255, 2. *Swinford* c 950, *Old Swynford* 1291: OE *brycg*, *swin, ford*]. See also Swineford.

Stourport-on-Severn Wo, 'port at confluence of Stour and Severn', but, like other names in -*port* (e g Ellesmere Port Ch, q v) celebrating the development of canal transport in the eighteenth century. The Staffs and Worcs Canal enters the Severn at Stourport [*Stourport* c 1775: OE *port*].

Stow LLi, — MLo, **Stow Bardolph** Nf, **Stow Bedon** Nf, **Stow cum Quy** C, **Stowe** Bk, — Sa, — St, **Stowe Nine Churches** Nth, **Stow Longa** Hu, **Stow Maries** Ess, **Stowmarket** Sf, **Stow-on-the-Wold** Gl. **Stowupland** Sf: 'place of assembly, holy place'. The additions Bardolph, Bedon, and Maries are manorial; others are descriptive or manorial. Stowe Nine Churches is said to be a reference to the lord's right of presentation to nine livings [OE *stōw*].

†**Strabane** Tyr, 'white riverside land' [I *srath, bàn*].

Strachan Knc, 'valley of the little horse' [*Stratheyhan* 1153: G *srath, eachain*].

Stradbroke Sf, 'stream by a Roman road' [*Statebroc* 1086, *Stradebroc* 1168: OE *strǣt, brōc*].

Straid Don, 'village' [I *sraid*].

Straiton Ayr, — MLo: 'village on a Roman road' [2. *Stratone* 1296: OE *strǣt, tūn*]. See also Stratton.

Strangeways La, '(place by a stream with) strong current' [*Strangwas* 1322: OE *strang, gewæsc*].

Stranraer Wig, 'thick promontory', possibly alluding to the Loch Ryan peninsula [*Stranrever* 1320: G *sròn, reamhar*].

Stratfield Mortimer Brk, **Stratfield Saye** Ha, **Stratfield Turgis** Ha: 'open country by a Roman road', the additions being all manorial. Radulf de Mortemer held the Berkshire place in 1086 and it remained in the family until the accession of Edward IV. Locally, only the feudal addition is used to designate the place, as in Virley Ess and Shendish Hrt (qq v). The Hampshire places are on the same Roman road, that from London to Silchester [1. *Stradfeld* 1086, *Stradfeld Hugonis de Mortemer* 1167, 2. *Stradfelle* 1086, *Stratfeld Say* 1277, 3. *Stratfeld Turgys* 1277: OE *strǣt, feld*].

Stratford Bd 1235, **Stratford Langthorne** Ess, **Stratford le Bow** Mx, **Stratford St Andrew** Sf, **Stratford St Mary** Sf, **Stratford sub Castle** W, **Stratford Toney** W, †**Stratford on Avon** Wa, **Fenny Stratford** Bk, **Stony Stratford** Bk, **Water Stratford** Bk, **Old Stratford** Nth: 'ford traversed by a Roman road', with descriptive, manorial, and topographical affixes. Stratford Langthorne was by a place marked by a tall thorn bush; Stratford le Bow adjoined an arched bridge over a tributary of the river Thames. Stony Stratford lies on Watling Street, at the crossing of the Ouse, and Old Stratford is on the Northamptonshire side of the river, west or 'in front of' Stony Stratford [2. *Strætforde* 1067, 4. *Straffort* 1086, 6. *Stratford under the Castle of Old Sarum* 1353, 8. *Stretfordæ* c 700,

Ufera Stretford bi Eafene 845, 9. *Fenni Stratford* 1252, 10. *Stani Stratford* 1202: OE *strǣt, ford, fennig, stānig, uferra*]. See also Strefford.

Strathallan Pth, 'valley of the Allan Water', applied to the area between Auchterarder and Dunblane; the river bears a name similar to a number· of others in Britain. The meaning is uncertain, but it has been suggested that its origin is in a British root meaning 'to drive, to push'. [*Strathalun* 1187: B *elā-*].

Strathavon Bnf, 'valley of the river Avon' [*Strathouen* c 1190: G *srath*, B *abonā*].

Strath Beag Ros, — Sut, **Strath Beg** Sut: 'little valley' [G *srath, beag*].

Strathblane Stl, '(place in) valley of the little flowers', so that the name is not to be associated with Kilblane or Dunblane, the second element of which is the personal name Blaan [*Strachblachan* c 1200, *Strachblahane* 1238: G *srath, blāthan*].

Strathbogie Abd, 'valley of the river Bogie, i e river with bag-shaped pools' [*Strabolgin* 1187, *Strabolgy* 1335: G *srath*, OG *bolg*].

Strathbran Ros, 'valley of the burn called Bran', the stream-name meaning 'raven' [G *srath*, OW *bran*].

Strathbrora Sut, 'valley of the river Brora (q v)' [G *srath*].

††**Strathclyde,** 'valley of the Clyde (q v)' [*Stratcluddenses* c 900: G *srath*].

Strathdon Abd, 'valley of the river Don (q v)' [G *srath*].

Strathearn Pth, 'valley of the river Earn (q v)' [*Sraithh'erni* c 950, *Stradearn* 1185: G *srath*].

†**Strathkelvin** Dnb, 'valley of Kelvin, i e narrow stream' [*Kelvyn* 1208: G *caol, abhuinn*].

Strathkinness Fif, 'valley at the head of the waterfall' [*Stradkines* 1144: G *srath, ceann, eas*].

Strathmiglo Fif, 'valley of the river Miglo', actually the upper reach of the river Eden. The change of name can be accounted for in the marshiness of the area in former times. The stream was probably lost in the surrounding mire, becoming a bog-loch (W *mig-llwch*). Other names in the area indicating boggy terrain include Myres Castle and **Pitgorno,** 'portion of the boggy place' [*Scradimigg-lolk* c 1200: G *srath*, W *mig, llwch*].

Strathnaver Sut, 'valley of the river Naver (q v)' [*Strathnauir* 1268: G *srath*].

Strathpeffer Ros, 'valley of the river Peffer, i e radiant stream' [*Strathpefir* 1350: G *srath*, P *pevr*].

Strathwhillan (Arran) Bte, possibly 'land of Cuilean', alluding to a tenth-century king of Alban [*Terrquhillane* n d: G *tir*].

Strathy Sut, '(place) in the valley' [G *srath*].

Stratton *freq*, 'farm on or by a Roman road', with a range of affixes similar to those of Stratford. An unusual descriptive addition is found in **Stratton Strawless** Nf, evidently an infertile place [OE *strǣt, tūn*].

Streat Sx, **Street** He, — K, — So (x 2): '(place on) Roman road' [1. *Estrat* 1086, 2. *Strete* 1086, 3. *Strǣt* c 1018, 4. *Stret* 725, 5. *Strate* 1086: OE *strǣt*].

Streatham Sr/GL, 'homestead on a Roman road', the road being Stane Street, from Chichester to London. Other Roman roads also bear this name, which means 'stone-paved road' [*Estreham* 1086, *Streteham* 1247: OE *strǣt, hām*].

Strefford Sa, 'ford traversed by a Roman road', a variant of Stratford (q v) and of **Stretford**, occurring in Herefordshire and Lancashire. Stretford He is on the Roman road from South Wales to Chester; Stretford La is on the road from Chester to Manchester, at the point where it crosses the river Mersey [1. *Straford* 1086, *Streford* 1255, 2. *Stratford* 1316, 3. *Stretford* 1212: OE *strǣt, ford*].

Stretton *freq*, 'farm on or by a Roman road', with manorial and topographical additions in various counties [OE *strǣt, tūn*].

Stroan Ant, — Cav, — Klk: '(place by a) little stream' [I *sruthan*]. See also Struan.

Stroma *isld* Cai, 'island in the current', the Pentland Firth being said to run like a river [*Straumsey* 1150: ON *straumr, ey*].

Stromness (North Ronaldsay) Ork, 'headland of the current' [*Straumsness* 1150: ON *straumr, nes*].

Strone Arg, — Dnb, — Inv (x 2), **Strone Point** Arg (x 2); 'headland' [2. *Strohon* 1240, *Stron* c 1400: G *sròn*].

Stronsay Ork, 'star island', perhaps alluding to its shape [*Stiornsay* 1150: ON *stjarna, ey*].

Strood K, †**Stroud** Gl, **Stroud Green** Mx: 'boggy place overgrown with brushwood' [1. *Strod* 889, 2. *La Strode* 1221, 3. *Strodegrene* 1562: OE *strōd*].

Struan (Skye) Inv, **Struan** Pth: '(place by) a little stream' [G *sruthan*]. See also Stroan.

Struie Ros, **Struy** Inv: 'stream place'. The Ross-shire name, in Edderton, is

locally applied to the granite hill above it, in full *Cnoc na Strùigh* [G *sruthach* ocative *sruthaigh*].

Strumble Head Pmb, meaning uncertain. No forms earlier than the seventeenth century are known. ON *muli*, 'promontory' may be the second element; the first may be OE **strump* or a Norse cognate, meaning 'stump' [*Strumble headde* 1602].

Sudbury Db, — Sf, — Mx: 'southern fortified place' [1. *Sudberie* 1086, 2. *Sudberi* 798, 3. *Sudbery* 1294: OE *sūð, burh*].

Suffolk, 'south folk', the southern group of East Anglian tribes whose territory was that of the modern county, and whose name became a place-name without further addition [*Suthfolchi* 895: OE *sūð, folc*].

Sulby IOM, 'Soli's farm' [*Sulaby* 1370: ON *bý*].

Sulgrave Nth 1086, 'grove by a plough-land' [*Solegreue* c 1240: OE *sulh, grǣf*].

Sunderland Cu,† — Du, — La: 'territory separated from a main estate'. North Sunderland Nb, however, has to be rendered by the paradoxical 'north southerly land'. It should have developed into **Sutherland*; the proximity of Sunderland Du, doubtless, produced an identical form, to which *North* was added to prevent confusion with the Durham place [1. *Sunderland* 1332, 2. *Sunderland* c 1168, 3. *Sunderlond* 1262, 4. *Suðlanda* 1177, *Sutherlannland* 12c: [OE *sundor, land, sūðer*].

Sunningdale Brk, 'dale corresponding to Sunninghill', a name devised in the mid-nineteenth century for a parish formed from parts of Old Windsor and Sunninghill Brk, with portions of

Windlesham, Egham, and Chobham Sr.
Sunninghill Brk, 'hill of the people of
Sunna', alludes to a tribe whose name
occurs also in **Sonning** Brk and to the
Sonning Hundred in that county; an
even larger area was formerly so designated, possibly the whole of Berkshire
east of Reading [2. *Sunigehill'* 1185,
3. *Soninges* 1086: OE *-ingas, hyll, dæl*].

Surbiton Sr/GL, 'south corn farm,
outlying farm' [*Subertone* 1203: OE *sūð,
bere-tūn*]. See also Norbiton Sr.

Surrey, 'southerly district', an ancient
name alluding to the Saxons of the middle
Thames valley. North of the river they
were described simply as 'Middle' Saxons,
between Essex and Wessex; on the southern shore there were Jutes in Kent and
Sunnings in Berkshire, so that a name
indicating this middle position was not so
easy to contrive. The second element is
the archaic *ge*, related to Modern German
Gau, 'district' [*Suþrige* 722: OE *sūðer,
gē].

Sussex, '(territory of) the South Saxons',
like Suffolk and Somerset, primarily a
folk-name that became regularly used for
the land in which they settled [*Suþ
Seaxe* 722: OE *sūð*].

†Sutherland, 'southern territory' of the
Scandinavian settlers of the Shetlands and
Orkneys. To the Norsemen the Hebrides
(q v) were *Suðreyar*, 'southern islands',
from which is derived MnE Sodor
[*Suthernelande* c 1250: ON *sūðr, land*].

Sutton *freq*, 'south farm', a very common
name occurring in all the counties of
England and in a few in Wales. Affixes of
all types are found, in addition to the
simple name [OE *sūð, tūn*]. See also
Ashfield.

Swadlincote Db, 'Swartling's cottage', the
form given in Domesday Book not

being confirmed by subsequent forms
[*Sivardingescotes* 1086, *Suartlincote* 1208,
Swertlyngcote 1410: OE *cot*].

†Swale *riv* K, — *riv* NRY, 'rushing,
whirling river' [1. *Suualuue* 812, 2.
fluuio Sualua c 730: OE **swalwe*].

Swallowfield Brk, 'open land by the river
called *Swealwe*', a river-name that has
now been replaced by Blackwater (q v),
but which might have developed to yet
another Swale (q v) [*Sualefelle* 1086: OE
feld].

Swanage Do, 'outlying premises used by
herds', the seaside situation suggesting a
seasonal pasturage utilised by inland
farms. **Swanwick** Db and **Swanwick** Ha
are of the same origin [1. *Swanawic* 877,
2. *Swanwyk* c 1278, 3. *Swanewic* 1231:
OE *swān, wīc*].

†Swansea Glm, 'Sveinn's sea (place)'.
Forms with *-ey*, 'island' certainly exist
but did not appear until nearly two centuries after earliest spellings. This is one of
the numerous Scandinavian place-names
in the Irish Sea area [*Sweynesse* c 1165,
Sueinesea 1190, *Swanesey* 1322: ON *sǽr*].

Swift *riv* Lei-Wa, 'winding brook', not
indeed being 'swift' but pursuing a
sinuous course characterised by the
restlessness suggested by its earlier name
Wovere Watir, 'wandering, wavering
river' [*Swift* 1577: OE *swifan*]. See also
Lutterworth.

Swinden Gl, **Swindon** St, **Swindon** W: 'pig
hill', though **Swinden** WRY is 'pig
valley' [1. *Svindone* 1086, 2. *Swineduna*
1167, 3. *Svindune* 1086, 4. *Suindene* 1086:
OE *swīn, dūn, denu*].

Swineford Myo, **Swinford** Brk, **Kingswinford** St: 'pig ford'. **Old Swinford** Wo,
the parish in which Stourbridge (q v)
is situated, is also to be interpreted in this

way [2. *Swynford* 931, 3. *Svinesford* 1086, *Kyngesswynford* 1322: OE *swin, ford*].

Swineshead Bd, either 'pig headland' or 'pig's head'; the former supposes that a hill nearby resembles a pig's head, but the latter may allude to a sacrificial practice (cf Farcet) [*Suineshefet* 1086: OE *swin, hēafod*].

Swinton Ber, — La, — NRY, — WRY: 'pig farm', though the Berwickshire example may be 'Sveinn's farm' [1. *Suineston* c 1098, 2. *Suinton* 1258, 3. *Suintune* 1086, 4. *Suintone* 1086: OE *swin, tūn*].

Sydenham K/GL, probably 'Cippa's homestead', the modern form providing little evidence of the origin of the name, owing to quite recent alterations. The change from *Ch* - to *S*- is explicable by appeal on AN influence (as in Cippenham Bk), but the replacement of -*p*- by -*d*- can only be described as a recent error or arbitrary change [*Chipeham* 1206, *Cypenham* n d: OE *hām*].

Symington Ayr, 'Simon's farm', said to have been named after Simon Lockhart (c 1150) [*Symondstona* 1293: OE *tūn*].

Table Mountain Wic 1760, 'flat-topped hill', perhaps a transferred name from the mountain at the Cape of Good Hope.

Tackley O, **Takeley** Ess: 'pasture for young sheep'. The dialect word *teg*, 'young sheep', the first record of which is dated 1537, is usually supposed to be of Scandinavian origin—Swedish *tacka* 'ewe' being offered for comparison [1. *Tachelie* 1086, 2. *Tacheleia* 1086, 4. *Ta(c)keley* 1562: OE **tacca, *tacce, lēah, tūn*]. See also Acton Do.

Tacolneston Nf, 'Tatwulf's farm' [*Tacoluestuna* 1086: OE *tūn*].

Tadcaster WRY, 'Tata's Roman station', on an outcrop of magnesian limestone. It has been suggested that *Calcaria Civitas*, mentioned by Bede, was Tadcaster, though this is possibly a Latin translation of OE *Kælcacæstir*, identified with Kelk ERY. Tadcaster is on the Roman road from Lincoln to Corbridge [*Tatecastre* 1086: OE *ceaster*].

†**Taf** *riv* Glm, 'water, stream' [*Taf* c 1102, *Taph* 1191: B **tamos*].

Tafolog *mtn* Mgm, 'place of docks', alluding to plants of the *Rumex* genus [W *tafol, -og*].

Taghmon Wex, — Wme: 'St Munna's house', the Wexford place being the location of a monastery founded by Munna in 634 [1. *Teach-Munna* c 1250: I *teach*].

Tai-bach Dnb, — Glm; 'little houses' [W *ty, pl. tai, bach*].

Tain Ros, '(place of the) river', a merely possible interpretation of what is almost certainly a pre-Celtic name [*Tene* 1226, *Thayn* 1257].

Takeley Ess. See Tackley.

Talacre Flt, 'end or headland of the arable land' [W *tal, acer*].

Talgarth Bre, 'end of the hill' [W *tal, garth*].

Talisker (Skye) Inv, possibly 'shelf or ledge rock', modified under Gaelic influence [ON *hjalli, sker*].

Tallabheith Pth, 'crag of birchwood' [*An t'All a' Bheithe* n d: G *all, beithe*].

Tallaght Dub, 'burial ground for plague victims' [I *taimhleacht*[.

Talke St, **Talkin** Cu: 'white brow' [1. *Talc* 1086, 2. *Talcan* c 1195: W *tal can*].

Tallow Wat, 'little hill', the full Irish form meaning 'little hill of the iron', alluding to the iron-ore workings of the area [I *Teallach-an-iarainn*].

Tallowbridge Wat, 'bridge by a little hill' [I *teallach*, OE *brycg*].

Talmine Sut, 'level land' [G *talamh, min*].

Talsarn Crd, **Talsarnau** Mer: 'end of the causeway(s)' [W *tal, sarn* (pl. *sarnau*)].

Talwrn Agl, — Flt (x 4): 'threshing floor, exposed part of a hill' [W *talwrn*].

Talybont Bre, — Crd: '(place at the) end of the bridge' [W *tal, pont*].

Tal-y-llyn Bre, — Mer· 'end of the lake' [W *tal, llyn*].

Tamar *riv* Co-D, possibly 'dark one', though, as for the related name Taf, a meaning 'water, stream' has also been suggested [*Tamaros* c 150: B **tamos*].

Tame *riv* Ch-La-WRY, — *riv* NRY, — *riv* St-Wa, **Team** *riv* Du, **Thame** *riv* O-Bk, **Thames** *riv* Gl-North Sea: '(dark) river, stream', a merely probable interpretation, despite much detailed study by a number of scholars [1. *Tome* 13c, 2. *Tame* 12c, 3. *Tame* c 1025, 4. *Thamam* c 1190, 5. *Tame* 956, 6. *Tamesis* 51 BC, *Thamis* c 650: B **teme-*].

†**Tamworth** St, 'enclosure on the river Tame' [*Tamuuorði* 781: OE *worðig*].

Tanderagee Arm, 'backside to the wind' [I *ton-le-gaeith*].

Tandoo Wig, 'black backside' [G *ton, dubh*].

Tansley Db, either 'Tan's wood or clearing', the personal name being Anglo-Saxon, or 'wood or clearing from which sprouts or shoots were obtained' [*Taneslege* 1086: OE *tān, lēah*].

Taplow Bk, 'Tæppa's mound', identified as a barrow in the churchyard, in which burial treasure was found [*Thapeslav* 1086: OE *hlāw*].

Tara Mth, **Tara Hill** Wex: 'place commanding a fine prospect' [I *teamhair*].

Tarbat Ness Ros, **Tarbert** Arg, — (Harris) Inv, — (Jura) Arg, — Ker, **Tarbet** Dnb, — Inv, — Sut: 'isthmus, portage'. The places are either on narrow promontories or on necks of land separating lochs [G *tairbeart*].

Tarff *riv* Inv, **Water of Tarf** *riv* Ang, **Tarff Water** *riv* Pth, — *riv* Wig: 'bull (river)', the animal name alluding to the violence of the stream [G *tarbh*].

Tarporley Ch, 'peasants' clearing', an interpretation (based on Dodgson's analysis in PNCh iv 294-5) to be preferred to allusions to pear-tree clearings. The suggested meaning derives from a postulated form related to ON *þorpari* 'villager' [*Torpelei* 1086: OE **þorpere, lēah*].

Tarrant *riv* Do, 'trespasser, i e river liable to floods', a name related to Trent (q v). The river has provided, with various additions, nearly a dozen place-names along its course; of these, e g **Tarrant Hinton, Tarrant Keynston, Tarrant Launceston, Tarrant Monkton**, and **Tarrant Rawston**, most are manorial. **Tarrant Crawford**, however, was earlier merely Crawford, 'crow ford', the river-name having been prefixed. **Tarrant Hinton** and **Tarrant Monkton** allude to monastic ownership, by Shaftesbury Abbey and Tewkesbury Abbey respectively [1. *Terrente* 935, 2-7. *Terente* c 871, 2. *Tarente Hyneton* 1285, 4. *Tarente de Lawyneston* 1285, 5. *Tarente Monachorum* 1291, 7. *Crawan ford* 956: B *trisantōn*, OE *tūn, hīwān, munuc, crāwe, ford*].

Tarvie Pth, — Ros: 'bull place' [G *tarbhaidh*].

Taunton So, 'farm on the river Tone', the river-name meaning 'roaring stream'. The tautologous **Vale of** †**Taunton Deane** ('Taunton valley') provides a name for the local government District lying between the Quantocks and the Blackdown Hills [*Tantun* 722: OE *tūn, denu*, B *tan-*].

Tavistock D, 'secondary settlement by the Tavy', the place having probably originated as an outlier of Marytavy and Petertavy. These places, like the numerous places called Tarrant (q v), originally bore merely the name of the river, meaning 'dark stream' and related to Tamar and Tame (qq v); they were subsequently distinguished by additions indicating the dedication of their respective churches to St Mary and St Peter [1. *Tauistoce* 981, 2. *Tavi* 1086, *Tavymarie* 1412, *Marytauey* 1577, 3. *Tawi* 1086, *Petri Tavy* 1270, *Peterestavi* 1276: OE *stoc*].

Tawstock D, 'secondary settlement across the river Taw', opposite **Bishop's Tawton** D, 'village on the river Taw', held by the Bishop of Exeter in 1086. The river-name, which is related to Tay (q v), is found also in **North Tawton** and **South Tawton** D [1. *Tauestoca* 1086, 2. *Tautona* 1086, *Tautone Episcopi* 1304, 3. *Tawetona* 1086, *Nortauton* 1262, 4. *Suthtauetona* 1212: OE *stoc, tūn, norð, sūð*].

Tay *riv* Pth, 'powerful river', or possibly 'silent river' [*Taus* c 80, *Taoua* c 150: B *Tausos*].

Team *riv* Du. See Tame.

Tebay We, 'Tibba's island' [*Tibeia* 1179: OE *ēg*].

Teddington Mx, 'farm of the people of Tudda' [*Tudintun* 969; OE *-ingas, tūn*].

Tees *riv* Cu-NRY, 'boiling, surging river', an interpretation which seems to be confirmed by the waterfalls, rapids, and strong current [*Tesa* 1026: W *tes*].

Teigh R, 'enclosure' [*Tie* 1086: OE *tēag*].

Teign *riv* D, 'stream'. On the river stand **Bishopsteignton** D and **Kingsteignton** D, holdings of the Bishop of Exeter and of the king respectively. These with **Drewsteignton** D (held by one Drogo in 1262), were all originally *Teignton*, 'farm on the river Teign'. **Teigngrace** D was held by Geoffrey Gras in 1352; **Teignmouth** D is on the estuary. The District name †**Teignbridge** must also be added [1. *Teng* 739, 2. *Taintona* 1086, *Teygtone Episcopi* 1262, 3. *Teintone Regis* 1259, 4. *Teyngton Drue* 1275, 5. *Teyngegras* 1331, 6. *Tengemuða* 1044: B* *tagnā*, OE *tūn, mūða*]. See also Stokeinteignhead.

Teise *riv* K, back-formation from Ticehurst (q v).

Telford Sa, 'town named to commemorate Thomas Telford', honouring the great civil engineer (1757-1834), responsible in this area for the Ellesmere Canal and the Shrewsbury-Holyhead road.

Teme *riv* Sa-He, '(dark) river', a name possibly to be grouped with Tame (q v) [*Temede* c 760: B *teme-*].

Templand Dmf, **Temple** Co, — MLo, **Temple Combe** So, **Temple Ewell** K, **Temple Guiting** Gl, **Temple Sowerby** We, **Templeton** Brk 1242, **Templeton** D: 'land held by the Knights Templars', the military religious order, which held numerous great estates in many countries.

The order was suppressed in the fourteenth century and its property was transferred to other orders, particularly (as Temple Guiting Gl) the Knights Hospitallers. The Templars' properties were separately designated *Temple*, sometimes prefixed to an existing name, sometimes used as a simple name alone, sometimes suffixed to an existing name, e g **Rothley Temple** Lei, and occasionally combined with other elements suffixed, e g Templand and Templeton [1. 1329, 8. *Templington Templariorum* 1284, 9. *Templum* 1206: ME *tempel*, OE *land*, *tūn*]. See Combe, Ewell, Sowerby.

Templederry Tip, 'church of the oakwood' [I *teampull*, *doire*].

Templeetney Tip, 'church of St Eithne' [I *teampull*].

Templemore Lon, — Myo, — Tip: 'big church' [I *teampull*, *mór*].

Templeton Brk, — D: 'farm or estate held by the Knights Templars'. See Templand.

Tenbury Wo, 'fortified place on the river Teme (q v)', possibly alluding to the mound known as Castle Tump, on the Shropshire side of the river but formerly included within the bounds of Tenbury [*Temedebyrig* 11c: OE *burh*].

Tenby Pmb, 'small fortress', identical in origin and meaning with Denbigh, but evidently affected by Scandinavian influence [*Dinbych* c 1275: W *din*, *bych*].

Tenterden K, 'swine pasture for Thanet dwellers', alluding to the assignment of large blocks of woodland in the Weald to early communities in Kent. The termination -*den* (for OE *denn*, and so pronounced), is characteristic of names in Kent and East Sussex. Elsewhere the same termination in modern spellings is

normally derived from OE *denu* 'valley, [*Tentwardene* 1179: OE *wara*, *denn*]. See also Thanet, Benenden.

Test *riv* Ha, 'strong or swift runner' [*Terstan* 877: B **trest*-].

Tetbury Gl, 'Tetta's manor or establishment'. Tetta was a sister of King Ine of Wessex, whose reign is remembered for (among other things) a systematic organisation of the church in Wessex [*Tettan monasterium* 681, *Tettan byry* c 900: OE *burh*].

†**Tewkesbury** Gl, 'Téodec's fort' [*Teodechesberie* 1086: OE *burh*].

Thame *riv*, **Thames** *riv*. See Tame *riv*.

†**Thanet**, **Isle** of K, 'bright island, fire island' [*Tanatus* 3c: B **tan*].

Thatcham Brk, **Thaxted** Ess: 'river-meadow/place where thatch was obtained' [1. *þæcham* c 954, 2. *Tachesteda* 1086: OE *þæc*, **þæcðe*, (*hām*) *hamm*, *stede*].

Theale Brk, 'plank (place)', possibly alluding to a wooden structure used for meetings of the hundred [*Teile* 1208: OE *þel*].

Thinghill He, 'assembly hill', an instance of OE *þing*; many names of this type have ON *þing* as their first element, as **Thingwall** Ch, 'field of assembly', the meeting place of the *Thing* of the Scandinavian community in Wirral; across the Mersey, **Thingwall** La catered similarly for a Norse community in south-west Lancashire [1. *Tingehele* 1086, 2. *Tinguelle* 1086, 3. *Tingwella* 1177: OE *þing*, *hyll*, ON *þing-vollr*].

Thirlwall Nb, 'gap (in) wall', the wall being that of Hadrian. The gap may represent the reopening of some ancient track across the line of the wall [*Thurlewall* 1256: OE *þyrel*, *weall*].

Thirsk NRY, 'place by a fen' [*Tresch* 1086: ON **þresk*].

Thornborough Bk, **Thornbrough** NRY: 'thorn hill' [1. *Torneberge* 1086, 2. *Thornebergh* c 1190: OE *þorn, beorg*].

Thornbrough Nb, — WRY, **Thornbury** D, — Gl, **Thornby** Nth: 'fortified place with thorn bushes' the bushes probably having contributed to the protection of the place. Thornby is Scandinavianised to the point where it resembles Thrimby or Thurnby (qq v) [1. *Thorneburg* 1242, 2. *Torneburg* 1242, 3. *Torneberie* 1086, 4. *þornbyrig* 896, 5. *Torneberie* 1086, *Thirnebi* c 1160: OE *þorn, burh*].

Thornton *freq*, 'farm where thorn-bushes grew', with various affixes, including a large number with *-le-*, e g **Thornton le Moors** Ch, **Thornton le Moor** NRY, **Thornton le Beans** NRY, **Thornton le Clay** NRY, **Thornton le Street** NRY, **Thornton le Fen** LLi. Others are manorial, e g **Bishop Thornton** WRY, which was held by the Archbishop of York, and **Childer Thornton** Ch, owned by, or in trust for, the young monks of St Werburgh's Abbey [OE *þorn, tūn*].

Thoroton Nt, 'Þoroð's village' a 'Grimston hybrid' name, the personal element being Scandinavian [*Toruertune* 1086: OE *tūn*]. See also Grimston.

Thorp(e) *freq*, usually, 'outlying village, secondary settlement', but occasionally 'village', the latter derived from the rare OE *þorp, þrop*, as in **Castle Thorpe** Bk and possibly **Thorpe** Du, but not **Thorpe Bulmer** or **Thorpe Thewless** in the same county. Additions may be descriptive, e g **Thorpe Market** Nf and **Thorpe Thewless** Du, though Thewless (ME *Thewles* 'immoral') may be a nickname and the affix manorial; manorial additions include **Thorpe Arnold** Lei, **Thorpe Malsor** Nth, and **Thorpe Bochart** Nt. [OE *þrop*, ON *þorp*]. See also Throop.

Threapwood Ch, — Flt, **Threepwood** Ayr, — Ber, — Lnk, — Nb, — Rnf: 'disputed woodland', usually on a county boundary. Threapwood Ch, for instance, is partly in Flint; in former times it was outside almost all jurisdiction and no rates or taxes were payable on property in the area [1. *Threpewood* 1548, 3. *Trepewode* c 1230: OE *þrēap, wudu*].

Threave Kcb, 'farm' [G *treabh*].

†**Three Rivers** Hrt, a District name coined at the time of local-government re-organisation. The rivers referred to are Chess (q v), Colne (q v), and Gade (v Gaddesden). The area comprises Rickmansworth, Chorley Wood, Abbots Langley, Sarratt, and Oxhey.

Thrimby We, 'farmstead at a thorn-tree', showing a phonetic development found also in **Thrintoft** NRY, 'dwelling site by a thorn-tree' [1. *T'nebi* 1200, *Tyrneby* 1200, *Thrinneby* c 1255, *Thrimby* 1580, 2. *Tirnetofte* 1086: ON *þyrnir, bý, topt*].

Throop Ha, **Throope** W, **Thrup** O, **Thrupp** Brk, — Gl, — Nth: 'village, farm' [1. *La Thrope* 1274, 2. *Trope* 1185, 3. *Trop* 1086, 4. *Thrope* 1316, 5. *Thrope* 1359, 6. *Torp* 1086, *Trop* 1207: OE *þorp*].

Thunderfield Sr, 'open land sacred to Þunor', a similar dedication to that found in **Thundersley** Ess and **Thundridge** Hrt, respectively 'clearing or wood' and 'ridge' sacred to the god [1. *þunresfeld* c 880, 2. *Thunreslea* 1086, 3. *Tonrinch* 1086: OE *fēld, lēah, hrycg*]. See also Tuesley, Wednesbury.

Thurleigh Bd, '(at) the clearing or wood', of considerable interest in that the definite article is impacted with the naming element in the modern form; early spellings indicate that the phrase *æt þære lēage* is involved here [*La Lega* 1086, *Thyrleye* 1372: OE *lēah*].

Thurles Tip, 'strong fort' [OI *dur, las*].

Thurnham La. See Farnham Nb.

Thurnby Lei, 'farmstead at a thorn-tree, [*Turneby* c 1175: ON *þyrnir, bý*]. See also Thrimby.

Thurrock Ess. See Grays Thurrock.

Thurso Cai, '(place by) bull river', the Gaelic form of the name of the town being *Inbhir Thorsa*, 'mouth of the Thurso'. A connexion with Thor has been suggested in some interpretations of this name, but the meaning here is based on the name of a promontory nearby as given by Ptolemy, *Tarvedum*, representing OC **Tarvodūnon*, 'bull fortress' or 'fortress by river called "Bull" ' [*Thorsa* 1152: OC **tarvo-* ON *á*].

Thwaite Nf, — NRY, — Sf, **Thwaite St Mary** Nf: 'clearing' [1. *Dweyt* c 1045, 3. *Theyt* 1228, 4. *Thweyt* 1254: ON *þveit*].

Ticehurst Sx, **Tickenhurst** K, **Tickenhurst** Sx: 'wooded hill on which kids grazed'. Other names with the same first element include **Tichborne** Ha ('kid stream'), **Tickencote** R ('shed for kids'), **Tickford** Bk ('kid ford'), **Titchfield** Ha ('open land upon which kids grazed'), and **Titchwell** Nf ('kid spring') [1. *Tycheherst* 1248, 2. *Tikenherst* c 1075, 4. *Ticceburnan* 909, 5. *Ticheford* 1086, 6. *Ticefelle* 1086, 7. *Ticeswelle* c 1035: OE *ticcen, burna, cot, feld, ford, hyrst, wella*].

Tilbury Ess, 'Tila's fortified place' [*Tilaburg* 1086: OE *burh*].

Tilehurst Brk, 'wooded hill on or near which tiles were made'. Evidence of such manufacture in this area is on record from the twelfth century [*Tigelherst* 1167: OE *tigel, hyrst*].

Tinhead W, '(estate of) ten hides' [*Tunheda* 1190: OE *tēn, hid*]. See also Stokein-teignhead.

Tintagel Co, of uncertain meaning. The first element signifies 'fortress', but the second is obscure — possibly a personal name [*Tintaieol* 1205: Co **tin*].

Tintern Mon, 'king's fortress' [*Dindyrn* c 1150: OW **din, teryn*].

Tinwald Dmf, 'place of assembly' [*Tynwalde* c 1280: ON *þingvollr*].

Tipperary Tip, 'well of Ara, i e ridged place', referring to the territory in which the well was situated. The site of the well is known [*Tiobraid-Arann* n d: I *tiobraid, ara*].

Tipperty Abd, 'well place' [*Typpertay* 1501: OG *tiobartach*].

Tiptree Ess, 'Tippa's tree', like other *-tree* names having a personal name as first element (cf Braintree, Coventry) [*Typpetre* c 1225: OE *trēow*].

Tiree *isld* Arg, 'land of Ith', the bearer of the personal name not having been identified [*Tir Iath* c 850, *Tiryad* 1343: G *tir*].

Titchfield Ha, **Titchwell** Nf. See Ticehurst.

Tittenhanger Hrt, 'Tida's hill-slope' [*Tidenhangra* 1198: OE *hangra*].

Tiverton Ch 1253, 'farm where red lead was found', alluding to raddle or red ochre, a mineral dyestuff [*Tevreton* 1086, *Taverton* 1360: OE *tēafor, tūn*].

†**Tiverton** D, 'farm at Twyford, i e the double ford', alluding to the situation of the place at the confluence of the Exe and its tributary the Loman. **Twerton** So has the same meaning [1. *Twyfyrede* c 885, *Tovretona* 1086, 2. *Twertone* 1086: OE *twi-, ford, tūn*].

Tober Cav, 'well' [I *tiobar*].

Tobercurry Sli, 'well of the cauldron', said to be so named from its shape [*Tobar-an-choire* n d: I *tiobar, choire*].

Tobermore Lond, 'big well' [I *tiobar, mór*].

Tobermory (Mull) Arg, 'well of St Mary' [*Tibbermore* 1540: G *tiobar*].

Tokavaig (Skye) Inv, 'hawk bay', a Scandinavian compound affected by Gaelic influence [ON *haukr, vík*].

Tolsta Head (Lewis) Ros, 'Tolli's farmstead headland' [ON *bólstaðr*].

Tomich Inv, — Ros: 'place of knolls' [G *tomach*].

Tomintoul Abd, — Bnf: 'barn knoll' [G *toman t'sabail*].

†**Tonbridge** K, 'village bridge', i e bridge to the village from some other part of the manor [*Tonebrige* 1086: OE *tūn, brycg*].

Tongue Sut, 'tongue of land' [*Toung* 1542: ON *tunga*].

Toome Ant, '(place by a) tumulus' [I *tuaim*].

Tooting Sr/GL, '(place of) Tota's people'. There were two manors, Tooting Graveney, the lords of which were Grevenel in the twelfth century, and Tooting Bec, in the tenure of the abbey of Bec Hellouin (cf Weedon Bec) (*Totinge* 675: OE *-ingas*).

†**Torbay** D, 'bay near Torre'. The name originally referred to the bay itself, then became that of the County Borough formed from the towns around it and has now become that of the District. **Torquay** D is named from a quay built by the

monks of Torre Abbey in the parish of **Tormohan**, 'Mohun's manor in Torre, i e hill'. An earlier name for Torquay was *Fleet*, '(place by) a stream', probably commemorated in Fleet Street, near which a small brook formerly entered the sea [2. *Torkay* 1668, *Fleete otherwise Torkey* 1670, 3. *Torre* c 1195, 4. *Torre Moun* 1279: OE *torr*].

Torran Arg, — (Raasay) Inv, **Torrance** Stl, **Torrans** (Mull) Arg: 'little hill(s)', the third and fourth examples with English *-s* for the plural [3. *Torrens* 1554: G *torran*].

†**Torridge** *riv* D, 'rough one'. On the river stand **Black Torrington** D, **Great Torrington** D, and **Little Torrington** D 'farm by the river Torridge' [1. *Toric* 938, 2. *Torintona* 1086, *Blacketorrintun* 1219, 3. *Chippingtoriton* 1284, *Torytone Manga* 1366, 4. *Parva Toriton* 1242, *Little Torygton* 1411: B *Torric*, OE *tūn*].

Torridon Ros, 'portage place' [*Torvirlane* 1464: G *tairbheartan*].

Torrington D. See Torridge *riv* D.

Totnes D, 'Totta's headland', alluding to the promontory upon which the castle is built [*Totanæs* c 1000: OE *næss*].

Tottenham Mx, 'Totta's homestead' The early forms of **Tottenham Court** Mx show that the two places only have the personal name element in common, the second having been originally Tottenhale, 'Totta's nook of land' [1. *Toteham* 1086, *Totenham* 1265, 2. *Totehele* 1086, *Totenhale* 1254, *Totten-Court* 17c: OE *hām, halh*].

Tove *riv* Nth, 'slow one'. On the river stands **Towcester** Nth 'Roman station on the river Tove', the Romano-British *Lactodoron*, which means possibly much the same as Towcester but has the Celtic name for the river suffixed with -duro 'fort' [1. *Toue* 1219, 2. *Tofeceaster* c 925: OE **tof, ceaster*].

Tower Hamlets Mx, 'settlements belonging to the Tower of London'; Stepney, Bethnal Green, and Poplar were formerly under the jurisdiction of the Tower.

Tow Law Du, 'lookout mound' [*Tollawe* 1423: OE *tot, hlāw*].

Towyn Crd, — Den, — Flt, — Mer: 'seashore' [W *tywyn*].

†Trafford La, 'ford by a Roman road', showing not only consonantal assimilation, as in Strafford, -*tf*- becoming -*ff*-, but also a loss of *S*- before another consonant (cf Nottingham), due to Norman influence [*Stratford* 1206: OE *strǣt, ford*].

Tralee Ker, 'shore of or by the (river) Lee', alluding either to the river-bank or the seashore by which the mouth of the river is found [I *traigh*].

Tramore Wat, 'great shore' [I *traigh, mor*].

Tranent ELo, 'stream or valley farm' [*Tranent* 1210: W *tref, nant*].

Tranmere Ch, 'sandbank on which cranes were seen' [*Tranemul* 12c, *Tranemel* 1290: ON *trani, melr*].

Tredegar Mon, 'town established by the Tredegar family', giving rise to the transfer of a place-name within a single county. The industrial settlement was founded in the nineteenth century by landowners who derived their name from Tredega ('Tegyr's farm') near Newport Mon [2. *Tredegyr* 1550: W *tref*].

Trefeglwys Mgm, 'church farm' [W *tref, eglwys*].

Trefriw Crn, 'farm on the hill' [*Treffruu* 1254: W *tref, rhiw*].

Tregarth Crn, 'farm on a ridge' [W *tref, garth*].

Tremadoc Crn, 'Madoc's farm' [W *tref*].

Tremain Crd, **Tremaine** Co, **Triermain** Cu: 'farm of the stone' [3. *Trewermain* c 1200: W *tref, maen*, Co *trev, mên*].

Trent *riv* St-Db-Nt, 'trespasser', i e a river liable to floods [*Trisantona* c 115: B **trisantōn*].

Tresco *isld* (Scilly) Co, 'elder-tree farm', originally the name, not of the island, but of a farm, where the abbey was. Landscape changes in the Scilles, due to the sinking of the main island in particular, have brought about some naming anomalies, as here; the original name of the island was *Iniscaw* c 1540, 'isle of elder' [*Trescau* 1305: OCo *tref, *scaw, *enis*].

Tresimwn Glm. See Bonvilston.

Trim Mth, '(ford of the) elder-tree', so called from the trees marking the crossing of the river Boyne [† *ath, truim*].

Trimley St Martin Sf, **Trimley St Mary** Sf: 'Trymma's wood or grove', with church dedications [1, *Tremlega* 1086, *Tremle Sancti Martini* 1254, 2. *Tremle Beate Marie* 1254: OE *lēah*].

Trimmer Wex, **Trummer** *isld* Cla., **Trummery** Ant: 'place of elder-trees' [† *tromaire*].

Tring Hrt, 'tree-covered hillside', an interpretation which suits both the topography and the etymology suggested, viz an origin in OE *trēow-hangra* rather than ON *þriðjung*. In support of the ON derivation only a single spelling,

Tredung in Domesday Book (with analogous forms for the former Hundred of Tring) can be adduced; against this must be set historical difficulties, including a complete lack of evidence of any Scandinavian administrative arrangements that would make sense of the term here, as well as the possibility of error in DB forms [*Tredung* 1086, *Triangre* 12c, *Trehangre* 1265: OE *trēow, hangra*].

Troon Ayr, 'headland' [*Le Trone* 1371, *Le Trune* 1464: W *trwyn*].

Trossachs *mtns* Pth, 'cross places, transverse hills', the word being said to be a Gaelic adaptation of W *trawsfynydd*, or at least of the first element. The name applies particularly to the hills that run athwart Loch Katrine, dividing it from Loch Achray [G *Tròsaichean*].

Trout Beck *riv* Cu (x 3), **Trout Beck** *riv* We (x 2), **Troutbeck** We: 'trout stream' [2. *Trutebek* 1292, 3. *Troutebeck* c 1195, 4. *Trutebec* 1179, 5. *Trutebyk* 1292, 6. *Trutebek* 1272, *Troughtebek* 1437: OE *truht*, ON *bekkr*].

Truro Co, possibly 'three yardlands', a name of the same type as Fifield, Tinhead, etc, except that here the unit of measurement is Cornish *erow* [*Triuereu* 12c: Co *tri, erow*].

Tuam Gal, 'tumulus', in full 'tumulus of the two shoulders' [I *Tuaim-da-Ghualann*].

Tuesley Sr, probably 'grove dedicated to the god Tiw', doubts about this meaning coming mainly from inconsistencies in some early spellings. Pagan references are by no means rare in Surrey names, however, and the interpretation is almost certainly right [*Tiwesle* 1086, *Tewersle* 1313: OE *lēah*].

Tummel *riv*. Pth, 'darkness', alluding to heavily wooded gorges [*Abhain Teimheil* n d: OG* *temel*].

†**Tunbridge Wells** K, 'medicinal wells by Tonbridge (q v)'.

Tunstall Du, — ERY, — K, — La, — NRY (x 2), — Sf, — St (x 2): 'site of a farm' [1. *Dunstall* 1196, 2. *Tunestal* 1086, 3. *Tunestelle* 1086: OE *tūn-stall*].

Tunstead Milton Db. See Milton.

Turville Bk, 'dry open country', with the *feld/ville* development as in Enville [*Þyrefeld* 796: OE *þyrre, feld*].

Tutbury St, 'Stut's fortified place', initial *S-* having been lost owing to Norman influence (cf Nottingham) [*Toteberia* 1086, *Stutesberia* c 1150: OE *burh*].

Tweed *riv* Pbl-Slk-Rox-Ber-Nb, possibly 'powerful river' [*Tuidi fluminis* c 730, *Twiode* c 1025: B *Tuesis*].

Twerton So. See Tiverton D.

Twickenham Mx, 'riverside grassland at a confluence', the place being near the point where the river Crane joins the Thames [*Tuican ham* 704, *Tuicanhamme* 793: OE *twicce, hamm*].

Twyford Bk, — Brk, — Db, — Ha, — Lei, — Mx, — Nf: '(place by) a double ford'. In some instances the double ford is at a confluence, e g Twyford Brk where the Loddon joins the Thames; elsewhere the ford crosses the stream by way of an island [1. *Tveverde* 1086, 2. *Tuiford* 1170, 4. *Tuifyrde* c 960: OE *twī-, ford*]. See also Tiverton D.

Tyburn Mx, '(place at) boundary stream' [*Tiburne* 1086: OE *tēo, burna*]. See also Marylebone.

Ty-nant Den, — Mer: 'dwelling in the valley' [W *ty, nant*].

Tyne *riv* Cu-Nb-Du, 'water, river'. The vague local designation Tyneside has now become specific and official in the District names †**North Tyneside**, †**South Tyneside** of the Metropolitan County of ††**Tyne and Wear.** †**Tynedale** is a District of Northumberland [*Tina* c 150: B **ti-*].

Tyrone, 'Owen's country' [*Tir-Eoghain* n d: I *tir*].

Uamh Bheag *mtn* Pth, '(by or with) the little cave' [G *uamh, beag* (fem. *bheag*)].

Uckfield Sx, 'Ucca's open land'. OE *feld* originally denoted land cleared of trees, either by natural or artificial means, and occurs in this sense in Enfield Mx Sheffield WRY, Hatfield Hrt, etc. Personal names occur with *feld* fairly frequently, but the places concerned are usually small [*Uckefeld* 1220: OE *feld*].

Uffculme D, 'Uffa's (farm on) the river Culm'. The river-name means 'lopped, winding' [*Offecoma* 1086: W *cwlwm*, 'knot'].

Uig (Lewis) Ros, — (Skye) Inv: 'bay, nook'. The Gaelic word is an adaptation of ON *vik* [1. *Vye* 1549, 2. *Wig* 1512: G *ùig*].

Uisge Labhar *riv* Inv, 'noisy water' [G *uisge, labhar*].

Uist (North and **South)** *islds* Inv, 'inner abode' [*Iuist* 1282, *Ouiste* 1373: ON *í, vist*].

Ulbster Cai, 'Ulf's dwelling' [*Ulbister* 1538: ON *bólstaðr*].

Ulgham Nb, **Ulwham** Nb: 'marshy nook haunted by owls'. The second element is rather rare and found only in NCy names [1. *Wlacam* 1139, 2. *Ulgheham* 1479: OE *ūle*, ON *hvammr*].

Ullapool Ros, perhaps 'Olaf's dwelling' [*Ullabill* 1610: ON *bólstaðr*].

Ullesthorpe Lei, 'Ulf's outlying settlement' [*Ulestorp* 1086, *Olvestorp* 1278: ON *þorp*].

Ullock Cu, 'place where wolves played'. **Wooloaks** Cu has the same meaning [1. *Great Ulfelayth* 1235, *Ullaik* 1332, 2. *Wolfaykes* 1235, *Wllaykes* 1285: ON *ulfr, leikr*].

Ullswater *lke* Cu, We: 'Ulf's lake'. Both -*mere* and -*water* occur as lake-names in this area, sometimes simultaneously as in *Grassmeer-water* 1671 for the present Grasmere; *Routhmere* c 1273 has now become Rydal Water, and the present Windermere was *Winander water* in 1577. Like Windermere, Ullswater has a personal name as first element [*Ulueswater* c 1235, *Vllesmere* 1622, *Ulles Lake* 1727: OE *wæter*].

Ulster, 'place of the Ulaid tribe'. Like Leinster and Munster (qq .v), the name of this Irish province consists of a tribal name with ON -*staðr* suffixed. In addition to the six counties of the present 'Northern Ireland', the province formerly included also Donegal, Cavan, and Monaghan.

Ulverston La, 'Wulfhere's farm', the personal name being Scandinavianised by loss of *W-* [*Ulurestun* 1086: OE *tūn*].

Ulwham Nb. See Ulgham.

Unst Zet, 'eagle's dwelling-place' [*Ornyst* c 1200: ON *orn, vist*].

Unthank Cu (x 2), — Nb (x 2), — NRY, — Rox: 'place occupied by unauthorised tenants'. The element also occurs in **Newton Unthank** Lei [OE *unþanc*].

Uphill So, '(place) above the creek'

alluding to a pool in the river Axe [*Opopille* 1086, *Uppepull* 1197: OE *uppe*, *pyll*].

Up Holland La. See Holland.

Upminster Ess/GL, 'higher church' [*Upmynster* 1062: OE *upp*, *mynster*].

Uppingham R, 'homestead of the people on the higher land'. The folk-name *Yppingas* is derived from OE *upp* [*Yppingeham* 1067: OE *-ingas*, *hām*].

Upton *freq*, 'higher village'. Apart from numerous examples of the simple name, there are also many affixed forms, usually compounded with a family name, e g Upton Cheney Gl, Upton Noble So, Upton Scudamore W, and Upton Cressett Sa. The manorial name precedes in Walters Upton Sa, held by Walter Fitz-John in the twelfth century. Upton Snodsbury Wo unites two places originally separate; the second component means 'Snodd's fortified place' [OE *upp*, *tūn*]. See also Crediton.

Ure *riv* NRY, 'holy-river' or 'strong river' [*Earp*, i e *Ear w(æter)* c 1025, *Jor* c 1140, *Yor* c 1190: B **isura*]. See also *Isurium*, Jervaulx.

Urquhart Fif, 'portion of the cast or shot', originally a *pett-* compound alluding to a method of allocating land by such means [*Petnaurcha* 1128: P **pett*, OG *aurchoir*].

Urquhart Inv, — Mor, — Ros: '(place by) a thicket' [1. *Airchardan* c 1100, 3. *Urchard* 1340: B *air cardden*].

Ushaw Du, 'wolves' wood', from **Ulfa-skage*, a Scandinavianised form of OE *wulfa-sceaga* [*Ulveskahe* 12c: OE *wulf*, *sceaga*].

Usk Mon, 'place on river Usk, i e fish river' [2. *Iska* c 150: B **eiska*]. See also Brynbuga, *Burrium*.

Uttoxeter St, 'Wuttuc's heath'. Modern spellings suggest a derivation from OE *ceaster* (as in Exeter, Wroxeter) but early forms show that this is certainly not so [*Wottocheshede* 1086, *Uittokeshather* 1251: OE **hǣddre*].

Uxbridge Mx, 'bridge of the Wixan tribe'. The reference is to a small settlement of people well away from their home territory, which was probably in the Midlands. Another Wixan enclave is commemorated in Uxendon Mx, 'hill of the Wixan tribe' [1. *Wixebru* c 1145, *Uxebregg* 1200, 2. *Woxindon* 1258: OE *brycg*, *dūn*].

Uxellodunum. See Stanwix.

Valentia Ker, 'estuary of the island', the latter being Valentia Island [I *béal*, *inse*].

†Vale Royal Ch 1536, 'royal valley', the site of a monastery founded by Edward I [*Vallis Regalis* 1277, *Vau Real* 1300, *Valroyal* 1357: OF *val*, ME *vale*, OF *roial*].

†Vale of White Horse Brk, 'valley adjoining White Horse Hill' — on which a figure of a horse was cut [1. *Vale of Whithors* 1368, 2. *mons ubi ab album equum scanditur* 1170, *Whyte-Horse* 1322: OE *hwīt*, *hors*].

Vange Ess, 'fen district', like Ely, Surrey, and Lyminge, formed with the archaic element *gē* 'district' [*Fange* 963: OE *fen*, **gē*].

Vauxhall Sr/GL, 'Falkes's hall', named after Falkes de Breauté, who held the land in the early 13c [*Faukeshale* 1279: OE *heall*].

Vecta,Vectis. See Wight, Isle of.

Venta. See Gwent.

Venta Belgarum. See Winchester.

Venta Icenorum. See Caistor-by-Norwich.

Venta Silurum. See Caerwent.

Ventnor Wt, '(manor of) Vintner', the manorial name replacing the earlier *Holewey* [*Vintner* 1617].

Ver *riv.* Hrt, name derived by back-formation from *Verulamium* (q v).

Vernham's Dean Ha, 'valley in or by Vernham, i e, fern homestead'. The voicing of initial *F-* to *V-* is characteristic of southern dialects of English but occurs beyond the area of West Saxon speech (e g Vange Ess). Other examples are Vobster So and Verwood Do (qq v) [*Ferneham* 1219: OE *fearn, hām, denu*].

Verterae. See Brough under Stainmore We.

Verulamium Hrt, 'place (settled by followers) of Verolamos', the Roman city on the edge of St Albans (q v). The personal name is probably of the 'nick-name' type, meaning perhaps 'broad hand', from the Celtic roots **veru-*, broad, wide' and *lama*, 'hand', compounded with the locative suffix *-ion*, as in *Londinion*. *Verulamium* gave rise to OE *Verlamcaestir*, recorded in the eighth century.

Verwood Do, 'fair wood' [*Fairwod* 1329: OE *fæger, wudu*].

Vilanstown Wme, 'farm worked by villeins', in Irish *Baile na Bhileanach* [*Villenston* c 1590: ME *vilein*, OE *tūn*].

Vindolanda Nb, 'white enclosure' [B **vindo- *landa*].

Viriconium, Viroconium. See Wrekin.

Virley Ess, originally Salcott Virley, 'premises on which salt was prepared, held by de Verli'. The erosion of the name until only the feudal addition survives is paralleled in Shendish Hrt (q v) [*Salcota* 1086, *Salcote Verly* 1291: OE *salt, cot*].

Vobster So, 'Fobb's rocky peak' [*Fobbestor* 1234: OE *torr*].

Voe Zet, 'little bay' [ON *vágr*].

Vowchurch He, 'speckled church' [*Fowchirche* 1291: OE *fāg, cirice*].

Vyrnwy *riv* Mgm-He: perhaps 'milky stream'. The Welsh name Efyrnwy, misread as Y Fyrnwy ('the Fyrnwy') led to the common form, an Anglicised spelling of Fyrnwy. *Efyrnwy* is derived from a mutated form of W *Hafren* (i e Severn), and must be interpreted in a similar way to that river-name [*Y Vyrnwy* 13c, *Efyrnwy* 13c].

Waddesdon Bk, 'Weott's hill' [*Votesdone* 1086, *Wottesdona* 1168: OE *dūn*].

Wainfleet All Saints LLi, 'stream fordable by a wagon', the addition referring to the dedication of the church [*Wenflet* 1086: OE *wægn, flēot*].

Wakefield Nth,† — WRY: 'open land on which annual fairs were held', both being meeting places for Hundred or shire assemblies [1, *Wacafeld* 1086, *Wachefeld* 1158, 2. *Wachefeld* 1086: OE *wacu, feld*].

Walberswick Sf, 'specialised farm held by Waldberht' [*Walberdeswicke* 1199: OE *wīc*].

Walcot *freq*, 'cottage(s) of the serfs or Welsh' [OE *Walh, cot*].

Wales, '(land of) the foreigners', the peremptory description of the Celts of Britain by the Anglo-Saxons. **Wales**

WRY 1086 has the same meaning [OE *W(e)alh*, plural *W(e)alas*].

Wallasey Ch, 'island of Waley, i.e. island of the Welsh', a name of rather confused development, *ēg* having been added twice to the root word *Wala*, 'of the Welshmen'. The name is properly applied to the whole area at the tip of Wirral, cut off from the peninsula at high tide and time of flood [*Walea* 1086, *Walleie* c 1100, *Walleye* 1259, *Waleyesegh* 1351: OE *Walh*, *ēg*].

Wallington Ha, — Sr, **Wallingtons** Brk: 'village of the British' [1. *Walintone* 1288, 2. *Waletona* 1086, 3. *Waleton'* 1195 *Walyton'* 1327: OE *Walh*, *tūn*].

Wallop Ha. See Nether Wallop Ha, Farleigh Wallop Ha.

Walmer K, 'pool of the British' [*Wealamere* 11c: OE *W(e)alh*, *mere*].

†**Walsall** St, 'little valley of Walh', the personal name possibly indicating someone of British origin [*Waleshale* 1163: OE *halh*].

Walters Upton. See Upton.

Waltham K, — LLi, **Coldwaltham** Sx, **Bishops Waltham** Ha, **Great & Little Waltham** Ess, **Up Waltham** Sx, **White Waltham** Brk, **Waltham Cross** Hrt, **Waltham Holy Cross** Ess, **Waltham on the Wolds** Lei, **Waltham St Lawrence** Brk: 'homestead in or by a wood', with a variety of additions. White Waltham is on chalky soil, whereas its neighbour Waltham St Lawrence is not. The Abbey of Waltham Holy Cross Ess held an estate in Waltham St Lawrence, but the names are independent of this fact. Waltham Cross Hrt, however, is named because of its proximity to Waltham Ess. *Cross* in the Hertfordshire name refers to the last but one of the Eleanor crosses set up by Edward I to mark the places where the body of the queen rested for the night on its journey from Harby to London. Bishops Waltham belonged to the Bishop of Winchester [1. *Wealtham* 11c, 2, 4, 5, 6, 7, 9, 10. *Waltham* 1086, 3. *Uualdham* 683: OE *w(e)ald*, *hām*].

Walthamstow Ess/GL, 'Wilcume's holy place', the form of the name having been affected by a connexion with Waltham Holy Cross Ess (q v) [*Wilcumestouue* c 1067, *Welchamstowe*1 263, *Wolkhamstouwe* 1309, *Walthamstowe* 1446: OE *stōw*].

Walton Bk (x 2), — Lei (x 2), — Nth, — O, — Sa (x 3), — So, **East Walton** Nf, **Isley Walton** Lei, **Wenlock Walton** Sa, **Walton Cardiff** Gl, **Walton Grounds** Nth, **Walton in Gordano** So: 'village in or by a wood' [1. *Waltona* 1090, 2. *Waldone* 1219, 3. *Waltone* 1086, 4. *Walton* c 1220, 6. *Waltone* 1086: OE *weald*, *tūn*]. See also Easton.

Walton Db, — K, — Sf, — St (x 3), — Sx, — WRY (x 2), **Walton Inferior** and **Superior** Ch, **Walton on the Naze** Ess, **Walton on the Hill** La, **Walton on the Wolds** Lei, **Walton on Thames** Sr: 'village of the Britons' [1. *Waletune* 1086, 2. *Waltun* 11c, 3. *Waletuna* 1086, 4-6. *Waletone* 1086, 10. *Waletona* c 1158, *Netherwalton* 1295: OE *Walh*, *tūn*].

Walworth Du, — Sr: 'enclosure of the Britons' [1. *Waleworth* 1262, *Wealawyrð* 1006: OE *W(e)alh*, *worð*].

Wandle *riv* Sr/GL, back-formation from **Wandsworth** Sr/GL, 'Wændel's enclosure'. The river-name is not on record before the sixteenth century; a thousand years earlier it was called *Hlidaburna* 'stream from the slopes'. This seems a very general name today, but doubtless in earlier times it served to distinguish the rivulet which rose in the uplands near Croydon from the numerous local streams in the marshy area around its junction with the Thames [1. *Hlidaburna* 693, *Vandalis riuuluᶱ* 1586, *Wandal* 1612, 2. *Wendles wurð* 693, *Wandelesorde* 1086: OE *hlid, burna, worð*].

†**Wansbeck** *riv* Nb, meaning unknown. The second syllable did not become *-beck* until the sixteenth century [*Wenspic* 1137, *Wanspike* 12c].

†**Wansdyke** Ha-So, 'Woden's embankment', i e supposed to have been constructed by Woden, or (if folk-memory entered into the bestowing of the name) was the place at which Woden, the war-god, presided. The embankment seems to have been constructed in the fifth century and was probably designed to resist English invasion from the south [*Wodnes dic* 903: OE *dic*].

Wanstead Ess/GL, 'dwelling place by a hillock', a slight elevation in otherwise low-lying country being chosen as a settlement. The first element means 'lump, tumour' [*Wænstede* 1066: OE *wænn, stede*].

Wantage Brk, '(place by) diminishing stream' [*æt Waneting* c 880, *Wanetinz* 1086, *Wantenge* 1392: OE **wanotian*].

Warboys Hu, 'watch bush(es)' [*Wærdebusc* 1077, *Wardeboys* c 1150: ON *varði, buskr*, OF *bois*].

Warden K, — Nb, **Old Warden** Bd: 'watch hill', with a superfluous addition in **Warden Low** Du, 'watch-hill hill'. **Chipping Warden** Nth lost its right to a market, implied in the name, in the early thirteenth century [1. *Wardon* 1207, 3. *Wardone* 1086, 4. *Wardona* 1183: *weard, dūn, hlāw, cieping*].

Wardlaw Ros, 'watch hill' [*Wardelaue* 1210: OE *weard, hlāw*].

Wardle Ch 1184, — La: 'watch hill' [1. *Warhelle* 1086, *Wardhul* 1278, 2. *Wardhill* 1218: OE *weard, hull*].

Ware Hrt 1200, '(place by a) weir', alluding to 'stoppages, which there obstruct the river' mentioned by Fuller in the seventeenth century [*Waras* 1086, *Wares* c 1195: OE *wer*].

Wareham Do, 'homestead by a weir' [*Werham* 784, *Warham* 1086: OE *wer, hām*].

Wark Nb, 'fort' [1. *Werch* 1158, 2. *Werke* 1279: OE *(ge)weorc*].

Warminster W, 'church on river Were, i e rambling one' [*Worgemynster* c 910: OE *wōrian, mynster*].

Warrington La, 'farm by a weir or dam' [*Walintune* 1086, *Werington* 1246: OE **wering, tūn*].

Warsop Nt, 'Wær's little valley' [*Wareshope* 1086: OE *hop*].

Warwick Cu, 'dwelling or premises on a bank' [*Warthwic* 1131: OE *waroð, wīc*].

†**Warwick** Wa, 'dwellings or premises by a weir', the second element being in the plural in early forms [*Veri* 11c, *in Wærinc wicum* 1001, *on Wærrincwican* 1016, *Warvic* 1086: OE *wering, wīc*].

Wash, The LHo-Nf, 'low-water ford across a tidal estuary', now naming the estuary, which can no longer be forded. In Roman times the mouth of the Wash was only about two-thirds of its present width, and for centuries afterwards there were two fordable portions [*The Wasshes* c 1545: OE *(ge)wæsc*].

Washington Du, — Sx: possibly 'farm at a muddy place' [1. *Wassyngtona* 1183, 2. *Wasingetune* 1086: OE *wase, -ingtūn*].

Waterford Wat, 'inlet of the wether', one of the fairly numerous collection of Norse names in the Irish Sea area. The town owes its origin to the Norwegian Viking Turgeis, who established it as a fortified port in the ninth century [*Vadrefjord* n d: ON *veðr*, *fjórðr*].

Waternish (Skye) Inv, 'glove promontory' (*Watternes* 1501: ON *vöttr*, *nes*].

Watford Hrt 945, — Nth 1086: 'ford used by hunters' [1. *Wathford(a)* c 1180, 2. *Wathford* 1238: OE *wað*, *ford*].

Watling Street, 'Roman road to *Wæclingaceaster*, i e St Albans', applied first, probably, to the road between London and St Albans, and later used for other portions of the Roman road to Wroxeter. Like Ermine Street and Icknield Way, this name is also applied to entirely independent roads in other parts of England, e g the Roman road from York to Corbridge [*Wætlingstræt* c 885: OE *stræt*].

Watten Cai, '(place by) a lake', the definition exactly describing the position of the place. The lake is called, tautologously, Loch Watten [*Watne* 1230: ON *vatn*].

Weald, The K-Ha, 'upland wood(s)' [*Waldan* (dat. pl) 1185: OE *w(e)ald*].

Wear riv Du, 'river' providing a name for a District in County Durham (†**Wear Valley**) and contributing to that of a new county (†† **Tyne and Wear**) [*Ouedra* c 150, *Wiri* c 720: B **uisu*].

Wednesbury St, 'Woden's fortified place', the reference to the god indicating either that the place was sacred to Woden or that it was supposed to be his handiwork. Although Woden is principally remembered as a war-god, he had other functions

as well. He was regarded as the tutelary deity of shamans or seers, but even more notably as the protector of trade and commerce—a function he shared with the Roman god Mercury, with whom he is equated, rather than with Mars, to whom Tiw or Tig corresponds [*Wadnesberie* 1086, *Wodnesberia* 1166: OE *burh*]. See also Wansdyke.

Weedon Bk, **Weedon Beck** Nth, **Weedon Lois** Nth: 'temple hill'. OE *wig* or *wēoh*, meaning 'idol' or 'holy place, shrine' occurs also in **Weoley Castle** Wo, **Wyfold** O, **Weyhill** Ha, and **Wye** K; these places may have been the sites of temples or shrines which remained in use as pagan places of worship after the remainder of the country had become Christian. Weedon Beck was once held by the Abbey of Bec Hellouin (cf Tooting Bec); the addition in Weedon Lois seems to be connected with a holy well, St Loy's Well, that was reputed to cure the blind and leprous. It may have been, of course, a pagan sacred well associated with the shrine [1. *Weodun* c 945, 2. *Weoduninga gemære* ('bounds of the dwellers at Weedon') c 945, *Wedone* 1086, *Wedon Beke* 1379, 3. *Leyes Weedon* 1475, 4. *Welegh* 1264, 7. *an Uuiæ* 839, *Wi* 1085: OE *wig*, *wēoh*, *dūn*, *lēah*, *falod* *hyll*]. See also Wellington.

Welland riv Nth-LHo: 'fine stream' [*Weolud* 921: B **uesu*-].

Wellingborough Nth, 'fortified place of Wændel's people', embodying the personal name found also in Wandsworth (q v) [*Wendlesberie* 1086, *Wedlingeberie* 1086: OE *-ingas*, *burh*].

Wellington He, — Sa, — So: 'farm of the dwellers at a heathen sacred place' [1. *Weolintun* c 1035, 2. *Welintona* 1220, 3. *Weolingtun* 904: OE *wēoh*, *-ingas*, *tūn*].

Welshpool Mgm, 'pool across the Welsh

border'. Similar names occur elsewhere along this border, e g **Welsh Newton** He, which must have been Welsh territory at one time. Note also the pairs of names indicating the relative positions, **Welsh Frankton** Sa and **English Frankton** Sa, and **Welsh Bicknor** He and **English Bicknor** Gl [*Pola* 1253, *Walshe Pole* 1477: OE *welisc*, *pōl*]. See also Y Trallwng.

†**Welwyn** Hrt, '(place) at the willows', from an OE dative plural form. **Willian** Hrt, some miles to the north, is from the dative plural of a related element and has the same meaning [1. *ad Welingum* c 945, *Wellyen* 1428, 2. *Wilie* 1086, *Wilian* 1212: OE *welig*, *wylig*].

Wembley Mx, 'Wemba's grove or wood' [*æt Wemba lea* 825: OE *lēah*].

Wendover Bk, '(place by) white stream', though there is no record of the use of the name for a river. The second element is the British plural word meaning literally 'waters' found also in Dover and Andover (qq v) [*æt Wændofron* c 970: OW *winn*, B *dubro-*].

Wensum *riv* Nf, 'winding one' [*Wenson* 1096: OE *wændsum*].

Wenvoe Glm, possibly 'moorland plain' [*Wnfa* c 1160: OW *guoun*, B *magos*].

Weoley Castle Wo. See Weedon.

West Anstey D, '(place with) narrow path', *West* distinguishing the place from **East Anstey**, more than a mile away. Both are on hills, and the narrow paths alluded to lead to the respective churches [1. *Anestiga* 1086, *Westanostige* 1234, 2. *Estanesty* 1263: OE *west*, *ēast*, *ānstiga*].

Westbourne Mx, 'western stream' [*Westeburne* 1259: OE *west*, *burna*].

West Bromwich St (now ††West Midlands). See Castle Bromwich.

Westbury Bk, — Ha, — Sa, —So, — W, **Westbury on Severn** Gl, **Westbury on Trym** Gl: 'western fortified place', the two Gloucestershire examples being distinguished by river-names. The Trym ('strong (river)') is a short tributary of the Bristol Avon [1. *Westberie* 1086, 2. *Wesberie* 1086, 4. *Westbyrig* 1065, 5. *Westberie* 1086: OE *west*, *burh*].

West Coker So, 'westerly place on the crooked stream', Coker having been once the stream name; also on the little river are **North Coker** and **East Coker** [*Cochra* 1086; B **kukros*].

Wester Ross Ros. See Ross.

Westgate Du, — Nb, **Westgate on Sea** K: 'western gate or pass' [1. *Westyatshele* 1457, 3. *Westgata* 1168: OE *west*, *geat*].

West Grimstead W. See East Grimstead W.

West Grinstead Sx. See East Grinstead Sx.

West Ham Ess/GL. See East Ham.

West Kirby Ch. See Kirby.

†**West Lothian** WLo, 'western part of Lothian, i e territory of Leudonus,' formerly called Linlithgowshire, from its chief town, Linlithgow (q v) [*Loonia* c 891]. See also East Lothian, Midlothian.

††**West Midlands** (Metropolitan County), set up under the 1972 Local Government Act, consisting of Birmingham, Coventry, Wolverhampton, Walsall, Stourbridge, and small sections of the counties of Warwickshire, Worcestershire, and Staffordshire in the vicinity of the places named.

Westmeath, 'western part of Meath, i e middle province', a county created by statute in 1542. The same act of the Irish Parliament renamed the constituent baronies. The present boundaries were established about 1600 [I *midhe*].

Westminster Mx, 'western monastery', stating its position relative to London [*Westmunster* 785: OE *west, mynster*].

Westmorland, 'district of the people living west of the moors', alluding to the Pennines of North Yorkshire. At first denoting only the Barony of Appleby, in the north of the county, the name was applied to the whole county by the time of Henry II. It is now part of the new county of Cumbria (q v) [*Westmoringa land* c 1150: OE *west, mōr, -ingas, land*].

Weston *freq*, 'western farm', with numerous additions, manorial and topographical. The latter include **Weston upon Trent** Db, **Weston upon Trent** St, **Weston Underwood** Bk, **Weston Underwood** Db, **Weston Subedge** Gl ('... at the foot of a cliff or steep ridge'), and **Weston in Arden** Wa. There is a **Weston in Gordano** So corresponding to Easton in Gordano (q v) and in the same county the genuine Latin addition of **Weston Super Mare** ('... upon the sea') [OE *west, tūn*].

West Riding WRY, 'western third', the others being North Riding and East Riding of Yorkshire. There was also a West Riding of the Parts of Lindsey in Lincolnshire, the other two in that county being North Riding and South Riding. All show the same phonetic development [*West Treding* 1086: ON *vestr, þriðjung*]. See also East Riding, North Riding.

Westward Ho! D, name commemorating the novel of that name by Charles Kingsley. Many scenes of the story are set in the neighbourhood.

West Wittering Sx. See East Wittering.

Wetwang ERY, '(by the) wet field(s)', embodying an element *wang* which is quite common in field-names but hardly ever encountered in major place-names [*Wetwangham* 1086: OE *wēt, wang*].

Wexford Wex, 'inlet by the sea-washed sandbank', one of the Scandinavian names of the Irish Sea area. For the *x*, see Leix [*Weysford* 15c: ON *veska, fjórðr*].

Wey *riv* Do, — *riv* Ha-Sr, **Wye** *riv* Db, — *riv* He-Mon: 'running water, conveyor' [1. *Waye* 1244, 2. *Waie* 675, 3. *Wey* 1233, *Wæge* 956: OW **weg*].

Weybridge Sr, '(place by) bridge over river Wey (q v)' [*Waigebrugge* 675: OE *brycg*].

†**Weymouth** Do, '(place at) mouth of river Wey (q v)' [*Waimouþe* 939: OE *mūða*].

Whalsay *isld* Zet, 'whale island' [*Hvalsey* c 1250: ON *hval, ey*].

Whatstandwell Db, 'place named after Walter Stonewell', an interpretation which has all the appearance of one of the more extravagant types of baseless popular etymology, but which is supported by abundant documentary evidence. In the late fourteenth century a bridge was built over the river Derwent, and in the document recording an agreement between the Abbot of Darley and the intending builder, John de Stepul, there is a reference to premises held by Walter Stonewell. The bridge was sited at a spot known as *Wattestanwell ford* 1390. The name appears among witnesses to documents of forty or fifty years earlier [*Wattestanwell ford* 1390, *Watstandwell* 1444].

Whipsnade Bd, 'Wibba's detached clearing' [*Wibsnede* 1202: OE *snǣd*].

Whissendine R, 'valley of pirates', possibly representing an early settlement of Vikings, but embodying the OE word rather than the cognate ON *vikingr* [*Wichingedene* 1086: OE *wicing, denu*].

Whitburn WLɔ, 'white stream' [*Whiteburne* 1296: OE *hwīt, burna*].

Whitby Ch, 'white manor house or village', a name of different origin and meaning from Whitby NRY (q v). The Cheshire name originally had an OE termination, *-burh*, probably with the sense that the term acquired in the late Anglo-Saxon period; this was replaced in post-Conquest times by the common Scandinavian element *by* (cf Rugby Wa) [*Witeberia* c 1100, *Witebia* c 1100, OE *hwīt, burh*, ON *bý*].

Whitby NRY, 'Hviti's village' [*Witeby* 1086: ON *bý*].

Whitehaven Cu, 'haven by Whithoft i e white headland', the early name with four or five syllables and repetition of consonant-clusters being early reduced by the omission of its middle portion. The 'headland' is a large white rock, in the shelter of which a harbour was built at some time before 1150 [*quithofhavene* c 1135, *Wythauene* 1279: ON *hvít, hǫfuð, hafn*].

Whithorn Wig, 'white building', so called, according to Bede, because it was of stone [*Candida Casa* c 730, *æt Hwitan Ærne* c 890: OE *hwīt, ærn*].

Whitland Crm, 'white glade', a hybrid name, to be compared with **Blanchland** Nb, which retains its connexion with its Old French origin [1. *Alba Landa* 1214, *Whitland* 1309, *Blaunchelande* 1318, 2. *Blanchelande* 1165, *Alba Landa* 1203: OE *hwīt*, OF *blanc*(*he*), *launde*].

Whitstable K, '(place at) white post', possibly referring to the mark of a passage or landing-placé [*Witenstapel* 1086: OE *hwīt, stapol*].

Whitton *freq*, 'white farm', alluding probably to stone buildings [OE *hwīt, tūn*].

Whitwick Lei, 'white outlying farm' [*Witewic* 1086: OE *hwīt, wīc*].

Wick Cai, 'bay' [*Vik* 1140, *Weke* 1455: ON *vík*].

Wick Gl (x 2), **Wick by Pershore** Wo, **Wick Champflower** So, **Wick Episcopi** Wo, **Wick Hall** Brk, **Wick Hill** Brk (x 2), **Wick St Lawrence** So: 'outlying dairy farm', with various additions, topographical and manorial. Wick Champflower, like **Huish Champflower** ('household property', OE *hiwisc*) was held by the family of Thomas de Chanflurs in the thirteenth century. Wick Episcopi was granted to the Bishop of Worcester in the eighth century [1. *Wyk* 1253, 2. *Wic* 12c, 3. *Wiche* 1086, 4. *Wikechamflur* 1280, 5. *Wican* c 765, *Wisshopeswick* 1221, 6. *Le Wyk*' 1284, 7. *Wyke* 1330, 9. *Wike* 1225: OE *wīc*].

Wickham *freq*, 'homestead by a *vicus*, i e Romano-British village', a name of considerable archaeological interest, with which may be compared some at least of the examples of Witton (qq v). It has been found that places with the name Wickham were often, if not always, within a mile of a known Roman habitation site. The form Wycomb occurs in Gloucestershire, and Wykeham, Wykham, and Wyckham in other counties [OE *wichām*].

Wickhambreux K, 'Wickham held by de Brayhuse', like other instances of Wickham, with Roman archaeological material in the vicinity [*æt Wicham* 948, *Wykham Breuhuse* 1270: OE *wichām*].

Wicklow Wic, 'meadow of the Viking(s)' [*Wykynoelo* n d: ON *Víkingr, ló*].

Widnes La, 'broad promontory' [*Wydnes* c 1200: OE *wid, næss*].

Wigan Agl, — La: 'Wigan's (farm)', only the personal name remaining in the surviving forms, but supposing an element such as W *tref* in these undoubtedly Celtic names [2. *Wigan* 1199].

††**Wight, Isle of,** 'place of the division', alluding to the position of the island in the fork of the Solent [*Vectis* c 150, *Wiht* c 890: B **uekta-*].

Wigston Magna Lei, 'farm of the Viking'; **Wigston Parva** Lei, however, is '(place with or by) logan stone'. It is the former which is incorporated in the District name, †**Oadby and Wigston** Lei [1. *Wichingestone* 1086, 2. *Wicgestan* 1002: OE *wicing*, ON *vikingr*, OE *stān, tūn, wigga*].

†**Wigtown** Wig, 'Wicga's farm' [*Wigeton* 1266: OE *tūn*].

Willenhall St, 'Willa's nook of land' [*Willanhalch* c 733: OE *halh*].

Willesden Mx, 'hill with or by a spring' [*Willesdone, Wellesdune* 939: OE *w(i)ella, dūn*].

Willian Hrt. See Welwyn.

Wilmslow Ch, 'Wighelm's burial mound'. As the name was originally limited to the church and churchyard, it is possible that the church was actually built on the tumulus [*Wilmesloe* 13c: OE *hlāw*].

Wilton *freq*, mostly 'farm among willows', though **Wilton** So is 'farm with or by a well or spring'. **Wilton** W, on which the county name is based, is 'farm on the river Wylye, i e tricky stream'. **Wiltshire** is 'shire centred on Wilton' [2. *Wilton* 1249, 3. *Uuiltun* 838, *Wiltune* 1086, 4. *Wiltunscir* 870: OE **wilig, wiella, tūn*].

Wimbledon Sr/GL, 'Wynnman's hill' [*æt Wunemannedune* c 950, *Wimmeldun* 1212. OE *dūn*].

Wimborne Minster Do, 'monastery by †Wimborne, i e stream among the meadows', the river-name, now replaced by Allen, having as its first element the postulated form **winn*, which may be compared with recorded forms in other Germanic languages, e g Gothic *vinja*, ON *vin* [*Winburnan monasterio* 894, *Winburnan mynstre* c 1025: OE **winn, burna, mynster*].

†**Winchester** Ha, 'Roman station at *Venta*', the Romano-British name of the place being *Venta Belgarum*, '*Venta*, i e favoured place, of the Belgae'. This name is of a type that demonstrates that what was formerly often believed about the Anglo-Saxon settlement can hardly be true, viz that the British population was either entirely destroyed or driven out. Massacred or fleeing Celts were not likely to communicate the name of their towns to their Germanic pursuers, yet there is a substantial number of these names of Celtic origin to which OE *ceaster* was added as a specifying label, e g Manchester, Cirencester, and Exeter [*Ouenta* c 150, *Venta Belgarum* 4c, *Uintancaestir* c 730: OE *ceaster*, B **ventā*].

Windermere *lke* We, 'Vinand's lake', the personal name being, exceptionally among Scandinavian names in England, of Swedish origin [*Winendermer* c 1170: OE *mere*].

Windrush *riv* Gl-O, '(river of) white marsh' [*Uuenrisc* 779: B **ven-, *rei-*].

†**Windsor** Brk, 'windlass-place on a river bank', the machine for drawing the boats from the water being sited near a settlement [*Windlesora* c 1060: OE **windels, ōra*].

†**Wirrall** Ch, 'bog-myrtle nook'; it is possible that in this name the second element (OE *halh*) has developed the sense 'peninsula', which, of course, exactly describes the area — now a District of ††Merseyside [*Wirhealum* 984, OE *wīr, halh*].

Wisbech C, 'valley of the river Ouse (q v)' [*Wisbece* 1086: OE *bǣce*].

Wishaw Lnk, — Wa: 'wood by a curved place' [2. *Witscaga* 1086: OE **wiht, sceaga*].

Wiske *riv* NRY. See Danby Wiske.

Wiston Lnk, 'Wice's farm', but Wiston Sx is 'Wigstan's farm' [1. *Wicestun* c 1155, 2. *Wistanestun* 1086: OE *tūn*].

Withiel Co. See Lostwithiel.

Withiel Flory So, 'willow clearing', with the manorial addition indicating tenure by the family of Randulfus de Flury [*Wiðiglea* 737, *Wythele Flory* 1305: OE *wiðig, lēah*].

Witney O, 'Witta's island' [*æt Wyttanige* 969: OE *ēg*].

Witton Ch, — Wo: 'farm by a saltworks', in the vicinity of Northwich Ch and Droitwich Wo respectively [1. *Witune* 1086, 2. *Wittona* 716: OE *wic, tūn*].

Witton Nf,—NRY, **Witton le Wear** Du, **Long Witton** Nb, **Nether Witton** Nb: 'farm by a wood' [1. *Widituna* 1086, 2. *Wutun* 1202, 3. *Widtona* 1166, 4. *Wudutun* c 1050: OE *wudu, tūn*]. See also Wootton.

Witton Wa, possibly 'farm by a Romano-British village', the first element here being perhaps Latin *vicus*, as in names of the Wickham type (qq v). The existence of a Roman settlement at Holford, nearby, has been suggested [*Witone* 1086: OE *wic, tūn*].

Wittonstall WRY. See Rawtenstall La.

Woburn Bd, '(place by) crooked stream' [*Woburne* 1086: OE *wōh, burna*].

†**Woking** Sr, '(territory of) the people of Wocc', almost certainly the same folk as those referred to in Wokingham Brk, 'homestead of Wocc's people' [1. *Uuocchingas* c 710, 2. *Wokingeham* 1146: OE *-ingas, hām*].

Wolds, The ERY, — Lei, — LLi, — Nt: 'upland woods' [1. *Yorkwold* c 1340, 4. *Wolde* 1252: OE *wald*].

†**Wolverhampton** St, 'Wulfrun's Hampton, i e high farm', the second part of the name being identical in origin and meaning with **Hampton** Ch, **Hampton** Sa, **Great** and **Little Hampton** Wo, **Welsh Hampton** Sa, and **Hampton in Arden** Wa, all these being derived from the dative form, *hēan-tune*. Wulfrun was an identifiable woman of the tenth century, whose family held many properties in the Midlands [1. *æt Heantune* 985, *Wolvrene-hamptonia* c 1080, 2. *Hantone* 1086, 4. *æt Heantune* 780: OE *hēah, tūn*. See also Arden.

Woodbury Salterton D. See Budleigh Salterton.

Wooden Nb, 'wolves' valley' [*Wolveden* 1265: OE *wulf, denu*].

Wookey So, '(place of the) trap or snare' [*Woky* 1065: OE *wōcig*].

Wooloaks Cu. See Ullock.

Woolwich K/GL, 'loading place for wool' [*Uuluuich* 918: OE *wull, wic*].

Wootton *freq*, 'farm in or by a wood' [OE *wudu, tūn*].

†**Worcester** Wo, 'Roman station of the Wigora tribe', the main problem here being in the interpretation of the tribal name. A connexion with the name *Wyre* has been suggested; this is the name of the forest area that may at one time have included the site of Worcester, and is itself probably derived from a river-name meaning 'winding one'. The county name Worcestershire has been on record since the eleventh century [*Uueogorna civitate* 691, *Uuegorna cestre* 814: OE *ceaster*].

Workington Cu, 'farm of Weorc's people' [*Wirkynton* c 1125: OE *-ingas, tūn*].

Worksop Nt, 'Weorc's valley' [*Warchesoppe* 1086: OE *hop*].

Worms Head Glm, 'snake's or dragon's head', so called from its shape. Other headlands are similarly named, e g Great Orme's Head Crn (q v) [*Wormyshede* 15c: OE *wyrm, hēafod*].

Wormwood Scrubs Mx, 'woodland infested by reptiles', *scrubs* being a later addition ('rough woodland') felt to be necessary when the original *Wormholt*, manifestly a place-name, had developed into *Wormwood*, which would be confused with the term *wormwood*, a plant-name, and would therefore seem to need modification to be used as a place-name [*Wermeholte* 1200: OE *wyrm, holt, *scrubb*].

Worplesdon Sr, 'hill with or by a bridle-path', with a first element that occurs in a number of road-names in Surrey and other southern counties [*Werpesdune* 1086: OE **werpels, dūn*].

Worstead Nf, 'site of an enclosed farm', pronounced like *worsted*, the fabric originally made there, and named from the place. A fourteenth-century document mentions '*poueres overours des draps de Wurthstede en le Counte de Norff*' [*Wrðestede* c 1045: OE *worð, stede*].

†**Worthing** Sx, '(place of) Wurð's people' [*Ordinges* 1086, *Worthinges* 1288: OE *-ingas*].

Wotton Sr, **Wotton under Edge** Gl, **Wotton Underwood** Bk: 'farm by a wood', a variant of Wootton (q v). The Bucks name alludes to **Bernwood Forest** ('wood on or by a burial mound') [1. *Wodetone* 1086, 2. *æt Wudetune* 940, 3. *Wudotun* 848, *Wotton under Bernwode* 1382: OE *wudu, tūn, byrgen*].

Wrath, Cape Sut, 'headland at the turning-place' [*Wraith* 1583: ON *hvarf*].

†**Wrekin, The** Sa, of unknown meaning. It represents an early English adaptation of *Viriconium*, the source also of **Wroxeter** Sa, 'Roman station at Viriconium', nearby [1. *Viriconium* 4c, *Wrocene* 975, 2. *Ourikonion* c 150, *Rochecestre* 1086: OE *ceaster*].

Wrexham Den 1186, 'Wryhtel's river-meadow', the English form surviving attempts to give the name a Welsh appearance during the Middle Ages [*Wristelsham* 1161, *Gwregsam* 1291: OE *hamm*].

Wrockwardine Sa, 'enclosure near the Wrekin (q v)', with the second element in its customary WMidl form, as in **Bredwardine** He, **Cheswardine** Sa, and **Bedwardine** Wo [*Recordine* 1086, *Wroch Wurðin* 1169: OE *worðign*].

Wrotham K, 'Wrota's homestead' [*Uurotaham* 788: OE *hām*].

Wroxeter Sa. See Wrekin.

Wrynose *mtn* Cu, 'stallion's neck', the second element being used both in its anatomical and its topographical senses [*Wreineshals* c 1160: ON *vreini, hals*].

Wychwood O, 'forest of the Hwicce tribe'; as the woodland was outside the general tribal area (Gloucestershire, Worcestershire and western Warwickshire), it may no doubt be regarded as of the same type of forest pasture as Tenterden K (q v) [*Huiccewudu* 840: OE *wudu*].

Wyckham Sx, **Wycomb** Gl, — Lei, **Wykeham** LLi, **Wykham** O. See Wickham. See also High Wycombe.

Wycliffe NRY, 'cliff by a river-bend' [*Wigeclif* c 1050, *Witcliue* 1086: OE *wiht, clif*].

Wye K, '(place by) pagan shrine or temple' [*an Uuiæ* 839: OE *wēoh*].

Wye *riv* Db, — *riv* He-Mon. See Wey *riv*.

Wykeham LLi, **Wykham** O. See Wickham.

Wylye *riv* W. See Wilton.

Wymeswold Lei, 'Wigmund's wood' [*Wimundeswald* 1086: OE *wald*].

Wymondham Lei, — Nf: 'Wigmund's homestead' [1. *Wimundesham* 1086, 2. *Wimundham* 1086: OE *hām*].

†**Wyre** *riv* La, 'winding one'. With this may be connected †Wyre Forest Wo-Sa, which supplies a District-name to the new county of Hereford and Worcester [1. *Wir* c 1180, *Wyr* c 1200, 2. *Wira* 1177: B*uigora*].

Wyvis Lodge Ros, 'dwelling-place by Ben Wyvis, i e mountain of the spectre' [*Weyes* 1608: G *fuais, beinn*].

Yafforth NRY, 'river ford', the apparent tautology of which can be resolved by the presence nearby of fords across stretches of water other than rivers [*Iaforde* 1086: OE *ēa, ford*].

Yalding K, '(territory of) Ealda's folk', a tribe name applied to the area of their settlement [*Hallinges* 1086, *Ealding* 1207: OE *-ingas*].

Yapton Sx, 'farm of the people of Eabba' [*Abinton* 1197: OE *-ingas, tūn*].

Yar *riv* Wt, possibly a back-formation from an obsolete name of a place on the river, *Yarnford*, 'eagles' ford' [OE *earn, ford*].

Yardley Ess, — Wo, **Yardley Gobion** Nth, **Yardley Hastings** Nth, **Yarley** So: 'wood or clearing from which yards or staves were obtained'. The Northants additions are manorial; the Hastings family is first mentioned in connexion with *Est Yerdele* in 1250; the other Yardley Nth was *Yerdele iuxta Potterespyrye* in occasional references until the manorial suffix was added in the fourteenth century [1. *Gerdelai* 1086, 2. *Gyrdleah* 972, *Ierdele* 1220, *Jordele* 1255, *Zerdeleye* 1291, 3. *Gerdeslai* 1166, *Yerdeleie Gobioun* 1353, 4. *Gerdelai* 1086, *Yardele* 1314, 5. *Gyrdleh* 1065: OE *gyrd, lēah*].

Yare *riv* Nf, is a back-formation from (Great) Yarmouth, itself derived from the old form of the river-name, *Gerne*, interpreted as 'roaring, rushing river' [*Gariennou* c 150, *Gerne* c 1150, *Yare* 1577: B **gar*-]. See also *Gariennos*.

Yare *riv* Wt. See Yarmouth Wt.

Yarmouth Wt, 'gravelly estuary', from which the river-name Yare has been derived by back-formation (cf Yare *riv* Nf). The first element is OE *ēar*, 'gravel' or an adjective derived from it, *ēaren*

[*Ermud* 1086, *Eremue* 1196, *Errenmuth* 1235: OE *ēar/ēaren, mūða*]. See also Great Yarmouth Nf.

Yarrow Slk, **Yarrow** *riv* La, **Yarrow Water** *riv* Slk: 'rough river'. Yarrow Slk is also known as St Mary's Kirk of Lowis, i e 'St Mary's church of the loch', alluding to St Mary's Loch, from which the Yarrow Water flows on its way to join the Ettrick Water near Selkirk. Lowis is from Old Northumbrian *luh*, adapted from Gaelic *loch* [1. *Gierwa* c 1120, 2. *Yarwe* 1190: W *garw*].

Yaxley Hu, — Sf: 'cuckoo wood or clearing' [1. *æt Geakeslea* c 955, *Iacheslei* 1086, *Yakesle* 1302, 2. *Jacheslea* 1086: OE *gēac, lēah*]. See also Exceat Sx.

Yeading Mx, '(place of) Geddi's people' [*Geddinges* c 757: OE *-ingas*]. See also Middlesex.

Yealm *riv* D, possibly 'kindly one', but complimentary names were sometimes given in order to appease an ill-disposed divinity [*Yhalam* 1309: B **alm-*].

Yeaton Sa, 'farm beside a river', being on the river Perry. This name is a variant of Eaton (q v) [*Eton* 1327: OE *ēa, tūn*].

Yelden Bd, 1390, 'valley of the Gifle tribe i.e. dwellers on the river Ivel' [*Giveldene* 1086, *Yueldene* 1315, *Yeveldene* 1316: OE *denu*]. See Ivel *riv* Bd.

Yell *isld* Zet, 'barren' [*Jala* c 1250: ON *gelld*].

Yelvertoft Nth 1314, perhaps 'Geldfrið's dwelling place'. [*Celvrecot* 1086, *Gelvrecote, Givertost* 1086, *Gelvertoft(e)* 12c: ON *topt*].

Yen Hall C, 'nook of land on which young lambs were kept' [*to Eanhale* 974: OE **ēan, halh*].

Yeo *riv* D, 'yew river', the interpretation of one example only, viz the tributary of the Creedy. Other instances in WCy are 'river', except for another special case, the river on which †Yeovil So stands. This one is identical with Ivel *riv* Bd, the folk-name Gifle being the earlier name of this river also. Yeovil was *Gifle* in the late ninth century, and the *-vil* is not a form of the *-ville* termination in some modern names [1. *on eowan* 739, Iouwe 1238, 3. *Yevel* 878, *Gifle* 933: OE (1) *ēow*, (2) *ēa*].

Yerbeston Pmb, 'Gerbard's farm', a characteristic Pembrokeshire name in which a Norman or continental Germanic name is followed by *-ton* [*Jerbardeston* 14c: OE *tūn*].

Yes Tor *mtn* D, 'eagle's hill' [*Ernestorre* 1240: OE *earn, torr*].

Yetlington Nb, ' farm of Geatela's people' [*Yettlinton* 1187: OE *-ingas, tūn*.]

Yiewsley Mx, 'Wifel's wood or clearing' [*Wivesleg'* 1235: OE *lēah*].

Ynys Cantwr *isld* Pmb, 'precentor's island', formerly owned by the precentor of St David's. It is an islet off Ramsey Island. [W *ynys, cantwr*].

Ynys-ddu Mon, 'black island' [W *ynys, du*].

Ynysdullyn Pmb, 'island in the black lake' [W *ynys, du, llyn*].

†**Ynys Môn.** See Anglesey.

Yoker Lnk, 'low-lying ground' [*Pont Yochyrr* 1505: G *iochdar, iocar*, 'bottom'].

†**York** Y, 'Eburos's place', interpreting the earliest forms from which the modern

name can be traced in direct and contin-
uous descent. Successive invaders and
settlers made their own modifications to
the name; the Angles did their best with
the Celtic *Eburāc* or *Evorōc*, but could
manage only *Eofor-wic*, breaking the
first vowel into a diphthong and changing
the second part of the word into a place-
name termination to which they were accustomed. 'Boar farm' made good enough
sense. Centuries after the Anglo-Saxon
settlement, Scandinavian invaders set up
a kingdom in York. They changed the
termination to ON *-vik*, even though
the topography of York hardly justified
a reference to 'an inlet of the sea'. Perhaps
because of this, the final syllable was
rapidly eroded, and monosyllabic forms
very similar to the modern name came
into existence in the thirteenth century
[*Eborakon* c 150, *Eburacum* 4c,
Eoforwicceaster 644, *Iorvik* 962, *Euruic*
1086, *Ʒeorc*, *Ʒorc* 1205, *Ʒork* 1338]. See
also East Riding, North Riding, West
Riding.

York Town. See Camberley.

Youghal Crk, '(place by) yew wood'
[*Eochaill* 1450: I *eochaill*].

Ysgeifiog Flt, — Pb, **Llanfihangel Ysgeifiog**
Agl: 'abounding in elder-trees' [1.
Schiviau 1086, *Esceiuaus* 1284: W
ysgaw, 'elder']. See also Llanfihangel.

Ystwyth *riv* Crd, 'sinuous river' [*Ustwith
River* 1536: OW **estuctia*].

Y Trallwng Mgm, 'the pool', the Welsh
name for Welshpool (q v), formerly
Trallwng Llywelyn, 'pool of Llywelyn'
[*Trallwg Llywelyn* 14c: W *trallwng*].

Zeal D, **South Zeal** D: '(place with or by)
a dwelling'. South Zeal was also known
as *Zele Tony*, from the family holding
the manor [2. *La Sele* 1168: OE *sele*].

Zeal Monachorum D, 'monks' willow
(place)', held by Buckfast Abbey in 1086.
L *monachorum* is retained in this name
and in Buckland Monachorum D; it
occurs in medieval forms of some others,
e g Monken Hadley Hrt (*Hadley
Monachorum* 1485) [*at Seale* 956, *Sele
Monacor*' 1275: OE *sealh*, L *monachus*].

Zeals W, 'willows', cf Zeal Monachorum.
Zeals is not far from **Selwood Forest,**
'willow wood' [1. *Sela* 1086, 2. *Sealwyda*
878: OE *sealh, wudu*].

Zennor Co, '(church of) Saint Senara',
about whom nothing is known. The
voicing of initial *S* to *Z* is characteristic
of the area [*St Sinare* 1235, *Zenar* 1534].

Zetland, 'hilt land', alternatively **Shetland.**
The *Z-* represents the medieval letter *Ʒ*
(which normally =*gh*) used here to express
the sound *hj* [*Haltland* c 1100, *Shetland*
1289, *Zetlandie* 1403: ON *hjalt, land*].

Glossary of Common Place-Name Elements

á ON: river
aber OW: confluence, estuary
*abonā B: river
āc OE: oak
achadh G: field
æcer OE: arable land
ærn OE: building, dwelling
æsc OE: ash tree
æt OE: at
ǽwell OE: stream
ǽwelm OE: spring, source of a river
afon W: river
àirigh OI: shieling, (shelter on) upland
  pasture
ald, eald OE: old
allt G: stream
alor OE: elder tree
ān OE: one, single, solitary
ard G: height, promontory
ath OI: new, repeated
ath G: ford
austr ON: east

bach W: bæc OE: hillock
bæce, bece OE: stream
bala W: outlet of a lake
ban G: fair, white
bangor W: rod in wattle fence
bar Co, barr G: top, summit
*barrāco- B: hill-top
*barro- B: hill
beag G: little
bearu OE: wood, grove
beau, bel OF: fine, beautiful
beinn G: mountain
beithe G: birch
be(o)rg OE: mound, hill
betws W: chapel
beul G: mouth
blaen, pl blaenau W: highland
bo G: cow
ból ON: farm
bólstaðr ON: homestead
boðl, bōtl, bold OE: building
brād OE: broad

bre W: hill
breac G: speckled
breiðr ON: broad
brende, brente ME: burnt
brigā B: hill
brith W: speckled
brōc OE: stream
brōm OE: broom, (occasionally) bramble
brycg OE: bridge
bryn W: hill
burh OE: fortified place, manor, chartered
  town
bý ON: farm, settlement
bychan W: little, tiny

*cadeir OW: chair, lofty place
cair OW, caer Co, W: fortified place
caiseal G: stone fort
cald, ceald OE: cold
caled W: hard
calu OE: bare
cam Co, G, W: crooked
camas G: channel
*cambo B: crooked
*canto- B: edge, rim
caol G: strait, firth
capel OF, W: chapel
*carn B, carn Co, G, W: heap of stones,
  round, rocky hill
carrec OW, carreg, W carreg OCo.: rock
cat G, OE: cat
cēap OE: trade, merchandise
ceaster OE: Roman station, old
  fortification
*cēd B: wood
celli W: grove
celynnen W: holly tree
cill G: church, burying place
cirice OE: church
cisel, ceosol OE: gravel
cladach G: shore
clif OE: cliff
*clōh OE: ravine
*clop OE: lump, hillock
cluain G: pasture

195

cniht OE: youth, servant, soldier, knight
cnoc G: hillock
cnocc OI: hillock
cnoll OE: hill-top, summit; (later) hillock
coed W: wood
coille G: wood, forest
coire G: round hollow in mountain-side
comar G: confluence
copp OE: summit, peak
creag G: crag
croh OE: saffron
crois G, OF, cros OI, ME: cross
*crouco B, cruc OW: hill, barrow, mound
cruach G: heap, stack
cū OE: cow
cum Lat: with
cumb OE: hollow, valley
*cunāco B: hill
cwead OE: dirt, mud
cyln OE: kiln
cyne OE: royal
cyning OE: king

dà G: two
dæl OE: valley
dail G: field
dâr W: oak
darach G: oak
dearg G: red
denn OE: woodland pasture
denu OE: valley
dēop OE: deep
dēor OE: animal, beast; deer
derne, dierne OE: hidden, blind, i e overgrown with vegetation
*dervā B: oak
dic OE: ditch, trench; embankment
din Co, OW: fort
djúr, dýr ON: animal, beast; deer
doire G: grove
donn G: brown
dorn G: fist, fist-stone
drochaid G: bridge
druim G: ridge
*dubo B, du W, dubh G: black
*dubro, *dubrā B, dour Co, dwfr W: water
dūn OE: hill
dūn G, OI: fort
*dūno B: fort, hill
*duro B: gate, walled town

ēa OE: river, stream
èar I: east
ēar OE: gravel, 'mud
earn OE: eagle
eas G: waterfall
ēast OE: east
*ēcels OE: land added to an estate
ecg OE: edge
*eclēsia B, eaglais G, eglos Co, eglwys W:
   church
ēg OE: island, land partly surrounded by
   water, dry ground amid fen
eið ON: isthmus
eilean G: island
eithin W: furze
ellern OE: elder tree
ende OE: end, extremity of an estate
enis OCo: island
eochail G: yew wood
eofor OE: wild boar
episcopus Lat: bishop
erg ON: shieling, (shelter on) upland
   pasture
ermitage OF, hermitage ME: hermitage
ey ON: island

faar ON: sheep
fada G: long
fæger OE: fair, pleasant
fæsten OE: stronghold
fāg OE: variegated, multi-coloured
fald, falod OE: fold, small enclosure for
   animals
fas G: stance, level spot on a hillside
fearn G: alder
fearn OE: fern
feld OE: open country, tract of land
   cleared of trees
fen ON, fenn, fænn OE: fen, marsh
   marshland
fennig OE: dirty, muddy
ferja ON: ferry
ffin W: boundary
fforest W: park, forest
fif OE: five
fionn G: white, fair
fjall, fell ON: rough hill
fjórðr ON: inlet of the sea
fleot OE: estuary, inlet, creek, stream
flint OE: hard rock, flint

ford OE: shallow place in a river
fors ON: waterfall
fraoch G: heather
frater Lat, frere OF, ME: brother, friar, member of religious or military order
frith G: wood, deer-forest
fugl ON, fugol OE: bird
fūl OE: foul, dirty, muddy
funta OE: spring
(ge)fyrhð OE: wood(land)
fyrs OE: furze

gaineamh G: sand
gall G: stranger, lowlander
garbh G: rough, coarse
gardd W: fold, enclosure
garðr ON: enclosure
garth Co, W: hill, promontory
garw W: rough, coarse
gāt OE: goat
*gē OE: district, region, territory
geac OE: cuckoo
geard OE: yard, enclosure
geat OE: gate, gap
gil ON: ravine
glan W: bank, river-bank, hillock
*glassjo- B, glais W: stream, river
*glasto- B, glas W: blue, green, grey
*glennos B, glen Co, ME, glyn W, gleann G: glen, valley
gobhal G: fork
gobhar G: forked
gobhlach G: forked
gorm G: green, blue
græf OE: trench, pit, digging
grāf OE: grove, copse
grēot OE, grjót ON: gravel
grianan G: sunny hillock
gwern W: alder-swamp
gwydfa W: mound, tumulus
gwyn W: white
gwyrdd W: green

hæfen OE, hafn ON: harbour, haven
(ge)hæg OE: enclosure
hægstald, hagustald OE: warrior, bachelor, younger son without inherited property
*hæs OE: brushwood
hæsel OE: hazel

hæð OE: heather, heath, uncultivated ground overgrown with heather
haga OE: hedge, hedged enclosure
halh OE: nook, corner of land, land in the bend of a river
hallr ON: slope, hill, boulder
hām OE: homestead, dwelling-place, village, manor
hamm OE: enclosure, meadow, water, meadow, land in the bend of a river
*hamol OE: maimed, multilated, broken
hām-stede OE: homestead, site of a dwelling
hām-tūn OE: home farm, enclosure in which homestead stood
hár ON: high
haugr ON: mound, tumulus
hēafod OE: head, headland, end of a ridge
hēah OE: high
hearg OE: heathen temple
heli W: brine
helyg W: willow
hen Co, W: old
hid OE: hide, amount of land for the support of one free family and its dependents (about 120 acres)
hir W: long
hiwan OE: household, members of a family; religious community
hiwisc OE: household; amount of land for the support of a family
hjalt ON: hilt
hlāw, hlæw OE: mound, tumulus
hlinc OE: ridge, bank
hof ON: pagan temple
hōh OE: heel, spur of land, steep ridge
holmr ON: small island, water-meadow
holt OE, ON: wood, thicket, copse
hop OE: enclosed plot in marshes; small enclosed valley
hóp ON: bay, inlet
hris OE, hrís ON: brushwood, shrubs
hrycg OE, hryggr ON: ridge
hūfe OE: hood, shelter
hvarf ON: corner, bend, nook
hwit OE: white
hyll OE: hill
hyrst OE: hillock, wooded hill
hȳð OE: port, haven, landing-place on a river bank

idel OE: empty, useless
inferior Lat: lower
-ing OE: (suffixed to names of plants or animals)—place in which plants etc are found
-ingas OE: people of—
ingtūn OE: place associated with—
inis OI, G, OW: island, river-meadow
*iscā B: water
iw, ēow, *ig OE: yew tree

kalfr ON: calf, small place (esp island) beside larger one
karl ON: freeman of the lower class
key OF, key ME: wharf, quay
kirkja ON: church
kjarr ON: brushwood, bog overgrown with brushwood
konungr ON: king
kringla ON: circle
krókr ON: bend, crook
kví ON: fold, enclosure for cattle

lacu OE: stream, watercourse
(ge)lād OE: watercourse; passage over a river
lag(an) G: (little) hollow
lágr ON: low
lamb OE: lamb
land OE: tract of country; estate; cultivated land
*landā B, *lann OW, llan W: enclosure, church
lanerc P: glade
lang OE, langr ON: long
*lannerch OW, OCo, llanerch W, lanergh Co: glade
las OI: fort
lax ON: salmon
lēah OE: clearing, wood, woodland pasture, grove
learg G: plain
leikr ON: playing place
leitir G: slope
*lemo- B: elm tree
*lēto- B, *lēd OW, llwyd W, luit OCo: grey
lettir OI: slope
*lindo- B, *linn OW, llyn W, linn G: pool

*lis OW, OCo, llys W, lis, les Co: hall, court
ló ON: glade, meadow
loch G: lake
lon G: marsh
long G: ship
lost Co: tail
lùb G: bend
lundr ON: small wood, grove; sacred grove, sanctuary
lȳtel OE: small, little

mægden OE: maiden
mǣl OE: cross, crucifix
*magestu B, *maes OW, OCo, maes W, mês Co: plain, field
*magno B, *main OW, OCo, maen W, mên Co: rock, stone
magnus Lat: great
*mailu B, *mēl OW, moel W, *moil OCo: bald, bare of vegetation
mare Lat: sea
marr ON: fen, marsh
meadho I: middle
meall G: lump, rounded hill
mearc OE: march, boundary
medume OE: middle, of medium size
melr ON: sandbank
micel OE: great
mjór ON: narrow
*moniio- B, minid OW, mynydd W: mountain
mont OF, ME: mount, hill
*mōr OW, mawr W, mêr Co, mór G: great
muir G: sea
múli ON: snout, promontory, rocky headland
munuc OE, mynach, mynych W: monk
mūða OE: estuary, mouth of a river
myln OE: mill
myncen OE: nun
myrr ON: bog, mire, marsh
(ge)mȳðe OE: confluence, junction of river and tributary

næss OE: promontory, headland
nant W: stream
*nanto- B, nant OW, OCo: glen
nes ON: headland, cape

198

newydd W: new
norð OE, ON: north

ob G: bay
ofer OE: slope, ridge, hill
ōra OE: bank, border, margin
ord G: round hill
ord OE: point, projecting ridge
òs G, ós ON: river mouth, sluggish stream
oxa OE: ox

pæð OE: track, path
*panto- B, pant W: valley
park OF, ME: land enclosed for hunting
parvus Lat: small
*pēac OE: hill, peak, knoll, pointed
   summit
pearroc OE: fenced enclosure
*penarth Co: promontory, headland
*penno- B, pen OW, penn W, Co: hill,
   height, hill-top
*pert P, *perth OW, perth W: wood,
   bush, scrub
*pett P, peit G: portion, share, croft
pevr P: brilliant
plega-stow OE: sport place, place where
   people gathered for play
pōl OE, poll OW, OI, G: pool, pond, pool
   in a river
pòr G: pasture
port OE: (1) haven, harbour (2) town,
   market, market-town
porth Co, W: harbour, estuary
preas G, pres, prys W, *pres, *pris Co:
   brushwood, thicket
pwll W: pool
pyll OE: tidal creek, pool in a river

rá(1) ON: roe, roebuck
rá(2) ON: boundary
rann G: division
ràth G: circular fort
rauðr ON: red
rēad OE: red
repaire OF: retreat, secluded residence
rex Lat: king (gen sing regis: king's, of
   the king)
riabhach G: brindled, greyish
rinn G: promontory, headland

risc, rix, rysc OE: rush, bed of rushes
rið OE: stream
ròn G: seal
ros OW, G, Co, rhos W: moor, heath,
   headland, promontory
röst ON: whirlpool, strong sea current
ruadh G: red, brown
rubha G: cape, point

sadol OE: saddle, saddle-shaped ridge
sǣ OE, sær ON: sea
sǣte (pl sǣtan) OE: dweller, settler
sǽtr ON: shieling, upland pasture
salh OE: willow
sand OE, ON: sand
sarn W: causeway
sauðr ON: sheep
*scaw OCo: elder trees
sceaga OE: small wood, copse, strip of
   undergrowth
scēap OE: sheep
scēat OE: corner of land, projecting wood
   or other land
*scēla OE: hut, hovel, shieling
scir OE: shire, county, administrative
   division
seileach G: willow
seofon OE: seven
set-berg ON, set-copp OE: flat-topped hill
sgeir G, sker ON: skerry, sea rock
sgorr G: rocky peak
sid OE: spacious, long
sidh G: hillock, fairy knoll, haunted hill
sigl W: morass
skáli ON: temporary hut, hut on pasture
   on mountainside
sliabh G: mountain, hill-side
srath G: valley, strath
sròn G: nose, point
stān OE: stone
staðr ON: place, site
stede OE: place, site
steinn ON: rock, stone
steort OE: tail or tongue of land
stig OE, stígr ON: path, narrow road,
   mountain track
stoc OE: place, secondary settlement,
   religious site
stocc OE, stokkr ON: stump, stock,
   tree-trunk, log

199

stoð ON: landing-place, jetty

stōw OE: place, assembly-place, holy place

strǣt OE: Roman road, paved road

strōd OE: marshy land overgrown with brushwood

sub Lat: under, beneath, below

sundor, synder OE: asunder, land detached from an estate

super Lat: above, upon

superior Lat: higher, upper

sūð OE: south, southern

svín ON, swin OE: pig, swine

sych W: dry

tairbeart G: isthmus, neck of land across which boats were carried

tān OE: sprig, shoot

tarbh G: bull

teampull G: temple or church

temple ME: property of the order of Knights Templar

tig OW, ty W, chy Co: house

tiobhar, tobhar G: well

tir G, W: land, territory

tòn G: buttock

topt ON: site of a house

torr OW, OE, G: heap, hill, rocky outcrop, peak

towyn, tywyn W: strand, seashore

traeth W, treath, trêth Co; strand

tref, tre W, trey, tre Co: farmstead, homestead, hamlet

tri G: three

tuath G: north

tulach G: hillock

tūn OE: enclosure, farm, estate, village

twi- OE: double

twisla OE: fork of a river

tyddyn W: small-holding

tyle W: hill, slope

tyno W: meadow, plain

þing-vollr ON: field where an assembly met

þorn OE, ON: hawthorn or other thorn tree

þorp ON: secondary settlement, dependent farmstead or hamlet

þriðjung ON: third part (of a shire)

þrop OE: hamlet

þveit ON: clearing, meadow, small enclosure

uaine G: green

uamh G: cave

uchd G: slope, bank

uchel W: high

uisge G: water

upp OE: upper, higher

ùruisg G: goblin, monster

ūt OE: outside, on the outskirts

*uxello B: high

vágr ON: bay, creek, inlet of the sea

varða, varði ON: cairn, heap of stones

vað ON: ford

vatn ON: fresh water, lake

*ventā B: (possibly) favoured place, chief town, market town

*verno- B, *wern OW, gwern W: alders, alder-thicket

vestr (comp vestri, vestari) ON: west (more westerly)

vík ON: inlet, creek, bay

vindo B: white

viðr ON: wood

wād OE: woad

wæter OE: water, pool, lake, stream

wald, weald OE: woodland, forest, upland forest

walh OE: stranger, Celtic-speaking foreigner, serf

–ware OE pl: inhabitants, dwellers

wella OE: spring, well

welm, wielm OE: surging of water, spring

wer OE: weir, river-dam, fishing-pool in a river

wic OE: outlying farm, dwelling, premises used for special purposes

*wic-hām OE: settlement near a Romano-British village

*wilig OE: willow-tree

*winn OE, gywn W: white, holy, fair

wōh OE: crooked, twisted

worð, worðig, worðign OE: enclosure

wudu OE: wood, grove, forest

wulf OE: wolf

wyrm OE: reptile, snake, dragon

y W: the
ych W: ox
*yfer OE: brow of a hill
ynys W: island, river-meadow

ysbyty W: hospice, hospital
ysgol W: ladder, terraced mountain-side
ystrad W: valley, river-meadow
ytri ON: outer

Appendix

Regions, Counties and Districts in Great Britain and Northern Ireland

Names of Districts are marked with an obelisk (†) in the Dictionary. Names of Counties and Regions brought into existence under the reorganisation of local government are marked with a double obelisk (††). See also page 13.

England: Counties and Districts

AVON: BATH, BRISTOL, Kingswood ('wood in the tenure of the king'), North AVON, WANSDYKE, Woodspring ('wood grouse copse')

BEDFORDSHIRE: BEDFORD, LUTON, Mid-Bedfordshire, South Bedfordshire

BERKSHIRE: BRACKNELL, NEWBURY, READING, SLOUGH, WINDSOR and MAIDENHEAD, WOKINGHAM

BUCKINGHAMSHIRE: AYLESBURY Vale, BEACONSFIELD, CHILTERN, MILTON KEYNES, Wycombe (v High Wycombe)

CAMBRIDGESHIRE: CAMBRIDGE, East Cambridgeshire, FENLAND, HUNTINGDON, PETERBOROUGH, South Cambridgeshire

CHESHIRE: CHESTER, CONGLETON, CREWE and NANTWICH, ELLESMERE PORT, Halton ('village by a nook of land'), MACCLESFIELD, VALE ROYAL, WARRINGTON

CLEVELAND: HARTLEPOOL, Langbaurgh ('long mound or hill'), MIDDLES-BROUGH, STOCKTON ON TEES

CORNWALL: CARADON, CARRICK, KERRIER, North Cornwall, PENWITH, RESTORMEL

CUMBRIA: Allerdale ('valley of river Ellen'), BARROW IN FURNESS, CARLISLE, Copeland (v Bolton in Copeland), EDEN, South Lakeland (v Lake Country)

DERBYSHIRE: AMBER VALLEY, Bolsover ('Bol's slope'), CHESTERFIELD, DERBY, EREWASH, HIGH PEAK, North East Derbyshire, South Derbyshire, West Derbyshire

DEVON: East Devon, EXETER, North Devon, PLYMOUTH, SOUTH HAMS, Teign-bridge (v Teign), TIVERTON, TORBAY, TORRIDGE, West Devon

DORSET: BOURNEMOUTH, CHRISTCHURCH, North Dorset, POOLE, Purbeck ('ridge frequented by bittern or snipe'), West Dorset, WEYMOUTH and PORTLAND, WIMBORNE

DURHAM: CHESTER LE STREET, DARLINGTON, Derwentside (v Derwent), DURHAM, Easington ('estate associated with Esa or Esi'), Sedgefield ('Cedd's or Secg's open country'), Teesdale ('valley of the river Tees'), WEAR Valley

EAST SUSSEX: BRIGHTON, EASTBOURNE, HASTINGS, HOVE, LEWES, Rother (river-name, back-formation from Rother Bridge, 'ox bridge'), Wealden (v Weald)

ESSEX: Basildon ('Beorhtel's hill'), BRAINTREE, BRENTWOOD, Castle Point, CHELMSFORD, COLCHESTER, EPPING FOREST, HARLOW, MALDON, Rochford (possibly 'ford of the hunting-dog'), SOUTHEND ON SEA, Tendring (possibly 'people of the beacon'), THURROCK, Uttlesford ('Udel's ford')

GLOUCESTERSHIRE: CHELTENHAM, COTSWOLD, FOREST OF DEAN (v Dean), GLOUCESTER, STROUD (v Strood), TEWKESBURY

HAMPSHIRE: BASINGSTOKE, East Hampshire, EASTLEIGH, FAREHAM, GOSPORT, Hartley Wintney ('stag wood held by Wintney Abbey'), HAVANT, NEW FOREST, PORTSMOUTH, Rushmoor ('waste land overgrown with rushes'), SOUTH-AMPTON, TEST Valley, WINCHESTER

HEREFORD AND WORCESTER: BROMSGROVE, HEREFORD, LEOMINSTER, MALVERN Hills, REDDITCH (v Reddish), South Herefordshire, WORCESTER, Wychavon

HERTFORDSHIRE: BROXBOURNE, DACORUM, East Hertfordshire, Hertsmere ('boundary of Hertfordshire'), North Hertfordshire, ST ALBANS, STEVENAGE, THREE RIVERS, WATFORD, WELWYN-HATFIELD

HUMBERSIDE: BEVERLEY, BOOTH FERRY, CLEETHORPES, GLANFORD (v Brigg), GRIMSBY, HOLDERNESS, KINGSTON UPON HULL, North WOLDS, SCUNTHORPE

ISLE OF WIGHT: MEDINA (v Meden), South Wight

KENT: ASHFORD, CANTERBURY, DARTFORD, DOVER, GILLINGHAM, Gravesham (early spelling of Gravesend), MAIDSTONE, MEDWAY, Sevenoaks ('by or near seven oak trees'), Shepway, SWALE, THANET, TONBRIDGE and MALLING, TUNBRIDGE WELLS

LANCASHIRE: BLACKBURN, BLACKPOOL, BURNLEY, CHORLEY, FYLDE, Hyndburn, LANCASTER, PENDLE, PRESTON, RIBBLE Valley, Rossendale, South RIBBLE, West Lancashire, WYRE.

LEICESTERSHIRE: BLABY, CHARNWOOD, HARBOROUGH (v Market Harborough), HINCKLEY and BOSWORTH, LEICESTER, MELTON, North West Leicestershire, OADBY and WIGSTON, RUTLAND

LINCOLNSHIRE: BOSTON, East LINDSEY, LINCOLN, North KESTEVEN, South HOLLAND, South KESTEVEN, West LINDSEY

GREATER MANCHESTER (Metropolitan County): BOLTON, BURY, MANCHESTER, Oldham ('old or former island'), ROCHDALE, SALFORD, STOCK-PORT, TAMESide, TRAFFORD, WIGAN

MERSEYSIDE (Metropolitan County): Knowsley ('Cynewulf's wood'), LIVERPOOL, ST HELENS, Sefton ('farm where rushes grew'), WIRRAL

NORFOLK: BRECKLAND, Broadland ('region of the Broads, i e wide stretches of water'), GREAT YARMOUTH, North Norfolk, NORWICH, South Norfolk, West Norfolk

NORTHAMPTONSHIRE: CORBY, DAVENTRY, East Northamptonshire, KETTERING, NORTHAMPTON, South Northamptonshire, WELLINGBOROUGH

NORTHUMBERLAND: ALNWICK (v Alnmouth), BERWICK UPON TWEED, BLYTH VALLEY ('valley of the pleasant river'), Castle MORPETH, TYNEdale, Wansbeck (river-name of unknown meaning)

NORTH YORKSHIRE: Craven (possibly 'garlic place'), Hambleton ('Hamela's farm'), HARROGATE, RICHMONDshire, RYEDALE (v Rievaulx), SCARBOROUGH, SELBY, YORK

NOTTINGHAMSHIRE: ASHFIELD, Bassetlawe ('hill of the dwellers in land cleared by burning'), Broxtowe ('Brocwulf's place'), Gedling ('Gedel's people'), MANSFIELD, NEWARK, NOTTINGHAM, Rushcliffe ('hill among brushwood')

OXFORDSHIRE: Cherwell ('winding river'), OXFORD, South Oxfordshire, Vale of White Horse ('valley in which turf-cut figure of a white horse can be seen'), West Oxfordshire

SALOP: BRIDGNORTH, North Shropshire, Oswestry, SHREWSBURY and Atcham ('village of Eata's people'), South Shropshire, THE WREKIN

SOMERSET: MENDIP, Sedgemoor ('boggy area in which sedges grew'), TAUNTON Deane, West Somerset, YEOVIL (v Yeo)

SOUTH YORKSHIRE: (Metropolitan County): BARNSLEY, DONCASTER, ROTHERHAM, SHEFFIELD

STAFFORDSHIRE : CANNOCK CHASE, East Staffordshire, LICHFIELD, NEWCASTLE UNDER LYME, South Staffordshire, STAFFORD, Staffordshire Moors, STOKE ON TRENT, TAMWORTH

SUFFOLK: Babergh ('Babba's mound'), Forest Heath (v Breckland), IPSWICH, Mid-Suffolk, ST EDMUNDSBURY, Suffolk Coastal, Waveney ('river by a quaking bog')

SURREY: Elmbridge ('bridge over misty river'), EPSOM and EWELL, GUILD-FORD, MOLE VALLEY, REIGATE and Banstead ('bean place'), RUNNYMEDE, SPELTHORNE ('thorn-tree at which speeches were made'), Surrey Heath, Tandridge (possibly 'ridge with swine pastures'), Waverley ('wood by marshy ground'), WOKING

TYNE AND WEAR: GATESHEAD, NEWCASTLE UPON TYNE, North TYNEside, South TYNEside, SUNDERLAND

WARWICKSHIRE: North Warwickshire, NUNEATON, RUGBY, STRATFORD ON AVON, WARWICK

WEST MIDLANDS: BIRMINGHAM, COVENTRY, DUDLEY, Sandwell, SOLIHULL, WALSALL, WOLVERHAMPTON

WEST SUSSEX: ADUR, Arun (back-formation from Arundel, 'hoarhound valley'), CHICHESTER, CRAWLEY, HORSHAM, Mid-Sussex, WORTHING

WEST YORKSHIRE (Metropolitan County): BRADFORD, CALDERdale, Kirklees ('wood belonging to a church'), LEEDS, WAKEFIELD

WILTSHIRE: KENNET, North Wiltshire, SALISBURY, Thamesdown ('hill by river THAMES'), West Wiltshire

Northern Ireland: Districts

ANTRIM, ARDS, ARMAGH, BALLYMENA, BALLYMONEY, Banbridge ('bridge over river Bann, ie goddess'), BELFAST, Carrickfergus ('Fergus's rock'), CASTLEREAGH, COLERAINE, COOKSTOWN, Craigavon, DOWN, Dungannon ('Geannann's fort'), FERMANAGH, LARNE, Limavady ('fort of the dog'), Lisburn (uncertain, but formerly Lisnagarvey, 'fort of the gamesters'), LONDONDERRY, Magherafelt ('plain of Fiolta's house'), Moyle ('place by the strait of the promontory'), NEWRY and MOURNE, NEWTOWNabbey, North DOWN, OMAGH, STRABANE

Scotland: Regions and Districts

BORDERS: BERWICKSHIRE, ETTRICK and LAUDERDALE, ROXBURGH, TWEEDdale

CENTRAL: CLACKMANNAN, FALKIRK, STIRLING

DUMFRIES AND GALLOWAY: Annandale and Eskdale ('valleys of ANNAN and ESK'), Nithsdale ('valley of Nith'), STEWARTRY (v Kirkcudbright), WIGTOWN

FIFE: DUNFERMLINE, KIRKCALDY, North-East FIFE

GRAMPIAN: ABERDEEN City, BANFF and BUCHAN, Gordon, KINCARDINE and DEEside, MORAY

HIGHLAND: BADENOCH and Strathspey ('valley of hawthorn river'), CAITHNESS, INVERNESS, LOCHABER, NAIRN, ROSS and CROMARTY, SKYE and Lochalsh ('foamy lake'), SUTHERLAND

LOTHIAN: EAST LOTHIAN, EDINBURGH City, MIDLOTHIAN, WEST LOTHIAN

ORKNEY

SHETLAND

STRATHCLYDE: ARGYLL and BUTE, Bearsden and MILNGAVIE, CLYDEbank, CUMBERNAULD and Kilsyth ('church of St Sadb'), Cunningham (meaning uncertain), Cunnock and DOON Valley, DUMBARTON, EAST KILBRIDE, Eastwood, GLASGOW City, HAMILTON, Inverclyde ('mouth of the Clyde'), KILMARNOCK and Loudon ('fort of Lugus'), KYLE and CARRICK, LANARK, Monklands, MOTHERWELL, RENFREW, STRATHKELVIN

TAYSIDE: ANGUS, DUNDEE City, PERTH and KINROSS

WESTERN ISLES

Wales : Counties and Districts

CLWYD: ALYN AND DEESIDE, COLWYN, Delyn, Glyndwr ('valley of the Dee'), RHUDDLAN, WREXHAM-Maelor ('territory of the prince')

DYFED: CARMARTHEN, CEREDIGION, Dinefwr ('yew fort'), LLANELLI, Preseli

GWENT: BLAENAU GWENT, Islwyn ('below the grove'), MONMOUTH, NEWPORT, Torfaen ('stone gap')

GWYNEDD: ABERCONWY, ARFON, Dwyfor ('great water'), Meirionnydd ('seat of Meirion'), Ynys Môn ('Isle of ANGLESEY')

MID-GLAMORGAN: Cynon Valley, MERTHYR TYDFIL, Ogwr ('sharp river'), RHONDDA, RHYMNI Valley, TAF-Eli ('running water')

POWYS: BRECKNOCK, MONTGOMERYshire, RADNOR

SOUTH GLAMORGAN: CARDIFF, Vale of GLAMORGAN

WEST GLAMORGAN: AFAN, Lliw Valley ('valley of bright stream'), Neath ('shining river'), SWANSEA

Bibliography

The dates are those of editions consulted. Place of publication is London unless otherwise noted.

Brøndsted, J. *The Vikings*, Baltimore, 1965

Cameron, K. *English Place-Names*, 1963
——. (*ed*) *Place-Name Evidence for the Anglo-Saxon Invasion*, 1975
——. *The Significance of English Place-Names*, 1976
Chadwick, N. *The Celts*, 1970
Charles, B.G. *Non-Celtic Place-Names of Wales*, 1938
Coates, R. *The Place-Names of Hampshire*, 1989

Davies, E. *Flintshire Place-Names*, Cardiff 1959
Dillon, M. and **Chadwick, N.** *The Celtic Realms*, 1973

Ekwall, E. *Concise Oxford Dictionary of English Place-Names*, Oxford 1951
——. *English River-Names*, Oxford 1968

Fellows-Jensen, G. *Scandinavian Settlement Names in the East Midlands*, Copenhagen 1978
——. *Scandinavian Settlement Names in the North West*, Copenhagen 1985
Field, J. *Discovering Place-Names, Tring* 1971, 2nd ed 1975
——. *English Field-Names: a Dictionary*, Newton Abbot 1972 (cited as EFN)
——. *Place-Names of Greater London*, 1980
——. 'What to Read in Place-Names in Britain', *Local Historian* 17 (1986–7), 396–404

Gelling, M. 'English place-names derived from the compound *wīchām*', *Mediæval Archæology* XI: 87–104, 1967
——. 'Place-names of the Isle of Man', *Journal of the Manx Museum*, VII: 130–9, 168–75, Douglas 1971 (cited as PNIOM)
——. *Place-Names in the Landscape*, 1984
——. *Signposts to the Past: Place-Names and the History of England*, 1978; 2nd edn Chichester 1988

Jackson, K. 'The Britons in Southern Scotland', *Antiquity*, XXIX: 77–88 London 1955
——. *Language and History in Early Britain*, Edinburgh 1953
——. 'On some Romano-British Place-Names', *Journal of Roman Studies*, XXXVIII
Johnson, J.B. *Place-Names of Scotland*, East Ardsley 1972
Jones, G. *History of the Vikings*, 1973
Joyce P.W. *Irish Names of Places*, East Ardsley 1972

Kneen, J.J. *Place-Names of the Isle of Man*, Douglas 1925–9

Matthews, C.M. *Place-names of the English-Speaking World*, 1972
Mills, A.D. Dorset Place-Names: Their Origins and Meanings, Wimborne 1986

Nicolaisen, W.F.H. 'Gaelic place-names in southern Scotland', *Studia Celtica*, V: 15–35, 1970 (cited as GPNSS)
————. 'Norse settlement in the Northern and Western Isles: the place-name evidence', *Scottish Historical Review*, 48: 6–17, 1969
————. 'P-Celtic Place-Names in Scotland: a reappraisal', *Studia Celtica*, VII: 1–11, 1972
————. *Scottish Place-Names*, 1976
————. (*ed*) (with **M. Gelling** and **M. Richards**) *Names of Towns and Cities in Britain*, 1970 (cited as NTC)

Padel, O. *Cornish Place-Name Elements* (EPNS LVI/LVII), 1985
————. *A Popular Dictionary of Cornish Place-Names*, Penzance 1988
Pierce, G. *Place-Names of Dinas Powys Hundred*, Cardiff 1968
Price, L. *Place-Names of County Wicklow*, Dublin 1945–67

Reaney, P.H. *Origin of English Place-Names*, 1964
Rivet, A.L. and **Smith, C.** *Place-Names of Roman Britain*, 1979

Smith, A.H. *English Place-Name Elements*, EPNS XXV, XXVI, Cambridge 1956
Spittal, C.J. and **Field, J.** *A Reader's Guide to the Place-Names of the United Kingdom*, Stamford 1990

Treharne, R.F. and **Fullard, H.** (*eds*) *Muir's Historical Atlas*, 1973

Wainwright, F.T. *Archæology and Place-Names and History*, 1962
————. (*ed*) *The Problem of the Picts*, Edinburgh 1955
Walsh, P. *Place-Names of Westmeath*, Dublin 1957
Watson, W.J. *History of the Celtic Place-Names of Scotland*, Shannon 1973

In addition to the above, the county volumes of the English Place-Name Society's survey have been consulted. References to these are abbreviated to PN followed by the contracted form of the county, e g PN Brk ii 507 is to be read as *The Place-Names of Berkshire*, Part ii, page 507.